Muhammad Ali Aziz holds a PhD from the University of Michigan, Ann Arbor. He has taught at Princeton University and the University of Michigan. He currently teaches at Yale University and is translating some of the medieval treatises of Ibn ʿAlwān.

RELIGION AND MYSTICISM IN EARLY ISLAM

Theology and Sufism in Yemen

The Legacy of Aḥmad Ibn ʿAlwān

MUHAMMAD ALI AZIZ

I.B. TAURIS
LONDON · NEW YORK

Published in 2011 by I.B.Tauris & Co Ltd
6 Salem Road, London W2 4BU
175 Fifth Avenue, New York NY 10010
www.ibtauris.com

Distributed in the United States and Canada
Exclusively by Palgrave Macmillan
175 Fifth Avenue, New York NY 10010

Library of Middle East History 26

ISBN: 978 1 84885 450 5

This book was published with the assistance of the Frederick W. Hilles Publication Fund of Yale University.

A full CIP record for this book is available from the British Library
A full CIP record for this book is available from the Library of Congress
Library of Congress catalog card: available

Printed and bound in Great Britain by CPI Antony Rowe, Chippenham
from camera-ready copy edited and supplied by the author

MIX
Paper from responsible sources
FSC
www.fsc.org
FSC® C013604

To the memory of my father

CONTENTS

ILLUSTRATIONS

List of Maps

List of Tables

List of Images

NOTE ON TRANSLITERATION AND DATES

In transliterating Arabic words, I have followed the system of the *International Journal of Middle East Studies* (*IJMES*). For the sake of brevity, I have dropped the Arabic closed "*tā.*" However, if it appears in a construct status, I retain the original "*tā.*" I differentiated between the sun letter "*lām*" (i.e., *al-lām ash-shamsiyya*) and the moon letter "*lām*" (i.e., *al-lām al-qamariyya*) according to spoken Arabic. I dropped the two "*lams*" completely from the Bibliography.

All dates are given according to the Muslim lunar calendar (*hijra*), which are followed by a backlash and the Common Era (C.E.) equivalents. Occasionally, if the lunar year is not mentioned, I rely on C.E. Finally the word "Ibn" in Arabic, which means *son,* will be abbreviated as (b.). For example, Aḥmad Ibn 'Alwān will be (Aḥmad b. 'Alwān).

ACKNOWLEDGMENTS

This book could not have been written without the generous support of a number of individuals and institutions. First, I must acknowledge a very deep indebtedness to my teachers at the University of Michigan, Ann Arbor: Alexander Knysh, Michael Bonner, Sherman Jackson, and Juan Cole. I am truly obliged to extend my special thanks to Alexander Knysh, who has provided me with genuine intellectual and personal support. Without his meticulous and insightful commentary, endless patience, and sincere encouragement, this book would have never been written. I am sure he could have written a book of his own instead of spending time preparing me to write mine.

I am also grateful to Brinkley Messick for his assistance and constant support before, during, and after my work. I am thankful for his inestimable guidance, profound suggestions, and thorough comments on this project. Without his insistent motivation and warm friendship, this book would not have come to light.

There are many scholars as well as administrators in the department of Near Eastern Studies in Ann Arbor who provided me with assistance during my graduate studies, including Kathryn Babayan, Norman Yoffe, Gary Beckman, and especially Raji Rammuny for his immeasurable help and encouragement. My thanks are due to my Egyptian friend, Khālid Sallām, who provided me with pages of Ḥamūd al-Qiyarī's study on Ibn ʿAlwān.

While I was a lecturer of Arabic at Princeton University (2004–2005), Michael Cook read an early draft of this book and made some important comments that I have taken into consideration and I thank him profoundly. I also thank all the faculty and staff of the department of Near Eastern Studies at Princeton University, especially Nancy Coffin.

My deep indebtedness goes to the two distinguished Sufi figures in Yemen, the contemporary ʿAbd as-Salām Muḥammad Qāḍī and the deceased Muḥammad b. Qāyid al-ʻAwāḍī (d. 2005) for their significant thoughts and suggestions regarding some Sufi and theological views. I would like to express my profound appreciation for the deceased local scholars of Ibb, ʻAbd Allāh b. Yaḥyā al-ʻAnsī (d. 1996) and ʻAlī b. ʻAlī Mutī‘ (d. 2003) for teaching me the principles of Arabic grammar, recitation of the Qur'ān (tajwīd), and other Islamic topics. I am grateful to Aḥmad Muḥammad al-Ḥadā'ī (d. 2008), ʻAbd al-Jabbār Sa‘d, ʻAbd al-Ḥamīd Mulhī, and Ḥamūd al-Bizāz, Muḥammad Eissa for the many vital discussions we had together on Sufi literature and the circles of God's remembrance (dhikr). My deepest thanks are due to the contemporary scholar, critic, and historian ʻAbd Allāh Muḥammad al-Ḥibshī whose book entitled *al-Ṣūfiyya wa-l-fuqahā' fī-l-Yaman* was the cornerstone on which I have based many topics. Similarly, I made extensive use of Alexander Knysh's book entitled *Ibn ʻArabī in the Later Islamic Tradition.* I am grateful to Abdallah Ḥasan al-Ḥadā'ī for accompanying my brother Walid to Yafrus in order to take photographs of the tomb of Ibn ʻAlwān.

I would like to thank all the faculty and administration in the Department of Near Eastern Languages and Civilizations at Yale University for their support and for creating a pleasant environment in which to write this book. I am indebted to the chair, John Darnell. My personal thanks go to the former chair and former acting chair Benjamin Foster and his wife, Karen Foster, for their continuous encouragement and support. I would like to thank the former director of graduate studies Echart Frahm; the current director, Bentley Layton; and the former director of undergraduate studies (DUS) and former chair Beatrice Gruendler, who encouraged me immensely and provided academic advice. Without Beatrice Gruendler's encouragement and support, this book would not have come to light. I am particularly thankful to the Arabic committee for their constant support and especially former chair Dimitri Gutas, who encouraged me enormously and provided profound academic advice along with current DUS Coleen Manassa and former DUS Hala Nassar and business manager Susan Hart. I would like to thank my colleagues Ghassan Husseinali, Shady Nasser, Shadee Elmasry, Hasmik Tovmasyan, and Sarab Al Ani along with Ayala Dvoretzky and Fereshteh Amanat-Kowssar. Bassam Frangieh read an early draft of this book and for that I am grateful. My thanks to Munzer Elby who helped in the location of some sources. I would also like to thank William Whobrey and all the staff of the Yale Summer Session for their constant support, especially Cristin Siebert. I am grateful for the assistance given by the Yale Center for Middle East Studies, particularly by the acting chair Frank

Griffel, former chair Ellen Lust-Okar, Kira Gallick, and new staff including the current chair Marcia Inhorn. My thanks also go to all the staff at the Center for Language Study, particularly Nelleke Vandeusen-Scholl, Suzanne Young, and Howard Barnaby; the staff at the faculty support at Yale University; and the staff at Yale library, especially Simon Samoeil.

I would like to thank my wife, Eyman al-Mashragi, for putting up with me for many years. In addition, I thank my daughter, Aysha, my sons Yousif, Qasim, Abdulwadood, Zakarya, and Adam for their unwavering love.

I would like to express my gratitude to my brothers and sisters whose hearts and love accompany me all the time. My thanks go particularly to Nabīl, who helped me with the search and delivery of some sources from Yemen, including electronic manuscripts. Similarly, my thanks go to Walīd, who provided the image for the jacket, some photos, and other documents pertaining to this study. My thanks go to my stepmother, Malika; my sister Ghrām; my brothers Fouad, Abd al-Karīm; my sister Karīma; my brothers Bashīr, Akram; my sisters Samīḥa and Sumayya; and my brother Abd as-Salām. I am grateful to all of them for their love and unwavering support.

It also gives me pleasure to thank my Yemeni friends for their moral support during the period when this book was being written: Rasheed Sāliḥ al-Nuzylī, Muḥammad Aḥmad al-Dues, 'Abd al-Ḥakīm Aḥmad al-Sāda, Muḥammad Ḥasan, Aḥmad Nu'mān, Muhammad Mansur, Khālid al-Qusaymī, Najeeb al-Ḥarīrī, Fawāz, Alī, Bilāl, Adel, and Sādiq al-Dues, Sādiq al-Shu'aybī, Hāfiẓ Sharf ad-Dīn azzubair, Najīb Asaad Shaḥra, Aḥmad al-'Ammārī, 'Abd al-'Azīz al-'Āṣimī, Jamīl al-Maitamī, Ṣalāḥ al-Shibāmī, 'Abd al-Walī al-Ṭahayf, Salīm al-Muṣannif, Ibrahīm Muḥarram, Aḥmad al-Awādi, Muḥammad 'Alī al-Qaḍḍābah, Muḥammad Fayṣal Maṭar, Muḥammad al-Ḥudād, and Aḥmad 'Alī Luṭf al-Sāda, Muḥammad al-Ghurbānī, Muhammad Eissa, Ismā'īl al-Muqaddam, my brother-in-law Qāsim al-Manṣūb, Abd al-Jabbār ar-Rūdī, Muhammad al-Muhtadī, Alī Amīqa, Muhammad al-Burayhī, Muhammad Sāleh al-Hāj, Abd Allāh al-Wahābī, 'Alī Abd al-Karīm aṣ-Ṣabāḥī, 'Abd as-Salām Ḥusayn al-'Ansī, 'Alī Qāsim al-'Ansī, Muḥammad Aḥmad Bā Salāmah, Ahmad ar-Rawāj, Muḥammad Abd al-Karīm al-Manṣūb, Ash-Shaykh 'Abd al-'Azīz al-Ḥubayshī, Aḥmad Kalaz, Abd al-Malik as-San'ānī, Ismā'īl as-San'ānī, Abd al-Walī al-Warāfī, Yahya al-Hushaee, Jamīl al-Hindī, Abd al-Ilāh al-Mawshikī, Jamīl, Yāsir, Bashīr and Muhammad al-Bizāz, 'Alī Muhammad 'Alī aṣ-Ṣabāḥī, Abdulwahhāb and Aḥmad aṣ-Ṣabāḥī, Khālid and Walīd Muhyi ad-Dīn al-'Ansī, Aḥmad Ṣabbān, Ali al-Hamdānī, 'Abd Allāh Ḥamūd al-Ghurbānī, 'Alī Ḥasan al-Ḥadā'ī, Abd al-Wahhāb Muqbil, Ismā'īl as-Sūswa, Muṭahhar as-Sayyid Ḥusayn, Adnān and Ḥusayn as-Sayyāghī, and the Jordanian Khāled al-Masrī.

My thanks also go to the personnel at the Graduate Library at the University of Michigan and especially Jonathan Rodgers, who has been greatly helpful in providing me with information regarding references central to my project. My gratitude also goes to the members of the Sweetland Writing Center who assisted me in editing some sections of earlier drafts of this work. In addition, I extend my gratitude to the Sterling Memorial and Bienke libraries at Yale University for providing the necessary references and adequate resources. At Yale, my thanks go to Anne-Marie McManus, who helped in the primary editing of an early draft of this book. Finally, I am thankful to the funding agencies that assisted me during my graduate studies. Particularly, I would like to thank the school of graduate studies, Rackham at the University of Michigan, for its generous financial support. I would also like to thank the Fulbright program for granting me a scholarship for two years (1995–1997). I particularly thank the staff of Amideast in Ṣan'ā' and Washington, D.C. Thanks are also due to the Department of Near Eastern Studies, Center for Middle East and North African Studies, and International Institute, all at the University of Michigan. In Yemen, I would like to thank Ṣan'ā' and Ibb Universities (particularly 'Abd ar-Raḥmān 'Abd Rabbuh, Muḥammad Sharfuddīn, and Abd al-Aziz ash-Shu'aybī), the Ministry of Education in Ṣan'ā', the Ministry of Higher Education in Ṣan'ā', and the Embassy of the Republic of Yemen in Washington, D.C. Finally, this book was published with the assistance of the Frederick W. Hilles Publication Fund of Yale University. I am gratefully indebted to its chair John MacKay and business manager Susan Stout at the Whitney Humanities Center at Yale University.

INTRODUCTION

This book explores the development of Islamic mysticism in Yemen from the beginning of Islam until the demise of the Ottoman Empire and into the modern period. It focuses on the religious-political struggle; the interplay between the Shīʿī, Sunnī, and Sufi traditions; and the cultural and intellectual debates. It also describes the rise and development of Sufi institutions with special attention to the theology, Sufism, and legacy of perhaps the greatest religious and mystical thinker of premodern Yemen, Aḥmad b. ʿAlwān (d. 665/1266).

Ibn ʿAlwān lived during the period of Yemen's momentous transition from the rule of the Egyptian Ayyūbid dynasty (569–626/1173–1228)[1] to that of their Rasūlid lieutenants (626–858/1228–1454), who declared their independence from the Egyptian Ayyūbids in 632/1234. As a renowned scholar and mystical visionary, Ibn ʿAlwān's interactions with the ruling elites of both dynasties were marked by tension and ambiguity. Their representatives held him in high regard and listened carefully to his advice and admonitions, yet they resented his critique of their governance. Ibn ʿAlwān's contribution to the development of Islamic mysticism, theology, and spirituality in Yemen was wide-ranging and varied. He left behind a substantial body of writings on various aspects of Islamic mysticism, theology, law, and Qur'ān exegesis, and he was also an accomplished mystical poet, whose poems have continued to enjoy great popularity among Yemeni Muslims up to the present day. Although Ibn ʿAlwān died seven and a half centuries ago, his tomb remains the object of a colorful annual pilgrimage attended by hundreds of visitors from far and wide. This fact alone serves as the best testimony of his continual relevance to the lives and aspirations of all in Yemen, from the rural peasant to the urban intellectual.

Given Ibn ʿAlwān's great stature as an intellectual and spiritual beacon of the Yemeni nation, it is not surprising that his life and work have become the subjects of many academic studies in Yemen and other Arab countries. However, these studies have not yet succeeded in placing his intellectual and spiritual legacy into the broader historical, political, and social context of his epoch. They are, for the most part, thoroughly descriptive and do not depart substantially from the legendary image of Ibn ʿAlwān constructed by medieval Yemeni chronicles and hagiographies. Nor is there any comprehensive examination of his religious and social convictions and their impact on the religious and intellectual life of Yemen in the subsequent centuries. This study not only rectifies this omission by reconstructing his historical persona but also demonstrates the ways in which Ibn ʿAlwān's semilegendary image has been appropriated by representatives of various political, religious, and intellectual trends in modern Yemeni society, from Islamists to secular nationalists.

In seeking to adjust Ibn ʿAlwān's figure to their disparate polemical and ideological agendas, the spokesmen of these movements have produced an extremely diverse array of images of the medieval Sufi master. Some have seen him as a courageous defender of the downtrodden against the depredations of the oppressive and unscrupulous Rasūlid rulers, while others portray him as an otherworldly recluse and visionary who took little interest in the affairs of the imperfect world around him. My study examines these varied images of Ibn ʿAlwān, and juxtaposes them with his persona as described in medieval chronicles and biographical collections to better understand the construction of his legacy in Yemen.

Paradoxically, despite his ubiquitous presence in Yemeni folklore and intellectual discourse, it is only quite recently that some of his major literary, theological, and mystical works have been edited and published. Prior to the democratic revolution of 1962, those works were banned by the conservative Zaydī (Shīʿī) rulers of Yemen who took a dim view of Sufism, which had traditionally derived its vitality from the Sunnī community of the country. After the revolution, Ibn ʿAlwān's legacy was resurrected and, before long, became embroiled in the debates over the future of the country among secular Marxists, liberal nationalists, and staunch advocates of an Islamic order.

In dealing with Ibn ʿAlwān's life and work I briefly examine the history of Sufism in Yemen and beyond. Since this history is yet to be written, I hope that my study of one of Yemen's most consequential representatives will become an important first step in this direction. Emphasis will be placed on the creative aspects of Ibn ʿAlwān's intellectual output. Studying Ibn ʿAlwān's thought through his poetry is a key point of entry to situate his work in the spiritual and intellectual context of his age. Although his work mainly focused on mystical ideas, one can also observe Ibn 'Alwān's thought in his fearless attitude toward the rulers of the Rasūlid dynasty. This book is also designed to identify and analyze the status of Sufism in Yemen before, during, and after the Rasūlid dynasty. If this study contributes to a better understanding of the society of Rasūlid Yemen and Ibn 'Alwān's theological and Sufi teachings, its purpose will have been served.

Chapter 1 is a general survey of the intellectual, cultural, and political atmosphere of Yemen leading up to the prosperity of the Rasūlid age. I discuss Yemen's political and social environment in the early moments of Islam and explore how the Rasūlid princes came to power as a result of a coup d'état. The rulers of this dynasty evolved into generous patrons of literature, arts, and religious establishments, creating the ideal conditions for the emergence of Yemen's Sufi movement. I portray the relationship between the Rasūlid authorities and the Sufi masters in light of their mutual interests, and examine why the cosmopolitan environment of Rasūlid Yemen was quite appealing to some "monastic" Sufi masters.

The cultural milieu of medieval Yemen, particularly its theological and juridical schools, receives significant attention. I examine the significance of the Shī'a as represented by two major sects, the Ismā'īlīs and the Zaydīs. Both sects are studied from the viewpoint of theology, doctrine, and literature. I conclude the chapter with a brief discussion of the history of the Sunnī community in Yemen and its doctrines, with special reference to the four major Sunnī schools of law, the Shāfi'īs, the Ḥanbalīs, the Ḥanafīs, and the Mālikīs.

Chapter 2 traces the origins of Yemeni Sufism from the earliest days of Islam, when Sufism as a coherent set of practices had not yet emerged, to the seventh/thirteenth century and the rise of the Rasūlid dynasty. Here I explain the latent forms of asceticism in Yemen that provided the foundations for the formation of mystical tradition that culminated in the age of Ibn 'Alwān. This chapter charts the reasons for the decline in Yemen's intellectual and cultural life between the first/seventh century and fourth/tenth century, before stability returned, which paved the way for the rise of saintly miracles (*karāmāt*) during the sixth/twelfth century and ended up with the prosperous, powerful Rasūlid dynasty (626–858/1228–1454).

Chapter 3 focuses on the legacy of Ibn 'Alwān. First, I discuss his biography with special reference to the role of his father. Then, I analyze an "incident" (*'āriḍ*) that medieval hagiographies portray as a major turning point in Ibn 'Alwān's life. My discussion also provides a cursory glance at his education, including teachers and disciples. Then, I discuss the relationship between Ibn 'Alwān and the Rasūlid princes, focusing on his courageous attitude. After that, I provide a detailed analysis of his major works, both published and in manuscript, beginning with the most influential book *The Supreme Union.* I follow with his second indispensable literary *diwān* (collection), concentrating on the debate around his miraculous language. Then, I turn to small treatises, "The Festival" and "The Unfamiliar Diverse Sea," and conclude with some remarks about his manuscript known as "The Appropriate Answers on the Outstanding Questions."

Chapter 4 deals with Ibn 'Alwān's theological views. I present his doctrine in his own words, emphasizing his Sunnī position, and his support of the Rightly Guided Caliphs. This chapter also tackles some difficult doctrinal issues addressed in Ibn 'Alwān's works, such as the relationship between God and human action, free will and predestination, his attitude toward speculative theology (*kalām*), the vision of God, the createdness of the Qur'ān, the Mu'tazilites, and, finally, his purported sympathy with some Shī'ī concepts.

Chapter 5 examines the relationship between Ibn 'Alwān and the Sufi tradition, beginning with his relationship with his popular Sufi rival Abū al-Ghayth Ibn Jamīl (d. 651/1253). I also discuss the relationship between Ibn 'Alwān and as-Sayyid Aḥmad al-Badawī (d. 675/1276). Although existing sources do not provide us with information about the influence of al-Ghazālī (d. 505/1111) on the theology and Sufism of Ibn 'Alwān, I argue that one can sense a spiritual affinity between them through a comparative study of their major works. In addition, this chapter critically examines the link between Ibn 'Alwān and al-Ḥallāj (d. 309/922) posited by Louis Massignon. Finally, I conclude with a refutation of the views of some modern scholars who ascribed Ibn 'Alwān's mystical ideas to the influence of Ibn 'Arabī (d. 638/1240).

Chapter 6 treats Ibn 'Alwān's Sufi thought. I begin with the most important feature of his thought, namely, the use of the Qur'ān and the Prophet's Sunna. By basing his teachings on the Qur'ān and the Sunna, Ibn 'Alwān placed himself squarely in the mainstream of Islam. Then, I discuss the controversial status of the Sufi concert (*samā'*) and Ibn 'Alwān's polemic against those who prohibited it. An analysis of Ibn 'Alwān's theory of the relationship between the Sufi master and his disciple follows. I also explore Ibn 'Alwān's analysis of Sufi epistemology and his tripartite classification of Sufi knowledge: the knowledge of divine essence, the knowledge of divine attributes, and the knowledge of divine actions. Since the Sufi concept of "unveiling" (*kashf*) is an indispensable theme in Ibn 'Alwān's legacy, I provide a brief survey of its development in the works of some major Sufi authorities, including al-Kalābādhī (d. 380/990), al-Qushayrī (d. 465/1072), al-Hujwīrī (d. 469/1077), al-Anṣārī (d. 481/1089), and al-Ghazālī (d. 505/1111). I also analyze Ibn 'Alwān's views of the concept of *kashf*. This chapter concludes with a discussion of Ibn 'Alwān's views of the possibility of mystical union with God on the condition that the Sufi follows the teachings of the Qur'ān, emulates the exemplary piety of the Prophet, and follows in the footsteps of the "friends of God" (*awliyā'*).

Chapter 7 provides a discussion of the Islamic concept of sainthood, particularly in the works of ash-Sharjī (d. 893/1487) and ash-Shawkānī (d. 1250/1834). I also examine Ibn 'Alwān's saintly miracles (*karāmāt*) in light of the views of premodern hagiographers. This chapter concludes with a discussion of the controversy around Ibn 'Alwān's tomb and the veneration of "friends of God."

Chapter 8 focuses on the protracted conflict in Yemen between the Sufi masters and the Zaydī imams, which began in the era where we first encounter charismatic Sufi leaders such as Abū l-Ghayth b. Jamīl (d. 651/1253) and Aḥmad b. 'Alwān (d. 665/1266). The Sufi masters' popularity with Yemen's people made them valuable political allies for the Zaydīs, even as doctrinal disputes sometimes tore the groups apart. While the intensity of this conflict varied over time, and certainly not all Zaydī imams opposed Sufism, it is nevertheless central to understanding the tensions that shaped medieval Yemen's religious and political environment.

Chapter 9 deals with the development of Sufism in Yemen from the demise of Ibn 'Alwān until the fall of the Ottoman Empire. I provide a brief survey of the connection between major Sufi orders in the Islamic lands and their representatives in Yemen. I outline the rise and subsequent history of some Yemeni Sufi orders including the Qādiriyya, Rifā'iyya, Shādhiliyya, Suhrawardiyya, Naqshabandiyya, 'Alawiyya, Yāfi'iyya, Aḥmadiyya, and the now extinct 'Alwāniyya. After the establishment of the Sufi orders, Yemen entered a new phase of fierce scholarly debates over the monistic ideas of Ibn 'Arabī (d. 638/1240). I conclude with a brief discussion of Sufism in Yemen after the end of these debates, focusing on two major representatives of tenth/sixteenth-century Sufism in Yemen: 'Abd al-Hādī as-Sūdī (d. 932/1525) in Ta'izz and 'Umar Bā Makhrama (d. 953/1545) in Ḥaḍramawt.

1

ISLAM IN MEDIEVAL YEMEN

Yemen, like many other areas of the Islamic world, was part of the Umayyad caliphate (40–132/660–749) and then part of the succeeding 'Abbāsid dynasty (132–656/749–1258). Yemen's governors were appointed by both dynasties. Despite the strength of these centralized caliphates, Yemen's remote location singled it out as a refuge for rebel groups and mutineers. Rebels from the central lands of Islam took advantage of the country's distance from the capital of Baghdad and made Yemen the trying ground for their political ambitions. They were also encouraged by Yemen's rugged terrain, which made it impregnable against invading armies.[1] At the beginning of the second/eighth century, Yemen became a veritable refuge for the Shī'a, and it is likely that at that time the first conflict began among three theological schools (*madhhabs*): the Zaydī, the Ismā'īlī, and the Sunnī. This tension defined Yemen's religious environment for centuries, creating conflicts on the one hand and producing a uniquely fertile intellectual and spiritual atmosphere on the other. This atmosphere helped the celebrated Yemeni Sufi and thinker Aḥmad Ibn 'Alwān (d. 665/1266) synthesize his original and pious theology. The following history will set the stage for his emergence in the sixth/twelfth century.

When Abbāsid authority weakened, these tensions in Yemen exploded to leave the country chaotically fragmented into independent states. This began with the rebellion of the Ashā'ir tribe against the 'Abbāsids in Zabīd at the end of the second/eighth century, and then a rebellion by the 'Alids in 203/818 under the leadership of Ibrāhīm b. Musā al-'Alawī, known as al-Jazzār.[2] In response, the 'Abbāsid caliph al-Ma'mūn (198–218/813–835) dispatched an army led by Muḥammad b. Ziyād (d. 245/859), who captured the Tihāma and its surroundings in 204/819. Ibn Ziyād took advantage of the situation and expanded his territory to include Ḥaḍramawt, Laḥj, Aden, al-Janad, Ṣan'ā', and as far as Sa'da. He reintroduced the name of the 'Abbāsid caliph during the Friday prayers (*khuṭba*) in the territories under his control. Taking advantage of the power vacuum created by conflicts inside the 'Abbāsid court, Ibn Ziyād grew powerful and his allegiance to the 'Abbāsids became merely nominal. He passed what had become a semi-independent state onto his sons, who did not remain long in power due to two factors: the political and religious activities of the Ismā'īlī religious mission (*da'wa*) around the country on the one hand, and the establishment of the Zaydī state in Sa'da in 284/897 by Imam al-Hādī Yaḥyā b. al-Ḥusayn (859–910) on the other.[3] There is no doubt that the struggle among the Ismā'īlīs, the Zaydīs, and the Sunnīs was severe and at times brutal.[4] Supporters of each *madhhab* tried to expand geographically at the expense of their rivals, which weakened Yemen's economic and political structures. The effects of the conflict were exacerbated by Yemen's difficult terrain and the weakness of 'Abbāsid rule to the extent that the country was left in a state of chaos.

Yemen entered a new phase of its history, which is often described as the age of independent states. There was an absence of central authority due to the fragmentation of petty states weakened by domestic isolation and debilitating internal wars. In the north was the Zaydī state, particularly in Sa'da, the Banū Ḥātim, rulers of the historical capital, Ṣan'ā', and along the southern coast the Zuray'id state, whose leanings were towards Ismā'īlī teachings. Among the independent states is the first Ismā'īlī dynasty, which was founded by the two *dā'īs* 'Alī b. al-Faḍl (d. 302/914) and al-Ḥasan b. Ḥawshab (d. 303/915).[5] The second Ismā'īlī state, and perhaps the most significant, was established by 'Alī b. Muḥammad aṣ-Ṣulayḥī (439–459/–1045–1066), who unified Yemen for the first time. In addition, we witness the emergence of the Sulaymānī *ashrāf* north of Najrān and as far as Ḥaraḍ in the south of Tihāma. Finally, one should not overlook the two Sunnī states, the Banū Mahdī (554–569/1159–1173) and the Najāḥids (412–551/1021–1156), who were in constant conflict with the Zaydī's on the one hand and the Ismā'īlīs on the other. This chaotic and unstable political condition paved the way for the powerful Sunnī Ayyūbids to invade Yemen, remaining in power from 569/1173 until 628/1228 (see Table 1).

The Ayyūbids

The Ayyūbids invaded Yemen in 569/1173 at a moment when the country was torn apart by constant infighting among its main theological and

Table 1. Ayyūbid Rulers of Yemen

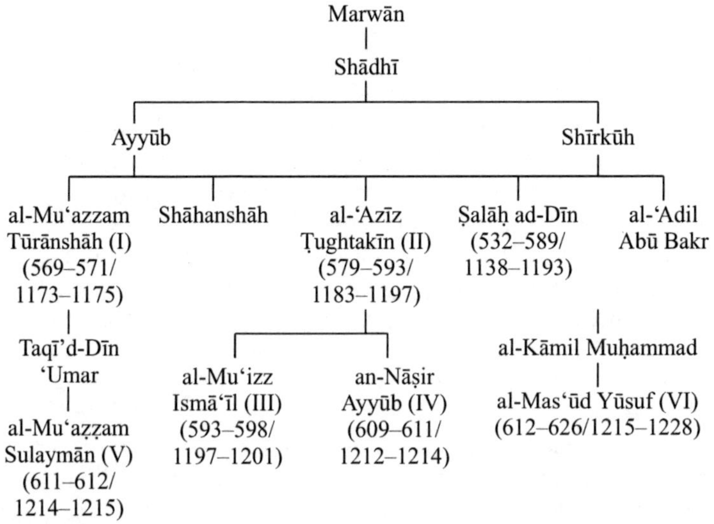
Marwān
Shādhī
Ayyūb
Shīrkūh
al-Mu'azzam Tūrānshāh (I) (569–571/ 1173–1175)
Shāhanshāh
al-'Azīz Ṭughtakīn (II) (579–593/ 1183–1197)
Ṣalāḥ ad-Dīn (532–589/ 1138–1193)
al-'Adil Abū Bakr
Taqī'd-Dīn 'Umar
al-Mu'izz Ismā'īl (III) (593–598/ 1197–1201)
an-Nāṣir Ayyūb (IV) (609–611/ 1212–1214)
al-Kāmil Muḥammad
al-Mas'ūd Yūsuf (VI) (612–626/1215–1228)
al-Mu'aẓẓam Sulaymān (V) (611–612/ 1214–1215)

political factions. There is no doubt that the Ayyūbids contributed significantly to the development of the Yemeni politics and culture, not least because their lieutenants were to usher in one of the most brilliant dynasties in Yemeni history, the Rasūlid dynasty (626–858/1228–1454), which declared independence from the Egyptian Ayyūbids in 632/1234. It is against the cultural and political backdrop of these cataclysmic changes in Yemen that the heritage of Aḥmad b. 'Alwān (d. 665/1266) unfolds. Before turning to Ibn 'Alwān, however, we explore the entrance of the Ayyūbids onto Yemen's political landscape.

First, why did the Ayyūbids invade Yemen? The motives behind this conquest have been a subject of debate among historians since the medieval period. This study has benefited from G. Rex Smith's excellent research in his edition of Ibn Ḥātim, Badr ad-Dīn's *Kitāb as-simṭ al-ghālī ath-thaman fī akhbār al-mulūk min al-ghuzz bi'l-Yaman* and the second volume of his *The Ayyūbids and Early Rasūlids in the Yemen*. Smith's contribution lies in the fact that he was able to scrutinize critically both medieval and modern sources. In his overall assessment of the Ayyūbid occupation of Yemen, Smith provides a religious motive to be rid of the Khārijī, 'Abd an-Nabī b. Mahdī.[6] Removing 'Abd an-Nabī b. Mahdī is considered by far the most significant reason for the Ayyūbid conquest as it is explained in medieval sources.[7] Thus, the Zaydī scholar

Yaḥyā b. al-Ḥusayn describes the Banū Mahdī, rulers of the Tihāma and Zabīd, by saying:

> As for their *madhhab*, it was said that they were followers of Abū Ḥanīfa in *furū'*[8] and followers of Khawārij in *uṣūl*.[9] They regard sinners as disbelievers and they punish them with death penalty. They kill and allow sexual intercourse with the wives of those who disagree with their *madhhab*. They enslave their offspring, and regard their land as an abode of war. …They killed those who were defeated among their soldiers, they killed fornicators, and those who were late to the congregational prayer and those who were late to attend their places of worship. These rules were implemented against their soldiers, but the subjects (*ar-ra'iyya*) were subject to lesser punishment.[10]

This highlights the unjust conditions in coastal areas of Yemen prior to the Ayyūbid occupation. However, the characterization of Ibn Mahdī in these sources is somehow exaggerated perhaps because he belonged to a Sunnī school of law, namely, the Ḥanafī *madhhab*.

In addition, Smith selects another feasible reason for the conquest given by H. A. R. Gibb, suggesting that Saladin (1138–1193) sent a large army led by Tūrānshāh (d. 1180) to Yemen to ease the tremendous financial burden of Saladin's army in Egypt. Smith concludes that the two chief motives for the conquest appear to have been trade and finding a secure place of refuge in the event of the dynasty coming under threat. A minor motive was the desire to drive out the Ismā'īlīs from Yemen. All the other reasons given in the sources, argues Smith, were incidental, though they should not be discounted.[11]

After leading the successful conquest, Tūrānshāh returned to Egypt, leaving his Mamlūk governors in a state of chaos. Each governor acted independently and soon was competing against the others. The deteriorating political situation in Yemen compelled Saladin to send another army under the leadership of Ṣafī ad-Dīn Khiṭilbā. After taking control of the country, he fell ill and died. The situation returned to chaos and again Saladin dispatched his other brother, Ṭughtakīn b. Ayyūb (better known as al-'Azīz), with troops to reassert Ayyūbid control over Yemen. Ṭughtakīn was not only able to wrest most strongholds from the local Yemeni tribes, but profited greatly from annual revenues and newly conquered areas.[12] When Ṭughtakīn had eliminated his rivals, he established a new and firm system of taxation policy. He is described in medieval sources as a just leader who dug wells and planted trees to boost agricultural production. Moreover, he is reported to have punished some of his soldiers for their abuses in the country.[13] Ṭughtakīn and other Ayyūbid princes built fortresses and castles for their military protection. After the death of al-ʿAzīz Ṭughtakīn in 593/1197 power shifted to his son al-Muʿizz Ismāʿīl b. Ṭughtakīn (593–598/1197–1201) who is said to have fallen out with his lieutenants, which led to a conflict within the ruling elite. Some of his former commanders were defeated and joined the Zaydī imam, ʿAbd Allāh b. Ḥamza (d. 614/1217), who was at war with al-Muʿizz. After the assassination of al-Muʿizz in 598/1202, conditions continued to deteriorate under his successor, an-Nāṣir Ayyūb b. Ṭughtakīn (609–611/1212–1214), who was poisoned in a conspiracy by his vizier, Badr ad-Dīn Ghāzī b. Jibrīl in 611/1214. Sulaymān b. Shāhinshāh was immediately installed as sultan in the same year.[14]

Owing to the provocation of various groups, conditions again deteriorated during this period until 612/1215 when the ruler of Egypt, al-Malik al-Kāmil, dispatched his son al-Masʿūd (d. 626/1228) with a military force to settle issues in Yemen. It is important to mention that al-Masʿūd had a very close relationship with the father of Aḥmad b. ʿAlwān who eventually served as a royal scribe to king al-Masʿūd. Al-Masʿūd remained in power for ten years until he died in Mecca on his way to Egypt in 626/1228. Before leaving Yemen, he had appointed Nūr ad-Dīn ʿUmar b. ʿAlī b. Rasūl as his deputy.[15] In the absence of an Ayyūbid sovereign, Nūr ad-Dīn was able to take control of the country and protect it against an uprising in the Tihāma as well as from a Zaydī offensive in the north.[16] The Ayyūbids were preoccupied with internal as well as external problems, which distracted their attention from the already volatile situation in Yemen. In the meantime, Nūr ad-Dīn was astute enough to replace the Ayyūbid military leaders, who were in charge of the fortresses and towns, with his loyal retinues.[17] When he made sure that the whole country was in his grip, he threw off his allegiance to his Ayyūbid masters and proclaimed himself an independent ruler with the title al-Manṣūr.[18] "To legitimize his new status, in 632/1234, he obtained an investiture from the ʿAbbāsid caliph in Baghdad, al-Mustanṣir."[19] He remained in power until he was assassinated in 647/1250 in a conspiracy planned by his nephew, Asad ad-Dīn Muḥammad b. al-Ḥasan b. ʿAlī b. Rasūl, who had been threatened with a discharge from the governorship of Ṣanʿāʾ.[20] Al-Manṣūr's son, Yūsuf, with the title al-Muẓaffar (647–694/1249–1295), assumed power and was able to defeat the assassins of his father and outmaneuver his rival, Fakhr ad-Dīn b. Badr ad-Dīn.[21]

With the establishment of al-Muẓaffar's rule in Yemen, I turn to the Rasūlid dynasty and its cultural, religious, and intellectual impact on Yemen. A description of this dynasty elucidates the broader context for the works of Aḥmad b. 'Alwān and his contribution to the political, cultural, religious, and intellectual life of medieval Yemen.

The Rasūlids

The genealogy of the Rasūlids can be traced in two ways: first, to the Turkomans, and second, to the pre-Islamic Yemeni tribe of Azd, specifically, to the time of the destruction of the Mārib Dam. The Rasūlids are said to have moved constantly through the centuries, stopping at the Tihāma and Ḥijāz, residing in Syria, Constantinople, Central Asia, Baghdad, and Egypt.[22] According to Smith, "those who did not know the Rasūlids traced their ancestry back to the Turkomans, while those who did know them acknowledged their Arab origin and called them Ghassānīs."[23] Although they were employed by the Ayyūbids in Egypt and Syria, they were so powerful that the Ayyūbids feared them as potential rivals and therefore dispatched them together with Tūrānshāh's expedition to conquer Yemen (see Table 2).

Rasūlid reign in Yemen began with Nūr ad-Dīn, who was succeeded by his son al-Muẓaffar Yūsuf (d. 694/1295), whose reign lasted for almost half a century. Commenting on his long rule, Alexander Knysh says: "Yemen witnessed an unprecedented political and social stability which led to the consolidation of the new state and its economy."[24] Another important feature of al-Muẓaffar's long reign has been observed by Daniel Varisco: "Yemen had achieved a unity not seen since the pre-Islamic kingdoms and not to be achieved again until the unification of the Yemen Arab Republic and Peoples Democrat[ic] Republic of Yemen in 1990."[25] The Rasūlid state after al-Muẓaffar reached its peak due to the rapid growth of trade and agriculture.[26] The last ruler of the Rasūlid dynasty was an-Nāṣir Aḥmad (d. 827/1424) whose death coincided with the dynasty's collapse. The repeated revolts of slaves and rebellious tribes equally contributed to the collapse of the Rasūlid dynasty.[27] The Rasūlid house was succeeded by the Ṭāhirids, whose rule was brought to an end by the first invasion of the conquering Ottomans in 945/1538.[28]

The era of the Rasūlids is described as "one of the most brilliant of Yemeni civilization."[29] Medieval as well as modern sources describe the Rasūlid sultans as noted for their erudite knowledge and love of scholarship. These rulers generously patronized scholars specializing in numerous religious and secular disciplines including history, biography,

Table 2. Rasūlid Rulers of Yemen

- Rasūl (Muḥammad b. Hārūn)
  - 'Alī
    - al-Ḥasan
    - Abū Bakr
    - al-Manṣūr 'Umar (1) (628–647/1230–1249)
      - Asad ad-Dīn Muḥammad
      - Fakhr ad-Dīn Abū Bakr
      - al-Muẓaffar Yūsuf (II) (647–694/1249–1295)
        - al-Ashraf 'Umar (III) (694–696/1295–1296)
        - al-Wāthiq Ibrāhīm
        - al-Mu'ayyad Dāwūd (IV) (694–721/1296–1322)
          - al-Mujāhid 'Alī (V) (721–764/1322–1363)
            - al-Afḍal al-'Abbās (VI) (764–778/1363–1377)
              - al-Ashraf Ismā'īl (VII) (778–803/1377–1401)
                - an-Nāṣir Aḥmad (VIII) (803–827/1401–1424)
                  - al-Manṣūr 'Abd Allāh (IX) (827–830/1424–1427)
                    - al-Ashraf Ismā'īl (X) (830–831/1427–1428)
                      - aẓ-Ẓāhir Yaḥyā (XI) (831–842/1428–1438)
                        - al-Ashraf Ismā'īl (XII) (842–845/1438–1441)
                      - 'Umar
                        - al-Muẓaffar Yūsuf (XIII) (dispute of power)
      - al-Mufaḍḍal Abū Bakr
      - al-Fā'iz Aḥmad
    - Mūsā

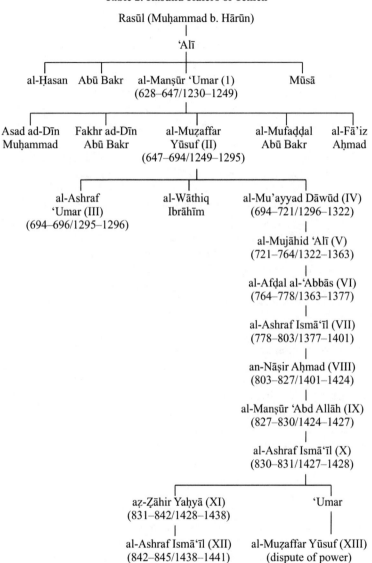

genealogy, astrology, Sufism, medicine, agriculture, furriery, equine, and veterinary. Rasūlid sultans themselves were students of first-rank scholars and were known for their prolific writings on a wide variety of subjects.[30] Emulating the Ayyūbid policies, the Rasūlid sultans built colleges, libraries, and international centers of Islamic education. The contemporary scholar, historian, and critic 'Abd Allāh al-Ḥibshī states that the Rasūlids were tolerant toward charismatic Sufi leaders, and frequently exempted them from land taxes. However, al-Ḥibshī argues, this tolerance (*tasāmuḥ*) was not based on religious motives; rather it was motivated by political interests.[31] Sufi masters enjoyed a high reputation among the peasants, and the Rasūlids cultivated friendship with them to benefit from their spiritual authority (*jāh*).[32] Some Rasūlids, it will be recalled, not only collected Sufi works but diligently studied Sufi philosophy.[33] The officials of the state imitated their rulers in reading speculative Sufism. For instance, Ibn 'Arabī's *Fuṣūṣ al-ḥikam* and the monumental *al-Futūḥāt al-makkiyya* enjoyed high regard at the Rasūlid court.[34]

Clearly, scholars were held in great respect at the Rasūlid court. Many scholars came from different parts of the Islamic world looking for opportunities offered by the enlightened Rasūlids.[35] Among them were Muḥammad Ibn Abī Bakr al-Fārisī (d. 675/1276), the great Egyptian biographer and *muḥaddith*, Ibn Ḥajar al-'Asqalānī (d. 852/1449), who eventually declined the post of the supreme *qāḍī* of Yemen, the celebrated lexicographer Majd ad-Dīn al-Fayrūzābādī (d. 815/1415), the acclaimed Meccan biographer and historian al-Fāsī, the renowned *hadīth* collector Ibn al-Jazarī (d. 833/1429), the great Muslim traveler Ibn Baṭṭūṭah (d. 779/1377), the Sufi writer 'Abd al-Karīm al-Jīlī (d. 832/1428), and others.[36] Under Rasūlid influence Yemen's cultural milieu changed drastically, setting the stage for the emergence of a scholar like Ibn Alwan. However, Yemen's cultural fabric was also shaped by the complex interactions between the major Islamic sects, including the Ismā'īlīs, Zaydīs, Ibāḍīs, and Sunnīs.

Yemen's Cultural Milieu

The Ismā'īlī Movement in Yemen

The Ismā'īlīs are a major branch of the Shī'a with numerous subdivisions. Its followers branched off from the Imāmiyya by tracing the imamate through Ismā'īl, the elder son of Imam Ja'far aṣ-Ṣādiq (d. 148/765). Nothing is known about the history of the Ismā'īlī movement until after the middle of the third/ninth century, when it appeared as a secret revolutionary organization carrying on intensive missionary efforts in many regions of the Muslim world.[37] All sources that deal with the subject of the Ismāʿīlīs in Yemen agree that the two missionaries (*dāʿīs*) ʿAlī b. al-Faḍl al-Khanfarī (d. 302/914) and al-Ḥasan b. Ḥawshab (d. 303/915), known as Manṣūr al-Yaman, were collaborating in the early stages of the nascent Ismāʿīlī movement to advance the cause (*ad-daʿwa*) and prepare for the accession of the future Fāṭimid caliph, whose enemies called him ʿUbayd Allāh al-Mahdī (297–322/909–934).[38] Whereas ʿAlī b. al-Faḍl preached his *daʿwa* at al-Janad, Ibn Ḥawshab established himself at ʿAdan Lāʿah near the mountain of Maswar, in the province of Ḥajja. In 299/913 ʿAlī b. al-Faḍl renounced his allegiance to ʿUbayd Allāh al-Mahdī and began to fight against his companion, the loyal Ibn Ḥawshab. The latter succeeded in spreading the *daʿwa* to the Maghrib and Sind, and Ibn al-Faḍl was depicted in Zaydī sources as a "Qarmaṭian." These sources attributed to him the most heinous of crimes, such as the approval of adultery, incestuous marriage, wine drinking, and outlawing the pilgrimage to Mecca.[39] According to a modern Yemeni commentator, ʿAbd Allāh ash-Shamāḥī, the reason for these allegations was Ibn al-Faḍl's intention to unify Yemen and suppress the conflict between sectarian *madhhabs*.[40] When Ibn al-Faḍl died in 302/914, his followers rapidly disappeared. Consequently, the Ismāʿīlī *daʿwa* weakened and went into steep decline following the death of Ibn Ḥawshab (d. 303/915).

Although the Yaʿfurid *amīr* ʿAbd Allāh b. Qaḥṭān, the ruler of Ṣanʿāʾ, who wrested Zabīd from the Ziyādids, supported the *daʿwa* from 379/989 to 387/997, it had suffered major setbacks.[41] It is not until 429/1038 that we hear about the founder of the Ṣulayḥid dynasty and missionary (*dāʿī*), ʿAlī b. Muḥammad aṣ-Ṣulayḥī, who fortified himself at the Masār mountain of Ḥarāz after establishing contacts with the Fāṭimids in Egypt. Ṣulayḥid rule over Yemen lasted for almost one century until 532/1138.[42] Aḥmad ash-Shāmī and R. B. Serjeant in their article, "Regional Literature: The Yemen," describe the Ṣulayḥid era as one of the most fruitful ages in Yemeni history. According to them, "despite the violent political confusion and destructive sectarian quarrels that marked it, learning, literature and verse flourished, colleges and mosques were built, roads constructed. Most rulers of the time—imams, sultans, or princes—were scholars of distinction, orators, poets, and authors in a great variety of fields."[43]

After the death of the eighth Fāṭimid caliph al-Mustanṣir in Egypt in 487/1094, the Ismāʿīlīs split up into two main groups, presided over by al-Mustanṣir's sons, Nizār and Aḥmad. In spite of al-Mustanṣir's designation of his eldest son, Nizār, as his heir, the vizier al-Afḍal supported Aḥmad, the younger son, to take the throne with the title al-Musta'lī. Nizār was defeated and fled to Alexandria. His right to inherit the throne was upheld by the Persian Ismā'īlīs under the leadership of Ḥasan-i Ṣabbāḥ, who, in the absence of Nizār, became the supreme chief claiming the rank of *ḥujja*.[44] Both Nizār and al-Musta'lī had devotees in different parts of the Islamic world. Al-Musta'lī was recognized by most Ismā'īlīs in Egypt and India, many in Syria, and by the whole community in Yemen. The Musta'lian Ismā'īlīs experienced further division after the assassination of al-Musta'lī's son and successor al-Āmir in 524/1130. The latter's son, aṭ-Ṭayyib (whose existence is questioned by some historians), had been proclaimed as heir eight months before his father's death. Despite the suppression of the infant's name and the succession of regents on the throne in Cairo, some Musta'lian communities in Egypt, Syria, and most of the leaders of the established *da'wa* network in Yemen continued to advocate the rights of aṭ-Ṭayyib.

The Ṭayyibī *dā'īs* worked successfully in Yemen with the support of the Ṣulayḥid queen, Arwā bint Aḥmad aṣ-Ṣulayḥī (d. 532/1138). After her death, another branch of *da'wa*, the Ḥāfiẓī, was supported by the Zuray'ids in Aden and some of the Hamdānid rulers of San'ā', but they lost state support after the Ayyūbid conquests. However, the Ṭayyibī community, as portrayed by historians, was on good terms with the Ayyūbids, Rasūlids, and Ṭāhirid rulers.[45] The position of the chief missionary (*dā'ī muṭlaq*) remained among the descendants of Ibrāhīm b. al-Ḥusayn al-Ḥāmidī (d. 557/1161) until 605/1209, when it passed to 'Alī b. Muḥammad of the Banū 'l-Anf family. It continued with this family until 946/1539 with two interruptions in the seventh/thirteenth century. The Ismā'īlī *da'wa* in Yemen established its headquarters in the stronghold of Ḥarāz mountains, though there were scattered communities in other parts of the country. In 1050/1640 the position of *dā'ī muṭlaq* passed on to Ibrāhīm b. Muḥammad b. Fahd of the Makramī family. The Makramī *dā'īs* established themselves in Najrān where they were supported by the tribe of Banū Yām. Sometime before 1131/1719 they conquered the mountain of Ḥarāz, which became their stronghold and which allowed them to resist the attempts of Zaydī imams to expel them. The attempt of the *dā'ī* al-Ḥasan b. Hibat Allāh (d. 1189/1775) to conquer Ḥaḍramawt was successful; however, his advance toward Central Arabia and his struggle against the rising Saudi dynasty ended in failure. In 1289/1872 the Ottoman general Aḥmad Mukhtār Pasha perfidiously killed the *dā'ī* al-Ḥasan b. Ismā'īl Āl-Shibām al-Makramī and expelled the Makramīs from Ḥarāz. In 1940, the *dāʿī muṭlaq* of the Sulaymānīs was Jamāl ad-Dīn ʿAlī b. al-Ḥusayn al-Makramī, who succeeded his father in 1939.[46] After this period, the *daʿwa* went into hiding, or occultation (*ghayba*)—if I may borrow this classical term from early Shīʿism—since the political as well as cultural atmosphere was no longer hospitable to such activities.

Ismāʿīlī Doctrine and Literature

Ismāʿīlī doctrine and literature had an important influence on the religious environment of Yemen both within and beyond the Ismāʿīlī community. For example, the Sufi figure Ibn ʿAlwān, while not directly linked to the Ismāʿīlīs, refers to them indirectly in his works and was clearly aware of their legacy.[47] Such instances, exemplified in a figure such as Ibn ʿAlwān, point to the complex interweaving that made up medieval Yemen's religious environment.

The early doctrine of pre-Fāṭimid Ismāʿīlīs, which was formulated during the second half of the third/ninth century, drew a sharp distinction between *aẓ-ẓāhir*, exterior or exoteric knowledge, and *al-bāṭin*, inward or esoteric knowledge. This doctrine seems to have been shared by many Shīʿī sects as well as Sufis, including Ibn ʿAlwān. *Bāṭin* consists of two main parts: an allegorical interpretation of the Qur'ān and the Sunna, and second, the "true realities" (*ḥaqā'iq*). This duality presupposes that the Ismāʿīlī system of philosophy and science can be reconciled with their religious beliefs. It is intended to prove the divine origin of the institutions of the imamate and the exclusive rights of the Fāṭimids to it.[48]

Ismāʿīlīsm tried to find in Neoplatonic philosophy a synthesis between the concept of monotheism and the plurality of the visible world. Moreover, the natural philosophy of Ismāʿīlīsm, with its ideas of the organic and inorganic world, psychology, and biology, is to some extent based on Aristotle's work and partly on Neo-Pythagorean and other Greek philosophical speculations. The probable aim of this theoretical framework was to reconcile religion with philosophy. The Ṭayyibī community in Yemen and India retained an interest in the gnostic cosmology and cyclical history of the Fāṭimid age. Unlike the traditional Fāṭimid cosmological system, the Ṭayyibī doctrine modified the cosmological system of the *dāʿī* Ḥamīd ad-Dīn al-Kirmānī (d. about 411/1021). His system describes ten intellects in the spiritual world rather than the traditional duality of the intellect and the soul. This modification was achieved by introducing a mythical "drama in heaven," first portrayed by the second *dā'ī muṭlaq* Ibrāhīm al-Ḥāmidī, whose thought shaped the Ṭayyibī concept of gnosis.[49] Finally, "the Ṭayyibī doctrine maintained the equal validity of [knowledge from both] *ẓāhir* and *bāṭin* and repudiated antinomian trends. Al-Qāḍī an-Nu'mān's [(d. 363/974)] *Da'āim al-Islām* remained the authoritative work of *fiqh*."[50]

It is with the *Rasā'il ikhwān aṣ-ṣafā'* (Epistles of the Brethren of Purity) that the relationship of the Ismā'īlī sect to the great medieval Yemeni scholar and devout Sufi Ibn 'Alwān becomes clearer. Not only were the Ismā'īlīs a prominent theological and political school in the medieval history of Yemen, but their literary works are mentioned in the poetry of Ibn 'Alwān. These epistles were controversial encyclopedic work, regarded by the Musta'lians as a compilation by the second son of the concealed imam, Aḥmad. These epistles are significant for the purposes of this study because their authors are occasionally mentioned in a commendable tone in the poetry of Aḥmad b. 'Alwān.

There is a vast body of literature dealing with the Ismā'īlī doctrine and the Ṭayyibī *da'wa* in Yemen and India, and here I shall confine myself to those issues relevant to the Ṭayyibī community of Yemen. The great works of the *dā'ī* authors in this community continued to preserve the literary heritage of the Fāṭimid *da'wa* of Egypt after the Fāṭimids had lost their political power. These are: *Dīwān* and *Ghāyat al-mawālid* by Ṣulṭān al-Khaṭṭāb al-Hamdānī (d. 533/1138), *Kanz al-walad* by the second *dā'ī muṭlaq* Ibrāhīm b. al-Ḥusayn al-Ḥāmidī (d. 557/1161), *Majmū' at-tarbiyya* by Muḥammad b. Ṭāhir al-Hārithī (d. 584/1188), and *Tuḥfat al-qulūb* and *al-Majālis* both by Ḥātim b. Ibrāhim al-Ḥāmidī. To these can be added *Kitāb 'uyūn al-akhbār* (seven volumes), and *Kitāb nuzhat al-afkār* (two volumes) all by the prolific *dā'ī*, Idrīs 'Imād ad-Dīn al-Anf (d. 833/1428). They are, according to the modern writer Ḥusayn b. Fayḍ Allāh al-Hamdānī (d. 1961), not only relevant to the Fāṭimid period but contain information based on earlier sources and information so intimately bound up with the *da'wa* that it is not possible to find it elsewhere.[51] Another later work, al-Hamdānī concludes, is also valuable for earlier Fāṭimid times, namely the *Kitāb al-azhār* ("Book of Flowers"), in seven volumes by the Indian *dā'ī* Ḥasan b. Nūḥ (d. 939/1533). Sections from some rare or lost works of the earlier Fāṭimid period are preserved in it.

In conclusion, the history, doctrine, and literature of the Ismā'īlīs have been extensively studied by Western scholars interested in so-called deviant Islamic doctrines, which Knysh describes as "a hobby-horse of European Islamology since its inception."[52] According to

Knysh, "this obsessive preoccupation with 'deviancy' has led them to neglect the 'platitudes' of mainstream Sunnīsm that was professed by the majority of medieval Yemenis."[53] From the Ismā'īlīs I turn to their opponents within the Shī'ī movement, the Zaydīs.

The Zaydī Movement in Yemen

The topic of the Zaydīs is so vast and complex that several large volumes would be required to do it justice. According to Alexander Knysh, "Zaydīsm has consistently received the lion's share of academic attention."[54] Here, I will confine myself to some important issues such as the doctrine of the imamate, imitation (*taqlīd*), and its refutation. This latter is relevant to the Sufi movement in general and to the study of Ibn 'Alwān in particular, who refers to them as Rawāfiḍ.[55]

The practical group of Shī'ism is distinguished from the Ithnā'ashariyya (Twelvers) and the Sab'iyya (Ismā'īlīs) by its recognition of Zayd b. 'Alī b. al-Ḥusayn b. 'Alī b. Abī Ṭālib (d. 122/740).[56] Zayd was the first to revolt against the Umayyads after the tragedy of Karbalā in 61/680 during which the Prophet's grandson al-Ḥusayn was killed. Zayd was induced by Kūfans to publicly put himself forward as imam. Sources say that he spent a year in Kūfa in secret preparation, then came forward openly only to be killed in street fighting around 122/740.[57] His followers continued their struggle after Zayd's death and took part in several uprisings in favor of the 'Alid clan, though they were not organized under any unified leadership. Their unification is attributed to the work of the two Zaydī leaders: (1) al-Ḥasan b. Zayd, who founded the Zaydī state south of the Caspian Sea, namely, Ṭabaristān, in 250/864. In the same year, another revolt took place that was considered to have been in line with Zaydī principles, during the caliphate of al-Musta'īn, led by Yaḥyā b. 'Umar (d. 250/864), who descended from al-Ḥusayn b. 'Alī (d. 61/680). (2) The second important Zaydī leader is al-Hādī ilā l-Ḥaqq Yaḥyā b. al-Ḥusayn (d. 298/910), the grandson of al-Qāsim b. Ibrāhīm ar-Rassī (d. 246/860), a descendant of al-Ḥasan b. 'Alī b. Abī Ṭālib (d. 50/670).

Zayd b. 'Alī (d. 122/740) was influenced by his teacher Wāṣil b. 'Aṭā (d. 131/748), the famous founder of the rationalist school of thought, Mu'tazila. After the demise of Zayd, the Zaydīs embraced Mu'tazilī theology and became its ardent followers. The school founded by ar-Rassī (d. 246/860) and developed by his successors is now the only surviving school: it is Mu'tazilite in theology and anti-Murji'ite in ethics, with a puritanical peculiarity in its repudiation of mysticism.[58] Their rejection of mysticism has been noticed through their activities such as the destruction of saints' tombs, including the tomb of the Sufi Ibn 'Alwān.

A number of Zaydīs propounded the doctrine of the "imamate of the inferior" (*imāmat al-mafḍūl*): that it was possible for a man of lesser excellence to be appointed as an imam during the lifetime of a man of greater excellence.[59] According to the contemporary historian and literary critic, Ḥusayn b. 'Abd Allāh al-'Amrī, the question of the theory of the imamate became diverse and complicated.[60] However, the genuine beginning of Zaydī history in Yemen took place with the establishment of the first Zaydī state in Ṣa'da by its founder Imam al-Hādī ilā 'l-Ḥaqq Yaḥyā b. al-Ḥusayn (245–298/859–910). Following his death, the Zaydī community continued to develop until the present day. However, in their historical development they have become less well-defined as a group, and have been observed vacillating between moderates and extremists (*ghulā*). Indeed, W. M. Watt asserts that the history of the Zaydīs is so complex that it is difficult to make generalizations.[61]

In his *Maqālāt al-islāmiyyīn wa'khtilāf al-muṣallīn*, Abū al-Ḥasan al-Ash'arī (d. 324/935) classifies the Zaydī sects in six groups: al-Jārūdiyya,[62] as-Sulaymāniyya (or al-Jarīriyya),[63] al-Butriyya,[64] an-Nu'aymiyya,[65] those who repudiated the caliphate of Abū Bakr and 'Umar but did not deny the return of the dead before the day of Judgment, and finally al-Ya'qūbiyya.[66] However, the heresiographer ash-Shahrastānī (d. 548/1153) in his *al-Milal wa n-niḥal* and the medieval Yemeni scholar, Nashwān b. Sa'īd al-Ḥimyarī (d. 573/1177) in his *al-Ḥūr al-'īn* choose to recognize only the first three sects of Zaydīs.

It is widely known in literature and practice up to the present day that the Zaydī school (*madhhab*) is the closest Shī'ī *madhhab* to the four Sunnī schools (the Ḥanafī, the Mālikī, the Shāfi'ī, and the Ḥanbalī). In his al-*Muntaza' al-mukhtār min al-ghaith al-midrār*, the Zaydī scholar 'Abd Allāh b. Miftāḥ (d. 877/1472) provides a vivid picture of the similarity between the Zaydī *madhhab* and the four Sunnī *madhhabs*. Greater conformity can also be found in the official textbook, *Kitāb al-azhār fī fiqh al-a'immah al-aṭhār* (The Book of Flowers), by Aḥmad b. Yaḥyā al-Murtaḍā (d. 836/1432), "a deposed Imam who composed his work while in prison."[67] "A chapter devoted to the *Imamate* represents the mainstream Zaydī position on qualifications and activities connected with this position. There are more than thirty commentaries and glosses on this authoritative manual, among them separate multi-volume commentaries by the original author and by his sister."[68] Al-'Amrī argues that those who commented on *al-Azhār* or *al-Baḥr az-zakhkhār* of al-

Murtaḍā reject his argument that the imam must be from the family of ʿAlī.[69] The essential demands on the imam were: (1) membership of the Ahl al-Bayt without any distinction between Ḥasanids and Ḥusaynids; (2) ability to resort to the sword if necessary for offense or defense; (3) necessary religious learning. If the qualifications for the imamate are not completely achieved, one cannot be recognized as a full imam.[70] The Zaydī *madhhab*, according to Muḥammad Abū Zahra (d. 1974), is quite similar to that of Abū Ḥanīfa. But the Zaydī *madhhab* is more extensive in the use of three legal principles: *al-maṣlaḥa al-mursala* (public interest), *al-istiṣḥāb* (presumption of continuity), and the use of *al-ʿaql* (intellect) if there were no indications (*adilla*) from the sources.[71]

Given all the above facts, it is important to survey the views of the historian and literary critic, Ismāʿīl al-Akwaʿ (d. 2008), who published *az-Zaydiyya: nash'atuhā wa muʿtaqadātuhā*. In this book, al-Akwaʿ provides a brief historical background on the rise and doctrine of the Zaydī sect. He begins his discussion by saying that there is little research on the Zaydī sects and its branches.[72] This claim is in contrast to the argument noted above, that studies on az-Zaydiyya have been extensive, especially when compared to studies of their opponents, the Sunnīs. This bias, as has been illustrated, was due to European interest in deviant sects. The Zaydīs as a *madhhab* have not attracted sufficient attention, in the opinion of al-Akwaʿ. An exception was given in a book titled *The Support of the Zaydī Schools* (*Nuṣrat madhāhib az-zaydiyya*), which had been attributed to aṣ-Ṣāḥib b. ʿAbbād (d. 385/995), the vizier of Buwyhid dynasty.[73] Al-Akwaʿ seems to be disposed to suspect whether this book might have been the same as *Kitāb az-zaydiyya* mentioned by the *Fihrist* of Ibn an-Nadīm under the biography of Ibn ʿAbbād. The content of the book revolves around the preference of ʿAlī b. Abī Ṭālib and the legitimacy of his predecessor.[74]

Al-Akwaʿ goes on to mention those Western scholars who have contributed to the study of the Zaydīs, such as R. Strothmann (d. 1960), who wrote about Zaydīs from a purely historical perspective. Among the Arab historians who have tackled the question of Zaydīs is the Iraqi Faḍīla ʿAbd al-Amīr ash-Shāmī who wrote *Tārīkh al-firqah az-zaydiyya* (1974). Her focus was on the Zaydīs of Jīlān and Daylamān during the second and third centuries A.H. As for the Zaydīs in Yemen, the lengthy book of Aḥmad Maḥmūd Ṣubḥī, a visiting scholar at the University of Ṣanʿāʾ, entitled *az-Zaydiyya*, was received with admiration by the followers of the Zaydī-Hādawī *madhhab*.[75] This admiration, argues al-Akwaʿ, sprang from the fact that Ṣubḥī uncritically praised some Zaydī ideas. Ṣubḥī thought that the Zaydīs of the late third century A.H., whose ideas have remained important up to the present, were an extension of the Zaydīs of the second century A.H., who appeared in Kūfa under their founder Zayd b. 'Alī (d. 122/740). This is not true, al-Akwa' says, because the relationship between the Zaydīs of Yemen and the Zaydīs of Kūfa had been cut off since the third/ninth century. Although this judgment by Ṣubḥī, al-Akwa' argues, was based on some Zaydī sources, Ṣubḥī apparently neglected to consult neutral sources pertaining to his subject.

Al-Akwa' proceeds to say that Zaydī scholars (*'ulamā'*) should have made an effort to fully identify Zaydīs in reference to the differences between the past Zaydīs at Kūfa and the Zaydīs of Yemen, and to clarify the relations between the Zaydīs and the Twelvers. According to Al-Akwa', this has not yet been done. He then criticizes some Zaydī works, such as the introduction of *Bayān Ibn Muẓaffar* by al-Qāḍī Ḥusayn as-Sayāghī (d. 1407/1987) for its inadequacy and *az-Zaydiyya: Theory and Practice* by 'Alī b. 'Abd al-Karīm al-Faḍīl for its digression.[76]

Following several definitions of az-Zaydiyya and the analysis of its branches, al-Akwa' mentions the jurisprudential (*fiqh*) sources of Imam al-Hādī ilā al-Ḥaqq Yaḥyā b. al-Ḥusayn (d. 298/910). Al-Akwa' states that Aḥmad b. Yaḥyā al-Murtaḍā (al-Imam al-Mahdī) in his *Ghāyat al-amānī*, quoted al-Hādī: "they—[the people of Sunna]—have two books called '*ṣaḥīḥayn*' [i.e., Bukhārī and Muslim] and I swear that they are devoid of truth."[77] This, al-Akwa' argues, is supported by Aḥmad b. Sa'd ad-Dīn al-Maswarī (d. 1079/1668) who says in his *ar-Risāla al-munqidha min al-ghiwāya fī ṭarīq ar-riwāya* that "everything in the six [Sunnī] collections of Ḥadīth (*al-ummahāt as-sit*) are lies and cannot be taken as a source of proof (*lā yuḥtajju bihi*)." This opinion was held because Imam al-Hādī and his followers did not regard them as true, because their transmitters were not Shī'īs.[78]

The point mentioned above is not only pertinent to the Zaydī *madhhab* but can also be prevalent in some other *madhhabs*. This, al-Akwa' says, is attested by Imam ash-Shawkānī (d. 1250/1834) in his *Adab aṭ-ṭalab* when he discusses the doctrine of blind imitation (*taqlīd*) in all Islamic *madhhabs* by saying: "they [i.e., the *muqallidūn*] believed that their Imam is the most knowledgeable of the proofs (*adilla*) in the Book and Sunna. . . . If they were informed of a proof in the Book of Allāh [i.e., Qur'ān] or in the Sunna of the Prophet, they reject it."[79] The *muqallidūn* argue that if proof from the Qur'ān or Sunna had been more significant (*rājiḥ*), then their imam would have adhered to it. They emphasized that their imam abandoned this Qur'ānic proof only because it was insignificant in his eyes, had less weight in scholarship, and another proof may have carried more evidence (*arjaḥ*). Ash-Shawkānī states in the same book: "If someone says to them: follow this verse from the Qur'ān or this sound Ḥadīth, they say: 'You are not more knowledgeable than our Imam so that we would follow you. If this was true as you claim, the one whom we imitate [i.e., the Imam] would not have departed it. He would not have been at variance with it, but rather left it to what seemed to him to have more evidence (*arjaḥ*).' "[80]

Finally, al-Akwa' supports his thesis with a long quote from ash-Shawkānī's *Adab aṭ-ṭalab*, particularly with regard to the doctrine of *taqlīd* within the Zaydī *madhhab*. I present the argument as it appears in *Adab aṭ-ṭalab*, which talks about the "followers" or "imitators" (*muqallidūn*; pl. *muqallid*)[81] among the Zaydīs of Yemen. According to ash-Shawkānī, the *muqallidūn* in Yemen were misled by a devilish pretext (*dharī'a iblīsiyya*) and a pessimistic excuse, namely, that the biographical dictionaries (*dawāwīn*) of Islam—the six books and what is added to them such as the *masānīd* and the *majāmī'* comprising the Sunna—were not only written by non-Shī'īs but also studied by those who do not follow the Prophet's family (*ahl al-bayt*). By this cursed pretext, ash-Shawkānī argues, they nullified the entire body of the pure Sunna. According to ash-Shawkānī, there is no Sunna except what is in these collections. Despite the fact that some scholars consider ash-Shawkānī a moderate Zaydī, he must be regarded as a Sunnī scholar since he defended the Sunna. Ash-Shawkānī criticizes the *muqallidūn* of the Zaydī *madhhab*:

> Although the *muqallidūn* are not considered among the people of knowledge, and do not even merit to be mentioned, and it is not worthwhile to display their ignorance and to record their stupidity, they nevertheless have pretended to be among the people of knowledge, carrying notebooks, attending mosques and schools to the extent that the populace believed in them as belonging to the people of knowledge and, hence, accepted their instructions. So they themselves went astray and deluded others. . . . With them, the calamity was aggravated and because of them disaster prevailed.[82]

Ash-Shawkānī maintains that the people of imitation (*taqlīd*) in every *madhhab* glorify the books of Sunna, acknowledge their eminence, and believe that they are the sayings and the deeds of the Prophet. Moreover, they are the *dawāwīn* of Islam, which scholars have depended on. Ash-Shawkānī further discusses the status of the *muqallidūn* of the Zaydī *madhhab*, who added to the repulsiveness of *taqlīd* another ugliness, more repugnant, and to the heretic bigotry another heresy, yet more abominable, specifically, the rejection of the Sunna. Ash-Shawkānī disparagingly says:

> If only they [i.e., Zaydī *muqallidūn*] had had a little bit of knowledge and a little bit of understanding, they would have come to know that the intention of writing these books was to collect what reached them [i.e., their authors] from the Sunna according to their capabilities and utmost of their knowledge. They were not bigots to a [particular] *madhhab*, and they did not confine themselves to what may appeal [more] to some *madhhabs* than others. Yet, they collected the Prophet's Sunna for the *umma* so that every scholar would learn from it in accordance with his knowledge and his preparation. Whoever does not understand this, does not deserve to be addressed as a human being.[83]

This statement represents the doctrine of *taqlīd* versus *ijtihād* not only within the Zaydī *madhhab*, but also within the cultural milieu of the Islamic world as a whole. There is no doubt that ash-Shawkānī was not the first to address this topic. He was preceded by Muslim scholars from different schools, who dealt with the topic of *taqlīd* versus *ijtihād*. For instance, pertaining to our purpose, Ibn 'Alwān rejected the concept of blind imitation, particularly in Sufism where he instructed his disciples that it is unnecessary to follow their Sufi masters if they are able themselves to follow the Qurān and Sunna. Nonetheless, six centuries later, ash-Shawkānī's era in Yemen was full of blind imitation (*taqlīd*) that probably exceeded all other parts of the Islamic world.

Criticism of the Zaydī-Hādwī *madhhab* has become prominent due to the efforts of the contemporary historian and Yemeni critic 'Abd Allāh ash-Shamāḥī. According to another contemporary Yemeni literary critic and historian Aḥmad Muḥammad ash-Shāmī (d. 2005), ash-Shamāḥī's study is the first scientific, historical, and political criticism of al-Hādī's theory of the imamate.[84] Later on, Aḥmad ash-Shāmī undermines ash-Shamāḥī's argument in relation to the Zaydī theory of imamate. Ash-Shamāḥī shows his astonishment that the Hādawīs would not understand that the confinement of the imamate to the Fāṭimids would harm them, their cause, and society.[85] He argues that Imam Zayd b. 'Alī was more farsighted than al-Hādī since Zayd did not embrace the doctrine of confining the caliphate to the sons of his grandmother Fāṭima az-Zahrā, the daughter of the Prophet.[86] Ash-Shamāḥī explains the consequences of the Zaydī dilemma as follows:

> The confinement of leadership (*at-taḥajjur fī az-za'āma*) led the Yu'firids, Āl ad-Da''ām of the Arḥab tribe, Āl aḍ-Ḍahḥāk of the Ḥāshid tribe, Āl Abī al-Futūḥ of the Khawlān tribe and their like among the people of *ijtihād* to oppose the Zaydī doctrine. This confinement also led all the Yemeni forces such as Āl Ḥātim, Āl al-Ghashm, al-Khaṭṭāb, Āl Zuray', Ṣulayḥids, Yāmids, Hamdānids, and others to stand against the Zaydī *madhhab*. These [Yemeni forces] opposed Zaydīs in favor of Ismā'īlīs.[87]

The confinement (*at-taḥajjur*) has been the obstacle behind the dissemination of the Hādawī *madhhab*. Ash-Shamāḥī describes al-Hādī's *madhhab* as follows:

> It is a real *madhhab*, full of truth and not imagination, not ecstatic propositions and dreams, not a *madhhab* with riddles and puzzles, not a *madhhab* of miracles and infallible Imams, not a *madhhab* of mediation between the servant and his Lord except the deed of the servant and his faith. It is a *madhhab* of worship as well as social customs and personal behavior (*mu'āmalāt*). Its rules reached the juridical and legislative accuracy, with comprehensiveness, susceptibility to develop and readiness to accept every new development, which contemporary laws have not reached. It is a *madhhab* of religion and worldly life, faith and deed, activity and seriousness, justice and altruism, *jihād* and *ijtihād*. In it the human being is free, not predestined, to obey God and to care for His servants. It is a *madhhab* that calls for intellectual liberation and profundity in beneficial knowledge. It prohibits blind imitation (*taqlīd*) in doctrines and religious scientific rules. It necessitates *ijtihād* on the basis of the Qur'ān and Sunna in worship and *mu'āmalāt*. It calls for strength and sacrifice. It enjoins obedience, discipline, and cooperation. It enjoins rebellion against the unjust Imams, revolution against social injustice and individual oppression. It does not accept, for its followers, humiliation, laziness, subjection and surrender except to God and His teachings. It is a *madhhab* that respects

the predecessors (*salaf*) in that they are humans, susceptible to criticism including the Companions and the sons of Fāṭima. Some members of the Fāṭimids are like the Companions in that they perform good deeds whereas some clearly wrong themselves.

All the above features of the Hādawī *madhhab* described by ash-Shamāḥī are meant to prepare the reader for the critical attack on the *madhhab*. However, ash-Shamāḥī exaggerates his description of the *madhhab* probably to avoid criticism due to his severe censure of the theory of imamate in the *madhhab*. He argues that the confinement of imamate reflects a weakness of the Hādawī *madhhab*. According to ash-Shamāḥī, the Hādawīs consider 'Alī, Fāṭima, Ḥasan, and Ḥusayn infallible like the prophets. Their consensus (*ijmā'*) after the demise of Prophet Muḥammad is a proof (*ḥujja*) [i.e., as the Qur'ān or Sunna] because they are alone the Prophet's family (Āl Muḥammad). Similarly, their educated sons have the authority of consensus because of their lineage. Ash-Shamāḥī argues that this narrow thinking, which is unfamiliar in the Hādawī *madhhab*, led the Fāṭimids to confine the imamate to themselves only. In addition, the Hādawī *madhhab* would have been stronger and more liberal if it had turned away from the theory of the imamate and its interference.[88]

Ash-Shamāḥī holds the view that the real setback behind the Zaydī failure in applying the Islamic theory of imamate was the theory's genealogical "confinement." He did a thorough investigation to discover the reasons behind the monopoly of leadership and how it was restricted to a particular group of people, thereby denying the right of others to participate in that process. Ash-Shamāhī, however, does not provide alternatives, as is evident from some reactions to his work presented by the Yemeni scholar and critic Aḥmad ash-Shāmī (d. 2005).

Aḥmad ash-Shāmī points out that the sectarian narrowing (*al-ḥaṣr aṭ-ṭā'ifī*) by al-Hādī (d. 298/910) and others of the imamate to either the "Qurashiyya" or the "Fāṭimiyya" is not the chief reason behind tragedies, whether in Yemen or elsewhere in the Islamic world. The "confinement" has been observed in the reality of Islamic history across the ages; a monopoly on authority has been seen in the families of every leader, caliph, king, or sultan. This is evident from the experience of the Umayyads, 'Abbāsids, Fāṭimids, Banū Ḥamdān, Mamlūkes, Saljuqs, and Ottomans. Similarly, this has been the case in Yemen, which was ruled by more than twenty families. The rich and powerful passed on their power and authority within their clans, such as the Banū Ziyād, the

Yu'firids, the Banū Najāḥ, the Ṣulayḥids, the Ayyūbids, the Rasūlids, the Hādawīs, and others until the revolution of 1382/1962.[89]

On the other hand, in an attempt to refute ash-Shamāḥī's thesis, Aḥmad ash-Shāmī discussed in detail the failure of the Zaydī theory of imamate and brought two questions to the fore: Why did the Zaydī imams fail continuously to apply their Islamic theory? Why did they succeed in formulating the theory but fail to apply it? The answer, according to Aḥmad ash-Shāmī, does not lie in ash-Shamāḥī's explanation that the theory has been distorted by genealogical factors. Despite the partial admission of ash-Shamāḥī's ideas, Aḥmad ash-Shāmī attributed the incapability of the Zaydīs and the Hādawīs to apply their theory of succession to several reasons. The most important reason is the freedom the theory grants to whoever believes himself able to meet the conditions of assuming power such as wielding the sword and calling people to follow him. But the real problem, argues Aḥmad ash-Shāmī, is the lack of a system represented by institutions to legislate the theory, explain it, and uphold it. Were such a system to be instituted, every member of Yemeni society would be comfortable because the peaceful transfer of power would be protected by institutions. Aḥmad ash-Shāmī concludes his remarks by noting that this is how civilized countries, whether in the East or the West, currently practice and live.[90] These are the major issues imbued in the Zaydī school of Yemen and—I believe—they are sufficient background for further research. The relationship between the Zaydi imams and the Sufis of Ibn Alwan's era will be discussed at length in Chapter 8 of this book. Now, in keeping with the aim of providing an image of medieval Yemen's diverse religious milieu, I turn to a discussion of another significant group, the Sunnīs.

The Sunnī Movement

An Overview

The term "Sunna" has multiple meanings.[91] In the Qur'ān, the most common meanings are "the wont of the ancients" (*sunnat al-awwalīn*)[92] and "the wont of God" (*sunnat Allāh*).[93] Other meanings are way, method, law, conduct of life, behavior of life, established rule, and established mode of conduct. The meaning of Sunna as an established mode of conduct appears in the Prophetic tradition (*ḥadīth*), "I am leaving with you two things: you shall never go astray as long as you adhere to them: the Book of Allāh and the Sunna of His Prophet."[94] According to Marshal G. M. Hodgson, "the term Sunnī is short for men of the Sunna and the Jamā'a. This name was first adopted by only one faction among those who accepted the 'Abbāsids—a faction which stressed continuity with the Marwānid past (and was not especially friendly to the 'Abbāsids as such) and combined this with a special interest in the Sunna practice as expressed in *ḥadīth* reports about the Prophet. But since that faction eventually was specially recognized as representing the Jamā'a position, the term has come to refer not necessarily to all that faction's complex of teachings, but simply to the acceptance of the Jamā'a principle in contrast to the 'Men of the Sharī'a', the 'Alid- loyalist party."[95]

There is much dispute about the beginnings of the process of recording traditions in Islam. However, a half century after the death of Muḥammad b. Idrīs ash-Shāfi'ī (d. 205/820), scholars produced what came to be known as the standard collections of authentic *ḥadīth*. These books are the two *Saḥīḥs* by al-Bukhārī (d. 257/870) and Muslim (d. 262/875), and the four *Sunans* by Ibn Māja (d. 273/886), Abū Dāwūd (d. 275/888), an-Nasā'ī (d. 303/915), and at-Tirmidhī (d. 279/892). All these books are known to Muslim scholars as "the six books" despite their rejection by some Shī'ī scholars. Of course there are other books, which are recognized by scholars, such as the *musnad* of ad-Dārmī (d. 256/869), the *musnad* of Aḥmad b. Ḥanbal (d. 241/855), the *Muwaṭṭā'* of Mālik b. Anas (d. 179/795), and others, but the priority of the Sunnī view has always rested upon "the six books." This corpus of traditions is recognized by everyone except the Shī'a.[96] The people who have transmitted or critically compiled traditions are known as "traditionists." It should be noted that scholars differentiate between "traditionists" and "traditionalists." The latter are those who have recognized religious knowledge derived from the Qur'ān, the Sunna, and the consensus (*ijmā'*) and given priority to these sources over reason in treating religious matters. Similarly, scholars have identified those who attack the "traditionalists" as the "rationalists" or speculative theologians (*mutakallimūn*), be they Mu'tazilites, Ash'arites, Mātūridites, or other groups. It should be noted, however, that the boundaries between "traditionists" and "traditionalists" are not always precisely marked.[97]

With the support of the 'Abbāsid caliph, al-Ma'mūn (d. 218/833), the Mu'tazilites required the Ḥadīth folk to admit that God had created the Qur'ān. The people of Ḥadīth refused such admission and instead emphasized the supremacy of God over all things, insisting that He alone created human acts, including a person's evil acts. God was above any human criteria of good or evil, of just or unjust because all things sprang from Him. The argument between the Mu'tazilites and the people of Ḥadīth was aggravated by the Mu'tazilī assertion of freedom of the human will, which would be rewarded necessarily by God's justice. The Ḥadīth folk felt that this was an insult to God, rendering Him powerless.[98] In the end, the Mu'tazilites were permitted to persecute the leaders of the Ḥadīth folk. The consequence of this was the famous inquisition (*miḥna*) of Aḥmad b. Ḥanbal (d. 241/855). The Mu'tazilites remained prevalent until Abū al-Ḥasan al-Ash'arī (d. 324/935) recanted his Mu'tazilī doctrine and was able to employ the debating techniques of the Mu'tazilites to produce a rational defense of tradition.[99] Al-Ash'arī's theological position became the standard view of almost all the Sunnī schools of law, including the Mālikīs, Shāfi'īs, Ḥanbalīs, and Ẓāhirīs. The orthodoxy of these Sunnī schools was recognized by the overwhelming majority of its membership.[100]

The Sunnīs in Yemen and Their Literature

According to Ibn Samura al-Ja'dī (d. 586/1190), the majority of Sunnī schools of law in Yemen in the third/ninth century were the Mālikīs and the Ḥanafīs. Before that time, the sources of Islamic law were taken from the work of Ma'mar b. Rāshid al-Baṣrī (d. 153/770), the work of Sufyān b. 'Uyayna (d. 198/813), the work of Abū Qurra Mūsā b. Ṭāriq al-Laḥjī (d. 203/818), the reports in *al-Muwaṭṭā*, the work of Abū Muṣ'ab az-Zuhrī (d. 242/856), the reports transmitted by Ṭāwwūs b. Kaysān (d. 106/724) and his son Abd Allāh b. Ṭāwwūs (d. 132/749), and the work of al-Ḥakam b. Abān al-'Adanī (d. 154/770), and others.[101]

Although Muḥammad b. Idrīs ash-Shāfi'ī (d. 204/820), the founder of the *madhhab*, visited Yemen in 179/790 and remained there for quite some time, his *madhhab* entered Yemen only in the third/ninth century, spreading in al-Janad, Ṣan'ā', and particularly in the south of Yemen (al-Yaman al-Asfal). Later on, it gained wide acceptance in Ḥaḍramawt.[102] Shāfi'ī *madhhab* was prevalent in the fourth/tenth century and came to prominence in the first half of the fifth/eleventh century.[103] Ibn Samura provides us with a brief account of the early Shāfi'īs who actively participated in the development of the Shāfi'ī *madhhab*.[104] The most noted scholar from the third generation of Shāfi'īs was al-Qāsim b. Muḥammad b. 'Abd Allāh al-Jumaḥī al-Qurashī (d. 437/1045) who played an important role in disseminating the Shāfi'ī *madhhab*.[105] Shāfi'īsm became popular when the Rasūlid sultan al-Manṣūr 'Umar converted from the Ḥanafī school to the Shāfi'ī *madhhab*.[106] The first Shāfi'ī book to arrive in Yemen was a summary of the Shāfi'ī precepts by Ismā'īl b. Yaḥyā al-Muzanī (d. 264/877), known as *Mukhtaṣar al-Muzanī*. It was introduced into the Yemeni scholarly milieu by Ḥusayn b. Ja'far al-Murāghī

(d. 324/935).[107] Ibn Samura (d. 586/1190) points out that people in Yemen took their source of Islamic law (*fiqh*) from *Mukhtaṣar al-Muzanī* and the principles of jurisprudence (*uṣūl al-fiqh*) from ash-Shāfi'ī's *Risāla*. According to Ibn Samura, the Yemenis relied on the books of al-Ghazālī (d. 505/1111), Abū 'Alī aṭ-Ṭabarī (d. 350/961), Ibn al-Qaṭṭān al-Miṣrī (d. 407/1016), and al-Maḥāmilī (d. 415/1024) until the arrival of the influential Shāfi'ī manual *al-Muhadhdhab* by Abū Isḥāq ash-Shīrāzī (d. 476/1083).[108] Ash-Shīrāzī's book was fashionable even after the compilation of *al-Bayān* by the Yemeni scholar Yaḥyā b. Abī al-Khayr al-'Imrānī (d. 558/1162). However, when books of an-Nawawī (d. 676/1277) such as *al-Minḥāj*, *al-Majmū'*, *Rawḍ aṭ-ṭālibīn,* and others came to Yemen, they superseded all the earlier sources that were developed by the Shāfi'ī school of law.[109]

It is important to note that the celebrated Sunnī traditionist Aḥmad b. Ḥanbal (d. 241/855) visited Yemen. He studied under 'Abd ar-Razzāq aṣ-Ṣan'ānī (d. 211/827) and was influenced by the latter's *al-Muṣannaf.* Another famous Yemeni traditionist worth mentioning is Muḥammad Ibn Abī 'Umar (d. 320/932), the chief judge of Aden. He compiled a collection of *hadīths* arranged according to the chain of transmitters known as *musnad*. The celebrated Sunnī *ḥadīth* collectors, Muslim b. al-Ḥajjāj al-Qushayrī (d. 261/874), the author of *Ṣaḥīḥ Muslim*, and Abū 'Isā at-Tirmidhī (d. 279/892), the author of *as-Sunan,* collected their traditions from him and relied heavily on his expertise in the field of *ḥadīth*.[110] Another prominent scholar from the late third/ninth century is 'Ubayd b. Muḥammad al-Kashwarī (al-Kishwarī) whose history has not come down to us, but is quoted by the prolific writer and historian al-Ḥasan b. Aḥmad b. Ya'qūb al-Hamdānī (d. 334/945) in his *al-Iklīl* and by Aḥmad b. Abd Allāh ar-Rāzī (d. 460/1068) in his *Tārīkh Madīnat Ṣan'ā'*.[111] Al-Kashwarī was one of the teachers of the well-known traditionist aṭ-Ṭabarānī (d. 360/970).

Due to the intellectual tensions between the Shāfi'īs and the Ḥanafīs in Yemen, and since the Ḥanafīs were close to the rationalist precepts of the Mu'tazilīs, the Shāfi'īs adopted the creed (*'aqīda*) of Ibn Ḥanbal (d. 241/855). They opposed speculative theology (*'ilm al-kalām*) and rejected the Mu'tazilite doctrine of the createdness of the Qur'ān. The Shāfi'īs went even further to refute the rationalistic tendencies advanced by the Mu'tazilites as can be seen in the polemical treatise titled *al-Intiṣār fī ar-radd 'alā 'l-Qadariyya al-ashrār* written by the foremost formidable authority of the Shāfi'ī school during the 'Abbāsid era, Yaḥyā b. Abī 'l-Khayr al-'Imrānī (d. 558/1162). Al-'Imrānī is also the author of an eleven-volume work titled *al-Bayān*, which is considered Yemen's most celebrated Shāfi'ī manual.[112] "Another Shāfi'ī scholar was Isḥāq b. Yūsuf aṣ-Ṣardafī (d. 500/1107) who lectured at a school established in the Mosque of aṣ-Ṣardaf and was an expert on arithmetic (*ḥisāb*) and the law of inheritance, on which he compiled *al-Kāfī fī 'l-farā'iḍ*."[113] Among the Sunnī scholars who participated in polemics against the Mu'tazilite doctrine were Manṣūr b. Jabr (d. 657/1258) in his *ar-Risāla al-muzalzila li-qawā'id al-Mu'tazila* and the Sufi scholar 'Abd Allāh b. As'ad al-Yāfi'ī (d. 768/1366) in his *Marāhim al-'ilal al-mu'ḍila fī ar-radd 'alā al-Mu'tazila*.[114]

Ḥanbalism in Yemen flourished at the hands of Aḥmad b. Muḥammad b. 'Abd Allāh al-Burayhī (d. 586/1190), known as the "Sword of the Sunna" (*sayf as-Sunna*). He was known for his asceticism (*zuhd*) and scrupulousness (*wara'*).[115] According to Ibn Samura, he was a disciple of Yaḥyā b. Abī al-Khayr and the second in rank after him.[116] Students came to study with him from far and wide. Al-Janadī (d. 732/1331) emphasizes his proficiency in *fiqh*, grammar, language, the principles of jurisprudence, and the principles of *hadīth*. He wrote books in refutation of the doctrines of Mu'tazilism and Ash'arism.[117] He left a considerable body of writing, much of which is still in manuscript. There are two lines of poetry in every book he left behind, warning, "This book should be confined to the Sunnīs; it should not go to the deviant Ash'arites nor those who have gone astray [i.e., the Mu'tazilites]."[118] Al-Ḥibshī, the contemporary historian and literary scholar, quoting Abū Makhrama's *Tārīkh thaghr 'Adan*, states that people had adhered to Ibn Ḥanbal's *'aqīda* until the age of al-Janadī (i.e., the eighth/fourteenth century) whereupon some scholars (*'ulamā'*) converted to the Ash'arite school of theology. The first scholarly tension between the Ḥanbalites and the Ash'arites, says al-Ḥibshī, was when Ṭāhir b. Yaḥyā al-'Imrānī abandoned his father's *madhhab* (i.e., the Ḥanbalites) and joined hands with the Ash'arites. Many *'ulamā',* including his father, rose against him until he was forced to leave Yemen for Mecca. When he came back after a long time they forced him to change his creed and to publicly retract his Ash'arite beliefs from the pulpit of the city's main mosque. The chief instigator of his retraction was the Ḥanbalī scholar, Sayf as-Sunna, Aḥmad b. Muḥammad al-Burayhī (d. 586/1190).[119]

Before the Ayyūbid conquest of Yemen, education was confined to a few mosques that served as schools (*madāris*, sing. *madrasah*). When the Ayyūbid ruler al-Mu'izz b. Ismā'īl b. Ṭughtakīn (d. 598/1202) assumed power, he built the first religious college in Zabīd in 594/1197, which was named after him (*al-mu'izziyya*).[120] The college resembled, to a certain extent, those found in Syria and Egypt about that age. The Rasūlids followed in their footsteps. They built colleges, mosques, and libraries throughout the country, making Zabīd and Ta'izz major international centers of Islamic learning.[121] Due to the fame of these centers, scholars came "from distant Muslim lands in search of the opportunities for advancement offered by the enlightened Rasūlid rulers."[122]

As mentioned above, Ash'arite theology became standard in lower Yemen, where the majority of Sunnī schools of law were located. (Ash'arism was embraced by Yemeni Sufis in the seventh/thirteenth century and continues to be an important part of the Sufi doctrine.) On the other hand, people in the northern part of the country, especially Ṣa'da and Ṣan'ā', have adhered to the Zaydi school of law, which has close ties with the Mu'tazilite-Hādawī school of theology. This geographic split is still in place at the present time.

Conclusion

During the 'Abbāsid caliphate, the majority of Yemenis adhered to Sunnīsm. Yemen's relative isolation and difficult geography prevented the 'Abbāsids from bringing it under centralized authority,[123] and so it became a refuge for Islamic sects to establish independent religious communities. Thus, Yemen became a veritable preserve of the Shī'a, represented by the Zaydīs and the Ismā'īlīs. Although these two sects shared some religious principles, they vied with one another for the political control of the Yemeni hinterland, and this competition prevented them from converting the country to either version of Shī'ism.[124]

The Ayyūbid invasion in 569/1173 returned some stability to Yemen.[125] The Ayyūbids suppressed the Ismā'īlīs and most of the sultanates, but failed to subdue the Zaydīs. Most important for our story are the Ayyūbids' energetic promotion of Sunnī learning and Sufi lodges and generous funding of their construction. They also exempted the lands of Sufi masters from taxation. In return, Sufi masters assisted authorities in quelling rebellions and mediated the frequent conflicts between the rulers and semi-independent tribal leaders. When the Rasūlids seized power they continued this trend, building colleges, encouraging intellectual activities and individual scholars, and advancing religious studies, Islamic mysticism in particular. In their era of stability and prosperity scholars came to Yemen from distant Muslim lands to enjoy the lavish rewards offered by Rasūlid princes.[126] It was under these conditions of state patronage that Yemen's ascetic movement began to flourish.

Here I have shown the historical and cultural development of Yemen in its broader perspective, introducing the various Islamic communities and showing Yemen's diversity. Armed with this understanding of the numerous strands of Islam shaping the medieval Yemeni environment and the influence of political dynasties on Islamic learning, I begin to trace the development of Yemeni asceticism. The following chapter explores the rise of the Sufi movement in Yemen from early Islam to the lifetime of Aḥmad b. 'Alwān, elucidating the connections between Yemen's complex religious environment and its nascent Islamic ascetic movement.

2

SUFISM IN YEMEN PRIOR TO THE SEVENTH/THIRTEENTH CENTURY

This chapter explores the origins of the Sufi movement in Yemen from the beginning of Islam to the rise of the Rasūlid dynasty in the seventh/thirteenth century, focusing on the era of Aḥmad b. ʿAlwān (d. 665/1266).[1] I outline the development of the ascetic movement in Yemen beginning with the first generation of Muslims, followed by the second generation of "successors." Although Sufism as a practice had not yet been defined, these early ascetics were crucial authorities in the formation of Yemeni Sufism. Thus, I portray in detail the lives and practices of select central figures in early Yemeni asceticism, such as Abū Hurayra (d. 59/713) and Abū ʿAbd Allāh ʿAmr b. Maymūn al-Awdī (d. 75/694).

I then proceed to discuss the factors—ranging from economic to religious—that caused a decline of intellectual activity in Yemen's major cities between the first/seventh century and fourth/tenth century, and refute the claim, based on the alleged influence of Dhū'n-Nūn al-Miṣrī (d. 245/860), that there was transference from asceticism to mystical tendencies during the third/ninth century. It is important to note that in these early moments of Yemeni Sufism it is almost impossible, and indeed unproductive, to erect strict boundaries between the practices of asceticism and mysticism. Nevertheless, for the purposes of this discussion I treat them as two stages on a path: an individual begins as an ascetic, and only after mortifying his body and adhering to Islamic teachings does he reach the stage of mysticism. Mysticism can also be understood as the science, or pure rationality, of asceticism. The trajectory that unfolds in an individual seeker's life will be mirrored, to an extent, in the development of Yemen's Sufi movement.

With the revival of economic activity in Yemen there was a concomitant flourishing in Yemen's nascent Sufism. As stability returned to

Yemen, culminating in the rich Rasūlid era, intellectual debate and state support for universities and mosques revitalized Yemen's spiritual environment. I introduce the major ascetics and prominent mystics, such as Aṣ-Ṣayyād (d. 579/1183), who were credited with the spread of Islamic saintly miracles (*karāmāt*). These were the trademarks of the ascetics and mystics across centuries, but became more prevalent beginning in the sixth/twelfth century. As the spiritual authority of these mystics grew, so did their influence as the Yemeni people flocked from far and wide to hear them preach. I conclude by introducing the three most celebrated figures of Yemen's religious and cultural history: Aḥmad b. 'Alwān (d. 665/1266), his rival Abū al-Ghayth b. Jamīl (d. 651/1253), and Muḥammad b. 'Alī al-'Alawī known as al-Faqīh al-Muqaddam (d. 653/1256) from Ḥaḍramawt.

Sufism: An Overview

Literary evidence shows that the term "Sufism" was not in circulation until the first half of the third/ninth century.[2] The preceding period witnessed the emergence and the rapid spread of various groups of Islamic ascetics (*zuhhād*) and devout men (*nussāk*). Although the Prophet and some of his companions were often portrayed in Sufi literature as the first Sufis, the actual founder of theosophical Sufism was the Nubian Dhū'n-Nūn al-Miṣrī (d. 245/860).[3] Sufism in Yemen, as elsewhere, began with prominent ascetic manifestations, which then, as they developed, permeated wider society until Sufism became a salient feature of Yemeni society in the late third/ninth century.

Among the first ascetics of the Prophet's companions, whose genealogy trace back to Yemeni origins, are Abū Mūsā al-Ash'arī (d. 44/664), Abū Hurayra (d. 59/713), and Uways al-Qaranī (d. 37/657). These companions should not be regarded as Sufis because Sufi concepts, which were not articulated until later generations, did not form part of their asceticism. In their affinity to asceticism they sought to fulfill their religious duties. Furthermore, "they paid close attention to the underlying motives of their actions and sought to impregnate them with a deeper spiritual meaning."[4] Their objective was accomplished by a scrupulous meditation on the revealed text, the Qur'ān, a comprehensive imitation of the Prophet's piety, a meticulous examination of the inner intentions of their deeds, a preference for poverty over wealth, and a constant chastisement of their souls as well as their bodies. Here are a few representatives of this devotional piety in the first Islamic generation.

Yemeni Ascetic Companions

After his conversion to Islam, Abū Mūsā al-Ash'arī (d. 44/664) was given permission from the Prophet to migrate along with other converts to Abyssinia, where he remained until the conquests of Khaibar in 7/629. Later on, he was sent to his homeland to propagate the Islamic teachings. Abū Mūsā was able to convert more than fifty men and upon his arrival in Madina, the Prophet looked at his companions and said: "People have come to you from Yemen. They are the most amicable and gentle-hearted of men. Faith is of Yemen, and wisdom is Yemeni."[5] At the battle of Ṣiffīn between 'Alī and Mu'āwiya in 37/657, Abū Mūsā al-Ash'arī was trusted by the majority of combatants as an impartial arbiter along with 'Amr b. al-'Āṣ (d. 43/663). Yet because Abū Mūsā was a prominent Yemeni, a people portrayed by the Prophet as "gentle-hearted," he was outwitted by 'Amr, and his political career was brought to an end.[6] This should not be taken as a defect in his character, for he was implementing Islamic morals and representing the utmost inner doctrine of the ascetic (*zuhd*) movement. Regardless of this, the arbitration was decided, with the help of 'Amr's politics, in favor of Mu'āwiya. Abū Mūsā spent the rest of his life in Mecca worshipping God and renouncing worldly pleasures. His exemplary piety and ascetic tendencies were directly influenced by the outstanding personalities, the Prophet and Imam 'Alī.

Another example of the early devotional type of the ascetic movement is Abū Hurayra (d. 59/713) who was the most important propagator of the Prophet's words and deeds. When he was asked by some companions about his ample transmission of Prophetic *hadīths,* he answered them that the Prophet was preaching one day and said: "Who will lay down his cloth until I finish my talk, and then will grab it so that he will not forget anything he heard from me?" Abū Hurayra spread out his cloth and the Prophet preached to him; then Abū Hurayra pulled it to himself, thus assuring faithful remembrance of what he had heard. Then, Abū Hurayra swore by God that if it were not for a verse in the Qur'ān, he would not have preached anything at all. The verse runs, "Those who conceal what we revealed of the proofs and guidance after we have clarified it for the people, those, God will curse and the cursers will curse them [too] (2:159).[7] Abū Hurayra's profound interest in the Prophetic *hadīth* convinced him to follow an ascetic path of life; his permanent presence with the Prophet was the major reason for his scrupulousness, piety, and asceticism.

Alongside Abū Mūsā and Abū Hurayra, one should mention the mystic beloved in Yemeni tradition, whose name (as was noted above) is connected to the Prophet: the celebrated recluse Uways b. ʻĀmir al-Qaranī (d. 37/657). The sources at our disposal agree that Uways lived most of his life in Yemen and that he never met the Prophet. And yet Uways's piety is revealed by the Prophet's famous words: "The breath of the Compassionate (*nafas ar-Raḥmān*) comes to me from Yemen."[8] Commenting on these elegant words, Shimmel argues that they have "become, in poetical language, the symbol for the act of divine guidance, which, like the morning breeze, opens the contracted bud of the human heart."[9]

Al-Janadī (d. 732/1331) reports that ʻUmar b. al-Khaṭṭāb (d. 3/644), the second caliph of Islam, used to inquire about Uways b. ʻĀmir al-Qaranī, whenever he received reinforcements (*amdād*) from Yemen. As soon as ʻUmar saw Uways, he asked him, "Do you have a mother?" "Yes," said Uways. Then, ʻUmar related to him what he heard from the Prophet:

> Uways b. ʻĀmir will come to you with reinforcements from Yemen, from Murād and from Qaran. He had had leprosy but was recovered except for a little spot. He has been kind and obedient (*barr*) to his mother. If he is to ask God, may He be exalted and Glorified, God will answer his prayer. So, oh ʻUmar, if you are able to ask him to pray for you, do that.[10]

Then, ʻUmar asked Uways to pray for him and Uways did. After that, ʻUmar asked him: "Where are you going?" "Kūfa," Uways responded. ʻUmar said, "Can I write to its governor to take care of you?" Uways replied, "I would love to be among the ordinary people."[11] This story of Uways reveals not only his extreme piety but also the concept of knowing the Prophet through a spiritual rather than physical connection. Uways was the first representative of a later Sufi order named after him, known as Uwaysiyya.[12] The adept who does not have a direct master is frequently called Uwaysī, or in Turkish, *veysi meshreb*. The Arabic term for this is *Uwaysi mashrab* and it refers to the mystic who has reached a state of illumination outside the regular mystical path, and without the spiritual support or guidance of a living Sufi master. The concept that a disciple can follow the Sufi path without a spiritual guide will be explained when I discuss Ibn ʻAlwān's Sufi thought.

Many sources portray Uways as a friend of God (*walī*).[13] The evidence of his friendship with God (*walāya*) is unmistakably attested by the fact that the Prophet ordered ʻUmar b. al-Khaṭṭāb and ʻAlī b. Abī

Ṭālib to look for Uways and to ask for his blessings and supplication.[14] This action by the Prophet meant that Uways was one of those chosen men, whose prayers God answers. One can deduce from the reports the importance of Uways who had not seen the Prophet, but whose uncompromising spirituality made him known not only as one of the companions, but as a very special one. The Prophet's foreknowledge of him is by itself a miracle (*karāma*). What is more important for our discussion of his character is the Prophet's foretelling that God would honor Uways's intercession in the hereafter for as many as the two Arabian tribes of Rabīʿa and Muḍar to enter Paradise.[15]

Islamic Influence on Sufism

The influence of Islam on the Sufi movement can be seen in the acts of penitence, self-renunciation, self-purification, self-improvement (*jihād an-nafs*), meticulous meditation on the Qur'ān and Sunna, fear of God, and exemplary piety. These pious features are considered attitudes conducive to the mystical goal, even though they remained underdeveloped in the early centuries of Islam. The distinctive features of asceticism in the first century of Islam were practiced by many companions, if not all, including those from Yemen. The characteristics that unified them were fasting, abstinence from meat and wealth, and wearing coarse wool.[16] This latter became a dominant characteristic of Islamic asceticism by the third/ninth century, and later exponents of the Sufi movement considered it to have been one of the defining practices of Sufism. This explains why later Sufi writers tend to tie the Prophet and his companions to the Sufi movement.[17] The ascetic movement in Yemen after the third/ninth century was a continuation of these inherited ascetic tendencies and can be traced back as far as the pre-Islamic period. Yet the scripture of Islam itself was a helping factor in the promotion of mystical dimensions, which encouraged Yemeni as well as many other ascetics (*zuhhād*) and devout men (*nussāk*) from all over the Islamic lands to participate in the development of asceticism. It is significant to note that although mystical practices emerged in Yemen in the third/ninth century, at that time they did not gain popular recognition as a unified movement.

Yemeni Ascetic Successors

In the second generation of Islamic ascetics, which was known as the generation of successors (*tābiʿūn*), there emerged a number of Yemeni ascetics whose exemplary piety was undisputed. Among them is the most famous ascetic, Abū ʿAbd Allāh ʿAmr b. Maymūn al-Awdī (d.

75/694). Besides his asceticism, he was one of the major transmitters of the *ḥadīth*. He accompanied a number of the Prophet's companions and narrated the *ḥadīth* on their authority. There is no doubt that his asceticism was influenced by his profound meditation on the Qur'ān and the extreme piety of the companions. It has been said in traditional Sufi literature that all the Prophet's companions were considered ascetics (*zuhhād*) and friends of God (*awliyā'*).[18] Although Al-Awdī is counted among the successors, his spirituality elevates him to the rank of the companions because he followed in their footsteps and paid no significant attention to material concerns.

Ṭāwūs b. Kaysān (d. 106/724) is another successor known for his asceticism and indifference to wealth, as the following anecdote illustrates. Ibn al-Jawzī (d. 597/1201) reports on the authority of an-Nu'mān b. az-Zubair that Muḥammad b. Yousuf and Ayyūb b. Yaḥyā, two leading politicians of the caliphate of al-Walīd b. 'Abd al-Malik (d. 96/714) sent five hundred dinars to Ṭāwūs, promising the envoy that he would be rewarded by the emir if Ṭāwūs accepted it. The envoy tried hard to convince Ṭāwūs but with no avail, so he hid the money in Ṭāwūs's house and falsely reported to the politicians that Ṭāwūs had accepted the money. Sometime later, when the politicians heard something unpleasant about Ṭāwūs, they sent another man to retrieve the money. However, Ṭāwūs denied having taken it. The two politicians knew that Ṭāwūs was honest, but they decided to confirm this by sending the former envoy to ask Ṭāwūs about the money. The envoy admitted that Ṭāwūs had accepted no money from him, and so Ṭāwūs asked the envoy, "Did you leave the money in the house?" The envoy pointed to the corner of his house and saw it lying there, covered with cobwebs because Ṭāwūs never touched it and never looked at the corner of his house. The envoy took the money and returned it to them.[19] This story reveals the asceticism of Ṭāwūs and his exemplary piety. First, he instinctively abstained from worldly pleasures, and second, he refused money from political authorities because of the popular belief that such money is morally compromised.

Ascetic practices appear in the lives of all the central figures of the first and second generation of Islam. Thus, most biographies of these personalities report the same ascetic practices such as love for contemplation of the Qur'ān, rejection of wealth, introspection, and uncompromising piety. The following Yemeni ascetics share all these features and seem to have been in the same sanctimonious rank, including Wahb b. Munabbih (d. 116/734), al-Mughīra b. Ḥakīm aṣ-Ṣan'ānī, al-Ḥakam b.

Abān al-'Adanī (d. 154/770), Ḍirghām b. Wā'il al-Ḥaḍramī, al-Khansā' bt. Khidām, and others.[20] These people were representatives of the distinctive devotional type of piety that characterizes asceticism, not mysticism. The boundary between these two concepts is thin and ambiguous, but it can be said that mysticism represents a more advanced, purely rational stage of asceticism. Most Islamic mystics experience in their early spirituality all the stages of asceticism—specifically, the acts of penitence, self-renunciation, self-purification, and self-improvement—before ascending to mysticism. These ascetics (*zuhhād*), while not mystics, were known as renouncers of worldly delights and devout men (*nussāk*), who lived pious lives and engaged in meticulous contemplation of the Qur'ān, God-fearing, and the Prophet's exemplary deeds.

Factors of Mystical Decline

The spiritual period in Yemen between the first/seventh century and the end of the fourth/tenth century was characterized by a tremendous deterioration in intellectual activity. The factors contributing to this decline include the transference of world trade routes from Yemen and the Red Sea to Iraq and the Persian Gulf. This economic shift began in the second/eighth century and lasted until the fourth/tenth century, causing financial and literary depression in Yemen. Another factor causing the decline of the literary and political atmosphere was Yemeni migration, especially in the first century of Islam, due to the Arab conquests (*futūḥāt*). When the early community of Islam spread to Iraq, ash-Shām (i.e., Syria), Egypt, Khurāsān, and other Muslim lands, the Yemeni state became isolated; due to the deterioration of economic resources, it was entirely neglected.[21]

This period is depicted by some historians and Yemeni chronicles as a period of intellectual and cultural stagnation. Contemporary Yemeni scholars have attempted to link the third/ninth century worshippers and pious men, discussed above, to the Sufi movement.[22] However, this is not accurate as there is no indication of any doctrines, literatures, or concepts (whether theoretical or practical) that could have been representative of the Sufi discourses. One can deduce from the medieval sources that ideas and discussions in Yemen after the third/ninth century started to shift gradually from asceticism into early moderate mysticism. This transformation was caused first by the assimilation of the Islamic culture, and second by the influence of foreign cultures, which came through converts to Islam from India and Persia who carried with them their old beliefs and doctrines that began to spread over the Islamic world, including Yemen. In addition, the translation movement from Greek into Arabic during the early 'Abbāsid rule was a major contributor in transforming classical Islamic notions into more sophisticated philosophical doctrines.[23] For the first time, mystical thinkers and poets such as Rābi'a al-'Adawiyya (d. 185/801) and Dhū'n-Nūn al-Miṣrī (d. 245/860) expressed divine love or annihilation (*fanā'*) in God. Such concepts were not familiar to the earlier ascetics and devout men.

Between Asceticism and Mysticism

One way to characterize the fine line between the interrelated terms of asceticism and mysticism is defining asceticism as an early stage of self-preparation that would lead to mysticism. For example, it is very rare that a well-recognized and established mystic would go back to asceticism, and conversely, an ascetic person may strive to be able to reach mysticism. While I must acknowledge the complexity of this fine distinction, the prevailing notion in the Sufi literature is that asceticism is merely a phase leading to long-lasting mysticism. Indeed, mysticism should be considered the rational outcome of pure asceticism.

Al-Yāfi'ī (d. 768/1367) reports a story that represents an early crystallization of nascent Yemeni mysticism. In the story, Dhū'n-Nūn al-Miṣrī (d. 245/860) experiences a vision during his visit to Yemen in the third/ninth century. Dhū'n-Nūn's desire to meet a wise mystic in Yemen is evidence of Dhū'n-Nūn's mystical mind, and also evidence of the emergence of mysticism in Yemen. The following is my translation of al-Yāfi'ī's story:

> It was described to al-Yāfi'ī that a man from the masters (*sāda*) of Yemen had surpassed the God-fearing people and exceeded ardent worshippers (*mujtahids*). He is known to the people, and he is described as sage, wise, modest, and humble. Dhū'n-Nūn said: "I went on a pilgrimage to the house of God (*al-bayt al-ḥarām*), and when I finished the pilgrimage, I and some people who were seeking blessing like me, went to visit him in order to hear something of his words and benefit from his exhortation. There was a young man with us, who had the characteristics of *ṣāliḥūn* and the look of a God-fearing man. He was pale without sickness, bleary-eyed without ophthalmia. He loved solitary places (*khalwa*), and was intimate with loneliness. . . . He was with us until we arrived in Yemen. We asked about the Shaykh's house and we were led to it. Then, when we reached him the young man started talking to the

> Shaykh . . . and asked him: 'What is the sign of the fear of God, may He be exalted?' The Shaykh said: 'Fearing God secures you from every fear save the fear of Him.' The young man was afraid and fell down into a trance, and when he recovered said: 'God bless you, when does the servant make sure of his fear of God?' He said: 'If he puts himself in the worldly life like a patient [who is] sick. . . .' The young man cried aloud until we thought his soul had departed. Then [the young man] said: 'God bless you, what is the sign of the love of God, may He be exalted?' He said: 'Oh Beloved, the rank of God's love is high.' The young man said: 'I love that you describe it to me.' The Shaykh said: 'Oh Beloved, the lovers of God, may He be exalted—their hearts are opened, [they] watch by the light of their hearts the Majesty of the Greatness of the Beloved God. Their souls become spirits, their hearts become veils, their minds become heavenly and travel among the rows of the eminent angels, and see those divine wonders with certitude and observation.' They worshipped Him as far as they could; [they would not serve God out of] desire for his reward and fear of his punishment." The young man, then, groaned loudly and immediately died.[24]

If the story is authentic and the transmitters are reliable, then I could say that the borderline that divides asceticism from mysticism is crossed in the narrative. However, the evidence is unsatisfactory because the story is an isolated event, and more importantly, there was no dissemination of Sufi ideas after Dhū'n-Nūn's visit to Yemen. Whether Dhū'n-Nūn's visit was due to his escape from the inquisition of the createdness of the Qur'ān or due to his efforts to establish the foundation of Sufism in Yemen is of no great significance.[25] Despite his eagerness to find out the mysteries behind an anonymous Yemeni Shaykh who, in Dhū'n-Nūn's eyes, was qualified to promulgate Sufi thought, one does not see any developments of these ideas. Thus, the claim that Dhū'n-Nūn made an impact on Yemeni Sufism cannot be documented, and on the contrary asceticism remained primitive, in the strict sense of the word, until the emergence of celebrated Sufis in the seventh/thirteenth century.

Further links in the development of nascent Yemeni Sufism emerge in the work of Aḥmad b. 'Abd Allāh ar-Rāzī (d. 460/1068), notably in his legendary book *Tā'rīkh madīnat Ṣan'ā'*. In it, one finds a group of ascetics who lived in the second to third/eighth to ninth centuries, but did not seem to have developed mystical ideas. A representative of these is

Muḥammad b. Bisṭām aṣ-Ṣan'ānī who was reported to have made his living through hard labor and was very cautious in the way he earned his income. According to ar-Rāzī, aṣ-Ṣan'ānī used to spend part of his earnings on bread made of barley and then donate the rest to the poor.[26] In these two centuries one finds other names connected with jurisprudence (*fiqh*) and *ḥadīth* literature, which can be found in separate biographies. Some of these scholars experienced asceticism in their lives as part of a general Islamic piety. In a similar vein, the fifth/eleventh century witnessed a new wave of Yemeni ascetics, most of which came from the plateaus parallel to the coastal areas of Tihāma and Ta'izz. A representative of these regions is the venerable recluse Abū Muḥammad Sawd b. al-Kumayt or al-Kamīt (d. 436/1044). The medieval biographer ash-Sharjī (d. 893/1487) states that Sawd renounced earthly delights and preoccupied himself with spiritual knowledge (*'ilm*).[27] Every year he spent the revenues of his land in service of God as a sign of his piety. Some of his descendants are well-known scholars, ascetics, and recluses.

Up to this point, there is no concrete information to explain the development of Sufi ideas that emerged in the third/ninth century through the anonymous Yemeni mystic whom Dhū'n-Nūn (d. 245/860) specifically traveled to see. Mystical ideas did not spread and were confined to a small circle. Scholars generally agree that, as noted above, intellectual activities were deteriorating due to Yemen's political and economic isolation, which in turn resulted in the isolation of Sufism. Nevertheless, the sixth/twelfth century witnessed the emergence of a group of intellectuals who were widely known for their combination of Islamic jurisprudence (*fiqh*) and tenuous asceticism. Their biographies can be found in the biographical dictionaries of Islam (*ṭabaqāt*) and jurisprudence.[28] The reason for this combination is that asceticism appeared to have been classified under other Islamic sciences and was marginalized due to the growth of dry scholasticism and the ascendancy of jurists (*fuqahā'*).

Yet an ascetic movement had been growing quietly within Islamic communities even though the debates and discussions were dominated by juridical-minded scholars. Among these juridical ascetics is the distinguished scholar Zayd b. 'Abd Allāh al-Yafā'ī (d. 514/1120).[29] According to al-Janadī (d. 732/1331), al-Yafā'ī started his early religious education in al-Janad and traveled to Mecca to broaden his knowledge in Shāfi'ī *fiqh* under the famous Shāfi'ī scholars, aṭ-Ṭabarī (d. after 500/1106) and al-Bandanījī (d. 500/1106).[30] Upon his return, he drew large crowds of disciples exceeding three hundred who flocked from far and wide to study in his circle. He was the first person to bring the books of

Abū Isḥāq ash-Shirāzī (d. 476/1083) such as *al-Muhadhdhabb* and *al-Bayān* in the Shāfi'ī *fiqh* to Yemen. During this time, Yemen's political atmosphere was shaped by competition among the three main theological and juridical schools—the Zaydīs, the Ismā'īlīs, and the Sunnīs—which was described in detail in the previous chapter. Ash-Sharjī (d. 893/1487) mentions that al-Yafā'ī abstained from socializing with the authorities of the time and instead engaged in abundant worship of God, which resulted in his ability to perform miracles (*karāmāt*). For instance, when he intended to leave his house during the quiet hours of the night heading to the mosque, the door opened itself for him with no assistance.[31] Then, he would pray and return home, in the same manner.[32] Al-Janadī asserted that al-Yafā'ī's tomb had been a site of visitation.[33]

Another worshipper and devout man in the same century is 'Abd Allāh b. Yazīd al-Qasīmī (d. 526/1131) nicknamed Abū Sa'īd. It was reported on the authority of authentic transmitters that al-Qasīmī saw the Night of Decree (*laylat al-qadr*) and that he asked God to provide him with licit income (*rizq ḥalāl*) and pious sons. God responded to his supplication and granted him, after quite some time, a farm of bees that produced more honey than usual bees, and also provided him with pious progeny.[34] The idea that someone has observed the Night of Decree is considered a miracle in the popular beliefs of Muslims. The holy Qur'ān was sent down on that night because God honored it, favored it, and selected it for its significance over any other night. Thus, He says: "Behold, We sent it down on the Night of Decree; and what shall teach you what is the Night of Decree? The Night of Decree is better than a thousand months; in it the angels and the Spirit descend, by the leave of their Lord, upon every command. Peace it is, till the rising of dawn."[35] According to the Qur'ān and the Prophetic tradition, anyone exposed to that night is granted the opportunity to make a wish that will be unquestionably fulfilled by the permission of God. Al-Qasīmī was chosen, thus becoming one of the friends of God (*awliyā'*).

The second half of the sixth/twelfth century, however, witnessed the emergence of a multitude of ascetics, some of whom were familiar with basic mystical elements that contributed to the development of the nascent Sufi movement. Abū al-'Abbās Aḥmad b. Abī al-Khayr, better known as aṣ-Ṣayyād (d. 579/1183), is one of the best representatives of this group because he was considered not only a friend of God (*walī*) like classical ascetics, but also a spiritual mystic. In his early life, aṣ-Ṣayyād was one of the common folk in Zabīd. His story of Sufi conversion reminds us of an earlier Sufi, al-Fuḍayl b. 'Iyāḍ (d. 188/803) and of a much later Yemeni Sufi, the celebrated Abū al-Ghayth b. Jamīl (556–651/1160–1253). Each of these Sufis shared a common feature of the Sufi conversion, but their stories differed in details. At the age of twenty, aṣ-Ṣayyād is reported to have received a pious vision. Once, while he was sleeping, someone said to him: "Stand up oh Ṣayyād and pray." He got up immediately and started to learn how to perform ablution and prayer, and eventually ended up practicing all the Islamic religious teachings, which bequeathed in him the characteristic of piety.[36]

Later on, as a sign of his sincere piety, aṣ-Ṣayyād frequently experienced the Sufi state of annihilation (*fanā'*). For instance, he once was lying in the desert for several days in the state of annihilation causing the wind to blow dust on his body and allow the grass to grow on it.[37] Ash-Sharjī (d. 893/1487) states that aṣ-Ṣayyād used to praise the coastal areas, especially the area between al-Mabrak mosque to Mocha (*al-Mukhā*) mosque and from Mu'ādh mosque to al-Fāza mosque, since these were, in his view, spiritual places where pious people (*ṣāliḥūn*) could practice constant worship. Similarly, he praised the Kamarān Island for its sanctity and for being a sanctuary of righteous worshippers of God (*'ibād Allāh aṣ-ṣāliḥīn*). When aṣ-Ṣayyād moved to Zabīd, he began to experience divine gifts, or saintly miracles (*karāmāt*), which attracted him a great number of admirers. One of these *karāmāt* is reported by an anonymous righteous man who came with a group of people to visit aṣ-Ṣayyād. They found him living with a young man and inquired whether he was his student. Aṣ-Ṣayyād did not reply. The group, then, asked the young man who answered affirmatively. Turning toward aṣ-Ṣayyād they said sneeringly: "Now you have disciples!" He was angry and said, "Yes." The group challenged him to command the young man to walk on water, using the shaykh's spiritual influence. He responded to their demands, asking the young man to walk on water. The young man carried out the spiritual order and walked on the water. They were stunned and begged the young man to come back but he did not. Then, they begged aṣ-Ṣayyād for the young man's return. He called him back, and the young man returned. The group regretted deeply their behavior and asked for forgiveness, which he eventually granted them.[38]

Aṣ-Ṣayyād frequently preached mystical ideas. Once he was asked, "Who is higher, the Gnostic (*al-'ārif*) or the lover (*al-muḥibb*)?" He replied, "The Gnostic, because the lover is preoccupied with love while the Gnostic is preoccupied with the beloved (*al-maḥbūb*)." His student Ibrāhīm b. Bashshār al-'Adanī compiled a manuscript that contains aṣ-

Ṣayyād's biography and his miracles. Before joining aṣ-Ṣayyād and benefiting from his friendship, Al-'Adanī had been a follower of the famous Qādirī order. He received the Sufi cloak (*al-khirqa*) directly from 'Abd al-Qādir al-Jīlānī (d. 561/1166), the founding father of the influential Qādiriyya brotherhood.[39] Al-'Adanī followed in the footsteps of his master and became a celebrated Sufi in his own right who was capable of producing miracles.

Factors of Mystical Revival

As the nascent Sufi movement began to flourish in Yemen beginning with the age of Aḥmad aṣ-Ṣayyād (d. 579/1183), it is noteworthy to discuss the factors that contributed to such a revival. Of particular interest here is Yemen's intellectual and cultural revival after its period of stagnation. First, the return of world trade routes through Yemeni ports and the Red Sea helped in the dissemination of books and the attraction of scholars to major cities. As a result of the return of vital commercial shipping, Yemen became less economically isolated. Second, one of the main reasons for the revival of intellectual activities was the rise of local Yemeni states, including the Ziādids (203–409/818–1018), the Yu'firids (232–387/847–997), the Najāḥids (412–551/1021–1156), the Ṣulayḥids (439–532/1047–1138), the Sulaymanids (c. 462–569/c. 1069–1173), the Zuray'ids (473–569/1080–1173), the Hamdanid sultans (492–569/1099–1173), and the Mahdids (554–569/1159–1173). This period flourished with the arrival of the Ayyūbids (569–628/1173–1228) and culminated with the most brilliant period ruled by the Rasūlids for two centuries (626–858/1228–1454). These states contributed to the development of local resources, relative stability, and the encouragement of Islamic and scientific learning. Third, the intellectual debates among the various Yemeni theological as well as juridical schools promoted the flourishing of scientific and intellectual movements. Finally, the end of migration and the return of some migrants alongside the revival of the economic and cultural activities are important factors behind Yemen's educational and cultural growth, which prompted interest in Sufism.[40] All the above factors contributed significantly to the boom of the intellectual and the cultural movement from around the beginning of the fourth/tenth century to the sixth/twelfth century and culminated with the brilliant period of the Rasūlid reign in the seventh to eighth/thirteenth to fifteenth centuries. Yemen was no longer isolated from the major intellectual, political, social, cultural, and economic activities of the Islamic world.

As has been discussed in the previous chapter, there is no doubt that the Ayyūbids were among the most important factors contributing to the flourishing of Sufism. In Yemen as elsewhere, they supported Sufism by building Sufi lodges throughout the country. The Rasūlids followed in their footsteps, building colleges and mosques, and cultivating Sufi masters in order to legitimize their rule. As a result, the seventh/thirteenth century witnessed the progress of mystical doctrines, followed by the establishment of Sufi institutions (*arbiṭa,* or *zawāya'*).

Circulation of Miracles

One of the most important mystics of this period was 'Alī b. 'Umar b. Muḥammad al-Ahdal (d. 602/1205), who was reported to have been the first person in the family of al-Ahdal to embrace mystical doctrines. (His grandfather came from Iraq with two cousins, all known for their knowledge of Sufism. These men became the grandfathers of most of the Sayyid families in Yemen.)[41] Al-Ahdal was noted for his saintly miracles and was one of the main teachers of the celebrated Sufi, Abū al-Ghayth Ibn Jamīl (d. 651/1253).

To mention one of his miracles, ash-Sharjī (d. 893/1487) reports that al-Ahdal predicted that a certain man of his village who worked with the authorities would die that night. The man and his family spent the night in agony. Some people told them to pay alms so that God might rescue him. They paid fifteen dinars, a considerable sum at that time. In the morning, the man came to pray with the shaykh, and the people awaited the shaykh's words. Al-Ahdal then sent one of his disciples to the man's house and instructed him to fold up a straw mat, which the man had slept on, and to speak to the snake beneath it to answer the call of the shaykh. The disciple implemented the order of the shaykh. The snake came crawling with the disciple to the shaykh's house and put its head on the shaykh's prayer rug. Al-Ahdal put his hand on its head and said: "The appointed time of death (*ajal*) was decreed tonight upon this man, but fifteen dinars were paid in alms-giving and therefore God has extended his life fifteen years." He then addressed the snake, "But he is yours and you are his." After fifteen years, the same snake killed the man while he was irrigating his land. When one looks back at this miracle, one has to remember that it took place at a time when miracles were eulogized and thus should not be judged by our contemporary standards.

The period of the seventh/thirteenth century is characterized by a multitude of mystics who had a divine opportunity to perform miracles according to the constant demands of their communities. 'Īsā b. Iqbāl al-

Hattār (d. 606/1209) was counted among them and was known as the second teacher of the celebrated mystic, Abū al-Ghayth Ibn Jamīl. Al-Hattār was portrayed in medieval hagiographical sources as a man of numerous *karāmāt* and Sufi unveiling (*kashf*). One of his miracles is reported to have taken place when he was approached by a promiscuous woman seeking his blessings. A glance from al-Hattār was sufficient reason for her immediate repentance, and soon al-Hattār married her to one of his disciples. On the day of her wedding, one of the emirs of the country, who used to have sexual intercourse with her, sent two bottles of wine as gifts—knowing that it is forbidden in the Muslim society—in order to mock her wedding. As soon as the messenger came, al-Hattār took the two bottles and poured them on the porridge. The wine transformed into ghee and honey. Al-Hattār asked the messenger to eat with them in order to show him how the invisible hand of God transformed the essence of the material objects, not mentioning that this happened due to his spiritual influence. When the emir learned what had happened, he came to the shaykh and apologized for his misbehavior.[42]

In general, all mystics of this century are credited with *karāmāt* and instances of Sufi unveiling (*mukāshafāt*). There was no single famous mystic who did not perform a miracle or at least predict the future. Exemplary mystics of this period include the two distinguished figures Abū 'Abd Allāh Muḥammad b. Abī Bakr al-Ḥakamī (d. 617/1220) and Muḥammad b. Ḥusayn al-Bajalī (d. 621/1224) who were known in medieval biographies as "the two people of the village of *'awāja*" (*ṣāḥibayy 'awāja*), for their miracles and spiritual influence. These were like the pair of compasses: if one of them was mentioned, the other would come to the mind involuntarily. Although their names were intertwined, each one had his distinguished personality and was able to perform saintly miracles alone.

Conclusion

Many Sufis contributed to the manifestation of Yemen's nascent Sufism, but I shall conclude here by introducing the three major representatives of this period: Abū al-Ghayth b. Jamīl (d. 651/1253), Aḥmad b. 'Alwān (d. 665/1266), Muḥammad b. 'Alī al-'Alawī, known as al-Faqīh al-Muqaddam (d. 653/1256). In the age of these three charismatic leaders, Yemen witnessed a rapid growth of Sufi institutions, or the *ṭarīqa* network. I have discussed here the rise of saintly miracles and revival of mystical activities due to competition between the flourishing Yemeni states and the boom in economic and political stability. However, the

Image 1. A contemporary poem by Muhammad al-Junayd in praise of Ibn 'Alwān.

real establishment of Sufism in Yemen started with the coming of the Ayyūbids and later culminated with the Rasūlids, who went a step further by encouraging the local inhabitants to take part in the nascent Sufi movement and participated in building Islamic centers of learning, colleges, and Sufi lodges (*arbiṭa*). These three charismatic leaders are the most prominent figures to emerge from the sociopolitical and religious conditions of their historical moment in Yemen. Their lives, works, and influence are the focus of the remainder of this work. In the following chapter I provide a comprehensive overview of the life and work of the most significant of these three, Aḥmad b. 'Alwān.

3

THE LIFE AND WORKS OF IBN 'ALWĀN

Abū al-Ḥasan, or Abū al-'Abbās[1] Aḥmad b. 'Alwān, was born around 600/1203[2] in Dhū al-Janān, a village situated between the mountains of Ṣabir and Dhakhir in what is now known as Jabal Ḥabashī. He was raised in 'Uqāqah, a village on the outskirts of Ta'izz, the capital of Yemen during the Rasūlid dynasty (632–827/1234–1424). (See Map 1.) According to a manuscript found in the *waqf* library at the Great Mosque in Ṣan'ā', Ibn 'Alwān descended from 'Alī b. Abī Ṭālib (d. 40/660), the Prophet's son-in-law and the fourth caliph of Islam. The manuscript was written by Muḥammad b. Aḥmad Ibn 'Anqā' (d. 996/1587),[3] who provided the following genealogy of Ibn 'Alwān: Abū al-Ḥasan Ṣafī ad-Dīn Aḥmad b. 'Alwān b. 'Aṭṭāf b. Yūsuf b. Muṭā'in b. 'Abd al-Karīm b. Ḥasan b. Ibrāhīm b. Sulaymān b. 'Alī b. 'Abd Allāh b. Muḥammad b. 'Îsā b. Idrīs b. 'Abd Allāh b. 'Îsā b. 'Abd Allāh b. al-Ḥasan (al-Muthannā) b. al-Ḥasan (as-Sibṭ) b. 'Alī b. Abī Ṭālib.[4] Another version of Ibn 'Alwān's genealogy with a slight variation in the middle of the tree can be found in the manuscript, *Fatḥ al-karīm al-jawād al-mannān bi-wāsiṭat 'iqd sayyid az-zamān fī ba'ḍ manāqib Aḥmad b.'Alwān* by Ja'far b. al-Ḥasan al-Barzanjī (d. 1079/1765).[5] This genealogy reads as follows: Ṣafī ad-Dīn Abū al-'Abbās as-Sayyid Aḥmad b. 'Alwān Khaṭṭāf[6] b. 'Abd al-Karīm b. Ḥasan b. 'Îsā b. Sulaymān b. 'Alī b. 'Abd Allāh b. Muḥammad b. 'Îsā b. 'Abd Allāh b. 'Îsā b. 'Abd Allāh b. al-Ḥasan (al-Muthannā) b. 'Alī b. Abī Ṭālib.

Ibn 'Alwān's father, 'Alwān b. Aṭṭāf, was famous for his beautiful handwriting. He is said to have copied a ten-volume book on Shāfi'ī *fiqh,* known as *al-Bayān,* by the Yemeni juridical scholar Yaḥyā b. Abī al-Khayr (d. 558/1162).[7] His copy of *al-Bayān* was taken from Yemen to Iraq, where it gained much respect for its fine-looking calligraphy as

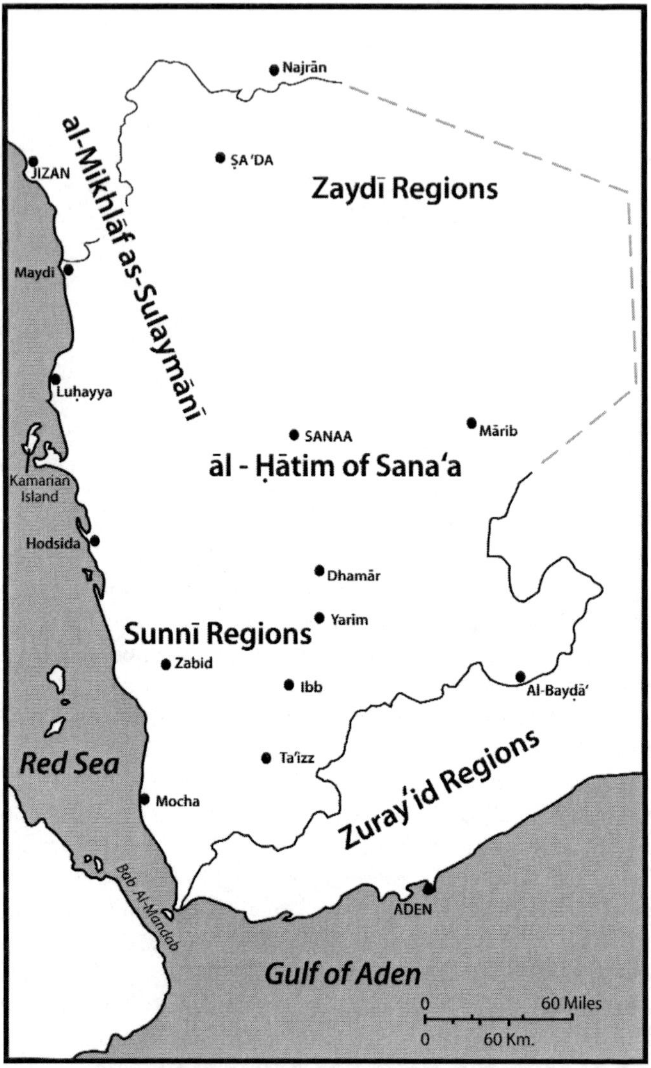

Map 1. Yemen before the arrival of the Ayyūbids, 569/1174

well as its content. 'Alwān was also an influential political figure in the Yemeni state because he served as a royal scribe (*kātib inshā'*)[8] for al-Mas'ūd b. al-Kāmil (d. 626/1228), the last ruler of the Ayyūbid dynasty in Yemen.[9] In his book *as-Sulūk fī ṭabaqāt al-'ulamā' wa l-mulūk,* Muḥammad al-Janadī (d. 732/1331) says, "It was narrated that Aḥmad b.

'Alwān's father traveled with al-Mas'ūd b. al-Kāmil, the king, to Ḥajja [a tribal town famous for its uneven mountains]; and a battle took place while 'Alwān was at the foot of a mountain. Suddenly, a landslide fell on him, as he was riding his female mule, causing his death; it was the last meeting between the king and 'Alwān."[10]

After his father's death, Ibn 'Alwān experienced financial difficulties that compelled him to meet with the ruler in hopes of obtaining a job or assuming his father's post. However, the course of his life changed because of an incident (*'āriḍ*) that occurred to him while he was on his way to the palace. According to al-Janadī (d. 732/1331):

> Some of the transmitters of his [Ibn 'Alwān's] works mentioned that his soul urged him in his youth to visit the Sultan's palace in order to follow in his father's footsteps to become a royal scribe. He left his village heading to the Sultan's palace. In the middle of his journey, a green bird landed on his shoulder and extended its beak to his mouth. The shaykh opened his mouth and the bird put something into it, whereupon the shaykh swallowed it. He then returned [to his village] and secluded himself in a spiritual retreat for forty days. Eventually, he came out and kneeled on a rock in order to worship God. The rock split and there appeared from it a hand. He then [heard a voice] commanding him to shake the hand. He said: "Who are you?" [The voice] replied: "Abū Bakr." He shook the hand. The voice said to him: I have appointed you as a shaykh (*naṣṣabtuka shaykhan*).[11]

This widely told anecdote serves as an explanation for the dramatic change in Ibn 'Alwān's life.[12] Like many other Sufis, he seemed to have undergone a major inner transformation. He no longer took an interest in the affairs of the unsatisfactory world; rather, he became an unearthly recluse and visionary. Little is known about his life before this incident. Ibn 'Alwān's biographers state that he had been well-educated before his conversion to Sufism and had extensive knowledge of Islamic religious sciences. Ibn 'Alwān's conversion story resonates with the spirit of the sixth–seventh/twelfth–thirteenth centuries, the golden age of the Sufi movement, when conversions to Sufism were quite common among both Muslim scholars and ordinary folk. Indeed, according to Jarāda: "The Sufi movement, during the age of Ibn 'Alwān had reached its culmination and prosperity, thanks to the Ayyūbids who encouraged it in every country under their rule, beginning with Egypt and ending with Yemen."[13] In addition, the story reveals the specific nature of Ibn

'Alwān's conversion to Sufism, namely, his shaking hands with the first caliph of Islam Abū Bakr aṣ-Ṣiddīq (d. 13/634). This indicates his strong allegiance to the Sunnī face of Islam, which did not preclude a sympathetic attitude toward the Shī'ī face of Islam, as discussed in the next chapter.

Education

As the son of a state official, Ibn 'Alwān received a formal Islamic education. He learned the basics of Islam, such as the Qur'ān and Sunna, jurisprudence (*fiqh*) and theology as well as the principles of the Arabic language (*'ulūm al-'arabiyya*), including phonology, morphology, syntax (*naḥw*), and rhetoric (*balāgha*). These disciplines seem to have formed the theoretical foundation on which he built his famous sermons. Ultimately, Sufism came to shape the spiritual dimension of his personality as well as his literary output. Thanks to his eloquent preaching, he came to be called "Jawzī al-Yaman." Al-Khazrajī (d. 812/1409) provided the reason for this moniker by saying that Ibn 'Alwān wrote a book of pious exhortations similar to that of the celebrated Ḥanbalī scholar and preacher Abū al-Faraj Ibn al-Jawzī (d. 597/1200).[14] It is known historically that Ibn al-Jawzī attacked Sufi excesses, an attitude that came to the fore in his book *Talbīs Iblīs.* It should be noted, however, that Ibn al-Jawzī was not opposed to Sufi ethics and self-discipline, provided that they did not contradict the Qur'ān and Sunna.[15] One should not forget that he wrote *Ṣifat aṣafwa,* which deals with the biographies of numerous friends of God (*awliyā'*). It is also believed that at the end of his life one hundred thousand men and ten thousand youth converted to a pious life.[16] Ibn al-Jawzī and Ibn 'Alwān were both successful preachers; however, Ibn 'Alwān's literary output is more narrow in scope than that of Ibn al-Jawzī, who wrote on a wide variety of topics and contributed to many fields of intellectual inquiry such as history, hagiography, *ḥadīth,* jurisprudence, and commentary on the Qur'ān.

Teachers and Disciples

According to biographers, one of Ibn 'Alwān's teachers was Abū al-Khaṭṭāb 'Umar Ibn al-Ḥadhdhā', a famous jurist (*faqīh*), an expert on *'ilm al-qirā'āt* (ten different recitations of the Qur'ān), and a man of miracles (*karāmāt*). Little is known about the relationship between Ibn 'Alwān and his teacher. His second teacher was the semilegendary Yemeni Sufi, Abū l-Ghayth b. Jamīl (d. 651/1253), nicknamed "the greatest sun" (*shams ash-shumūs*).[17] Ibn 'Alwān's third teacher was Abū

Ḥafs 'Umar b. al-Masan aṭ-Ṭayyār (d. 640/1242), a native of Dhubḥān, an area on the outskirts of Ta'izz, who had many followers in different places around the country. Some of these followers were described by al-Janadī as being "famous for their *karāmāt,*" which may indicate that they were accomplished Sufi masters.[18] Al-Masan was reputed for establishing a Sufi order known as "al-'Umariyya" after his first name. This Sufi order is now extinct. Al-Masan had a son called 'Abd Allāh, who married the daughter of Ibn 'Alwān. Their offspring have been in charge of hostels for itinerant Sufis (*arbiṭa,* sing. *ribāṭ*) and Sufi lodges (*zawāyā,* sing. *zāwiya*), which belong to the descendants of both shaykhs, al-Masan and Ibn 'Alwān, up to the present day.

One of the most prominent disciples and close friends of Ibn 'Alwān was Abū al-'Alā' as-Samkarī, known as as-Sulṭān 'Alā' (d. 680/1282).[19] Our sources say that they exchanged letters and visits.[20] For instance, if as-Sulṭān 'Alā' did not see his friend and teacher for a long time, Ibn 'Alwān would pay a visit to his village and spend time there. Al-Janadī (d. 732/1331) reports that as-Sulṭān 'Alā' asked Ibn 'Alwān (d. 665/1266) about the most hopeful verse in the Qur'ān. His answer was the following verse: "Say: Each one acts according to his disposition" (17:85). As-Sulṭān 'Alā' was not satisfied with this answer, which Ibn 'Alwān realized, and thus he interpreted the verse as follows: "If sin were determined by God eternally, it would not be affected by present accidental acts that cause God's anger. And if sin were determined by God eternally, it would not be affected by the recent accidental acts that please God. The sin of Adam and the obedience of Satan (*Iblīs*) serve as a sufficient proof of this [statement]. For when Adam descended to the earth of unhappiness from the fortress of his rank with all his progeny, the gifts of their Lover returned [to them] as God now is descending to the lowest heaven in His desire to be close to them and being unwilling to cause them pain . . . and God calls out: Is there a repentant one?"[21] This same question has a different interpretation in *Tuḥfat az-zaman fī ta'rīkh al-Yaman* by Ibn al-Ahdal (d. 855/1451). According to the latter, Ibn 'Alwān interpreted this Qur'ānic verse by saying: "If God's love were determined eternally, it would not be affected by the recent accidental acts that cause God's anger, and if God's aversion were determined eternally, it would not be affected by the recent accidental acts that cause [God's] love."[22] This account resembles the edited version of Ibn 'Alwān's famous book titled *al-Futūḥ*.[23] This interpretation alludes to the classical concept of God's determination of all events (*jabriyya*). However, Ibn al-Ahdal rejected Ibn 'Alwān's interpretation, citing the probability that Ibn 'Alwān might have borrowed these ideas from Ibn 'Arabī (d. 632/1242) and his followers. It seems that Ibn al-Ahdal had no proof, but at that time he was engaged in a polemical campaign against Ibn 'Arabī and had a grudge against all Sufis and their doctrines.

Another outstanding disciple of Ibn 'Alwān was the celebrated Sufi and scholar, Aḥmad b. Mūsā b. 'Ujayl (d. 690/1291), nicknamed "*al-faqīh.*"[24] The famous Yemeni town Bayt al-Faqīh is named after him. At the time of hardship, Sufis and non-Sufis used to seek refuge in this holy town because it was believed to be protected by Ibn 'Ujayl's blessings. Deeply influenced by Ibn 'Alwān, Ibn 'Ujayl emerges from Yemeni literature and folklore as a miracle maker and a friend of God. The famous hagiographer of medieval Yemen Aḥmad ash-Sharjī (d. 893/1487) provides accounts of some of Ibn 'Ujayl's *karāmāt* in his *Ṭabaqāt al-khawāṣṣ*. Here is an example:

> When he [Ibn 'Ujayl] came upon someone possessed with an evil spirit, he recited [aloud] the following Qur'ānic verse. "And ask: Has God commanded this, or you are imputing lies to God?"[25] The demon [who resided in the afflicted person] would cry out saying, "Oh by God, oh by God." The evil-spirit would then leave the possessed and would never come back to him as long as Ibn 'Ujayl was alive. However, when Ibn 'Ujayl died, the evil spirit returned. A certain man, who had attended the recitation when Ibn 'Ujayl recited the verse of the Qur'ān, claimed that he could recite the same verse upon the possessed. In fact, he went to the residence of the possessed and recited to him the same verse. Yet the evil-spirit sneeringly laughed at him and said, "The verse is the verse but the man is not the man."[26]

This demonstrates that Ibn 'Ujayl could not perform his miracles without God's sanction, because the attempt by others to use the same technique—the recitation upon the possessed—did not achieve the expected outcome. Miracles could not be performed without divine sanction.

In any case, Ibn 'Alwān had other disciples who are occasionally mentioned in his writings including Dāwūd an-Nassākh, 'Alī b 'Umar b. Aḥmad, Muḥammad b. 'Umar al-Ḥaḍramī, 'Ali b. Yaḥyā', the emir Shams ad-Dīn 'Alī b. Yaḥyā al-'Ansī, Shaykh 'Abd al-Wahhāb b. Rashīd, and others. However, it should be noted that there is a popular belief, which has been passed on from one generation to another since the time of Ibn 'Alwān's death, that no one has ever won the hearts and minds of more followers than Ibn 'Alwān. His charismatic character as a social reformer and spiritual leader has led numerous admirers to observe an annual gathering around his tomb. This fact can be seen nowadays as the best evidence of his relevance to Yemen's popular as well as intellectual traditions.

Ibn 'Alwān's Relationship with the Rasūlids

As mentioned above, Ibn 'Alwān renounced the world and spent his life meditating, preaching, and writing Sufi treatises. At the same time, he was deeply concerned with the sufferings of his fellow Muslims at the hands of unjust tax collectors (*al-qabbāḍīn*). Their depredations prompted him to write a letter to the ruler of Yemen, al-Manṣūr 'Umar b. 'Alī b. Rasūl (d. 647/1249),[27] asking him to abolish the newly introduced system of taxes, which was based on estimation rather than real output. This new policy was invented by individuals that Ibn 'Alwān described as "Rawāfiḍ." It is very hard to detect any connection between the Rawāfiḍ and tax collectors since the term "Rawāfiḍ" or "Rāfiḍa" literally means "repudiators" or "rejecters." Moreover, the term "Rāfiḍa" is said to relate to the proto-Imāmiyya and subsequently, to the Twelver Shī'a, and any Shī'ī group. The term also had wider applications. For instance, ash-Shahrastānī (d. 548/1153) includes the *ghulāt* (extremists) in the term "Rāfiḍa". Other scholars, including Ibn Ḥanbal (d. 241/855), Ibn Qutayba (828–889), 'Abd al-Qāhir al-Baghdādī (d. after 429/1037), and Abū l-Muẓaffar al-Isfarāyīnī, used the term to refer to the Zaydīs.[28] It seems highly likely that the term "Rāfiḍa" refers to the rejection of Abū Bakr (d. 13/634), 'Umar (d. 24/644), and some other companions of the Prophet by the early Shī'i groups.[29] Perhaps Ibn 'Alwān compared tax collectors in their aggressiveness to Rāfiḍa (the Rejecters) in that they repudiated the conventional rules of Islamic taxation (*zakā*) and replaced them with a new statistical system. Thus, the subjects (*ra'iyya* or *ra'āyā*) of the sultan used to pay *zakā* in kind (i.e., fruit, cows, calves, bulls, vegetables) according to what they possessed; but the tax collectors (*al-qabbāḍūn*) compelled them to pay in cash (*dīnār aw dīnārayn*) instead. Consequently, some subjects were unable to tolerate the new methods of excessive taxes and were forced to flee their lands. For this reason, Ibn 'Alwān launched a scorching diatribe against the economic conditions in the Yemeni state and advised the ruler al-Manṣūr 'Umar b. 'Alī b. Rasūl to redress the situation. At the end of his letter, Ibn 'Alwān wrote the following poem in which he summarized the miserable situation. The first line goes,

> The days of your life are the days that have a price: justice [which] should prevail, and an action all of [which] is good. . .

The following lines are from a later section of the poem:

> Continue to practice justice so that people may say: "Blessed is the king and blessed is Yemen."
> Oh! The third [after] the two 'Umars,[30] do as they did, so that your inward [intention] is similar to your outward deed.
> The Rawāfiḍ, may God obliterate their prop, were the first to plant this *ghars* [i.e., new taxation policy].
> They imposed a cash tax on the land due to their hatred of the adherents of Sharī'a and those who follow Sunna in their religion.
> They were indulgent with those who follow Rafḍ; but those who do not follow them are humiliated.[31]

In the second part of the poem, Ibn 'Alwān describes the wretched condition of the ruler's subjects in detail, clarifying the great gap in wealth between the king and the oppressed masses. He begins with the deplorable economic condition of the major cities and their inhabitants, urging al-Manṣūr to be lenient with his subjects and to treat them kindly. Then, Ibn 'Alwān launches a direct attack on the king, al-Manṣūr, accusing him of negligence because he never bothers to ask about the sources of his income. He draws a dramatic comparison between the king who lives in luxury and the ordinary people in his realm who are struggling to survive. Ibn 'Alwān concludes the poem by exhorting the king to remember the hereafter and reminding him that worldly life is trivial, treacherous, and unreliable. He says:

> This is Tihāma that has no money; neither has Laḥj, Abyan, Ṣan'ā' nor Aden.
> What is the fault of the poor of the mountains? They are your neighbors, allies and those whom you can rely on. . . .
> Have pity on them; God's eye is watching. You are their guardian and the Sultan is always trustworthy.
> Shame on you! You have erected palaces, but your subjects live in shacks.
> Do not take pleasure in accumulating money [without knowing where it came from]. For aren't you an intelligent and wise man?

You see thousands [of *dinars*], yet you do not ask the collector
from where they have come and how they were collected.
Whenever revenues increase, you should know that they were
exacted by force or injustice.
This is advice from one who knows for sure, not through a mere
rumor; it has been prompted by worries and sadness.
A king who thinks of nothing but his kingdom is similar to an
unfortunate insomniac.
You and I should stay away from worldly life. We should depart
this life empty-handed.
Do not rely on the worldly life because it has often spurned those
who relied on it.[32]

Due to the significance of this poem, the majority of Ibn ʿAlwān's biographers and modern Yemeni authors include quotations from it in their works. Although the whole poem is a critical attack on the dire economic conditions of Rasūlid Yemen, it reveals the political atmosphere of the Yemeni state, which may, even by our own standards, appear to be tolerant. In other words, the poem's daring and confrontational tone reflects a relative freedom of speech under the Rasūlid dynasty. Here, we witness the courageous voice of Ibn ʿAlwān, who was preoccupied not only with inward spirituality and Sufi teachings but also with the social and political conditions of his time. It is important to note that Ibn ʿAlwān never joined Yemeni court poets, who composed verses that praised the dynasts for their military exploits. On the contrary, his poetry is of a different kind, one that is not concerned with pleasing or placating the powers that be. Nevertheless, like many other Sufi masters, Ibn ʿAlwān played a significant role in mediating disputes among tribal leaders. To do so, he occasionally used letters in which he admonished the tribal leaders to purge their hearts of malice and cruelty, and encouraged them to be tolerant. In the end, he managed to resolve their long quarrels and to reconcile their differences. In addition, Ibn ʿAlwān frequently arbitrated between the Rasūlid rulers and some tribal leaders and regularly strove to protect the common people from the hostility of both.

Ibn ʿAlwān's Contributions to Sufi Thought

Ibn ʿAlwān's most influential books are *at-Tawḥīd al-aʿẓam* (The Supreme Union), *Kitāb wa-dīwān al-futūḥ* (The Book and Collection of Revelation), *al-Mahrajān wa-l-baḥr al-mushakkal al-gharīb* (The Festival and the Unfamiliar Diverse Sea), *al-Ajwiba al-lāʾiqa ʿalā al-asʾila al-fā'iqa* (The Appropriate Answers on the Outstanding Questions, a manuscript), and a treatise entitled *al-Kibrīt al-aḥmar* (The Elixir). There are seven other manuscripts, privately held and rarely circulated, which unfortunately are not available for study. These include *Qāmūs al-ḥaqā'iq* (The Dictionary of Realities), *Kanz al-'arsh* (The Treasure of the Throne), *al-Baḥr al-muḥīṭ* (The Surrounding Sea), *Wadā' Ramaḍān* (Farewell to Ramaḍān), *al-Hiwāya fī 'ilm al-ghayb* (The Hobby in the Unknown Knowledge), *al-Balāgha wa-t-taṣwīb* (Rhetoric and Rectification), *al-Ishrāq* (Illumination).[33] In what follows, I will confine myself to the most widely circulated books, which have had and continue to have a significant impact on the spirituality of the people of Yemen across the centuries.

At-Tawḥīd al-a'ẓam *(The Supreme Union)*

The editor of Ibn 'Alwān's books, 'Abd al-'Azīz Sulṭān al-Manṣūb, affirms that many who have dealt with Ibn 'Alwān's works have, for the most part, been unable to understand his ambiguous terminology and complicated arguments. Some scribes tampered with Ibn 'Alwān's writings, and others tried to make sense of his ambiguous texts, by imposing on them what they considered to be the correct language usage. A major expert on Ibn 'Alwān's legacy, al-Manṣūb has done a thorough investigation by comparing old manuscripts with their later versions. His prodigious efforts resulted in fairly reliable editions of Ibn 'Alwān's works.

The subtitle of *at-Tawḥīd al-a'ẓam* (The Supreme Union) is *Al-muballigh man la ya'lam ila rutbat man ya'lam* (the one who transfers those who do not know into the rank of those who know). Since the seventh/thirteenth century *at-Tawḥīd al-a'ẓam* has been one of the most influential sources of Sufi literature in Yemen even to the present day. It is held in high regard by Yemeni Muslims, especially in the Sunnī regions. It was believed among the populace, before this book was published, that any attempt to print it would fail due to its supernatural and magical nature. However, this belief has no grounds and the book's reputation relies primarily on its pious exhortations, poems, and Sufi themes. Ibn 'Alwān begins his book with a statement of his theological creed. He argues that the Truth (i.e., God) is obvious and that sound intellects (*'uqūl*) are unable to doubt His existence. If intellects travel through the horizons of vision to obtain knowledge of their essences (*ma'ārif*) and comprehend their attributes, they will eventually discover that they are reflections of His light. Their essences are related to His essence, their attributes are related to His attributes. The existence of their essences is His existence, and the denial of the reality of their being is equivalent to His denial. Whenever they tend to deny Him, the denial goes back to them. Whenever they tend to repudiate Him, the repudiation returns to them. As the *'uqūl* becomes aware of the sustained proof of their existence, they almost imagine that they were Him and He them. When the affinity between them and God becomes clear to them, they learn that they are only the shadows of His light, which show the way to Him.[34]

We have to understand that Ibn 'Alwān succeeded in refuting the thesis of those who claimed unrestricted union with God, such as al-Ḥallāj (d. 309/922), Ibn 'Arabī (d. 638/1240), and others. For Ibn 'Alwān, those who had reached that rank of closeness to God only imagined that their attributes became identical with His attributes and their essences with God's essence. According to this fine point, many Sufi travelers to God were mistaken when they claimed their unified affinity with God. As noted above, Ibn 'Alwān asserts that the intellects (*'uqūl*) of these path seekers of God are merely shadows of His light. The closest example that best describes this thesis is that the sun's beams are not the essence of the sun: they are only shadows and reflections of the sun. Ibn 'Alwān's uniqueness and distinctiveness can be understood from this argument. Many Sufi masters, if not all, fail to recognize the subtle difference between the essence itself and its reflection. They presumed that they reached to the essence of God whereas in fact they recognized the shadows that may lead to God.

At-Tawḥīd al-a'ẓam is divided into three chapters.[35] The first deals with the ninety-nine beautiful names of God. Before explaining each name Ibn 'Alwān uses the expression "Glory to You" (*subḥānaka*) as the key word for his interpretation, and he argues that the term carries the meaning of exalting and sanctifying God. His approach is unique because it peels away the layers of ego and pride that might accompany writing. It also shows the depth of Ibn 'Alwān's mystical knowledge and his unrivalled ability to present it to a wide audience of readers. In addition, his writing carries a profound message of teaching scholars how to treat divine names with absolute respect. His approach also tends to emphasize human deficiency and simultaneously alerts scholars to the significance and urgency of protection against errors.

Instead of philosophically explaining the meaning of each name, like the commentary of Abū Ḥāmid al-Ghazālī (d. 505/1111) in *al-Maqṣad al-asnā* or Fakhr ad-Dīn ar-Rāzī (d. 606/1209) in his *Sharḥ asmā' Allāh al-ḥusnā,* or *Lawāmi' al-bayyināt sharḥ asmā' Allāh ta'ālā wa-ṣ-ṣifāt,*

Ibn ʻAlwān describes the function of each divine name, leaving aside the classical method of Greek syllogism. Unlike al-Ghazālī or ar-Rāzī, Ibn ʻAlwān seems to avoid the complexities that stem from the explanation of metaphysical meanings of God's most beautiful names. In other words, Ibn ʻAlwān treats God's names from a practical and spiritual point of view, whereas ar-Rāzī, al-Ghazālī, and others tried to examine them from the viewpoint of speculative theology (*ʻilm al-kalām*) or philosophy. Thus, Ibn ʻAlwān's way is more appealing to all types of readers, rather than simply addressing a group of theologians or philosophers.

The second chapter deals with a variety of spiritual supplications and, to a great extent, the ʻAlwānī litanies (*awrād;* sing. *wird*) for assigned times of the day and night, which shaped his Sufi path (*ṭarīqa*). Ibn ʻAlwān introduces a short philosophical epistle, which deals with the concept of two images and two births, the soul and the flesh. There follows an essay on Sufi concerts (*samāʻ*), which may have been a significant part of the practice of the extinct ʻAlwānī brotherhood. In addition, Ibn ʻAlwān includes passages of supplications that may have constituted essential practices in his Sufi brotherhood. They are classified into a variety of general and specific supplications to be read after the five prayers. In other words, there is a supplication (*duʻāʼ*) after each canonical prayer beginning at dawn and ending at nightfall. The purpose of the abundant supplications is to keep the disciple (*al-murīd*) busy with the remembrance of God (*dhikr*) and to keep him from distractions.[36]

The third chapter consists of a collection of topics. It begins with a poem, which explains the primary stages of human creation, then an epistle concerning the methods of the path (*as-sulūk*). According to Ibn ʻAlwān, the path consists of: (1) obeying God's command; (2) following in the footsteps of the Prophet; (3) searching for a scholar who knows God's Book and the Prophet's code of behavior, and how to apply them to his personal life; (4) living with such a scholar or visiting him frequently. After that, we find a mixture of pious exhortations and poems. This section is followed by an epistle of advice to a certain Ibn Arḥab, who may have been one of Ibn ʻAlwān's disciples because he addresses him "*ayyuhā'l-walad.*" The form of this epistle resonates to some extent with that of al-Ghazālī (d. 505/1111) in his epistle *ayyuhā'l-walad.* Another epistle was addressed to Ibn Sālim, on whom we have no information except that he came from a tribal area. The next section deals with short exhortations and answers to questions presented to Ibn ʻAlwān regarding interpretations of some verses of the Qur'ān and explanations of Sufi terms.

These epistles are followed by a refutation of the thesis that some Sufis despised heaven. Ibn 'Alwān expresses his surprise at this critique of Sufism. He says, "If they renounce Paradise, do they renounce the neighborhood of the Imām as-Sunna and the noblest of all jinn and human, the Prophet?" He adds: "They desired union with God (*ittiḥād*) and were anxious to seek the Lord of worshippers from a different angle, from a different aspect, from a different presence (*ḥaḍra*), and from a different group."[37] According to Ibn 'Alwān, Sufis neither hold paradise in contempt, nor ridicule the torture of hell. Ibn 'Alwān contends that when a Sufi says, "We neither worship God in hope of His Paradise nor from fear of His Hell, but for His own sake,"[38] they mean to purify their deeds of evil accidents and to become sincere in their intentions. They want to follow the Prophet's advice: "Worship God as if you see Him, for if you do not see Him, He sees you." Ibn 'Alwān proceeds to explain the rationality of their position from a spiritual point of view. He states that if God is present and if He commands and prohibits those who see Him, their worship requires the quality of self-control or pious meditation (*murāqaba*) and contemplation (*an-naẓar*), and not fear of punishment or desire for divine reward. However, if He disappears from sight, their worship is determined by the expectation of divine reward (*thawāb*) and divine punishment (*'iqāb*).

The lengthy final chapter of *at-Tawḥīd* starts with exhortations and poems followed by a theological section on the Islamic caliphate and a panegyric poem praising the Prophet's family (*ahl al-bayt*).[39] There follows a section on the self or soul (*an-nafs*) along with the refutation of those who deny resurrection, eschatological events, and the return of souls to their bodies. In the next episode, Ibn 'Alwān talks about the manner in which nations will enter either paradise or hell after the resurrection. He argues that this kind of knowledge is inaccessible to scholars.[40] Then, he describes images from his inspired visions about the ways that believers will enter paradise, how the disbelievers will cross the threshold of hell, and how the disobedient believers will leave hell after a period of torture, and go to heaven. This section, however, is immediately followed by short refutations of philosophers, incarnationists (*ḥulūliyyūn*), and others. The next section is dedicated to the relationship between master (*shaykh*) and disciple (*murīd*), followed by excerpts from sermons and didactic poems.[41] At the end of *at-Tawḥīd,* the author states his doctrine and beliefs, which will be discussed at length in Chapter 5. *At-Tawḥīd* concludes with two short letters addressed to al-Muẓaffar Yūsuf b. 'Umar b. 'Alī b. Rasūl (d. 694/1295) in which Ibn 'Alwan asks him to redress grievances committed by his staff against his subjects. The last section of the book, as in many of his writings, consists of general exhortations.

It is very difficult to make judgments about the writing of Ibn 'Alwān, especially if we intend to tie his thought to the previous Sufi figures. However, it is safe to say that his way was distinctive in terms of his handling of ideas and theology, and, more important, in establishing a distinctively Yemeni Sufi lexicon.

Al-Futūh *(The Revelations)*

The manuscripts of *Dīwān al-futūḥ* have two different formats. The first format, according to Ḥamūd al-Qiyarī, a contemporary Yemeni writer, consists of two parts. The first part is composed of 127 poems, with no prose, whereas the second contains a mixture of prose and poetry. They cover ecstatic states (*mawājīd*), Sufi thoughts, and panegyric poems in praise of the Prophet. The second format divides *Diwān al-futūḥ* into four sections, and Al-Qiyarī states that there is no significant difference between the two formats except in arranging concepts, passages, and poems. He argues that the second format was adopted by a medieval writer, Abū al-Fatḥ b. 'Abd Allāh al-Jabartī al-'Aqīlī al-Baṣṣāl, whose biography is unfortunately not found in Yemeni literature. In the manuscript, the scribe says that the formatting by al-Baṣṣāl "became the original copy for later scribes."[42] However, the editor of Ibn 'Alwān's works, 'Abd al-'Azīz al-Manṣūb, rejects al-Baṣṣāl's copies due to many errors in form and content. Al-Manṣūb relies on other manuscripts that are older than al-Baṣṣāl's. It appears that both editors, al-Qiyarī and al-Manṣūb, have made use of the available manuscripts, and the latter had more access to earlier manuscripts. Owing to the interpolations of scribes, al-Qiyarī argues that *Diwān al-futūḥ* has actually been known under three different titles. Carl Brockelmann cites three books by Ibn 'Alwān that may have the same content: *Kitāb al-futūḥ aṣ-ṣāfī li-kull qalb majrūḥ* (Gotha), *Dīwān* (Cairo), and *al-Futūḥ al-maṣūna wal-asrār al-maknūna* (Paris).[43] Al-Qiyarī is also surprised that Khayr ad-Dīn az-Ziriklī's (d. 1976) *al-A'lām* and al-Ḥibshī's *Maṣādir al-fikr al-islāmī fī al-Yaman* mention *al-futūḥ* and *Dīwān shi'r* as two different books. Due to the corruption of Ibn 'Alwān's manuscripts by scribes and in order to find middle ground between conflicting views on this issue, al-Manṣūb has published Ibn 'Alwān's book under the title *Kitāb wa-dīwān al-futūh;* hence, for brevity, I shall call it *al-futūḥ*.

Al-Futūḥ is the second most important source of Ibn 'Alwān's Sufi legacy. It is, in many respects, similar to *at-Tawḥīd al-'aẓam* in form and content. The difference lies only in the number of poems included. *Al-Futūḥ* has more poems than *at-Tawḥīd,* which account for its being referred to as a *dīwān* (collection). In present-day Yemen, during the Sufi gatherings that take place during the *mawlid* or *tahlīl,* participants often recite excerpts from Ibn 'Alwān's *al-Futūḥ.*[44] To explain their choice of his poetry they cite its musicality, piety, and traditional Sufi themes, which focus on the relationship between the Divine Master and his human servant.

It is important to note that *al-Futūḥ* contains a number of poems composed in the form of quatrains (*rubā'iyyāt*), a form believed to be purely Persian. For instance, the famous British scholar E. G. Browne, says: "The quatrain may safely be regarded as the most ancient essentially Persian verse-form, while next to this comes the *mathnawī,* or poem in 'doublets,' which is generally narrative, and where the rhyme changes in each couplet."[45] A. J. Arberry argues that Browne's judgment regarding the origins of the quatrain as a product of the Persian genius stands unchallenged and indisputable.[46] It should be pointed out, however, that the Persians borrowed many features from the Arabs after the conquest of Persia, and the reemergence of Persian as a literary language. Not only were forms and genres borrowed, but many meters, with the exception of the *rubā'ī,* were likewise borrowed.[47] Ibn 'Alwān has been credited by a contemporary critic and prolific writer, 'Abd al-'Azīz Al-Maqāliḥ, as being the first Yemeni poet to introduce not only the form of the *rubā'iyyāt* (quatrain), but also *al-mubayyatāt* (a poem written in the vernacular and characterized by melodious nature), and *al-mukhammasāt* (stanzas that consist of five lines each). Al-Maqāliḥ argues that popular (*'āmmī*) or vernacular Yemeni poetry as well as *ḥumaynī* (a famous genre of lyric poetry) were originally introduced into Yemeni literature by no one other than Ibn 'Alwān. Al-Maqāliḥ adds that the variety of rhyme schemes found in Ibn 'Alwān's poetic legacy is unprecedented in Yemeni literature. Unfortunately, Al-Maqāliḥ forgets to mention Ibn 'Alwān's *thulāthiyyāt* (stanzas consisting of three lines each). Being a Sufi poet, Ibn 'Alwān was perfectly positioned, according to al-Maqālih, to explore new poetic fields and to be guided by lyrical rhythms that are perfectly suited to *dhikr* assemblies and the Sufi predilection for *samā'* and music.[48]

Ibn 'Alwān's language in general and in *al-Futūḥ* in particular has been described by some scholars as ambiguous and obscure. Medieval biographers portray his mystical writings as composed in "diverse languages" (*lughāt shattā*). When asked how Ibn 'Alwān learnt these languages without ever leaving his native country, one of the Sufi mystics (*ba'ḍ al-'ārifīn*) answered, "He learnt them through his visionary encounters with the spirits of foreign saints who visited him in his retreat."[49] Al-Ḥibshī, however, describes Ibn 'Alwān's language as "strange language" (*lugha gharība*) and argues that Ibn 'Alwān claimed to have invented it himself. He concludes that this process is no more than Ibn 'Alwān's immoderation in spiritual athleticism (*ifrāṭihi fī r-ryāḍa*).[50] Yet is it really a strange language? Here I will argue that it is in fact an ordinary language that makes use of new vocabulary, morphological inflections, and derivation. For instance, he created new verbal nouns that were unfamiliar in his cultural milieu, though he derived them from their common Arabic roots. For example, he used the noun pattern *bāhūt* from the verb "*bahita*" or "*bahuta*" (which means to be perplexed, startled, and amazed). The term "*bahūt*" with the short vowel "a" exists in classical Arabic but not with the long vowel "ā." Similarly, he used the verbal noun "*ghārūf*" (a deep well) instead of "*gharūf*." Moreover, some other verbal nouns, such as "*qāṭūf*" from the verb "*qaṭafa*," "*kāshūf*" from the verb "*kashafa*," demonstrate Ibn 'Alwān's ability to create new derivative patterns (*awzān*) unfamiliar to his contemporaries.

In his *Qaḍāyā wa-ishkāliyyāt at-taṣawwuf 'ind Aḥmad bin 'Alwān*, 'Abd al-Karīm Sa'īd has drawn up a list of these new words found in *al-Futūḥ* and other works of Ibn 'Alwān.[51] To make sense of these terms, one can divide each neologism into two recognizable words found in standard Arabic dictionaries. One example of this is the term "*haylahūt*": the first part is derived from "*hayla*," which means *hilāl Allāh* (the crescent of God), and the second is a suffix derived from the morphological pattern for exaggeration (*ṣīghat al-mubālagha*).[52] According to 'Abd ar-Raḥmān Ba'kar (d. 2007), a literary writer and critic, Ibn 'Alwān used the device of blending (*naḥt*),[53] which is fairly common in Arabic linguistics. It is employed to depict scenes of the hereafter and eschatological events in the Qur'ān.[54]

Another way of looking at these new terms is by determining their etymologies. As an example of this, one can cite some words of Persian origin such as "*dustukān*," which means a vase made of glass, and "*dustūn*," a colloquial form of the standard Persian "*dastān*," which means "story." I have noted earlier that Ibn 'Alwān's biographers emphasized the fact that he never left Yemen. Nevertheless, he might have learned these and other Persian terms from travelers or from Persian books that were circulated in Yemen during his time. It is also probable that the so-called Sons of Persians (*al-abnā'*), who had settled in Yemen before the advent of Islam, transmitted Persian terms into the Yemeni language. Finally, Ba'kar argues that Ibn 'Alwān must have known the Persian language along with some other languages. This view is captured in his statement, "If Ibn 'Alwān were not an intelligent gardener, he would not have picked flowers [i.e., beautiful vocabulary] from the gardens of Persia and Byzantium."[55] However, the fact remains that Ibn 'Alwān never left Yemen.

Ba'kar sees the use of non-Arabic words (*isti'jām*) in the poetry of Ibn 'Alwān in two ways. First, there is *isti'jām* that finds its expression in one word only, which can be found in many poems. Second, there is the less common *isti'jām* that encompasses a whole line. An example of the latter is a line from *al-futūḥ*, which reads: "*faqālat sāminū hānū sibhisāh sibhisānī.*"[56] Ba'kar states that al-Manṣūb, the editor of Ibn 'Alwān's works, has never commented on this line nor explained the alien words (*isti'jām*) of which it consists. However, Ba'kar did not comment on the line either. Here I suggest that the interpretation of this line falls under the Sufi notion of *ramz,* which, according to Abū Naṣr as-Sarrāj (d. 378/988), designates "an inner meaning hidden under the guise of outer speech, which no one will grasp except for its [intended audience] (*ahluhu*)."[57] Using this definition, I contend that all the incomprehensible words in Ibn 'Alwān's poetry can be seen as instances of his use of *ramz* as a rhetorical device. Thus, the line mentioned above may be interpreted as a response to an earlier line in the same poem, which reads: "*Faqultu al-hawn yā Sāmūn, siyāb al-ḥubb awhānī,*" meaning: "I said, be gentle to me, oh Sāmūn, [for] the captivity of love weakened me." The author requests Sāmūn, a symbol of God's love, to be easy on him, because excessive intimacy with God and love of Him have exhausted his soul. Sāmūn replies, "Take it easy, because we are in the same boat of love." In other words, Sāmūn implies that what has enchanted the speaker has also enchanted him. Perhaps Ibn 'Alwān is referring to the Qur'ānic verse: "God could verily bring (in your place) another people whom He would love as they would love Him."[58] Moreover, he may be alluding to the idea of the "unity of being" that was expounded by the writing of Ibn 'Arabī (d. 538/1240). Finally, this process of spiritual dialogues should be classified under his major theme of mystical moderation.

Ibn 'Alwān's use of "foreign languages" in *al-Futūh,* which is marked, like many Sufi narratives, by its open-endedness, does not extend to his other writings.[59] Most of the time the obscurity of his texts is a consequence of his constant use of Sufi symbols to convey his subtle and elusive mystical experiences. The fact that this new vocabulary was incomprehensible to some of the author's contemporary disciples does not constitute a major problem in the study of Ibn 'Alwān's Sufi legacy, nor does it prove his knowledge of the Persian language. His contribution lies in his creative ability to produce rare and unusual forms and patterns that were unfamiliar to the ordinary reader or listener and that aroused curiosity. It was thus a rhetorical device, not unlike the rare words and neologisms found in the Qur'ān, to awaken the reader or listener to the subtle truths about to be revealed. In conclusion, Ibn 'Alwān's heritage should be examined within the context of the Sufi literature of his age which, according to Marshall Hodgson, was characterized by pervasive use of obscure symbolism and allegorical style.[60]

Al-Mahrajān wa l-Baḥr al-mushakkal al-gharīb

In his introduction to *al-Mahrajān wa l-Baḥr al-mushakkal al-gharīb* (The Festival and the Unfamiliar Diverse Sea) by Ibn 'Alwān, the contemporary editor and critic, 'Abd al-'Azīz al-Manṣūb pointed to the fact that he combined the two separate treatises *al-Mahrajān* and *al-Baḥr al-mushakkal al-gharīb* into one book. Al-Manṣūb argues that the relatively small size of the two books tempted scribes to produce more copies, which rapidly led to their dissemination on the one hand, but resulted in considerable editorial differences and bad renditions on the other. Thus, al-Manṣūb found eight manuscripts of *al-Mahrajān* (The Festival), one of which is more than three hundred years old, and eleven versions of *al-Baḥr al-mushakkal al-gharīb* (The Unfamiliar Diverse Sea). Because the editor found a separate epistle, *al-Kibrīt al-aḥmar* (The Elixir), which is only six pages and not sufficient to be circulated as a separate copy, he added it as an appendix to the previous two treatises. He further appended a commentary on the Qur'ānic verse of the throne (*āyat l-kursī*) (2:256) as well as the opening chapter of the Qur'ān (*surat al-fātiḥa*) (1:1–7), both of which were found in a separate manuscript by Ibn 'Alwān. In addition, the manuscript of Egypt titled *Dīwān al-futūḥ* has an appended poem of nine verses, which al-Manṣūb added along with another long poem, to the new book *al-Mahrajān wa l-Baḥr al-mushakkal al-gharīb.* This long poem was discovered two hundred years after Ibn 'Alwān's death by Abū al-Fatḥ al-Jabartī al-'Aqīlī al-Baṣṣāl, who might have feared its loss and probably was certain that it belonged to Ibn 'Alwān. (Al-Manṣūb did not include this poem in his edition of *Kitāb wa-dīwān al-futūḥ*, in line with his overall approach to Ibn 'Alwān's legacy, which is aimed at purifying it of inauthentic material.) However, the poem was attached as an appendix to the two manuscripts *al-Mahrajān* and *al-Baḥr al-mushakkal al-gharīb* to form one book. The content of this poem is a refutation of the jurists (*fuqahā'*) of Banū Isḥāq, who had denounced the Sufi gatherings and concerts (*samā'*).

The content of Ibn 'Alwān's *al-Mahrajān* revolves around the portrayal of the characteristics of one who has achieved full knowledge of God, that is, the Sufi knower (*al-'ārif*). His style is similar to that of his other writings. On many occasions, we find ideas that were inspired by Sufi interpretations of some verses of the Qur'ān. Despite the relative shortness of *al-Mahrajān,* it covers four distinct topics: (1) exhortations; (2) Qur'ānic interpretations; (3) refutations of those who reject *samā';* (4) and, finally, a discussion of the strange sciences pertaining to the knowledge of the soul (*'ulūm an-nafs al-gharība*). Moreover, in *al-Mahrajān,* Ibn 'Alwān expresses thoughts concerning God's existence. This is a very comprehensive view that parallels the doctrine of "unity of being" (*waḥdat l-wujūd*) introduced by his contemporary Sufi and scholar Muḥyī d-Dīn Ibn 'Arabī (d. 638/1240), but it also resembles another mystical vision, "unity of witnessing" (*waḥdat ash-Shuhūd*) that was expounded almost four centuries later by Ahmad Sirhindī (d. 1034/1625).[61] Ibn 'Alwān's comprehensive vision of God and the world is as follows:

> There is nothing behind what God created except God, and there is nothing before what God created except God, and there is nothing within what God created except God. So, be with God behind everything that He created, and be with God before everything that He created, and be with God within everything that He created. You would be intimate with God in the diversity of His creation, and all that is dissimilar would become intimate with you.[62]

In the next section Ibn 'Alwān elaborates on the relationship among God, time, and place. He states that "God is not in a place, specified for Him, and is not in a time, specified for Him, but He has chosen from all the places, the hearts of knowers (*qulūb al-'ārifīn*) and from all the times, the times of those who remember Him (*adh-dhākirīn.*)"[63]

Similarly, *al-Baḥr al-mushakkal al-gharīb* begins with the classification of knowledge (*ma'rifa*) and the knower (*al-'ārif*) according to a *ḥadīth* whose chain of transmitters is relatively dubious (*fī isnādihi līn*). The import of the *ḥadīth* is that if one knows God totally (*ḥaqqa ma'ri-*

fatih), one can walk on water, and the mountains will shake as a result of one's supplications. Ibn 'Alwān continues his narrative by inviting the reader to travel along the path of the *'ārif.* To this end, he recommends the following: (1) to know the Blessing-Giver (*al-mun'im*); (2) to know grace (*an-ni'ma*); and (3) to know the enemy of both *al-mun'im* and *an-ni'ma.* As soon as the follower knows these three things and assimilates them, he will be able to experience "the sweetness of God's service and the fruit of worship and that his heart will be lit with the light of knowledge."[64] Ibn 'Alwān argues that this can be perpetuated through adopting acts of obedience and avoiding acts of disobedience. If the novice is not capable of experiencing these thoughts, he should know that his heart has hardened (*qāsī*).

The most essential theme in *al-Baḥr al-mushakkal al-gharīb* and perhaps the entire message of Ibn 'Alwān's thought is the idea of balance in the Sufi path. Few Sufi writers or practitioners have insisted upon this notion, but Ibn 'Alwān consistently urges followers to adopt it. He argues,

> If you are prevailed upon by the domain of fear, use the domain of hope. If you are prevailed upon by the domain of hope, use the domain of fear. If you are prevailed upon by the domain of love, use the domain of awe. If you are prevailed upon by the domain of awe, use the domain of love. Then, strive in that until fear is straightened with hope, and love with awe. Whenever you lose the balance of one of the domains—we have mentioned—one of the domains of the heart is shut and you become unworthy of knowledge [in God]. So my brother, look, do you find the domains of your heart proportionate in your heart? If they are proportionate, take your strife as long as they are proportionate. If they are not proportionate, your construction will be on waste.[65]

This passage conveys the essential message of his teachings. Sufi writers may have spoken about such balance among the spiritual states, but they never advise anyone who has reached the state of love to balance it with the state of awe. Despite the fact that the state of love is the ultimate station for any path seeker to attain, the parallel state of awe is inseparable from it in the thought of Ibn 'Alwān (d. 665/1266). This insistence on making proportionate the heart of the knower in God is the supreme message of Ibn 'Alwān, and he should be credited for this unique idea.

Al-Ajwiba al-lā'iqa 'alā al-as'ila al-fā'iqa

The manuscript of *al-Ajwiba al-lā'iqa 'alā al-as'ila al-fā'iqa* (The Appropriate Answers to the Outstanding Questions) has not been edited like the other works just mentioned.[66] This manuscript is found as an appendix to one of the manuscripts of *at-Tawḥīd al-a'ẓam* in the town of Ibb in Yemen. Al-Manṣūb has been unable to gain access to it there, nor has it been mentioned in 'Abd al-Karīm Sa'īd's *Qaḍāyā wa-ishkāliyyāt at-taṣawwuf 'ind Aḥmad b. 'Alwān* or by Ḥamūd al-Qiyarī in his M.A. thesis titled *Taḥqīq wa-dirāsat dīwān al-futūḥ* presented to the University of Cairo (1988). This manuscript was copied in 1370/1950 by Yaḥyā ad-Dalālī, a native of Ibb, who did not cite the source he took it from. Al-Falāḥī argues that this manuscript resonates, to a great extent, with the other works of Ibn 'Alwān. Thus, as no one has yet proved otherwise, it is safe to say that it is very likely one of the missing works written by Ibn 'Alwān. Due to the tampering of scribes, we find a poem in this manuscript identical to the first poem that appears in *at-Tawḥīd.*

This epistle is about Sufi questions presented to Ibn 'Alwān by Sharaf ad-Dīn Ḥasan al-'Ajamī.[67] The questions and Ibn 'Alwān's answers constitute the content of *al-Ajwiba al-lā'iqa 'alā al-as'ila al-fā'iqa.* Ibn 'Alwān deals with questions of how things emerged from their Maker and how the Maker can be known through the examination of their properties. What is the nature of this divine revealed knowledge? How is one to comprehend the demise of created things or their continuing existence? These questions also encompass how one can comprehend the existence of the Maker of created beings by examining the ways in which they point to Him. They also ask how it is possible to arrive at knowledge by examining your conspectus of the universe. Finally, this epistle contains a discussion of divine names, attributes, and actions, all of which will be discussed later.

Conclusion

This chapter has traced Ibn 'Alwān's life and works as they are described in the sources at our disposal. His important influence in Yemen is evident in the fact that some of his disciples became well-known saints in Yemeni Sufi literature and folklore, the most prominent example being Aḥmad b. Mūsā b. 'Ujayl. Perhaps even more significant for his place in Yemen's social history, Ibn 'Alwān did not shy away from confrontation with political powers in the name of the common people, as demonstrated by the poem he sent to the Rasūlid ruler, 'Umar b. 'Alī b. Rasūl (d. 647/1249). As we have seen, Ibn 'Alwān valiantly urged the ruler to stop his oppressive policies, remedy the grievances of the Yemeni peasants, and improve their dire economic conditions. Incidents such as these provide a holistic picture of Ibn ʻAlwān's role in Yemen's social and political environment and his commitment to justice.

I have discussed the most important works of Ibn ʻAlwān, particularly those that have been published, as well as those still in manuscript. In the following chapter I move away from Ibn ʻAlwān's role in Yemeni society to delve in more detail into the theological nuances of Ibn ʻAlwān's oeuvre in its own right, expounding his complex system of thought and showing its strong roots in Islamic scripture, the Qur'ān, and the *ḥadīth*. This exploration of Ibn ʻAlwān's work enables us to situate him within the larger religious debates of his era and articulate the various doctrinal positions he took in relation to contemporary Islamic movements such as the Muʻtazilites.

4

IBN ‘ALWĀN’S THEOLOGICAL VIEWS

In this chapter I provide a much-needed study of the content of Ibn ‘Alwān’s theology and literary production and address Ibn ‘Alwān’s inner religious motivations as well as his relationships to other Sufis and Islamic movements in Yemen and across the Arab world during the sixth/twelfth century. It will become clear that Ibn ‘Alwān developed an original system of Sufi thought that was strongly grounded in the Qur’ān and the *ḥadīth,* and in his praise for the Rightly Guided Caliphs he affirmed his allegiance to the Sunnī school of thought. Following a detailed overview of Ibn ‘Alwān’s philosophy of free will, good and bad deeds, and other important questions, I provide a summary of Mu‘tazilite theology, which Ibn ‘Alwān often wrote against, and speculative theology (*kalām*), which Ibn ‘Alwān strongly opposed for standing against revelation. I examine in detail Ibn ‘Alwān’s views on two branches of *kalām*—seeing God, and the createdness of the Qur’ān—and show that Ibn ‘Alwān’s Sunnī theology did not prevent him from espousing sympathy for certain Shī‘ī concepts. Indeed, Ibn ‘Alwān brought his insight and piety to bear on the multiple Islamic influences circulating in Yemen during his lifetime and synthesized a unique theology grounded firmly in Islamic scripture, a theology that continues to have resonance in Yemen today.

Doctrinal Views

Scholars who have studied the doctrine of Ibn ‘Arabī (d. 638/1242) found him deliberately elusive.[1] In his meticulous presentation of his doctrine and beliefs in *at-Tawḥīd al-a‘ẓam,* Ibn ‘Alwān reminds us of Abū Ḥāmid al-Ghazālī (d. 505/1111), who summarized his doctrine in his famous book *al-Munqidh min aḍ-ḍalāl.* The chief motive behind Ibn

'Alwān's presentation of his doctrine was his wish to purge from the hearts of his brothers the hostile insinuations of Satan.

Ibn 'Alwān begins his discussion by stating that God is one in essence, attributes, names, and verses. According to Ibn 'Alwān, God's existence is eternal with no limits or boundaries. His eternal existence is not subject to extinction, and there is no end to His overflowing bounty. Creation belongs to Him in form and design; command belongs to Him in planning and determination. He is knowledgeable, hearing and seeing without senses. He is speaking, the One who contracts (*al-Qābiḍ*), and the One who expands (*al-Bāsiṭ*) without having extremities of the body (*jawāriḥ*). No eyes can penetrate Him by describing Him (*waṣfan*), but He penetrates all eyes due to His subtlety (*luṭfan*). Ibn 'Alwān goes on to say that He created creatures neither for a motive nor for a reason. He did this in order to show His power and to carry out His will. The purpose of creation is not known to anyone or anything except God. Whoever tries to discover what lies beyond His verse—"I have not created the jinn and mankind except to worship Me"[2]—is subject to extreme temptation. The Qur'ān is His speech, which He revealed to the best of His creatures, the Prophet. In conclusion, Ibn 'Alwān states that whoever believes that the Qur'ān was created has departed from Islam. Ibn 'Alwān certainly was trying to refute the Mu'tazilite doctrine of the createdness of the Qur'ān.

In addition to his discussion of his belief about God's essence, attributes, and actions, Ibn 'Alwān notes that some Rāfida claimed that the Qur'ān was an invention (*qarīḥat*) of Muḥammad. He argues that such a doctrine constitutes a departure from Islam, and there is no distinction between saying that the Qur'ān was created or invented by Muḥammad. Both, in Ibn 'Alwān's view, are manifestations of disbelief because he equated the createdness of the Qur'ān with the assumption that the Qur'ān was the Prophet's speech: accordingly, he rejected them both.[3] It is possible that Ibn 'Alwān was referring to this much-debated topic in terms of the inimitability of the Qur'ān, as expounded by Abū Bakr Muḥammad b. aṭ-Ṭayyib al-Bāqillānī (d. 404/1013) in *I'jāz al-Qur'ān* (The miraculous character of the Qur'ān). Ibn 'Alwān's discussion of the unity of God also appears to resonate, to some extent, with the denial of anthropomorphism in *Maqālāt al-Islāmiyyīn* by Abū al-Ḥasan al-Ash'arī (d. 324/935) in which he dealt with the Mu'tazilite doctrine of *tawḥīd* as translated by W. Montgomery Watt:

> The Mu'tazila agree that God is one; there is nothing like him; he is hearing, seeing; he is not a body (*jism, shabaḥ, juththa*), not a

> form, not flesh, and blood, not an individual (*shakhṣ*), not substance nor attributes; he has no colour, taste, smell, feel, no heat, cold, moisture nor dryness, no length, breadth nor depth, no joining together nor separation, no movement, rest nor division; he has no sections nor parts, no limbs nor members; he is not subject to directions, left, right, in front of, behind, above, below; no place comprehends him, no time passes over him; inadmissible for him are contiguity, separateness and inherence in places; he is not characterized by any attribute of creatures indicating their originatedness, nor by finitude, nor extension, nor directional motion; he is not bounded; not begetting nor begotten; magnitudes do not comprehend him nor veils cover him; the senses do not attain him; he is not comparable with men and does not resemble creatures in any respect; infirmities and sufferings do not affect him; he is unlike whatever occurs to the mind or pictured in the imagination; he is ceaselessly first, precedent, going before originated things, existent before created things; he is ceaselessly knowing, powerful, living, and will not cease to be so; eyes do not see him; he is not heard by hearing; [he is] a thing, not as the things, knowing, powerful, living, not as [men are] knowing, powerful, living; he is eternal alone, and there is not eternal except him, no deity apart from him, he has no partner in his rule, no vizier [sharing] in his authority, no assistant in producing what he produced and creating what he created; he did not create creatures on a preceding model; to create a thing was no easier and no more difficult for him than to create another thing; he may not experience benefit or harm, joy or gladness, hurt or pain; he has no limit so as to be finite; he may not cease to exist nor become weak or lacking; he is too holy to be touched by women or to have a consort and children.[4]

The message of this passage was to show the transcendence of God, which has constantly been the major strand in Islamic thought. Like many Islamic scholars, Ibn 'Alwān's thought of the unity of God was commensurate with the ideas of the Mu'tazilites and particularly with the Ash'arites. As can be seen above, some of these ideas have their basis in the Qur'ān (e.g., "there is nothing like him"; "eyes do not see him").[5] Following his discussion of the unity of God, Ibn 'Alwan discusses the portrayal of the Prophet Muḥammad as the best Prophet and messenger of Allāh. God revealed His speech through the Prophet's mouth and supported him with noble ethics. According to Ibn 'Alwan, the Prophet was patient in the time of poverty, generous not only in the time of prosperity but also in the time of hardship. Among all prophets, he is the most knowledgeable in God and the most obedient.

In his discussion of the period of the Rightly Guided Caliphs (*al-khulafā' ar-rāshidūn*), Ibn 'Alwān argues that Abū Bakr was the first caliph of Islam to have been a protector and a friend of the Prophet. He accompanied the Prophet to the cave, where they were hiding from the unbelievers, during their migration from Mecca to Madina. Abū Bakr was a righteous imam who obliged obedience from anyone below him in rank. He was neither oppressor nor usurper. The honored group of *banū* Ḥāshim, such as 'Alī b. Abī Ṭālib, al-'Abbās b. 'Abd al-Muṭallib, and others, prayed behind him and fought under his banner with absolute loyalty. 'Umar b. al-Khaṭṭāb was the second caliph whose authority was similar to that of Abū Bakr in terms of justice and good qualities, and who likewise required obedience from those ranking below him. 'Uthmān, the third caliph, was also a righteous imam who obliged obedience from others: his rule was similar to his predecessors, and he was unjustly assassinated. Finally, 'Alī b. Abī Ṭālib, the fourth caliph of Islam, was a righteous imam who also required obedience from those below him in rank, and was like his predecessors in justice and sound judgment. He fought on the right path until he died. Ibn 'Alwān's praise of the Rightly Guided Caliphs appears to have been a definitive proof of his allegiance to the Sunnī community.

Regarding the relationship between God and human action, Ibn 'Alwān maintains that every action that causes its agent a punishment in the worldly life and torture in the hereafter can be attributed to both God and His servant, the actor. Action is seen in two ways: it is attributed to God in terms of knowledge, predestination (*qaḍā' wa qadar*), desertion (*khidhlān*), and hatred, but it is also attributed to the servant in terms of duty, love, choice, persistence, and obstinacy. Similarly, every action that causes its agent praise in the worldly life and a reward in the hereafter can be attributed to God in terms of knowledge, predestination, support, and love whereas it can be attributed to His servant in terms of duty, love, choice, and altruism.[6]

In his discussion on the concept of success (*tawfīq*) and desertion (*khidhlān*), Ibn 'Alwān states that *tawfīq,* which is granted by God, is coupled with repentance and regret. Thus, those who repent receive more guidance as expressed by God: "But those who are rightly guided will be given greater guidance by Him, and they will have their intrinsic piety."[7] However, *khidhlān* is coupled with insistence on accumulating sin and challenging religious instruction, as expressed in the Qur'ān: "God never leads men astray after guiding them, until He makes quite clear to them what they should avoid."[8] In his discussion of good and evil, Ibn 'Alwān maintains that good is a state in which bodies recover from illness, food becomes cheap, grazing livestock give milk, and years become fertile. All these qualities come from God in terms of His bounty and favor. On the other hand, Ibn 'Alwān argues, evil is when bodies become sick, food becomes expensive, grazing livestock give no milk, years become infertile, and so on. All these, too, come from God to remind people of His supervision and design of justice. God says: "Yet if some good comes their way they say: it is from God; and if it is evil that befalls them, they say: it is indeed from you. Say to them: everything is from God. O, what has come upon the people that even this they fail to understand! What comes to you of good is verily from God; and what comes to you of ill is from your own self (your actions)."[9]

One aspect of Ibn 'Alwān's discussion of good (*ḥasana*) and bad (*sayyi'a*) deeds requires careful attention. He states, "Every act of obedience (*ṭā'a*) that comprises every rational good deed is included in God's knowledge, will, love, praise, and contentment but excluded from his hatred, censure, and anger." In addition, "Every act of disobedience (*ma'ṣiya*) that comprises every irrational bad deed is included in God's knowledge, hatred, censure, and anger but excluded from His will, love, praise, and contentment."[10] According to Ash'arite theologian and Yemeni Sufi of the Shādhilī order Shaykh Aḥmad b. Qāyid al-'Awāḍī (d. 2005), scribes who wrote various manuscripts of *at-Tawḥīd* misplaced the term "excluded from" by placing it before "God's will." This view, argues al-'Awāḍī, is ascribed to the Mu'tazilites, who did not see any distinction between God's command and will (*al-amr wa-l-irāda*). According to al-'Awāḍī, Ibn 'Alwān was in support of the opposing doctrine. In order to understand Ibn 'Alwān's actual view, and to correct the scribes' distortion, says al-'Awāḍī, one should read the last line in the previous quotation: "The *ma'ṣiya* is excluded from God's love, praise, and contentment but not from His will."[11]

As for the doctrine of free will and predestination (*al-jabr wa-l-ikhtiyār*), Ibn 'Alwān positions himself between these two extreme schools of thought in line with Ash'arite theology. It is known that the Jabriyya sect, as described in heresiographical traditions, denied the freedom of human will, whereas their opponents—among them Ibn 'Alwān—held the view that man has a certain power over his actions. The Jabriyya found many verses in the Qur'ān to support their view. For instance, God says: "For God leaves to stray whom He wills, and guides whom He wills" (35:8), and in another verse: "God sends whomsoever He wills astray, and leads whomsoever He wills to the straight path" (6:39). Nevertheless, Ibn 'Alwān argues, these verses should not be interpreted in a way that would make us think of God as though He is intervening, as people do, in the real affairs of the world. Rather, they should be interpreted in terms of divine consequences in the hereafter. In other words, God does not force people in this world onto the wrong path, but instead informs us about punishments of the disobedient in the hereafter. Ibn 'Alwān adds that the previous verses and their like in the Qur'ān should always be read in terms of the unambiguous—or as it is known in the principles of Islamic jurisprudence as "perspicuous" (*muḥkam*), which is represented by the following verses: "God never leads men astray after guiding them until He makes quite clear to them what they should avoid" (9:115) and "God does not withdraw a favor bestowed upon people unless they change themselves, for God hears all and knows everything" (8:53).

As for the problematic verse—"But you cannot will except as God wills"[12]—and others like it in the Qur'ān, Ibn 'Alwān argues that their meaning can be summed up in two points. First, the servant has a trivial will that originates in his carnal appetite (*shahwa*); the carnal appetite incites caprice, and caprice causes disobedience. Second, God has a noble will based in His mercy; mercy brings guidance, and guidance prompts obedience. Thus, whoever does not know the meaning of the Qur'ān and does not understand what God wants assumes that the evildoer (*al-fāsiq*) is included in God's will. This means that the evildoer commits sins and attributes them to the unwillingness of God to guide him. This is a well-known view adopted by the classical Murji'ite school, which accuses God of the evil of compulsion (*iljā'*). Whoever adopts this view, Ibn 'Alwān argues, misunderstands God's message. God further clarifies in the following verse: "And there is not a thing except We have its treasures, and We do not send it down except in determined measure."[13] Ibn 'Alwān proceeds to explain that God has two kinds of will. One refers to His love of people and empowering them; it is the will of obedience required from every human being who is able to perform good or bad acts. The other will refers to His power and determination of events; this is the will that creates objects. He concludes his discussion by saying that God commanded but never forced anyone to obey His command, and prohibited but never forced anyone to abandon the acts He prohibited.[14]

In the last part of his profession of faith, Ibn 'Alwān informs us that he adheres to the *madhhab* of Imam Muḥammad b. Idrīs ash-Shāfi'ī (d. 204/820). Finally, Ibn 'Alwān invites his followers to correct his doctrine if they find anything wrong with it (*yuqīmū mu'wajjahā wa yuṣliḥū khalalahā*).[15] This invitation was probably inserted by scribes, and one must doubt the integrity of this section at least for the change of pronouns from "I" into "he" and the emphasis on the preference of the jurist ash-Shāfiī. In my view, either this section was written by someone other than Ibn 'Alwān, and very likely an adherent of the Shāfi'ī school, or it may have been written by Ibn 'Alwān but using a different style of narration such that the reader assumes that it was written about Ibn 'Alwān. In support of this latter thesis, the whole section is certainly commensurate with the overall writings of Ibn 'Alwān. For purposes of historical context it is important to understand that Ibn 'Alwān's ideas were a counterargument to the well-known views of the Islamic sect, the Mu'tazilites, whose views will be discussed here.

The Mu'tazilites

The origins of the Mu'tazilites date back to the reign of Hārūn ar-Rashīd (170–194/786–809) when a group of Hellenistic Iraqis and others of various backgrounds converted to Islam, carrying with them their old doctrinal beliefs. The influx of Greek philosophy into the Arab world was also spurred by the Greco-Arabic translation movement, which had been developing gradually for almost two centuries. According to Dimitri Gutas, the translation movement "was no ephemeral phenomenon."[16] Moreover, "it was supported by the entire elite of 'Abbāsid society: caliphs and princes, civil servants and military leaders, merchants and bankers, and scholars and scientists."[17] Furthermore, "It was eventually conducted with rigorous scholarly methodology and strict philological exactitude—by the famous Ḥunayn ibn-Isḥāq [(d. 260/873)] and his associates—on the basis of a sustained program that spanned generations and which reflects, in the final analysis, a social attitude and the public culture of the early 'Abbāsid society."[18]

The Mu'tazilites were preceded by the early exponents of speculative theology, Ḍirār b. 'Amr and Hishām b. al-Ḥakam, who started to employ Greek ideas in Islamic theological discourse.[19] After these two men, the main founders of the Mu'tazilites—Mu'ammar b. 'Abbād (d. 215/830), Abū-l-Hudhayl al-'Allāf (d. 227/841), Ibrāhīm b. Sayār an-Naẓẓām (d. 222/836 or 231/845) in Basra and Bishr b. al-Mu'tamir (d. 210/825) in Baghdad—began to use Greek philosophical and rhetorical techniques in their arguments and were successful in establishing the real beginning of so-called speculative theology (*'ilm al-kalām*).

The Mu'tazilite founders raised difficult theological questions in public places, often dealing with the nature of God and His attributes. These public debates unsettled the masses, and in turn concerned the rulers. The goal of this new theology was to purify Islam of those imported ideas brought by converts to Islam. Their task was to defend Islam from all the doubts circulating at that time. Later on, the Mu'tazilites defined themselves as adhering to five principles: *at-Tawḥīd* (unity of God), *al-'adl* (justice), *al-wa'd wa-l-wa'īd* (the promise and the threat), *al-manzila bayn al-manzilatayn* (the intermediate position), and *al-amr bi-l-ma'rūf wa-n-nahy 'an al-munkar* (commanding the right and forbidding the wrong). The most important of all these principles, according to one of the later leading Mu'tazilites, the Qāḍī 'Abd al-Jabbār (d. 415/1025), are *at-Tawḥīd* and *al-'adl* while the other principles are ramifications of these two.[20] Although they initially did not find support with political powers, when al-Ma'mūn began his reign (198–218/813–833) he found himself drawn to the rationalistic tendencies of the Mu'tazilites and brought them back to favor.[21]

Where did the name Mu'tazilite originate? When al-Ḥasan al-Baṣrī (d. 110/728), who had been brought up in Medina, moved to Basra, many students flocked to listen to his sermons at a mosque. One explanation for the origins of the name "Mu'tazilites," which remains under debate, derives from his life story. Once, someone asked al-Ḥasan whether the grave sinner (*murtakib al-kabīra*) is a believer or an unbeliever. While al-Ḥasan was thinking, a student in his circle Wāṣil b. 'Aṭā (d. 131/748), said: "I do not say that the grave sinner is an absolute believer or an absolute unbeliever, but that he is in an intermediate position (*fī manzila bayn al-manzilatayn*)."[22] Then, Wāṣil stood and withdrew (*i'tazala*) to one of the pillars of the mosque to share his response with a group of al-Ḥasan's disciples. Then, al-Ḥasan said: "Wāṣil withdrew from us (*i'tazala 'annā Wāṣil*)." Therefore, Wāṣil and his friends are called "Mu'tazila" (withdrawers).[23]

This story has been rejected by W. Montgomery Watt, who argues that the term *i'tazala* had been attributed to a number of people.[24] However, Watt's reasons for casting doubts on this story cited in *al-Milal wan-niḥal* by ash-Shahrastānī (d. 548/1153) prove weak, especially if we consider that the story existed in numerous versions far earlier than ash-Shahrastānī. In addition, another student, 'Amr b. 'Ubayd (d. 761), and not Wāṣil b. 'Aṭā, is said to have withdrawn, and that from the circle of

Qatāda, al-Ḥasan's successor. To further complicate the matter, sometimes Wāṣil (d. 131/748) and his contemporary 'Amr b. 'Ubayd are spoken of as Kharijites.[25] Nevertheless, Watt clarifies his argument on the acceptability of the anecdote by pointing to the connection between the Mu'tazilites and the disciples of al-Ḥasan al-Baṣrī (d. 110/728), among whom 'Amr was prominent. Despite the divergence in their views, these disciples continued to be on good terms with each other for at least forty years. Moreover, the wide circulation of the story and its acceptance in scholarly circles are strong reasons for accepting it as true and genuine.

Whatever its origins, the term "Mu'tazilite" became restricted to those who accepted the five principles outlined above. In his discussion of God's reward and punishment, Ibn 'Alwān seems to have agreed with the Mu'tazilite view that the worshipper who spends all his life sincerely worshipping God deserves heaven. Similar to the Mu'tazilites, who maintained that it was necessary for God to reward whoever obeyed Him and punish whoever disobeyed Him, Ibn 'Alwān discusses the concept of self-obligation (*naẓariyyat aṣ-ṣalāh wa-l-aṣlaḥ*), but with a subtle difference. He argues that God compelled Himself to reward the obedient by way of justice and favor.[26] The view of *ahl as-sunna wa-l-jamā'a* is that there is nothing to compel God to do anything because He is the creator. In his support of the Mu'tazilite's idea of self-obligation, Ibn 'Alwān seems to have deviated from *ahl as-sunna wa-l-jamā'a.* The only difference in this regard is that the Mu'tazilites deem it incumbent upon God to reward the obedient and punish the disobedient whereas Ibn 'Alwān speaks about the same result with the assertion that this incumbency comes from God Himself because He obligated Himself. Finally, Ibn 'Alwān strongly rejects their doctrine of the createdness of the Qur'ān and of seeing God in the hereafter. He also advocated the phenomenon of sainthood and *karāmāt,* which the Mu'tazilites rejected.

Ibn 'Alwān and Speculative Theology

As discussed in the first chapter, the Rasūlid dynasty in Yemen (626–858/1228–1454) energetically promoted learning by establishing schools (*madāris*) and allowing intellectual contests. By the seventh/twelfth century, public discussions of theology were rare in communities such as Zabīd because scholars did not want to involve the common people in discussions of God's essence, attributes, and actions lest they unintentionally blaspheme or corrupt their faith. Thus, some scholars prohibited public discussions of speculative theology (*kalām*). For example, despite Abū Ḥāmid al-Ghazālī's (d. 505/1111) moderate position between basic and advanced theological books in his *al-Iqtiṣād fī -l-I'tiqād* (The Economy in Creed), he prohibited common people from indulging in discussions of speculative theology. In this regard, al-Ghazālī wrote a treatise entitled *Iljām al-'awāmm 'an 'ilm al-kalām* (Reining in the Populace's Knowledge of Speculative Theology). Beyond speculative theology, al-Ghazālī wrote *Maqāṣid al-Falāsifa* (The Intentions of Philosophers) in which he explained the creedal positions of the philosophers,[27] however in *Tahāfut al-falāsifa* (The Incoherence of the Philosophers), he directly refuted certain philosophical trends including peripatetic philosophy.[28] A generation later Ibn Rushd, or Averroes (d. 595/1198) wrote *Tahāfut at-tahāfut* (The Incoherence of the Incoherence) in which he criticized al-Ghazālī and sought to revive peripatetic philosophy.[29] Despite the circulation of Ibn Rushd's work among Islamic rationalists, a half century later Ibn 'Alwān sought to revive al-Ghazālī's campaign to refute philosophy and speculative theology. In keeping with the generally antiphilosophical atmosphere, Ibn 'Alwān wrote a poem condemning philosophy and logic, and by extension, the theoretical foundation of speculative theology. This reflected his deeper desire to attack Greek philosophy and logic, which he argued stood against revelation. The following is an extract from his long poem:

> The illumination of the sun has reached the whole spherical world
> And you call me to darkness . . .
> The Prophet reports the precise statements revealed to him by God
> And you inform me about the philosophers of lies . . .
> The right speech among people is the Prophet's words,
> Not the logic of logicians who are disdainful and going astray . . .
> Their sayings are temptations for their followers
> And tempting words are inspired by Satan . . .
> O you, who are following them blindly,
> You are slaughtered but without a knife . . .
> They have fed you a poison.[30]

In this poem, as elsewhere, Ibn 'Alwān rejects speculative theology (*kalām*) or, as he called it, "speculative dialectic" (*jidāl*), because it leads to controversy and futility. Disputes among Muslims, he contends, after they have received guidance from God's book and the Sunna of the Prophet, allow corrupted leaders to rule. He urges people to disregard the temptations of philosophers and logicians, and instead return to

God's scriptures and His teachings. It should be noted that the above poem was written immediately after a refutation of the Rawāfiḍ doctrine, which might suggest that Ibn 'Alwān was referring to his contemporary radical Zaydī theologians and perhaps the extremist Ismā'īlī philosophers.[31] It is highly probable that Ibn 'Alwān was directing his criticism toward these two schools since both of them employed the techniques and methods of philosophy and speculative theology.

In what follows, I turn from a general discussion of speculative theology (*kalām*) to examine Ibn 'Alwān's views on the specific branches of *kalām,* including seeing God and the createdness of the Qur'ān. These aspects of Ibn 'Alwān's thought allow us to examine a unique aspect of Ibn 'Alwān's theology, that is, his blending of Sunnī thought with sympathy for Shī'ī concepts.

Seeing God

Seeing God in the hereafter is a matter of controversy between two dominant theological schools in Islam, the Mu'tazilites and the people of Sunna and unity (*ahl as-sunna wa-l-jamā'a*). The latter camp consists of the majority of Muslims, particularly those who follow the four Sunnī schools of law[32] and believe that God will appear on the day of judgment as He sees fit. In contrast, the Mu'tazilites denied that God is seeable either in this world or the next. They believe the verse: "No eyes can penetrate Him, but He penetrates all eyes" (6:103), and hold that when God said to Moses, "You cannot behold Me," the same denial applies to ordinary people. Relying on the concept of *ta'wīl* (allegorical interpretation), the Mu'tazilites interpreted verses that describe seeing God allegorically. For instance, they argued that the verse, "Some faces that Day will beam [in brightness and beauty] looking towards their Lord" (75:23), means that the faces await reward from their Lord. However, this interpretation would eventually lead to the draining of the experience of God of all content (*ta'ṭīl*). Despite their intention to preserve God's transcendence (*tanzīh*), they contributed to stripping away God's attributes and reducing them to philosophical abstractions.[33] However, the people of *as-sunna wa-l-jamā'a* hold that God will be seen in the hereafter by the believers according to scriptures. Later, some scholars allowed for the possibility of this vision "because He exists, and every existent [being] can be seen."[34]

Ibn 'Alwān took the position of *ahl as-sunna wa-l-jamā'a* because their view was supported by scriptures; they did not twist the meaning of the verses in the Qur'ān and the traditions of the Prophet, subjecting them to the concept of *ta'wīl* (allegorical interpretation), as was the case with the Mu'tazilites. Ibn 'Alwān argues God will be seen on the day of judgment in the way He wishes. Whoever denies this has no knowledge, and whoever asks how it will occur is ignorant of the true meaning of the scriptures.[35] In a different context, Ibn 'Alwān maintains that on the day of judgment human nature will fade away. At that time, God immediately talks to the believers and they talk to Him with no tongue; they look at Him and He looks at them with no eyes.[36] In this regard, Ibn 'Alwān's argument resembles the views advanced by Abū Muḥammad 'Alī b. Aḥmad, best known as Ibn Ḥazm aẓ-Ẓāhirī (d. 456/1064) who argues in *al-Fiṣal fī-l-milal wa-l-ahwā' wa-n-niḥal* that God will be seen in the hereafter with a faculty other than the current faculty of the eye. Ibn Ḥazm explained his view saying, "We know God, the Exalted, in our hearts with a true knowledge that is undoubted. Consequently, God, in the hereafter, will put in the visions a faculty that allows seeing God, as [the example of] the faculty He put in the heart in this world and as [the example of] the faculty He, the Exalted, put in the ear of Moses, peace be upon him, [in this world] so that he saw Him, heard Him and spoke to Him."[37] In his refutation of the Mu'tazilites, Ibn Ḥazm argues that it is obligatory to interpret words (*kalām*) according to their literal meaning, and that metaphorical interpretation is not permissible except by either a designation (*naṣṣ*)—i.e., by the Prophet—consensus (*ijmā'*) of the religious scholars, or by necessity (*ḍarūra*).[38] Later on, Ibn Ḥazm was criticized for being a literalist (*ẓāhirī*) in his overall legacy: hence his nickname aẓ-Ẓāhirī.

Ibn 'Alwān believed that the Qur'ān is God's speech. I discuss briefly the doctrine of the createdness of the Qur'ān and Ibn 'Alwān's refutation of that doctrine.

The Createdness of the Qur'ān

During the reign of Hārūn ar-Rashīd, a new type of devotion emerged to satisfy the hunger of most Muslims for accessible piety far from the mystically minded elite and away from secretive Shī'i doctrines. This devotion was founded on the discussion of the people of *ahl al-hadīth* (a group of people for whom *ḥadīth* reports about the Prophet formed the chief source of religious authority) who glorified the Qur'ān even when they carried it in their hands. Later, it was developed into a doctrine that saw the Qur'ān, God's word, to be as eternal as God Himself. The Mu'tazilites were horrified at this new doctrine that, according to their rationalistic thinking, made the Qur'ān a second divine being. They were so apprehensive of anthropomorphic notions of God that they denied that the divine had any human attributes at all. Thus, they developed specific interpretations of all the verses that allude to divine attributes. For instance, the Mu'tazilites argue that in the Qur'ānic episode when God spoke to Moses, God created speech in a tree, and Moses heard the voice from the tree. This interpretation maintains that the Qur'ān is the created word of God. The *ahl al-ḥadīth* insisted that the Qur'ān is uncreated, because saying otherwise would entail that the Qur'ān is a mortal entity like any created thing. Because the Mu'tazilites were close to the authorities, they had the power to persecute the people of *ḥadīth* and an inquisition (*miḥna*) ensued. A victim of this inquisition, Aḥmad b. Ḥanbal (164–241/780–855) represented the majority of people, including the people of *ḥadīth*. This happened during the reign of al-Ma'mūn (d. 219/833) and during the three succeeding 'Abbāsid caliphs.[39] Later, the *ahl al-ḥadīth* and the Mu'tazilites were reconciled by Abū al-Ḥasan al-Ash'arī (d. 324/935). He believed the Qur'ān is the uncreated word of God, but that the ink and paper of the book were created.

In his refutation of this dangerous doctrine, Ibn 'Alwān believed that any person who claims the createdness of the Qur'ān is a disbeliever. According to him, this was an abominable innovation because the Qur'ān is an attribute of God by which He created the universe and continues to recreate it with every new moment. With God's power of the word, He provides sustenance, gives life, and takes it away. The Qur'ān is an attribute of His essence, which is necessary like the attributes of His knowledge and life. Ibn 'Alwān maintained that whoever considers the Qur'ān to be created is equal in judgment to the Rawāfiḍ who believed that the Qur'ān had been fabricated by Muḥammad. These two doctrines were identical and led to atheism, disbelief, and error.[40]

Sympathy with Some Moderate Shī'ī Concepts

As established in Chapter 1, Yemen's religious environment during Ibn 'Alwān's life was characterized by three major Islamic factions: the Zaydīs, the Ismā'īlīs, and the Sunnīs. The Zaydī sect was, and still is, situated in northern Yemen, while the Ismā'īlī sect coexisted with the Sunnīs in middle and southern Yemen.[41] Ibn 'Alwān seems to have adhered to the Sunnī sect but was sympathetic to some Shī'ī concepts; this sympathy with Shī'ī thought can be traced from four different angles. First, Ibn 'Alwān was an ardent proponent of Sufi teachings, which support the duality between the manifest (*zāhir*) and the inward (*bāṭin*). This duality had some basis in Shī'ī thought, particularly that of the

Ismāʿīlīs, who developed their own *bāṭin* tradition based on a fundamental distinction between the exoteric (*ẓāhir*) and the esoteric (*bāṭin*) dimensions of religion.[42] Second, Ibn ʿAlwān was familiar with the Ismāʿīlī legacy, with which he likely became acquainted through the "Epistles of the Brethren of Purity" (*Rasāʾil Ikhwān aṣ-Ṣafā*). Ibn ʿAlwān mentions Ikhwān aṣ-Ṣafā on different occasions in his poetry. For instance, he says:

The pure morals of the Chosen (the Prophet)
The covenant of *Ikhwān aṣ-Ṣafā*
The string of intimacy and loyalty
The key to the lock of [God's] favors.[43]

In another poem, he says:

O agent of the Prophet
O specter of *Ikhwān aṣ-Ṣafā*
Loyalty should not be rewarded by estrangement.[44]

It has been well-established in scholarship that Neoplatonism, with its distinctive doctrine of emanation and hierarchism, was the dominant Greek philosophical influence on Ikhwān aṣ-Ṣafā.[45] The ultimate goal of this philosophy was to harmonize religion with philosophy in order to help human beings purify their souls and achieve salvation. However, it is not clear whether Ibn ʿAlwān really meant Ikhwān aṣ-Ṣafā, the well-known philosophical group who were linked to the Ismāʿīlī legacy. He may have been referring to his fellow Sufis, who were like brothers in purity.[46]

Third, there is a clear tendency in the thought of Ibn ʿAlwān to glorify the Prophet's family (*ahl al-bayt*) and to occasionally rank them first in the entire Islamic community, even above the Rightly Guided Caliphs (*al-khulafāʾ ar-rāshidūn*).[47] For example, in one of his supplications, Ibn ʿAlwān asks God to enable him to enter paradise with the Prophet, ʿAlī, Fāṭima, al-Ḥasan and al-Ḥusayn, Abū Bakr, ʿUmar, ʿUthmān, and the rest of the ten companions who were promised paradise.[48] On another occasion, he says: "If you follow righteousness, your Lord will elevate you to the high station, becoming a neighbor of the Prophet, ʿAlī, Fāṭima, al-Ḥasan and al-Ḥusayn."[49] However, these instances should not be read as conveying his preference for the Prophet's family over the Rightly Guided Caliphs, because many Sunnīs love the Prophet's family.

Finally, Ibn 'Alwān supported the view that a descendant of the Prophet was concealed due to "jealousy and the hardening of hearts."[50] Although Ibn 'Alwān did not explain what he meant by this phrase, it is highly probable that he was referring to the political atmosphere in relation to the Shī'ī twelfth imam, al-Qā'im Muḥammad b. al-Ḥasan al-'Askarī, who disappeared in Samarra in 260/874. Two major Shi'ī doctrines—the *ghayba* (occultation) and the *raj'a* (return) of the Islamic messiah (al-Mahdī) at an appointed time—shaped the idea of al-Mahdī. After the death of al-Mukhtār ath-Thaqafī (d. 68/687), and later Muḥammad Ibn al-Ḥanafiyyah, a son of 'Alī b. Abī Ṭālib by a woman other than the Prophet's daughter, the adherents of the concepts of *ghayba* and *raj'a,* who came to be known as the *kaysāniyya,* rejected Ibn al-Ḥanafiyyah's death. They argued that his demise should not be considered, "as a reality, and instead maintained that he was in hiding and would eventually return and fill this world with justice and equity, as it is now filled with injustice and oppression."[51] This idea continued to be ascribed to almost all the Shī'ī imams. However, it is widely used with reference to the major occultation of the aforementioned twelfth Shī'ī imam. In a poem, Ibn 'Alwān describes the future coming of the al-Mahdī and encourages people to wait for him.[52]

Although Ibn 'Alwān seems to have had sympathy for some Shī'ī concepts, he severely attacked the "extremists," the Rawāfiḍ. He based his attack on the hatred of the Rawāfiḍ for Abū Bakr, 'Umar, and 'Uthmān. According to Ibn 'Alwān, the Rawāfiḍ compared Abū Bakr to the idol Yaghūth, 'Umar with the idol Ya'ūq, and 'Uthmān with the idol Nasra. These three idols were worshipped before the advent of Islam. Ibn 'Alwān comments: "You are unfair to your master (i.e., 'Alī b. Abī Ṭālib) by slandering his friends (i.e., Abū Bakr, 'Umar, and 'Uthmān)."[53] In a poem in *at-Tawḥīd,* Ibn 'Alwān criticized those among the subsequent generation, who rejected the caliphate of Abū Bakr by claiming that Abū Bakr was unjust and 'Alī was just. Ibn 'Alwān argues that both were innocent of what was attributed to them, saying: "How preposterous! Does he ['Alī] oppress [people] or owe allegiance to an oppressor, and is he a courageous, daring hero? Nay! This one ['Alī] was not oppressed and that one [Abū Bakr] was not an oppressor. They were both guiltless."[54]

On the other hand, Ibn 'Alwān paints a very vivid picture that can be interpreted as evidence of his allegiance to the Shī'ī face of Islam. However, this should be examined carefully in line with his overall legacy. His assessment of the period after the Prophet's death is unique and unprecedented. First, he appears to have been a unifier of the two major Islamic sects, the Shī'a and the Sunnīs. Second, he argues that the Prophet had two distinctive powers within his personality: the power of physical conduct and the power of spiritual conduct. After the Prophet's death, it was necessary to have two leaders to assume the physical as well as the spiritual leadership of the Islamic community. The first, in his view, had to carry out the religious ordnances and control outward (*zāhir*) knowledge and practice. The second had to be in charge of unseen knowledge and control inward (*bāṭin*) knowledge and practice. The first was Abū Bakr aṣ-Ṣiddīq who became an imam and a pole of the physical world. The second was 'Alī b. Abī Ṭālib who became an imam and a pole of the world of spirits.

Having said this, Ibn 'Alwān asserts that the pole of the physical world (Abū Bakr) was a wing to the pole of the world of unseen spirits ('Alī). This relationship is as indispensable as the relationship between a bird and its wing. Thus, the pole of the unseen world is a partner with the pole of the physical world in his knowledge and practice because the former is the pivot of the latter's base in the inward poleship (*quṭbiyya*), neither disagreeing in words nor actions. Also, the pole of the physical world is a partner with the pole of the unseen world in that the former submits to the latter and learns from him because he is the head of his base in the outward poleship, neither disagreeing in words nor actions. With this conformity, Ibn 'Alwān contends, the authority of religion rose, after the death of the Prophet, among the four imams (or simply, caliphs), i.e., Abū Bakr, 'Umar, 'Uthmān, and 'Alī. They needed each other because the rank of the pole is less than the rank of the Prophet; and the rank of the wing is less than the rank of the pole because he cannot receive the emanation of the unseen world and the emanation of the physical world simultaneously combining knowledge and authority. The Prophet could combine knowledge and authority because God gave him the ability to bear revelation and supported him with tranquility and perfection. God described the Prophet in the Qur'ān: "Indeed, you have great morals."[55]

Ibn 'Alwan argues that after the death of the Prophet, God prepared two men to bear what is vital for the Islamic community (*umma*) of the Prophet's revealed message. If one of these two men were to be compared with the entire *umma,* he would outweigh them in virtues and divine knowledge. Thus, 'Alī was the pole who received the unseen knowledge of the Prophet mercifully and kindly. Abū Bakr was the wing who received the outward knowledge of the Prophet commandingly and forbiddingly. Then, 'Alī flew with the wing of Abū Bakr, providing sincere advice to the caliph and the Muslim community until Abū Bakr's life of justice and piety came to an end. When 'Umar took over, 'Alī flew with his wing, providing intercession and consultation until 'Umar died. The wing of 'Uthmān was the weakest due to his wealth and love of his kinship but 'Alī flew with his wing until 'Uthmān was martyred.[56] Ibn 'Alwan describes that 'Alī turned to find a wing to fly with, but as he did not find anyone he risked losing his luminous rank and found himself embroiled in a war imposed on him. He fought even though he would rather have witnessed God directly. Ibn 'Alwan writes that 'Alī was displeased with his demotion to the station of human nature (*nasūt*) from his higher station, by which he had been capable of experiencing the world of divine majesty and kingship (*al-jabarūt wa-l-malakūt*). If he had found a fourth wing (i.e., a fourth caliph), he would have remained in his shimmering status, possessing divine knowledge and the spiritual authority to intercede. However, Ibn 'Alwan says, it was incumbent upon 'Alī to fight because he was the only one qualified to perpetuate the era of the orthodox (*rāshidūn*) community. Thus, he became the pole and the imam at the same time, and acted like a lion in a fierce fight until his death.[57]

According to 'Abd al-Karīm Sa'īd, Ibn 'Alwān's views vacillate between Shī'īsm and Sunnīsm.[58] However, this paradox can be mitigated by considering several hypotheses. First, Ibn 'Alwān was in conformity with public opinion, which opposed the Rawāfiḍ (Zaydī theologians). Second, he may have opposed the Shī'a at the beginning of his life but probably changed his mind later on. Third, it is possible that opinions against the Shī'a were falsely ascribed to him.[59] While these hypotheses may be true, I contend that the real interest lies in the fact that Ibn 'Alwān was by no means a strict adherent of Sunnīsm. Rather, he adopted both views as long as they did not conflict with the Qur'ān or the Prophet's reports. Another example of this duality can be seen in a different context, specifically with regard to Sufi concepts such as self-annihilation in God (*fanā'*), survival in God (*baqā'*), exoteric knowledge (*ẓāhir*), and esoteric knowledge (*bāṭin*). He says in a poem: "I have two sides: hidden (*maknūn*) and visible (*bādī*); I have also two kinds of knowledge (*'ilmān*), one is partial while the other is comprehensive."[60] Again this duality does not necessarily prove that he positioned himself between Shī'ism and Sunnīsm, as suggested by some investigators.[61] All the evidence, as I have shown in this chapter and elsewhere, indicates that Ibn 'Alwān belonged to the Sunnī community.

Conclusion

As detailed in this summary of Ibn 'Alwān's doctrine, he placed himself within the debates of his historical moment by taking a series of intellectual and spiritual positions that were entirely original. He wrote in a style that was lucid and unequivocal, stressing the unity of God, the significance of the Prophet, and the status of the Rightly Guided Caliphs. This establishes Ibn 'Alwān's clear allegiance to the Sunnī face of Islam, and I have noted that many of his views, such as human action vis-à-vis God's action, and free will and predestination, were partially inspired by Ash'arite theology. While Ibn 'Alwān's Sunnī loyalties cannot be doubted, he nevertheless showed sympathy for Shī'ī concepts in Sufism, such as respect for the Prophet's family and the concealment of the Prophet's descendant (al-Mahdī). He theorized that following the Prophet's death there was a need for leadership in both the physical (*zahir*) and spiritual (*batin*) worlds, thus taking an innovative approach to the two faces of Islam. Furthermore, Ibn 'Alwān followed in al-Ghazalī's footsteps to oppose speculative theology (*kalām*), despite Ibn Rushd's re-establishment of peripatetic philosophy, and furthermore opposed the Mu'tazilites, notably criticizing the doctrine of the createdness of the Qur'ān. By placing Ibn 'Alwān in relation to his Islamic environment we are able to see the formation of his theology as one following in the footsteps of—and indeed defending—Islamic teaching, but fusing multiple aspects of Yemen's Islamic environment to create his Sufi theology.

Having provided here an in-depth analysis of Ibn 'Alwān's relationship to the many strands of Islamic thought making up Yemen's religious world in his lifetime, it is necessary now to turn to Ibn 'Alwān's specifically Sufi environment. Who were his contemporary Sufis, and what were the influences he shared with them? In the following chapter I discuss Ibn 'Alwān's theological and mystical inspiration in relation to the Sufis of his time, beginning with his closest rival, Abū l-Ghayth Ibn Jamīl (d. 651/1253).

5

IBN 'ALWĀN AND THE SUFI TRADITION

In this chapter I evaluate and analyze, one by one, the major Sufi influences on Ibn 'Alwān (d. 665/1266), both within and beyond Yemen's borders. In so doing, I not only clarify Ibn 'Alwān's intellectual and spiritual heritage but also trace the national and transnational Sufi networks of his era. What emerges is a picture of Ibn 'Alwān in his intellectual and spiritual environment, certainly studying and assimilating the ideas and works of other Sufis into his theology, but ultimately infusing his work with his own beliefs and local Yemeni practices to generate a unique body of Sufi thought that was bound neither to the local nor the transnational.

One of Ibn 'Alwān's most important peers in Yemen was Abū al-Ghayth Ibn Jamīl (d. 651/1253), who, like Ibn 'Alwān, founded a Sufi order and produced a volume of work on Sufism. The intellectual and spiritual relationship between these important Sufi thinkers has been a subject of debate since medieval times: was Ibn 'Alwān Abū al-Ghayth's disciple, or were they merely rivals? Here I show that Abū al-Ghayth and Ibn 'Alwān were peers who engaged in literary competition, and that Ibn 'Alwān far outstripped Abū al-Ghayth in popularity. Abū al-Ghayth's life and work are nevertheless crucial to gaining a fuller understanding of Yemeni Sufism. Beyond Yemen, I examine and ultimately reject the purported influence of the Egyptian Sufi al-Badawī (d. 675/1276) and clarify that the intense spiritual relationship between Ibn 'Alwān and the famous Abū Ḥāmid al-Ghazālī (d. 505/1111), whose books spread to Yemen, was nevertheless not based on direct textual sharing. Next I analyze Ibn 'Alwān's sensitive reading of al-Ḥallāj (d. 309/922), who he argues was trapped in the state of annihilation (*fanā'*), which Ibn 'Alwān had surpassed. Finally, I turn to perhaps the most famous Sufi in

Western scholarship, Ibn 'Arabī (d. 638/1240), a contemporary of Ibn 'Alwān's, and disprove with textual evidence the widely held assumption that Ibn 'Alwān was influenced by Ibn 'Arabī.

Abū al-Ghayth Ibn Jamīl

Medieval sources do not discuss in detail the relationship between Ibn 'Alwān and his contemporary, the Yemeni Sufi Abū al-Ghayth Ibn Jamīl. Instead, they only reproduce a poetic exchange, which goes back to the earliest source written by al-Janadī (d. 732/1331), between the two Sufis. Although there is very little information on the nature of their relationship, the story of Abū al-Ghayth's conversion to Sufism is well-known and resembles that of an earlier Sufi, al-Fuḍayl Ibn 'Iyaḍ (d. 188/803). Abū al-Ghayth was a highway robber, and once, while lying in wait for passersby he heard a voice (*hātif*) saying: "O eye-watcher, you are [yourself] being watched (*Yā ṣāḥib al-'ayn 'alayka al-'ayn*)."[1] This was the turning point in his life, which caused him to repent and embark on a godly life. Like al-Fuḍayl, Abū al-Ghayth sought out a Sufi shaykh to receive a Sufi cloak (*khirqa*). He found his contemporary, Abū al-Ḥasan 'Ali b. 'Abd al-Malik b. Aflaḥ, who instructed Abū al-Ghayth to serve at his Sufi lodge (*zāwiya*). This service is called *khidma*, and it should be accomplished according to the rules determined by the master. It may include such responsibilities as plowing, harvesting, wood collecting, and domestic chores.[2]

After serving in Ibn Aflaḥ's *zāwiya*, Abū al-Ghayth desired higher knowledge. This prompted him to join Shaykh 'Ali b. 'Umar b. Muḥammad al-Ahdal (d. after 600/1203), who trained him and provided him with the techniques of Sufi leadership. Abū al-Ghayth used to say, "I left Ibn Aflaḥ while I was a rough pearl, and al-Ahdal cultivated me."[3] After this religious and Sufi learning, Abū al-Ghayth was ready to carry out the Sufi rituals without assistance from his master. Owing to his readiness, al-Ahdal dispatched him, along with forty Sufi novices, to establish a new lodge (*zāwiya*) in Bayt 'Aṭā'.[4] A modern writer and historian of Jāzān, Muḥammad b. Aḥmad al-'Aqīlī, sees the dispatch of Abū al-Ghayth to the mountains as banishment by his two teachers, Ibn Aflaḥ and al-Ahdal. Al-'Aqīlī argues that Ibn Aflaḥ and al-Ahdal felt that Abū al-Ghayth was too ambitious and therefore a threat to their spiritual authority.[5] Al-'Aqīlī's analysis might be accurate but cannot be verified by textual evidence.

Contemporary writers, following the medieval historian, al-Khazrajī (d. 812/1409), support the view that Ibn 'Alwān received the Sufi cloak (*khirqa*) from Abū al-Ghayth. Yet al-Janadī (d. 732/1331), who was the earliest authority, tells us that Ibn 'Alwān came back from the town of Bayt 'Aṭā', the residence of Abū al-Ghayth, without receiving the *khirqa* from him (*'āda min bayt 'Aṭā' bighayr dustūr min Abū l-Ghayth*).[6] Al-Janadī quotes Abū al-Ghayth saying: "If the *jabalī* (Ibn 'Alwān) had stayed, he would have received the *qumāsh* (*khirqa*)."[7] Given the textual evidence, it is safe to say that Ibn 'Alwān was merely a rival of Abū al-Ghayth.

Medieval sources inform us that Ibn 'Alwān wrote two lines of poetry clarifying the spiritual state he had attained and sent them to Abū al-Ghayth. In reply Abū al-Ghayth composed two lines, indicating that he had reached a higher spiritual state than his peer. These poetic exchanges demonstrate that modern as well as medieval sources were interested in highlighting the bickering (*mumāḥakāt*) or literary contests between Ibn 'Alwān and Abū al-Ghayth. Here are the lines of Ibn 'Alwān:

> I passed through the stages of utterances, then through the letters,
> then to beyond until I [reached][8] the stage of creativity. /
> I do not seek help by calling "Laylā" when I journey through the
> night; certainly not even "Lubnā" raises my sail.[9]

The message in Ibn 'Alwān's lines is twofold. First, he mastered creative language, which means that he had a solid background in the sciences of phonology, morphology, and syntax. Second, not only did he master these sciences but also reached a level that placed him above all other writers and theorists. Moreover, he seems to have implied that in his spiritual seeking of God, he surpassed the beginners on the Sufi path who had been dwelling under the influence of such literary symbols as "Laylā" in describing their mystical experiences.[10] The appearance of Laylā's name in the third line does not signify the poet's recurring theme of love and separation as it was originally found in the legendary story of Laylā and her lover Majnūn.[11] Rather, Laylā's name in the third line and Lubnā in the last line suggest that Ibn 'Alwān reached the highest level of the Sufi path, which no longer requires the use of symbols to attain mystical and spiritual goals. Abū al-Ghayth retorted:

> The Eternal Name manifested itself to me,
> So that all names derive from my names.
> The King and Guardian has honored me and was content,
> So that the earth and heaven are mine.[12]

Here Abū al-Ghayth conveys that, while Ibn 'Alwān had attained linguistic mastery, Abū al-Ghayth had surpassed that level to achieve full control of the very source of language. In other words, if Ibn 'Alwān had reached the final stage of the Sufi spiritual path without difficulty, Abū al-Ghayth had outstripped him because he had attained the stage of complete unification with God. Therefore, the attributes of Abū al-Ghayth had become identical with those of God, such that he claimed all existing names were derived from his own names. Likewise Abū al-Ghayth claimed to own both heaven and earth. The difference between Ibn 'Alwān and Abū al-Ghayth, in this respect, is that the former described his progress along the stages of the Sufi path, whereas the latter portrayed only his unification with God, beyond which there is no further stage. A Sufi expression for this state is described by Ibn Arabi (d. 638/1240) as the "station of no station" (*maqām la maqām*).[13]

Both Sufi masters were on equal standing and the claims that Ibn 'Alwān was a disciple of Abū al-Ghayth cannot be substantiated, as the following anecdote from al-Janadī (d. 732/1331) confirms. Ibn 'Alwān met Abū al-Ghayth after their poetic exchange, and Abū al-Ghayth intuitively realized that Ibn 'Alwān was proud of his ability to speak on the knowledge of God. Ibn Jamil poured scorn on him by saying: "You are the nut of time (*jawzī al-waqt*) and I am its cycle (*dawratahu*) but I am afraid that my cycle breaks your nut (*dawrati taksiru jawzatak*)."[14] Afterward, Abū al-Ghayth asked one of the attendees to write down something, then turned toward Ibn 'Alwān and asked him to complete it. Ibn 'Alwān replied, "It is inappropriate for the slave to finish the speech of his master." He then took the paper and kissed it.[15] This should not be understood as a concession on the part of Ibn 'Alwān as being a disciple of Abū al-Ghayth, but rather that Ibn 'Alwān appears to have been well-mannered, opinionated, and respectful. His refusal to complete Abū al-Ghayth's note can be interpreted as a sign of independence, and his kissing the paper should also be viewed as a sign of respect.

The relationship between Ibn 'Alwān and Abū al-Ghayth can best be seen in the context of individual competition and Sufi rivalry. They both contributed to the development of Yemeni Sufism and have been highly respected in their homeland across the centuries. They founded two Sufi orders, known as al-Ghaythiyya and al-'Alwāniyya; unfortunately neither has survived. Although Ibn 'Alwān and Abū al-Ghayth were on an equal footing, the historical evidence shows that Ibn 'Alwān was more celebrated than his peer, and his impact on the Yemeni community is still palpable. Finally, Ibn 'Alwān left a substantial body of writings on various aspects of Islamic thought including mysticism, theology, law, and Qur'ān exegesis while Abū al-Ghayth left behind only one work.

Abū al-Ghayth's Life and Work

Medieval hagiographers report that Abū al-Ghayth described the Sufi as one whose heart is free of concerns and filled with moral lessons. The Sufi, too, is one who secludes himself and does not differentiate between gold and clay.[16] It is reported that Abū al-Ghayth used to say, "Relying on what you own is evidence that you have little trust in God. . . . Relying on people at the time of calamity is evidence that you do not know God. . . . Your delight with a material thing you get in this world is evidence that you have strayed from [the path of] God."[17] Al-Janadī (d. 732/1331) argues that these Sufi expressions may belong to Abū Yazīd al-Bisṭāmī (d. 234/848 or 261/875) or one of his contemporaries, but Ibn al-Ahdal (d. 855/1387), after quoting al-Janadī, maintains that these expressions are transmitted from the parables of the prophet David.[18] It is possible that the intention of these two medieval writers, al-Janadī and Ibn al-Ahdal, was to purify Yemeni literature of any Sufi ecstatic utterances (*shaṭaḥāt*). This objective was probably coupled with the assumption that Yemeni society at that time was primitive, and thus such ideas should only be attributed to non-Yemeni Sufi masters. Such an assumption is evidently baseless.

In a visionary dream, ash-Sharjī (d. 893/1487) reports that al-Yāfi'ī (d. 768/1366) heard the Prophet praising Abū al-Ghayth Ibn Jamīl. When he asked him why, the Prophet smiled and said, "Abū al-Ghayth becomes the protector of the one who has no family."[19] This mystical vision shows the saintly miracle (*karāma*) and spiritual authority that Abū al-Ghayth enjoyed in the Sufi community of Zabīd and along the coastal area of Tihāma. As a founder of a Sufi community, Abū al-Ghayth was continuously surrounded by numerous admirers who attributed to him a number of saintly miracles (*karāmāt*). Among his ardent friends and close disciples was Abū Muḥammad 'Isā b. Ḥajjāj al-'Āmirī (d. 664/1265), who is viewed as an accomplished Sufi master in his own right, and who, like his master, was admired for his *karāmāt*.

Despite that, Abū al-Ghayth was described as illiterate and uncultivated. In *Tuḥfat az-zaman*, Ibn al-Ahdal states, "Abū al-Ghayth did not know the terminology of the theologians, and did not read or write any books."[20] Not only did Ibn al-Ahdal denigrate Abū al-Ghayth, but he also called into question the authenticity of the latter's book, collected by his disciples. Ibn al-Ahdal argues that the manuscript was fabricated because it contains statements similar to the writing of Ibn ʿArabī (d. 638/1240). However, there is no basis for this judgment because Ibn ʿArabī's works were brought to Yemen by ʿUmar b. ʿAbd al-Raḥmān b. Ḥasan al-Qudsī (or al-Muqaddasī) (d. 688/1289) long after Abū al-Ghayth's death.[21] Ibn al-Ahdal even goes further and warns readers not to be misled by al-Yāfiʿī's *Mir'āt al-janān* and *Nashr al-maḥāsin al-ghāliya* for they both contain numerous sayings of Abū al-Ghayth.[22] On the other hand, Ibn al-Ahdal narrates on the authority of Muḥammad b. ʿUthmān b. Hāshim, an exponent of *ḥadīth* who lived sometime before Ibn al-Ahdal, the following statements of Abū al-Ghayth: "Whoever knows God, denies the existence of [His] creatures." He argues that Abū al-Ghayth used this expression without understanding its real meaning because, as Ibn al-Ahdal asserts, the denial of the existence of the creatures is nothing but the doctrine of the School of Absolute Unity (*madhhab ahl al-ittiḥād*). Because he is prejudiced against the works of Ibn ʿArabī, Ibn al-Ahdal casts doubt on the work of Abū al-Ghayth and denounces them both. He states,

> [Abū al-Ghayth's] sayings are reminiscent of those of Ibn ʿArabī and his followers in that they also deal with the union [of God with his creatures], the refusal to acknowledge that humans are responsible for their acts of disobedience, obedience and submission, the denial of the act of creation and of the Muslim religion, and [as a consequence] the denial that unbelief [really] exists.[23]

Moreover, Ibn al-Ahdal cites a commentary by the *ḥadīth* expert, Muḥammad b. ʿUthmān b. Hāshim on the notion of the "denial of existence of creatures." Ibn Hāshim asserted that this idea might mean either "a preference for spiritual retreat" or "the denial of the existence of the independent agency (*asbāb*) of creatures." Another example of Abū al-Ghayth's controversial thinking is his statement, "the people of Heaven and Hell came under my command." Ibn Hāshim relates these "extreme" statements to the use of metaphor (*majāz*) similar to the one found in a famous *ḥadīth* narrated by al-Bukhārī (d. 257/870): "When I love him [i.e., the servant,] I am his hearing with which he hears, his sight with which he sees, his hand with which he strikes."[24]

But Ibn al-Ahdal was not convinced by Ibn Hāshim's interpretations and insisted that such ecstatic outbursts could not have possibly belonged to Abū al-Ghayth. Immediately after asserting that these "ecstatic outbursts" had nothing to do with Abū al-Ghayth, Ibn al-Ahdal contradicted himself by saying that Abū al-Ghayth considered these "outbursts" to be sound and, therefore, uttered them without knowing that their meanings were untrue. Ibn al-Ahdal seems to have forgotten his claim earlier that Abū al-Ghayth was illiterate. Now, confusingly, Ibn al-Ahdal declares that he is not certain whether the statements in question belong to Abū al-Ghayth. Even if they were his, they should be interpreted as unsound and stemming from the doctrine of "Unity of Being" (*waḥdat al-wujūd*).[25]

Similarly, in his book *Kashf al-ghiṭā'*, which is a refutation of the philosophy of Ibn 'Arabī, Ibn al-Ahdal argues that the book of Abū al-Ghayth resembles Ibn 'Arabī's ideas. It is obvious that Ibn al-Ahdal's rejection of Abū al-Ghayth's contribution to Yemeni Sufism is part of his campaign against Ibn 'Arabī's mystical doctrine. Al-Ḥibshī, the contemporary writer and critic, states that Ibn al-Ahdal's argument lacks textual evidence. He suggests that Abū al-Ghayth may have produced his book in the form of dictation to one of his disciples as he did in his response to the letter of Imam Aḥmad Ibn al-Ḥusayn al-Qāsimī (d. 665/1266).[26] Finally, al-'Aqīlī, refuting Ibn al-Ahdal's argument, says that his claim that Abū al-Ghayth was illiterate has no basis.[27]

On the other hand, it is known that for centuries the relationship between the Sufis and Zaydī imams in Yemen was based on mutual mistrust and was frequently hostile.[28] When Imam 'Abd Allāh b. Ḥamza (d. 614/1217) was on the rise, he deemed it necessary to expand his territory toward the mountains of Tihāma in preparation of controlling all the coastal areas populated by Sunnīs. Hearing this news, the popular Sufi master Abū al-Ghayth came back to Bait 'Aṭā', a village in the Surdud valley of Tihāma, where he was not welcomed by some scholars who envied his popularity. In the meantime, the Zaydī Imam Aḥmad b. al-Ḥusayn (646–656/1249–1258) began his political campaign to draw Sufi leaders to his side in hopes that they would persuade their followers in Tihāma to fulfill his expansive ambitions. He sent one of his messengers with a letter to Abū al-Ghayth requesting his assistance to rally the disciples around his cause as a religious duty. The letter started with the following verse from the Qur'ān: "Say: 'People of the Book! Come now to a word common between us and you, that we serve none but God, and that we associate not aught with Him, and do not some of us take others as Lords, apart from God.' And if they turn their backs, say: 'Bear witness that we are Muslims.'"[29] Then, he ended his letter by clarifying his intention, which was unified power to command the right and forbid the wrong.[30] Although the meaning of the Qur'ānic verse goes directly to the people of the book, or the people of earlier revelations before Islam, the imam intended to wheedle Abū al-Ghayth into giving his support. Abū al-Ghayth understood the imam's goal and responded to his letter in the same polite manner by using a verse from the Qur'ān with a counter-meaning. The verse runs: "If God helps you, none can overcome you; but if He forsakes you, who then can help you after Him? Therefore in God let the believers put all their trust."[31] Then, Abū al-Ghayth continued his letter by praising God, the Prophet and his family, and the companions. After that, Abū al-Ghayth acknowledged the receipt of the letter, clarifying that the path of summoning to God had been trodden previously and was still desired by the majority of people. But, as Abū al-Ghayth had heard God say "to Him the call of Truth," he had no room left to respond to the summons of any creature.[32] He added that no one should unleash the sword upon himself or waste day after day. Finally, Abū al-Ghayth concluded his letter with the justification that he was too busy to accomplish the imam's aim and that the imam should find excuses. The implication of Abū al-Ghayth's letter is that despite its nature of spiritual exhortation, it carries further significance. His apology was witty, and he skillfully absolves himself from any affiliation with the imam.

As a result, the abiding hostility between the Sufis and the Zaydī imams was further aggravated.[33] The antagonism was dissimilar to the amiable relationships between Yemeni Sufis and the governors of the Rasūlid dynasty (626–858/1228–1454) who frequently summoned Sufi leaders to their palaces to seek their advice. Abū al-Ghayth benefited from his relationship with the Rasūlid court since he was instrumental in persuading the leaders of the Qarābīlī tribe of Tihāma, alongside other tribes, to support Sultạn al-Muẓaffar (d. 694/1295) in toppling a rebellion after the assassination of his father 'Umar b. 'Alī b. Rasūl (d. 637/1241), the founder of the Rasūlid dynasty. Abū al-Ghayth's participation in the political atmosphere of the Rasūlid dynasty can be discerned as a manifestation of a new strategy to mediate conflicts between rulers and tribal leaders while protecting the masses from the aggression of both. Suffice it to say that Sufi masters participated in local politics, which one does not find with foreign elements that have allegedly impacted the Sufi movement in Yemen. The next section treats such allegations, concluding that they were baseless and lack textual evidence. I discuss the relationship between Ibn 'Alwān and Aḥmad al-Badawī (d. 675/1276) and examine the allegations that Ibn 'Alwān was influenced by al-Badawī.

As-Sayyid al-Badawī

There is no reference in Ibn 'Alwān's works to as-Sayyid Aḥmad al-Badawī (d. 675/1276), the founder of the Badawiyya order in Egypt in the seventh/thirteenth century, and Yemeni historians argue that Ibn 'Alwān (d. 665/1266) never left Yemen.[34] However, there are three references to the alleged ties between Ibn 'Alwān and al-Badawī. Two of these are recent and depend on *al-Jawāhir as-saniyya fī n-nisba wa l-karāmāt al-Aḥmadiyya*, which was written by Abd aṣ-Ṣamad al-Aḥmadī in 1028/1619 and is dedicated to al-Badawī's genealogy and saintly miracles (*karāmāt*). In this text, al-Aḥmadī describes Ibn 'Alwān as one of the followers of al-Badawī. He emphasizes their friendship during the earlier period of al-Badawī's attraction to God (*awā'il jadhbih*) and before his departure for Iraq. Al-Aḥmadī then lists Ibn 'Alwān's *karāmāt* according to their popularity. One such *karāmā* is that sea travelers used to call on him if their boats were sinking, and their prayers are answered due to his spiritual influence.[35] No information is given about the extent of friendship between al-Badawī and Ibn 'Alwān or any indication of al-Badawī's Sufi influence on Ibn 'Alwān's Sufism. Similarly, in a manuscript by Ja'far b. al-Ḥasan al-Barzanjī (d. 1177/1763), recently found in Berlin, the nature of al-Badawī's influence on Ibn 'Alwān is not clear. According to al-Barzanjī, Ibn 'Alwān learned the Sufi path (*ṭarīqa*) and accepted the Sufi cloak (*khirqa*) at the hands of Abū al-Ghayth Ibn Jamīl (d. 651/1253) and then continued under the guidance of al-Badawī, Ibn 'Arabī (d. 638/1242), and others.[36] Al-Barzanjī did not provide any evidence to support his claims.

In his *Qaḍāyā wa ishkāliyyāt at-taṣawwuf 'ind Aḥmad b. 'Alwān*, 'Abd al-Karīm Sa'īd states that some scholars who are interested in the study of al-Badawī refer to *al-Jawāhir as-sanīya* by al-Aḥmadī as the chief source for the relationship between the two Sufis. In addition, Sa'īd cites the work of contemporary Yemeni scholar, Ḥamūd al-Qiyarī.[37] Both Sa'īd and al-Qiyarī attribute to al-Aḥmadī the claim that Ibn 'Alwān made a trip to Tanta,[38] yet al-Aḥmadī did not mention this trip in his book. He mentioned a similar trip to Tanta but under the entry of 'Awsaj al-Maṣrī, who is discussed immediately after Ibn 'Alwān's entry. Therefore, it appears that 'Abd al-Karīm Sa'īd and Ḥamūd al-Qiyarī made a mistake by attributing the Tanta trip to Ibn 'Alwān. The real problem, however, lies in the fact that Ibn 'Alwān stayed his entire life in Yemen. If this were the case, which is well-documented in medieval sources, al-Badawī (d. 675/1276) could have had no influence on Ibn 'Alwān (d. 665/1266) for the obvious reason that they never met. However, it may be possible that Ibn 'Alwān visited Mecca to perform a pilgrimage and, while there, met Ibn 'Arabī and al-Badawī. Yet this is a mere supposition. One may argue that Ibn 'Alwān and al-Badawī's alleged friendship could have been strengthened by their shared descent from the Prophet's family. The only difference is that al-Badawī's genealogy traces to the Ḥusaynī branch while Ibn 'Alwān belongs to the Ḥasanī branch (both Ḥasan and Ḥusayn were sons of 'Alī b. Abī Ṭālib, from the Prophet's daughter Fāṭima). In the end, there is no textual evidence that might serve as a sturdy proof of their presumed relationship. Hence, the idea that Ibn 'Alwān was influenced by al-Badawī should be rejected.

Abū Ḥāmid al-Ghazālī

The spread of Abū Ḥāmid al-Ghazālī's (d. 505/1111) books in Yemen might lead one to believe that his thought indirectly influenced the thought and Sufism of Ibn 'Alwān. Al-Ghazālī was the only scholar mentioned in the writings of Ibn 'Alwān as "Our Shaykh." In his discussion of the ranks of the soul (*'ilm an-nafs*) in *al-Mahrajān*, Ibn 'Alwān quotes al-Ghazālī's views on the categories of knowledge by saying: "Our Shaykh, Imam Muḥammad b. Muḥammad al-Ghazālī aṭ-Ṭūsī, may God be pleased with him, said: 'knowledge is threefold: that which is obligatory under the law (*Sharī'a*), that which is necessary according to Sufism (*ḥaqīqa*), and the knowledge of the *Sirr* (the innermost part of the heart).'"[39] Al-Ghazālī's severe attack on philosophy, particularly in his *Tahāfut al-falāsifa*, seems to have inspired Ibn 'Alwān, who wrote a poem rejecting philosophy and logic, discussed in Chapter 3. Simultaneously, Ibn 'Alwān ridicules speculative theology (*'ilm al-kalām*) and was a key figure in reviving al-Ghazālī's legacy, especially *Iljām al-'awāmm 'an 'ilm al-kalām* and *Tahāfut al-falāsifa*. However, Ibn 'Alwān's campaign against Greek logic, philosophy, and speculative theology was the direct result of his profound knowledge of Islamic teachings. He had studied the Qur'ān and the Prophet's Sunna deeply and based all his teachings upon them. He declared: "The Prophet reports precise statements on the authority of God and you inform me about the philosopher's lies. . . . The right speech among the people is the Prophet's words, not the logic of the logicians who are disdainful and going astray. . . . Their sayings are temptations for their followers, and tempting words are usually inspired by Satan."[40] Ibn 'Alwān urges people to avoid speculative dialectic (*jidāl*) and to focus instead on God's book and the Prophet's exemplary piety.

Moreover, it is not clear that al-Ghazālī's "Revival of Religious Sciences" (*Iḥyā' 'ulūm ad-dīn*) had a significant impact on Ibn 'Alwān's thought. The exhortations and sermons in *at-Tawḥīd* and *al-Futūḥ* do not for the most part resemble those found in the *Iḥyā',* which is a voluminous commentary on various aspects of Muslim life and learning. Although the *Iḥyā'* deals with numerous Islamic disciplines ranging from ethics to theology, from law to psychology, and from sociology to history, its main focus is mysticism. Textual evidence suggests that al-Ghazālī was heavily influenced by the ascetic ethos of "The Nourishment of the Hearts" (*Qūt al-qulūb*) by Abū Ṭālib al-Makkī (d. 386/966) and the mystical psychology of "The Book of Observance of What Is Due to God" (*Kitāb ar-ri'āya li-ḥuqūq Allāh*) by al-Ḥārith al-Muḥāsibī (d. 243/857). Even though Ibn 'Alwān may have read all these works, it appears they had no direct influence upon his works. Both al-Ghazālī and Ibn 'Alwān relied on other Sufi works, especially "The Epistle on Sufism" (*ar-Risāla fī at-taṣawwuf*) by 'Abd al-Karīm al-Qushayrī (d. 465/1072), "The Book of Flashes in Sufism" (*Kitāb al-luma' fī t-taṣawwuf*) by Abū Naṣr as-Sarrāj aṭ-Ṭūsī (d. 378/988), "The Unveiling of the Hidden" (*Kashf al-maḥjūb*) by 'Alī b. 'Uthmān al-Jullābī al-Hujwīrī (d. 465/1073 or 469/1077), "The Generations of Sufis" (*Ṭabqāt aṣ-Ṣūfiyya*) by Abū 'Abd ar-Raḥmān as-Sulamī (d. 412/1021), "The Decoration of Friends of God" (*Ḥilyat al-awliyā'*) by Abū Nu'aym al-Iṣfahānī (d. 430/1038), "The Stations of the Travelers" (*Manāzil as-sā'irīn*) by 'Abd Allāh al-Anṣārī (d. 481/1089), and others.

Al-Ghazālī's chief purpose in the *Iḥyā'* was to show "how a punctilious observance of the duties imposed by the *Sharī'a* could be the basis of a genuine Sufi life."[41] The *Iḥyā'* is divided into four main quarters: the first deals with cult practices and worship (*rub' al-'ibādāt*), the second with social customs and personal behavior (*rub' al-'ādāt*), the third quarter with vices and evil actions leading to perdition (*rub' al-muhlikāt*), and the fourth with qualities leading to salvation (*rub' al-munjiyāt*).[42] The parts of the book cover general Islamic teachings, similar to the message of Ibn 'Alwān in his various styles. However, each of the two scholars approached his subject distinctively. For instance, in *Fayṣal at-tafriqa*, al-Ghazālī classifies existence (*al-wujūd*) according to five levels: (1) ontological (*dhātī*); (2) sensory (*ḥissī*); (3) imaginative (*khayālī*); (4) noetic (*'aqlī*); and (5) analogous (*shabahī*).[43] However, Ibn 'Alwān classifies existence according to a very different system. First, the hierarchy of existence (*al-wujūd*) in the image of the Great World is divided into four levels: (1) The Exalted Lord (*ar-rabb subḥānahu*); (2) the angels; (3) the heavens; (4) the earth. Second, the hierarchy of existence in the image of the human being has four levels: (1) The Exalted Lord; (2) the Intellect (*al-'aql*); (3) the soul (*an-nafs*); (4) the body (*al-jism*).[44] This classification may remind us of the cycles of Ismā'īlī thought, and differs completely from al-Ghazālī's scholasticism.[45]

In conclusion, the spiritual relationship between al-Ghazālī and Ibn 'Alwān is profound and intimate, in spite of a century and a half between the two great Sufi scholars. Both of them produced clear accounts of their basic tenets as laid down in their major works, *al-Munqidh min aḍ-ḍalāl* by al-Ghazālī and *at-Tawḥīd al-a'ẓam* by Ibn 'Alwān. Both of them presented their doctrines in a clear style, unlike, for example, Ibn 'Arabī (d. 638/1240) and others. Their works are widely read by medieval and contemporary scholars, and highly respected in Yemen. Finally, the literary output of al-Ghazālī is much more substantial when compared to that of Ibn 'Alwān. However, the fact that al-Ghazālī wrote many works has led some scholars to call into question the authenticity of many of his books,[46] whereas, due to the prodigious efforts of 'Abd al-'Azīz al-Manṣūb, who edited most of the major works of Ibn 'Alwān, we have an authentic picture of Ibn 'Alwān's most important works.

Al-Ḥusayn b. Manṣūr al-Hallāj

In his comprehensive study of the legacy of al-Ḥusayn b. Manṣūr al-Ḥallāj (d. 309/922), Louis Massignon (d. 1962) considers Ibn 'Alwān one of the followers of al-Ḥallāj in Arabia.[47] This idea was reiterated by contemporary Yemeni writers, including 'Abd Allāh al-Ḥibshī, the historian and literary critic, in his book *aṣ-Ṣūfiyya wa l-fuqahā' fī l-Yaman*.[48] The reason that led Massignon to categorize Ibn 'Alwān among the followers of al-Ḥallāj is Massignon's reliance on the critical study advanced by Kratchkovsky (d. 1951) who discovered in the *Kitāb al-futūḥ* of Ibn 'Alwān an interesting statement about al-Ḥallāj. According to this statement, the sincere lover bears witness to his true beloved on the most direct route to knowledge of the compassionate companion.[49] Ibn 'Alwān was aware of al-Ḥallāj's tragic fate and, therefore, undertook a critical analysis of al-Ḥallāj's state of mind followed by an apology for his behavior. Ibn 'Alwān explains that al-Ḥallāj submitted his will to the divine light, citing the example of the philosophers (*ḥukamā'*) who inform us, according to Massignon, of "a ray of sunlight entering a recess in a wall like fresh water in a glass, consuming its substance; the house sparkles with this glory, and this is the light that expressed itself in al-Ḥallāj when he said: [I]."[50]

Ibn 'Alwān proceeds to explain how he himself was clothed by knowledge, after running in ignorance in search of God. This knowledge made him aware of the same feeling that al-Ḥallāj had. The difference between them is that Ibn 'Alwān surpassed the spiritual state of annihilation (*fanā'*) while al-Ḥallāj was trapped in it. This difference is considerable since it defines the borderline between the ultimate station of fixity (*tamkīn*) and the Sufi stations that come before it. It is also significant because all Sufi stations will end in a state of no more stations for the seeker (*maqām lā maqām*).

Ibn 'Alwān then describes a dialogue between two witnesses: the witness of *fanā'*, or the passing away of consciousness of selfhood, and the witness of *baqā'*, or the remaining consciousness of God and of the self. In the case of al-Ḥallāj, the two witnesses *fanā'* and *baqā'* were arguing in his mind as to whether he should die or not. The witness of *fanā'* approved the idea of al-Ḥallāj's execution in his mind before it was consummated in reality. So, al-Ḥallāj was crucified, though innocent of polytheism (*shirk*), in order to make sure that no one coming after him would ever dare to be as bold as himself. As soon as his blood was spilled, it formed the phrase: "*Ana Allāh qātiluh*" (it is I, God, his murderer).[51] However, the same experience that al-Ḥallāj went through is revisited by Ibn 'Alwān, who uses the metaphor of the two witnesses. He was wavering between *fanā'* and *baqā'*, and between "He" and "I" until he eventually agreed to abandon *fanā'* and to join *baqā'*. Thus, the witness of *baqā'* told him, "You have fallen from the sun into dust, and from holiness into prison." He responded, "Do you intend to kill me as you killed that soul the other day?"[52] And the witness of *baqā'* smiled and said, "That witness was about to hang you on the gallows of al-Ḥallāj." Ibn 'Alwān sums up the discussion in a poem:

> The two witnesses quarrel within my light of intellect; one gives
> me life, the other wants to kill me.
> I support the counselor (*al-mushīr*) (i.e., my interlocutor)
> [who advised me] to be [in the state of] self-manifestation
> (*tajallī*), and disregarded [the advice of] the counselor (*al-mushīr*) [who advised me to be in the state of] self-seclusion
> (*takhallī*).
> If I, indeed, were to utter [anything] in my state of annihilation,
> I would have said the words of al-Ḥallāj before me.
> But He, whom I love, supported me and sustained my purpose
> (*himma*) and helped my intellect.

Some parts of my character, with regard to love, are annihilated;
the remaining parts are among brothers and family.
I do not know whether I should remain for my brothers, for my
family, for God or for myself!
I have two sides: hidden (*maknūn*) and visible (*bādī*); I have also
two kinds of knowledge (*'ilmān*); one is partial (*juz'ī*) while
the other is comprehensive (*kullī*).[53]

This poem is the last portion of Ibn 'Alwān's discussion of al-Ḥallāj. Massignon did not mention it in his book, *The Passion of al-Ḥallāj*, though he mentioned a different poem concerning "excusing" al-Ḥallāj and conveying his ardent acceptance of punishment. As one can see, the poem starts with a quarrel of the two witnesses *fanā'* and *baqā'*, which takes place in Ibn 'Alwān's soul. These two witnesses are not explicitly mentioned in the poem, but they can be deduced from the preceding prose. Whereas *fanā'* wants to annihilate the poet, *baqā'* wants to save his life. Then Ibn 'Alwān proceeds to explain that he joined the station of self-manifestation (*tajallī*) after consulting the adviser (*al-mushīr*), who is his interlocutor, and rejected the station of self-seclusion (*takhallī*). After that, he goes on to argue that if he had spoken in the state of annihilation (*fanā'*), he would have said the words of al-Ḥallāj—that is "I am the One Real" (*Ana al-Ḥaqq*) or, in other words, "I am God." Ibn 'Alwān compares the stage he reached in his spiritual quest for God with that of al-Ḥallāj. The only difference that can be found in this comparison is that Ibn 'Alwān saved himself from the state of annihilation while al-Ḥallāj failed.

Al-Ghazālī (d. 505/1111) in his *Mishkāt al-anwār* also exonerates al-Ḥallāj of his words and states that the words of lovers who are passionate in their intoxication and ecstasy must be hidden and not made public.[54] Ibn 'Alwān's interpretation of al-Ḥallāj's state of mind is slightly different from that of al-Ghazālī. Al-Ghazālī exonerates al-Ḥallāj from the ignorant accusations by explaining away his mystical experience and arguing that the ecstatic utterances (*shaṭaḥāt*) and speech of lovers should be concealed. However, Ibn 'Alwān maintains that al-Ḥallāj's execution was meant to show his patient endurance and to prevent those coming after him from behaving with the same fearless abandon.[55]

In contrast, al-Baradūnī (d. 1999),[56] the great Yemeni poet, interprets the third line of this poem to mean that the tyranny and oppression of the rulers of the Rasūlid dynasty made it difficult for poets to express their feelings. Al-Baradūnī understands the term "annihilation" literally, not as a Sufi term, and therefore, he argues that Ibn 'Alwān was not able to express himself because of the tyranny of the despotic rulers. Later on, al-Baradūnī interprets the last three lines, which carry the meaning of indecision and wavering, as representing the variety of cultural surroundings in Rasūlid Yemen. This was characterized by the Shī'ī school, the Sunnī school (which was adopted by the Rasūlids who inherited it from the Ayyūbids), the Zaydī Mu'tazilite school, and finally the Ismā'īlī Bāṭinī legacy. All these diverse lines of Islamic thought, al-Baradūnī asserts, are implied in the poem of Ibn 'Alwān. With this in mind, one can see that al-Baradūnī exaggerates in his interpretations. He is right that the cultural milieu of the Rasūlid dynasty was diverse, but it is not accurate to assume that all the above ideas are implied in Ibn 'Alwān's poem for I have already mentioned (in Chapter 2) Ibn 'Alwān's courageous stance in dealing with the powers that be. The poem should be seen as a portrayal of Ibn 'Alwān's personal mystical experience.

Ibn 'Alwān describes the duality of his character, wondering whether he should remain alive for his brothers and his family or even for himself. He seems to have left the reader undecided so that the reader would figure out his mystical world-view and judge him accordingly. He concludes the poem pointing to his character, which represents two faces of the same coin: the manifest (*ẓāhir* or *bādī*) and the inward (*bāṭin* or *maknūn*). In addition, he mentions two kinds of knowledge: partial knowledge (*'ilm juz'ī*), which probably means jurisprudence (*fiqh*), and comprehensive knowledge (*'ilm kullī*), which can be found in juridical theology, speculative theology (*'ilm al-kalām*), and philosophy. Another better interpretation of these two kinds of knowledge would be the ritual observances, social customs, and ethical rules (*'ulūm al-mu'āmala*) and the knowledge of the secrets of true realities (*'ulūm al-mukāshafa*).[57] The underlying meaning of this classification is to show that Ibn 'Alwān was in complete union with God on the one hand, and in complete presence of mind with people and his family on the other. In the Sufi tradition, this state of irresolution is described in two terms: "*at-tafriqa*" (the "dispersion," or plurality of the empirical world) and "*al-jam'*" (the underlying unity of all created beings, or union with God).

Al-Ḥibshī states that Massignon credited Ibn 'Alwān with the authorship of a book entitled *Dhikrā al-Ḥallāj*,[58] but this is not accurate. In his book *The Passion of al-Ḥallāj*, Massignon relied on the research of Kratchkovsky, who discovered in the *Kitāb al-futūḥ* of Ibn 'Alwān an interesting passage dealing with al-Ḥallāj (d. 309/922). This passage about al-Ḥallāj by Ibn 'Alwān amounted to eight pages in his *al-Futūḥ*, not a separate book.[59] According to 'Abd al-Karīm Qāsim Sa'īd, the contemporary writer and critic, what has been said about Ibn 'Alwān's alleged book *Dhikrā al-Ḥallāj* can be attributed to the distortion of manuscripts by their copiers (*'abath an-nussākh*). This distortion is, Sa'īd argues, what Massignon meant when he spoke of a separate "book."[60] However, Massignon never credited Ibn 'Alwān with the authorship of a book describing "al-Ḥallāj's passions."[61] He simply mentioned an episode about al-Ḥallāj in his book *al-Futūḥ*. In the next chapter, I shall examine elements of the doctrine of incarnation (*ḥulūl*) and divine union (*ittiḥād*) in Ibn 'Alwān's thoughts, in an attempt to bring out possible similarities between Ibn 'Alwān (d. 665/1266) and al-Ḥallāj (d. 309/922).

Muhyī ad-Dīn Ibn 'Arabī

Contemporary Yemeni writers and literary critics tend to ascribe Ibn 'Alwān's mystical views to the influence of his contemporary Ibn 'Arabī (d. 638/1240) without providing any evidence to this effect. For instance, Muḥammad Sa'īd Jarāda argues that the evidence of Ibn 'Arabī's impact on Ibn 'Alwān is that the latter named his book *al-Futūḥ,* imitating Ibn 'Arabī's book, *al-Futūḥāt*, even though the contents of the two books are completely different.[62] Another example is 'Abd al-'Azīz al-Maqāliḥ, who sees that Ibn 'Arabī's stay in Mecca is proof that Ibn 'Alwān was influenced by Ibn 'Arabī.[63] Both writers have tried to establish some connection between Ibn 'Arabī and Ibn 'Alwān, and their assumptions spring from Ibn 'Arabī's great popularity and excellent reputation as a spiritual master. But is this a sound judgment or a mere supposition?

In addition, none of them came across the manuscript entitled *Fatḥ al-karīm al-jawād al-mannān* by Ja'far b. al-Ḥasan al-Barzanjī (d. 1079/1765) who claimed that "Ibn 'Alwān studied under Ibn 'Arabī and al-Badawī in Mecca."[64] Although, al-Barzanjī had no proof, our contemporary writers would still use his statement to demonstrate Ibn 'Arabī's alleged influence on the work of Ibn 'Alwān. If they had known about al-Barzanjī's manuscript, they would have argued that since al-Barzanjī was a premodern historian, he must have known the circumstances of the personal life of Ibn 'Alwān. But, is this in actuality a genuine case? In fact, there was a four century time difference between Ibn 'Alwān and al-Barzanjī. Thus, on the one hand, he was not living in Ibn 'Alwān's epoch, and, on the other, he was involved in the debates around the legacy of Ibn 'Arabī. It is highly probable that contemporary Yemeni writers are unfamiliar with the medieval sources, which assert that Ibn

'Alwān never left Yemen. They may even go further by arguing that Mecca was part of Yemen during the Rasūlid dynasty and, therefore, there was no conflict with the statement that Ibn 'Alwān never left Yemen. In the end, in order to be neutral and objective, one cannot rule out the possibility that Ibn 'Alwān may have studied under or been influenced by Ibn 'Arabī, yet we do not have substantial evidence to support it. According to Alexander Knysh, "his [i.e., Ibn 'Alwān] indebtedness to Ibn 'Arabī cannot be established via documents."[65]

Although Ibn 'Arabī visited Ḥijāz, Palestine, Syria, Iraq, and Anatolia, he never visited Yemen. This is, according to al-Ḥibshī, because he might have feared the anarchy in Yemen during that period.[66] His works were brought to Yemen by 'Umar b. 'Abd al-Raḥmān b. Ḥasan al-Qudsī (or al-Muqaddasī) (d. 688/1289).[67] One does not find any reference to Ibn 'Arabī in the writings of Ibn 'Alwān, but instead Sufi names such as al-Ḥallāj, Abū Yazīd al-Bisṭāmī, al-Ghazālī, an-Niffarī, and others are there. This absence is attributable to Ibn 'Arabī's books being brought to Yemen after the death of Ibn 'Alwān. Likewise, there is no mention of Ibn 'Alwān in the numerous writings of Ibn 'Arabī. This demonstrates that both were living at the same age but never met each other. Moreover, Ibn 'Arabī met a number of Yemenis, including the famous Yemeni traditionalist Abū 'Abd Allāh Muḥammad b. Ismā'īl b. Abī aṣ-Ṣayf (d. 609/1212) who is the only Yemeni scholar mentioned in *al-Futūḥāt*.[68] All the attempts of creating a connection between them are merely based on hypothetical assumptions. Little is known about the early lives of either of these Sufis. Interestingly, their conversions to Sufism were precipitated by heavenly voices commanding them to abandon their ungodly ways and to devote themselves fully to the service of God. Both Sufis immersed themselves in ascetic practices and pious meditations and were able to achieve an advanced degree of spiritual attainment.[69]

From the doctrinal point of view, it is hard to trace the basic tenets of Ibn 'Arabī because he did not provide us with an unequivocal summary of his views in his two major works: "The Bezels of Wisdom" (*Fuṣūṣ al-ḥikam*), and the monumental "Meccan Revelations" (*al-Futūḥāt al-makkiyya*). Unlike Ibn 'Arabī, Ibn 'Alwān (d. 665/1266) wrote a clear account of his basic tenets in his major book *at-Tawḥīd al-a'ẓam*. He is straightforward in presenting the gist of his doctrine, whereas Ibn 'Arabī is intentionally elusive. Both Sufi scholars seem to have been well-read in contemporary Sufi literature and left behind many writings, most of them on Sufism. Nevertheless, Ibn 'Alwān's literary output is much more narrow in scope when compared to that of Ibn 'Arabī, and studies of Ibn 'Alwān's legacy from the Western point of view are extremely rare. One may conclude that both Ibn 'Alwān and Ibn 'Arabī as Sufi masters and literary scholars were on equal footing and competent rivals. Yet the popularity of Ibn 'Arabī is larger due to his travels and reputation around most Islamic lands while the popularity of Ibn 'Alwān is limited to Yemen since he preferred humbleness (*khumūl*) rather than fame. Finally, one may argue that Ibn 'Arabī's popularity is reinforced by scholarship, whereas the popularity of Ibn 'Alwān is caused by his anthropological nature as a miracle worker and friend of God.

Conclusion

There is no evidence that Ibn 'Alwān was directly influenced by either local or foreign Sufi masters. Rather than jump to conclusions, as scholars have in the past, and assume that Ibn 'Alwān's work and thought must be ascribed to the influence of other, perhaps more well-known Sufi figures, here I have attempted to show a more nuanced picture of Ibn 'Alwān's intellectual heritage. In so doing, I have demonstrated Ibn 'Alwān both absorbing and critiquing the ideas that were circulating on the intellectual and spiritual map of Yemen and the Islamic world beyond. This goes beyond a simple model of imitation or influence; for example, Ibn 'Alwān may have availed himself of the works of al-Ghazālī, but nevertheless I cannot dismiss the distinctive styles and originality in each scholar. Finally, Ibn 'Alwān was, like al-Ghazālī, familiar with the development of the early Sufi literature and its presence in his works is undeniable.

His oeuvre displays distinctive features of local Yemeni Sufism, and the evidence shows that he can neither be linked to local hegemony nor to any foreign Sufi tradition. As I point out in the following chapter, his famous statement that a disciple can manage without a master if he follows the teachings of the Qur'ān and Sunna is compelling evidence that he was not affiliated with any Sufi master or brotherhood. As we explore the nuances of Ibn 'Alwān's Sufi thought we shall see that he opened the door for any disciple or path seeker to become free of the obligations of Sufi masters, with the stipulation that they follow sincerely the essence of the religious instructions laid down by the Qur'ān and the Sunna. Having derived, from this chapter, an accurate sense of Ibn 'Alwān's relationship to the major Sufi figures of his era I turn to the specifics of his own Sufi thought.

6

THE FUNDAMENTALS OF IBN ʿALWĀN'S SUFI THOUGHT

Any treatment of Ibn ʿAlwān's Sufi thought must grapple with his tremendous knowledge of the Qur'ān and the Sunna. In this regard, his Sufi thought is grounded in Islamic scripture on every point. His exegesis moves fluidly between literal meanings of God's word and Sufi interpretation. Furthermore, he shows himself as a Sufi poet who skillfully employs metaphor and imagery to convey what cannot be portrayed in ordinary language. I explore his more difficult and ambiguous verses on the subject of divine love, his awe of God, and Sufi knowledge *(ma'arifa)*. Ibn ʿAlwān makes use of his literary skill not only as a pedagogical device to explain difficult Qu'rānic verses but also to defend his views on such controversial issues as the Sufi concert (*sama'*). I dwell on this latter point, for Ibn ʿAlwān composed beautiful poetry on the concert as a path to the ecstatic remembrance of God, urging jurists not to close their hearts to it. I then turn to Ibn ʿAlwān's writings on the relationship between master and disciple, and the disciple's progression along the mystic's path. Ibn ʿAlwān advocated moderation in all things and justified his stance that a disciple might advance without a master in a manner entirely coherent with his overall Sufi theology: of primary importance to the disciple are the Prophet and Islamic scriptures—not a shaykh. Although Ibn ʿAlwān offers much guidance to his followers on ways to open their hearts to God, inevitably he returns to the ultimate condition of Sufi knowledge: following the teachings of the Qur'ān and the Prophet.

Several complex and important issues in Sufi thought—unveiling (*kashf*), passing away (*fanā'*), survival in God (*baqā'*), mystical union (*ittiḥād*), and incarnation (*ḥulūl*)—are treated at length here, first in the Sufi tradition in general, and then in Ibn ʿAlwān's theology. It becomes clear that Ibn ʿAlwān consistently provided a moderate interpretation of

Sufi doctrine, sometimes criticizing other Sufi thinkers, by advocating absolute reliance on Islamic scripture.

Qur'ān and Sunna

Sufism is seen by some Muslims as the heart of the Islamic tradition. Its teachings, which combine love of God with knowledge of His attributes, are founded on many of the most beautiful verses of the Qur'ān and the sayings of the Prophet Muḥammad. Ibn 'Alwān's Sufism is distinguished by his extensive use of Qur'ānic citations and Prophetic *ḥadīths*. The number of Qur'ānic quotations Ibn 'Alwān uses appears to be greater than the number of *ḥadīth* citations. Some scholars have counted the number of verses Ibn 'Alwān cites from the Qur'ān and found 290 quotes in *at-Tawḥīd* and 240 in *al-Futūḥ*.[1]

One example is Ibn 'Alwān's quotation of God speaking to the angels: "When I have shaped him and breathed into him of My spirit, you fall down, bowing before him."[2] In his interpretation, Ibn 'Alwān states that God meant the spirit of knowledge, not the spirit of life.[3] He argues that the spirit of life is not necessarily confined to Adam and his progeny but rather to all living creatures, and that this spirit is known as the sensual spirit (*nafs ḥissiyya*). To support his argument, Ibn 'Alwān interprets the verse, "Then He gave Adam knowledge of the nature and reality of all things and every thing,"[4] by saying that God created Adam's intellect (*al-'aql*), which understood what God taught it. This understanding, or—as Ibn 'Alwān puts it—spirit, which is able to distinguish and comprehend, is different from the spirit of senses and life. Ibn 'Alwān provides an analogy to show how the continuity of spiritual nourishment is significant. For instance, he argues, if you teach someone the following verse: "There is no God but Allāh," it functions like a sperm that has fertilized an egg. If the embryo's nourishment discontinues for any reason, it will become weak, cannot fully grow, and loses its similarity to the image of its father. Likewise, if spiritual nourishment is withdrawn from a spiritual seed, it will decompose and eventually turn into the dust of ignorance. Consequently, a spiritual seed needs constant nourishment, which is continuously remembering God's name (*dhikr*), meditation, and keeping company with scholars of revealed law (*sharī'a*), and those who have knowledge of Sufism (*al-'ārifīn bi'l-ḥaqā'iq wa'l-wāqifīn bi'd-daqā'iq*). These practices are necessary for the seed to grow until it achieves union with the One (God).

Part of the reason for the tremendous respect and awe for Ibn 'Alwān lies in his plumbing the depths of the Qur'ānic universe and his representation of that universe. Let us consider another example of Ibn ʿAlwān's Qur'ānic interpretation, which seems to go beyond the literal meaning:

> "It is He who created you from dust," of ignorance.
> "Then from a sperm-drop," then transferred you to the drop of education.
> "Then from a clinging-clot;" then elevated you to the clinging-clot of understanding.
> "Then He brings you out as a child;" [through giving you the ability of] contemplation.
> "Then you attain the age of maturity" through [the display of] knowledge.
> "Then [further] that you become elders" to educate [people].
> "And among you is he who is taken in death before [that]," i.e., before propagation.
> "You reach a specified term;" [as] a definite station and determined sustenance.
> "and perhaps you will use reason," to understand His speech and and read His Book.[5]

On many occasions, Ibn ʿAlwān addresses the literal and apparent meaning of the Qur'ān, whereas on other occasions he uses Sufi interpretations (*min bāb al-ishāra*). The Qur'ān is the true and authentic embodiment of God's speech. Its every letter is full of significance, and it is the source of all information because it is the concrete, linguistic expression of the Real Being, God Himself.[6] Here is another example of Ibn ʿAlwān's exegesis of the Qur'ān:

> "Say: O Lord of dominions," i.e., the Lord of kings.
> "You give kingship to whom You please," i.e., You give the power of knowing and obeying You to whom You please, through Your favor.
> "And You strip off kingship from whom You please," i.e., You strip off the power of knowing and obeying You from whom You please, through Your justice.
> "You exalt whom You please" through knowing and obeying You.
> "And debase whom You please" by being ignorant about You and disobeying You.

> "All goodness is Yours (entirely)" such as giving Your servant an intellect to clarify the way to knowing You, a knowledge to clarify the way to obey You, an obedience to necessitate Your complacency, and a contentment to necessitate Your heaven.
>
> "Indeed You have the power over all things" of graces.
>
> "You make the night succeed the day," just as the darkness of having not known You is followed by the light of knowing You.
>
> "You make the day succeed the night," just as the light of having known You succeeds the darkness of having not known You.
>
> "Raise the living from the dead," as You raise the life of faith from the death of disbelief.
>
> "The dead from the living," as You raise the death of disbelief from the life of faith.
>
> "And give sustenance to whom You please, without measure." You give the noble word to whomever is sincere so that he can gain the power of this world and the hereafter. [7]

These verses are examples of Ibn 'Alwān's mystical inspiration. In dealing with Prophetic *ḥadīths*, Ibn 'Alwān uses numerous examples to support his argument. When he discusses the Sufi path or something related to the Sufi states or stations, he always refers his readers to the following famous *ḥadīth* narrated by al-Bukhārī, which is used by the majority of *'ulamā'* (Sufi scholars and disciples):

> Allāh Almighty has said: Whosoever shows enmity to a friend of Mine, I shall be at war with him. My servant does not draw near to Me with anything more loved by Me than the religious duties I have imposed upon him, and My servant continues to draw near to Me with supererogatory works so that I shall love him. When I love him I am the hearing with which he hears, the seeing with which he sees, his hand with which he strikes. Were he to ask [something] of Me, I would surely give it to him; and were he to ask Me for refuge, I would surely grant it to him.[8]

This *ḥadīth* is repeatedly cited in most of Ibn 'Alwān's works.[9] Its significance lies in the fact that it carries metaphorical connotations and implications, which many writers cite in their ongoing debates. More often, one finds only the last part of the *ḥadīth*: "When I love him I am his hearing with which he hears, his seeing with which he sees, his hand with which he strikes." The primary importance of Prophetic knowledge, for Ibn 'Alwān, is to explain citations from the Qur'ān and the *ḥadīth*. These citations were among the most central points of intellectual reference for him and his generation—and they have remained as such for a large body of the human race.[10] It is almost impossible to think about Ibn 'Alwān's writing without references to either the Qur'ān or the Sunna. They form an integral part of his discussion and are the means by which he constructs his mystical theory. The use of the Qur'ān and Sunna is a recurrent theme, which overwhelmingly colors his literary style. It is safe to say that Ibn 'Alwān's Sufism is a direct reflection of his profound understanding on the thoughtful meaning of the Qur'ān and the Sunna.

Ibn 'Alwān's View of the Sufi Concert

Because the Qur'ān is recited in a musical way, it is important to clarify Ibn 'Alwān's attitude toward the Sufi concert (*samā'*). *Samā'* is not a Qur'ānic term, but it is found in classical Arabic literature in the sense of song or musical performance. While it is often employed in Islamic disciplines such as grammar and theology, it has a special meaning in Sufism.[11] Here, it generally denotes the act of listening to music, particularly a Sufi spiritual concert in a ritualized form.[12] Ibn 'Alwān pays special attention to the *samā'*, defending it against those who condemn it, specifically the *fuqahā'* of the tribe of Banū Isḥāq of Zabīd. Ibn 'Alwān begins his discussion by stating that the wise man should know that composed poetic lyrics, sung by melodious voices and accompanied by musical tunes, produce pleasure in the heart. He says: "I think that any being who has senses, be it a beast or human being, would be moved by an enchanting voice. If it is accompanied by meaningful words, it surely leaves a strong and splendid impression on the heart."[13] In other words, *samā'* is the "nourishment of the soul," or as it is perceived by many Sufi authors, a devotional practice that can induce intense emotional transport (*tawājud*), states of grace (*aḥwāl*), and trance or ecstasy (*wajd*; *wujūd*).[14]

Ibn 'Alwān elaborates on the concept of *samā'* as if it were a heavenly wind, which carries with it the keys to divine secrets. He compares it to a magnet that attracts everything near it, in the same way that sensual bodies are drawn to each other. Therefore, Ibn 'Alwān asserts, one may compare the motion of people in ecstatic states (*aṣḥāb al-mawājīd*) under the influence of intense emotional trance (*wajd*) and remembrance of God's name (*dhikr*) with the movement of nails when they are attracted by the magnet.[15] With this vivid picture, Ibn 'Alwān meant to show the inconceivable intensity of the Sufi state during *samā'*.

In one poem Ibn 'Alwān refutes the views of the *sharī'a*-minded scholars of Zabīd, particularly those of the tribe of Banū Isḥāq who criticized Sufi activities including *samā'*. He argues that only those who hate music hasten to say it is forbidden:

> If only you could taste its sweetness, you would have changed your mind.
> Indeed all hearts love to remember their Lord except a whimsical heart, which has been veiled [of remembering].
> You prohibited dancing and clapping, while it is lawful [in the view] of scholars.
> Intense emotional trance is permissible in our view.
> The twigs do not remain stable if [the wind of] trance moves the tree. Look carefully, oh people of reason, and consider the best opinion, for man is held accountable for his actions.
> Seek God's forgiveness for what you have said about them [i.e., the Sufis].
> Truth should be your aim and you could seek it from strangers (*al-ghurabā'*).
> You will be asked about them on the Last Day and they will be asked about you, but whoever is wrong will reap the pain [of Hell fire].
> If what I said is true, accept it! But if you deny it, God will punish the liar.
> As for those who are going astray and the ignorant, who are not among you, they are like butterflies, which are trying to put out the fire.[16]

In addition to poetry, Ibn 'Alwān dedicates a special section in *at-Tawḥīd* to establish the importance of *samā'*. He starts by giving an example of Adam in Paradise, when he sought the advice of Satan. As a result of Satan's deception, Adam was expelled from Paradise to be tested. While on earth, Adam knew no rest or contentment, longing for his previous noble station. Similarly, if the lover remembers his beloved, he abandons tranquility and becomes intoxicated; all his movements are dictated by the force of love. When he reaches this state, knowledgeable people (i.e., the Sufis) will exonerate and excuse him.[17] In his defense of *samā'*, Ibn 'Alwān addresses those who condemn the motions of a longing lover when he hears the name of his beloved. He depicts them as "sick people" because their hearts have turned away from God's remembrance (*dhikr*). Their hearts have been barred from the sweetness of His love and longing. He urges them to weep for their loss of love of God. Ibn 'Alwān invites them to heed the following Qur'ānic verse: "And when I have made him [i.e., Adam] and have breathed My spirit into him, you [the angels] fall down, bowing before him."[18] According to Ibn 'Alwān, no one can experience the trance of *samā'* unless he has the spirit of God in him, as Adam had.

As stated earlier, Ibn 'Alwān uses the Qur'ān to support his arguments and to show that his Sufism rests solely on the guidance of the Qur'ān and Sunna. He urges the jurists (*fuqahā'*) not to rush to negative judgments and instead try to understand the meaning of mysterious signs (*ishārāt 'ajība*) and unusual but sound analogies (*qiyāsāt muḥkama gharība*). In elaborating on the concept of *samā'*, Ibn 'Alwān describes love as the proper vehicle leading to the states of longing for God. Ibn 'Alwān argues that love is like a tree that grows in the heart. Its land is anxiety (*ashjān*), its water is the tear dropping from the eyelids, and its fruit is longing for a meeting with the Merciful. This tree of love is in itself motionless and can only move by listening to the melodies (*alḥān*) of remembering God (*dhikr*).

> So how do not I become delighted due to His *dhikr*!
> And drag the tails [of my garments and enjoy] intoxication in Him.
> He is the one who planted in me an aromatic plant
> and watered it by the intoxication of His wine.
> So do not blame me if I am addicted to [His] love
> because this issue [comes] from His command.[19]

Again, Ibn 'Alwān addresses those who object to *samā'*, warning them to preserve the sanctity of the lovers of God. He justifies his request by mentioning the Qur'ānic verse in which God asked His Prophet to: "Persevere with those who call on their Lord, morning and evening, seeking His face."[20] Ibn 'Alwān further argues that whoever cannot persevere with the lovers of God should leave them alone. Finally, Ibn 'Alwān concludes his discussion by citing another metaphor to clarify the difference between the hardened heart and the soft heart in relation to *samā'*. Thus, the breeze would move the soft twigs, which grow in the fertile beautiful gardens, but if the breeze meets a dry trunk there will be no motion, even if the wind is strong.

Because *samā'* is a feature of Sufi gatherings, and these gatherings are usually organized under the auspices of a master, it is necessary to describe how Ibn 'Alwān views the relationship between the master and his disciple.

Master and Disciple

Ibn 'Alwān wrote on the subject of the master/disciple relationship in response to debates among his fellow brothers concerning the person who claims to have received a miracle (*mawhiba*) from God without a human intermediary. In *at-Tawḥīd*, Ibn 'Alwān discusses the importance of the master (shaykh) and why he deserves this rank. He asks, is the word "shaykh" eternal or created? The word mastery, *al-mashyakha*, originates from the term for a certain age in human life. The derivative term is used in the context of construct status (*iḍāfa*) such as *shaykh qabīla* (master of a tribe), *shaykh māl* (master of wealth), *shaykh sinn* (master of age, i.e., an old man), and *shaykh ma'rifa* (master of knowledge). When God created Adam in accordance with the perfect image and the appropriate age, his body became the master of all bodies until the day of judgment. When Adam reached the rank of perfection, God made him the master and He made the angels his students. Then, God manifested some of His wonders, which the angels were not aware of, by making Adam ask them about what the Qur'ān terms "names of these" (*asmā' ha'ulā'*). The angels were not able to answer. God said:

> "O Adam! Convey to them their names". When he [Adam] had told them, God said: "Did I not tell you that I know the unknown of heaven and earth, and I know what you reveal and know what you conceal?"[21]

Therefore, Adam was the master of the angels because they lacked his knowledge, and it was incumbent upon them to glorify him immediately. When the angels were not able to understand, God commanded them to prostrate themselves before Adam, thereby teaching them that their rank was lower than his. Thus, according to Ibn 'Alwān, the authority of shaykhs in relation to divine knowledge has been asserted. Not only were shaykhs glorified and respected but also people humbled themselves before them, kissing their feet, and kissing the ground in front of them. Ibn 'Alwān compares the master/disciple relationship to that of an infant who needs nutrition from his mother.

In *al-baḥr al-mushakka al-gharībl*, Ibn 'Alwān provides a detailed explanation of the steps that the disciple should take to reach his mystical goal. In *at-Tawḥīd al-a'ẓam*, however, Ibn 'Alwān addresses theological questions pertaining to the relationship between the master and his disciple. The difference, in this respect, is that in *at-Tawḥīd* Ibn 'Alwān discusses the debate over whether the disciple needs a master, and how he can manage with or without a shaykh, whereas in *al-baḥr al-mushakkal* he discusses the aspects of the Sufi path on which the disciple should strive to attain his ultimate purpose. In *at-Tawḥīd*, he speaks of five steps that the master should keep in mind to cultivate and educate his disciple.[22] First, the master nourishes the disciple with spiritual milk, as it is known in the Sufi tradition, just as the mother feeds her infant. He should not overwhelm the disciple with Sufi knowledge at this point, for doing so might result in the disciple giving up and leaving his master. By treating him gently, the master ensures the disciple's progress along the spiritual path. The master may start by opening the disciple's heart to meditation about earth and heaven in a spiritual retreat (*khalwa*). The disciple should neither be too lonely nor too sociable. If he is lonely in his early initiation, he is more likely to be distressed or be in the state of "contraction" (*qabḍ*). If he were to become too sociable, he may be spoiled by excessive joy or "expansion" (*basṭ*). The disciple therefore must remain moderate. This idea of being a middle-roader is one of the central themes of Ibn 'Alwān's overall Sufi thought. In fact, his theology, thought, and Sufism are based on moderation and spiritual balance. Second, if the master recognizes that the disciple has assimilated all the above requirements, he should advance him to the second stage. This stage is known as youthfulness (*al-ghulāmiyya*), in which the master uses psychological knowledge to put his disciple in a state of neither feeling nor sensing. At this point, the master should clarify the subtle difference between the soul at peace (*an-nafs al-mutma'inna*) and the evil soul (*an-nafs ash-shaytāniyya*). He must explain the latter's shortcomings and its evil nature so that the disciple may reject it along with hatred. Third, the master elevates the disciple to the third stage, adulthood (*ash-shabāb*). In this stage, the master orders the disciple to destroy his lower soul and former ego (*qahr an-nafs*), which constantly strives to dominate him. The disciple must repress his lower soul, whose sharp edges are dulled by controlling one's evil habits (*qam' ḥiddat an-nafs*). The master should command his disciple to improve his good soul until he reaches perfection. Fourth, the master elevates his disciple to the stage of maturity (*kuhūla*), whereupon he reveals to him divine secrets and orders him to be grateful for the favors of God. The master also opens the disciple's heart to the essence of unity (*tawḥīd*) and discloses to him the secrets of *tajrīd* (total trust in God). Additionally, he should show him how to be independent and how to avoid emulation. Finally, the master promotes his disciple to the fifth stage, which is known as the station of mastership (*ash-shuyūkha*). In this final stage the master deems his disciple qualified to give *fatwās* (legal or mystical opinions) and to answer all questions raised by his fellows.[23] These five stages are central to the evolution of any Sufi order. Therefore, if we consider Ibn 'Alwān the master of a Sufi order named after him, these main stages constitute the pillars that ensure the continuity of his Sufi order.

Ibn 'Alwān asks when the disciple (*murīd*) needs a master (shaykh), and answers that if the *murīd* is ignorant of the Book of God, its meaning, and the Prophet's Sunna, he needs a shaykh to teach him. When he has studied these foundational matters, he may continue to the five stages mentioned above. Furthermore, Ibn 'Alwān asks if a *murīd* can manage without a shaykh, and answers that if the *murīd* is chosen by God and is proficient in God's book, follows the Prophet's Sunna, and takes the Prophet's deeds as an example, he will be granted primordial guidance, will, and wisdom. By these, God will elevate him to the station of those who are close to God (*muqarrabūn*), thus making the disciple independent of all creatures. Then, Ibn 'Alwān cites the famous *ḥadīth* to prove that the *murīd* does not necessarily need a shaykh: "My servant will not draw toward me with anything more than the religious duties I have imposed upon him, and my servant continues to draw toward me with supererogatory [acts] until I love him. If I love him I will be his hearing, sight, hand, and supporter."[24] He also poses the question as to whether this report is based on God's Book and the Prophet's Sunna or on the doctrines of people (i.e., Sufi masters). For Ibn 'Alwān, the priority should be given to the Qur'ān and Sunna.

Likewise, Ibn 'Alwān gives preference to the Prophet over the Sufi shaykh. He argues that nobody can approach God except through the door of the Prophet. Whoever thinks that he will come closer to God without following His Book or the model of the Prophet will not achieve his goal. Rather he will lose his senses and perish; the light of his mind will shrink and he will fall on the dung hill of his ignorance, as God says: "But no, by your Lord: They will not believe until they make you the judge regarding their disagreement."[25] Ibn 'Alwān goes on to say that God commands His creatures to follow the Prophet. No one can claim the Prophet's love unless he follows the Prophet's Sunna and applies its teachings to his actions, according to the Qur'ānic verse: "If you love God, follow me so that God will love you."[26] Thus, one cannot love God except through the pursuit of the Sunna of the Prophet. Finally, Ibn 'Alwān argues, every station (*kull maqām*) that the Sufi master conquers through mystical scrutiny, guidance, and God's assistance rests on a sincere imitation of the Prophet as well as abandoning the world of pleasures. Ibn 'Alwān ends this section with the following Qur'ānic quotation: "Do not exaggerate your religion except the truth."[27]

In his discussion of the master/disciple relationship, Ibn 'Alwān comments extensively on the dispute that arose among his disciples regarding the Sufi cloak (*al-yad* or *al-khirqa*). He denies that the Sufi *khirqa* originated with the imam of the path, Abū Bakr aṣ-Ṣiddīq.[28] To prove his point, Ibn 'Alwān cites the following verse from the Qur'ān: "Say: My way, and that of my followers is to call you to God with full perception."[29] Moreover, whoever follows the Prophet completely and takes his deeds seriously, whether obligatory or recommended, has the right to call other people to the Path of God because the Prophet says: "May God have mercy on someone who heard my message, comprehended it, and conveyed it to whoever would hear it; many a bearer [of good tidings] is more aware than a listener."[30]

As for the implication of the master putting his hand over the hand of the disciple, which is a symbol of allegiance (*sirr al-yad al-qābiḍa*), it is nothing but an emblem of friendship, which sustains relationships between brethren who serve in the path of God.[31] On the day of judgment, nobody will argue that they pledged allegiance to a master or wore a *khirqa* since neither of these actions will save them from God's punishment. Again, Ibn 'Alwān reminds his fellow brothers who pay special attention to the Sufi concept of *khirqa* that their argument has no proof. He draws a sharp distinction between the view of his brothers, with regard to the significance of the *khirqa* and the Prophet's message to his family: "O 'Abbās b. 'Abd al-Muṭṭalib, O 'Alī b. Abī Ṭālib, O Fāṭima bint Muḥammad, I have no power to get anything on your behalf from God."[32]

If the Prophet warned his family not to rely on their kinship, and to act righteously in order to obtain a place in Paradise, then the master should warn his disciples not to pin their hopes on their master. Total reliance on the teachings of the master will not lead them to heaven. Ibn 'Alwān goes on to explain that sometimes the *khirqa* may not be given to an adept who deserves it while it may be bestowed on someone who does not deserve it. Furthermore, there is no guarantee that a master/disciple relationship will lead to God's satisfaction and consequently to Paradise. To this effect Ibn 'Alwān quotes the Prophet as saying: "The spirits are like armies—those who know each other become friendly [with each other] and those who do not know each other become unfriendly [with each other]."[33]

Once more, as proof of the friendship between the Sufi master and his disciple does not necessarily entail God's forgiveness, Ibn 'Alwān narrated a story. Someone asked a Sufi master why he accepted the friendship of all those who came to him. The master replied: "We accompany the people of Paradise to it, and we accompany the people of Hell to it." This means, Ibn 'Alwān explains, that whoever follows our example will win Paradise, and whoever disagrees with us will go astray. Another interpretation runs, "whoever follows our Path will not be misled and will win our support (i.e., *ḥujja lahu*), and whoever disagrees with us may go astray, and thus will not enjoy our support (i.e., *ḥujja 'alayhi*)."[34] Notably, God abolished a family lineage because of doctrinal disagreement (*mukhālafa*) between a father and his son as the Qur'ān says: "O Noah, truly he is not of your family. He is surely the outcome of an impious act."[35] It then follows that He can abolish a friendship between a master and his disciple for the same reason. Finally, Ibn 'Alwān concludes his discussion by saying that God's support and protection (*wilāya*) accompany whoever follows the right path persistently, not whoever swears an allegiance and then deviates from it.

In conclusion, Ibn 'Alwān should not be thought of as rejecting the Sufi *khirqa* per se. Rather, his argument revolved around clarifying the misconception of his fellow brothers. He wanted to free them from the sense of commitment to a specific order or Sufi shaykh. His overall discussion did not presuppose his allegiance to a particular Sufi view. Finally, Ibn 'Alwān's description of the master/disciple relationship stems from his profound perception of the Qur'ān and the Sunna, as is evident in his extensive use of citations.

Sufi Knowledge (*ma'rifa*)

In Ibn 'Alwān's view intuitive knowledge (*ma'rifa*) was a necessity for the disciple. Like many Sufi scholars as well as ancient and medieval philosophers, Ibn 'Alwān classified Sufi knowledge, or "gnosis" (*ma'rifa*), into three types: knowledge of divine essence, knowledge of divine attributes, and knowledge of divine actions. This classification is based on Ibn 'Alwān's response to a question posed to him by a contemporaneous scholar, Sharaf ad-Dīn Hasan al-'Ajamī. Ibn 'Alwān began by saying that knowledge of divine essence is the most honorable and highest form of knowledge. However, its field is narrow, its meditative grasp is arduous, and it eludes rational discussion. For this reason it is said: "Meditate on the graces of God, but do not meditate on God."[36] The discussion of this knowledge, argues Ibn 'Alwān, entails investigating knowledge of transcendence (*tanzīh*), glorification, absolute sanctity, and knowledge of eternal existence. This latter includes knowledge of Oneness (*aḥadiyya*), everlasting-ness (*ṣamadiyya*), divinity (*ilāhiyya*), pre-eternity (*azaliyya*), eternity (*abadiyya*), self-subsistence (*qayyūmiyya*), and sanctity (*qaddūsiyya*). For further elaboration, Ibn 'Alwān asks the reader to consider the following lines of poetry:

Divine majesty that cannot be described by the intellects (*'uqūl*)
A sanctity, which neither changes nor ends
The attributes of essence are highly sanctified
An attempt to comprehend them leads to total bewilderment.[37]

In what follows, Ibn 'Alwān's explanation becomes enigmatic. He cites famous theological statements to show the difficulty of understanding divine essence. These statements, like intellectual puzzles, are as follows: "The inability to attain attainment is [by itself] an attainment" (*al-'ajz 'an darak al-idrāk idrāk*). "The claim of understanding by means of the sensual senses is polytheism" (*da'wā al-idrāk bi-ḥawās al-ḥiss ishrāk*). "Cutting off desire in the essence of knowledge is obstruction" (*qaṭ' aṭṭama' fī aṣl al-ma'rifa ta'ṭīl*). "The claim to have perfect knowledge—which comes from imagination—is anthropomorphism" (*da'wā kamāl al-ma'rifa min al-khayāl tashbīh wa tamthīl*). Afterward, Ibn 'Alwān admonishes his reader to accept, with full certainty, God's existence without anthropomorphism and to be confident in the divine greatness, sanctity, and transcendence because no one knows God, in reality, except God. Since this fine point is ambiguous, Ibn 'Alwān resorts to poetry to express his feelings on divine love:

The most painful condition of love I have encountered is the
  closeness of the beloved, but there is no way to reach Him.
This is similar to she-camels in the desert:
They get very thirsty while they carry water on their backs.[38]

Ibn 'Alwān concludes his discussion of the knowledge of essence by saying that linguistic expressions have been exhausted, mystical signs (*ishārāt*) have failed, and there is no way to describe that state. Only those who taste will know and those who turn away are ignorant.

Ibn 'Alwān then proceeds to discuss the knowledge of divine attributes. He states that its scope is larger, and discussion of such knowledge with both scholars and non-experts is allowed. According to Ibn 'Alwān, knowledge of divine attributes is mentioned in the Qur'ān and Sunna, and this knowledge is discussed by the knowers of God (*al-'ulamā' bi Allāh*). Examples of God's attributes are knowledge, power, will, life, wisdom, speech, hearing, and seeing. These attributes, Ibn 'Alwān argues, do not resemble in any way human attributes because God's essence does not resemble human essence. Ibn 'Alwān warns people not to worship these attributes because it is similar to idol worship. Nevertheless, Ibn 'Alwān distinguishes between the worship of individual divine attributes and knowing the mystical meanings of these attributes. He cites the following *ḥadīth* in support of his argument: "God has ninety-nine names; whoever counts them, enters Paradise."[39] Ibn 'Alwān comments on this *ḥadīth* by saying that some scholars interpreted the phrase "counts them" as to mean, "whoever knows their meaning." He concludes his discussion of God's attributes by saying that whoever knows the meaning of the divine names will know the origin of knowledge.

As for the knowledge of divine actions, Ibn 'Alwān argues that it is infinite. Examples of this knowledge are the tablet, the pen, the throne, the seat, paradise, hell, heavens and earth, angels and holy spirits, human beings and the jinn, Satans, Yajūj and Majūj, the world of images, the world of the known and the unknown, the world of changeable empirical appearances (*mulk*), the world of divine sovereignty (*al-malakūt*), and the world of life and the hereafter. It was said, Ibn 'Alwān states, that God has forty thousand or eighty thousand worlds; this universe is only one world, as God says: "None knows the armies of your Lord save Himself." Reflecting on this idea, Ibn 'Alwān quotes anonymous lines of poetry to convey his awe of God's greatness:

> Oh what a wonder, how the Lord is disobeyed!
> Or how could the unbeliever deny Him!
> For in everything there is a sign
> To indicate that He is the One.[40]

Finally, Ibn 'Alwān writes that there is no existence except for God and His actions, His actions are His predetermination of events (*maqdūrāt*), and His knowledge is endless. This doctrine might be read as a combination of monism, which maintains that there is only one entity of existence, and Ibn 'Arabī's theory of the "unity of being" (*waḥdat al-wujūd*) that entails God and his names. The difference is that Ibn 'Alwān's notion of existence is one ultimate reality manifested in the form of actions, which are predestined events, carried out by human beings. Ibn 'Alwān clarifies this doctrine by specifying the meaning of divine action, which constitutes all happenings in the world. Ibn 'Alwān concludes his argument with the following verses: "Say: If the ocean were ink (wherewith to write out) the words of my Lord, sooner would the ocean be exhausted than would the words of my Lord come to end, even if we brought another ocean like it, for its aid" (18:109); "My Lord comprehends in His knowledge everything" (6:80); "And not even a little of His knowledge can they grasp except what He will. His seat extends over heavens and the earth" (2:255); "And that you have been given but little knowledge" (17:85). Again, Ibn 'Alwān's thorough use of citations from the Qur'ān and Sunna emphasizes that his Sufism is firmly rooted in Islamic teachings. Moreover, his discourse rests on the Qur'ānic notion of God's uniqueness and absolute transcendence.

In his *al-Baḥr al-mushakkal al-gharīb*, Ibn 'Alwān's main focus is explaining divine knowledge. He provides numerous examples of approaches to divine knowledge. He talks about the fluctuation of the knower (*'ārif*) in the early stages of his quest as well as his ultimate goals. He discusses the preconditions of acquiring divine knowledge and the means of preserving it. In one example of Ibn 'Alwān's discussion he invites his disciple (*murīd*) to enter the path of the knower, and to achieve this one must know the bestower of bounty (*al-mun'im*), know his bounty (*an-ni'ma*), and know the enemy of both—that is, *al-mun'im* and *an-ni'ma*. If the disciple masters all this, Ibn 'Alwān argues, he will achieve his goal. For instance, the *murīd*—as a result of knowing the first type—receives "love" from the bestower of bounty; this leads to longing that in turn engenders "turning away from sin" (*ināba*). Then, the disciple will be grateful to the bounty, a feeling that engenders increase in knowledge. However, if the disciple comes to know the enemy of the bestower of bounty and the bounty, he will fear, and this leads to caution and good manners (*irab* or *adab*). As soon as the disciple realizes these three recommendations, he will be able to experience "the sweetness of God's service and the fruit of worship … and his heart will be lit with the light of knowledge."[41] Ibn 'Alwān maintains that this condition can be perpetuated by acts of obedience.

If the novice is not capable of experiencing these thoughts, he should know that his heart has hardened (*qāsī*). However, he can overcome this state (*qasāwa*) by avoiding the following sins: eating to excess, being unjust to others, delaying the times of prayers, and eating or drinking with the left hand. Immediately after clarifying the path to God, Ibn 'Alwān explains the reasons for the hardening of a heart. These are eating abundantly, conversing abundantly, laughing abundantly, sleeping abundantly, and worrying abundantly about one's nourishment. If one avoids these pitfalls, Ibn 'Alwān states, his heart is likely to revive. If one's heart is hardened, one should seek the light of knowledge by reading persistently the chapter of pure faith (*al-Ikhlāṣ*), eating little, keeping company with people of knowledge, eating the plants of the desert, and performing the night prayer. If the seeker of mystical knowledge follows these recommendations, he will find the sweetness of God's service and the fruit of worship. In addition, the trees of passionate longing for God, love, renunciation, contentment, and repentance (*ināba*) will spontaneously spring up in his heart.[42] If the follower, after making every effort possible, does not experience what has been described to him, he should know that his heart is barren. In order to revive his heart and allow the trees of knowledge to grow, he must put an end to the hardness of his heart by accompanying scholars (*'ulamā'*), tapping orphans on their shoulders (that is, paying attention to their needs), asking God's forgiveness in the early morning before dawn, abandoning evening and nighttime conversations, and fasting during the day.

Ibn 'Alwān concludes his narrative by asserting that all these Sufi thoughts were advised by the Prophet. In other words, Ibn 'Alwān's discussion stems from his understanding and interpretation of the Prophetic tradition. He then addresses the disciple by saying,

> If you follow these teachings and continue to do so, it is hoped that the orchard of knowledge will enter you[r mind]… and when it becomes visible to you, you should know that it has a spacious mansion, and you should employ every conceivable means to enter it with the intention to accomplish five steps: confirming without repudiation (*iqrār bilā juḥūd*), witnessing without denial (*shahāda bilā inkār*), religion without vacillation (*dīn bilā taraddud*), submission without doubt (*Islām bilā tashkīk*), and determination without alteration (*taqrīr bilā ta'dīl*). If these things come to dwell in you, then you are in the field of *ma'rifa,* which has trees, rivers, and fruits.[43]

Ibn 'Alwān warns that if one takes up the axe of disobedience, he will demolish the wall of knowledge and cut down the trees of God's love and longing. Consequently, God's aversion and curse will descend upon him, and God will neglect him through separation and alienation. Finally, Ibn 'Alwān discusses the meaning of the "trees, rivers, and fruits" until he warns the servant of God against sin. If the servant's knowledge is original, God will inspire him to repent, but if it is transitory, he will continue sinning until the light of knowledge abandons him and he is expelled from the court of happiness to the court of misery.

Unveiling (*kashf*) in the Sufi Tradition

Although there are three different levels of Sufi knowledge—divine irradiation (*tajallī*), direct witnessing (*mushāhada*), and unveiling (*kashf*)—the latter has the widest currency in Sufi literature and is often a synonym for the other two. *Kashf* was defined by al-Jurjānī (d. 816/1413), and it denotes "the act of lifting and tearing away the veil [which comes between man and the extra-phenomenal world]." As a technical term, it means, "to reveal in a complete and actual realization the mysterious meanings and realities which are hidden behind the veil."[44] In the Qur'ān, the verb *kashafa* occurs several times in the sense "to uncover"—that is, to remove misfortune, evil, danger, and torment. Nevertheless, two Qur'ānic verses were the basis of future elaborations along mystical lines: "We have lifted your veil (*kashafnā*), and today your sight is sharp" (50:22); and, "What is to come is imminent. There is no one to unveil it apart from God" (53:57–58). The experience of *kashf* brings about *mukāshafa*, which means unveiling in the sense of illumination or epiphany. These two notions are the antonyms of veiling (*satr*) or concealment (*istitār*), which imply the act of being banned from the knowledge of divine mystery and, eventually, of God.[45]

At the time of al-Hallāj, Sufi texts perceived "divine self-revelation" or "divine irradiation" (*tajallī*) as a synonym of unveiling (*kashf*). Al-Kalābādhī (d. 380/990) distinguished three types of *tajallī*: "revelation of the essence, which is unveiling (*kashf*), revelation of the attributes of the essence, which is illumination, revelation of the attribute (*ḥukm*) of the essence, which is the hereafter."[46] This idea was further elaborated in *ar-Risāla al-qushayriyya* by 'Abd al-Karīm al-Qushayrī (d. 465/1072), who identified three stages in the progression toward the reality. The first is the mystic, who positions himself vis-à-vis the objective he aspires to [i.e., God] (*muḥāḍara*). The path seeker in the state of *muḥāḍara* remains "behind the veil" due to his reliance on discursive proof (*burhān*) and the distraction of his intellect (*'aql*).[47] In other words, without God's support through His signs (*āyāt*), the mystic may not perceive God. The second stage, according to al-Qushayrī, is the uncovering of the veil (*mukāshafa*). At this stage, the seeker no longer searches for the path because discursive reasoning (*burhān*) gives way to evidential proof (*bayān*), and the indirect signs of God overshadow His attributes. Nevertheless, this remains an intermediary stage before the curtain is partially raised to uncover the divine mystery. This will lead the seeker to the third stage, the direct vision (*mushāhada*), where he no longer needs the mediation of proof because he is placed in the "presence of the Reality" (*ḥaqīqa*).

Another example of Sufi elaboration of the term *kashf* is the classification provided by the famous Ḥanbalī Sufi of Herat 'Abdallāh al-Ansārī (d. 481/1089). He described *kashf* and *mukāshafa* as a preliminary stage before the ultimate divine illumination. In *Manāzil as-sā'irīn*, al-Ansārī describes each "halting-place" (*manzil*) as having three progressive degrees. The first is "the knowledge of certainty" (*'ilm al-yaqīn*), which is the acceptance of the Word of God. The second is "visual certainty" (*'ayn al-yaqīn*), which goes beyond verbal argument. The third is "real certainty" (*ḥaqq al-yaqīn*), which marks the utmost level of realization.

Almost all Sufi writers depict *kashf* as a lightning-flash that permits the mystic to penetrate the world of mystery. There is no need for any kind of proof because God's "evidential proof" (*bayān*) is attained. It is no surprise that *mukāshafa* was defined as "a state [of divine presence] which *bayān* cannot in any way describe."[48] *Kashf* and *mukāshafa* are closely connected to the superior worlds of invincibility, or "divine majesty" (*jabarūt*) and "divine sovereignty" (*malakūt*), which lie beyond the appearances of the empirical world (*mulk*). The significance of the concept of *kashf* appears in the titles of Sufi works such as "The Unveiling of the Hidden" (*Kashf al-maḥjūb*) by 'Alī b. 'Uthmān al-Hujwīrī (d. 465/1073 or 469/1077), "The Unveiling of the Hearts" (*Mukāshafat al-qulūb*) by al-Ghazālī (d. 505/1111), and others. For al-Hujwīrī, the mystic's advancement toward the hidden true reality can be achieved through a progressive removal of veils. The raising of the veil will constitute the supreme state of enjoyment in paradise. In other words, the mystic will experience the state of *kashf* through which the miracles of saints (*karāmāt*) become possible. For example, the mystic in the state of *kashf* is able to read the thoughts of his disciples and to predict the future.[49] For al-Ghazālī, *kashf* establishes the basis of genuine knowledge (*yaqīn*) as opposed to acquired knowledge (*taqlīd*). The term "*kashf*" occurs frequently in al-Ghazālī's works such as "The Revival of Religious Sciences" (*Iḥyā' 'ulūm ad-dīn)*, "The Economy in Faith" (*Iqtiṣād fī al-i'tiqād*), "The Deliverance from Error" (*al-Munqidh min aḍ-ḍalāl)*, "The Niche of Lights" (*Mishkāt al-anwār*), "The Unveiling of Hearts"

(*Mukāshafat al-qulūb*), and others. In his *al-Munqidh min aḍ-ḍalāl*, al-Ghazālī discusses the notion of *kashf* by comparing it with the light (*nūr*) that God places in the hearts of His friends. Moreover, he distinguishes between knowledge of ritual observances, social customs, jurisprudence, and ethical rules (*'ulūm al-mu'āmala*) and the knowledge of the absolute truth (*'ulūm al-mukāshafa*). The latter belongs to "the sincerest ones" (*siddīqūn*) and "those who are close to God" (*muqarrabūn*). This knowledge does not stem from argumentation or from simple acceptance but is an intuitive and sure grasping of God's knowledge. According to al-Ghazālī, "by *'ilm al-mukāshafa* we mean the pulling aside of the veil so that the Real One shows Himself in all His splendor; this is effected with a clarity which sets the object right before the eyes, without any possible grounds for doubt."[50] For al-Ghazālī, *kashf* is a light, a given grace from God, which shines in the heart when it is purified from its reprehensible qualities and, in turn, grants its possessor a sure knowledge of God.[51]

Ibn 'Alwān's View on *Kashf*

Ibn 'Alwān opens his discussion of *kashf* by distinguishing it from the categories of Islamic duties. Muslims are not required to attain the state of *kashf* because it is the bequest of sincerity and religious striving (*mujāhada*). *Mujāhada* itself is not necessarily a stipulation to attain *kashf* because, like sustenance (*rizq*), it can come with or without cause. "This is the bounty of God; He gives it to whomsoever He pleases. God is master of great bounty."[52] Ibn 'Alwān then defines *kashf* in theological and mystical terms. In *at-Tawḥīd*, he provides the theological definition of *kashf* as, "the state of observing, by means of discursive proof, the mysteries of Satan's plotting."[53] In *al-Ajwiba al-lā'iqa*, he defines *kashf* mystically as God's unmediated revelation of His mysteries to His prophets and saints.[54] In other words, this knowledge is intuitive, does not require a cause, and inaccessible to the intellect (*al-'aql*). The Qur'ānic allusion to this type of knowledge can be drawn from the following verses in which God addresses the Prophet: "Then he drew near, and drew closer, and was at a distance of two bow-lengths or (even) nearer." (53:8–9) The allusion to this type of knowledge is revisited in poem 116 of *al-Futūḥ* where Ibn 'Alwān portrays the image of the coming closer to God and the Prophet. "He drew from the nearness of our closeness without width and without length. Neither low nor high; neither did he say it nor was it said. He revealed to him what He revealed like a subject to an object."[55] Clearly, these lines have an important message that refutes as anthropomorphic the majority of commentaries on the above Qur'ānic verses. Ibn 'Alwān, may God be pleased with him, showed that the image is free of the medium of space alluded to by words like width and height. In addition, the dialogue between the Prophet and God is attained without the medium of language. There is the language of divine revelation that cannot be subjected to human reasoning. Perhaps the poetic lines of Ibn 'Alwān need to be understood in the same way without falling into anthropomorphism.

In a similar vein, with respect to the intuitive knowledge of the "saint" (*walī*), Ibn 'Alwān cites the following verse: "Then they found one of our servants upon whom We had bestowed mercy from Ourselves and whom We had taught knowledge from Us" (18:65). This shows Ibn 'Alwān's dependence on the Qur'ān and the Sunna. He conveys to the reader that his affiliation with Sufism is derived from Islamic instruction, rather than foreign influence. The requirements (*adāb*) of *kashf*, according to Ibn 'Alwān, are a sincere and firm will (*'azīma*), persistence with God, and looking to none other than Him. For "neither did sight falter nor exceed the bounds" (53:17). Ibn 'Alwān argues that the person who reaches this, the highest station of knowledge, is a knower of God and is assisted by God in all his undertakings. The seeker is engulfed by divine majesty, his eyes are filled with the illumination of beauty, his characteristics are obliterated, and his mention is expunged from this world and the next (*al-kawnayn*). All individuals at this station are completely effaced except prophets and God's closest friends, whom God allows to return to this world for the purpose of preaching.[56] The returnee is honored by the qualities of God, so he hears by God and sees by God. He walks among God's creatures with the light of God, calling to God, and looking at God with the eye of God. Nothing obstructs him from God. Describing his state is difficult because his image has been transformed, in accordance with the Qur'ānic verse that addressed the Prophet: "Those who swear allegiance to you indeed swear allegiance to God" (48:10). Likewise, the Qur'ānic story of the *walī* who performed strange acts, such as making a hole in a ship and killing an innocent boy, while accompanying the Prophet Moses is another example of image transformation. Those acts were performed according to divine instructions, as the Qur'ān says: "So I did not do that of my own accord"(18:82). Ibn 'Alwān alluded to this transformation in Poem 229 of *al-Futūḥ*: "Until I am shown out of my intoxication and drunkenness, if you are mentioned I am with you. Thus, my occultation and bewilderment befall me, and the strings of my mind are rolled up. Then, my figure is transformed to other than my figure and my spirit is guided to your sublimity."[57]

Ibn 'Alwān concludes his discussion of *kashf* by saying that if God loves a person, He paves the way for him by guiding him to a master. Without a master, the disciple will encounter difficulties and impediments that will prevent him from attaining the goal of his mystical quest. Therefore, he is advised to have an accompanying fellow before embarking on the path. This does not contradict his view that a disciple may manage without a master in his quest for divine knowledge if he or she follows the teachings of the Qur'ān and Sunna.

Al-Fanā' and *al-Baqā'*

Since the goal of a mystical quest differs among religious traditions and mystical schools, I shall confine myself here to doctrines from the classical period of early Islamic mysticism, namely, the passing away (*fanā'*) and the survival or subsistence in God (*baqā'*), along with Ibn 'Alwān's views. The Sufi doctrine of passing away, or annihilation (*fanā'*) of human attributes through union with God, is usually a reflection of the verse: "Everything upon the earth passes away. And there survives the face of your Lord (with grandeur and glory)."[58] Beginning in the work of Abū Yazīd al-Bistāmī (d. 234/848 or 261/875) the doctrine of *fanā'*, along with *baqā'* (survival or continuance in God), assumed a central position in Sufi theory.[59] Al-Junayd of Baghdad (d. 298/910) developed the doctrine of *fanā'/baqā'* into an integral part of well-coordinated mystical insight.[60] When describing Sufism, al-Junayd says: "God should cause you to die to yourself and to live in Him." This dying-to-self is the meaning of *fanā'*, whereas "life in Him" is *baqā'*. Al-Junayd and his followers treated the experience of *fanā'/baqā'* as both antithetical and complementary. They are more or less similar pairs that portray the mystical vision of God and the world, namely, intoxication (*sukr*) and sobriety (*ṣaḥw*), unity (*jam'*) and separation (*tafriqa*), negation (*nafy*) and affirmation (*ithbāt*), unity (*waḥda*) and plurality (*kathra*), and the like.[61]

In his description of the mystical path, Ibn 'Alwān provided a new interpretation of *fanā'/baqā'*. He states, "If God descends upon you from within yourself, He will isolate you from the authority over yourself. When you lose control over yourself, He will provide you with the state of self-sufficiency. When you become self-sufficient [needing neither acts of obedience nor the help of others], He will annihilate you within His existence so that you will see neither your existing self nor other human beings. When the complete passing away is consummated, He will appear in your essence and in your attributes, becoming your hearing (by which you hear), your sight (by which you see), your tongue (by which you speak), your hand (by which you strike), your foot (by which you walk), and your spirit (by which you live). Then you become one of His houses—that is, one of the hearts—which contains Him."[62]

That God resides in the loving heart is expressed by another favorite *ḥadīth*: "Heaven and earth contain Me not, but the heart of my faithful servant contains Me." According to Annemarie Schimmel, the heart is the dwelling place of God, or, the mirror in which God reflects Himself. This mirror has to be polished by constant asceticism and acts of loving obedience until it can reflect primordial divine light.[63] In Ibn 'Alwān's view, the discussion of the doctrine of *fanā'/baqā'* is nothing but a one-sided interpretation of the Qur'ānic verses beginning, "Say O the Lord of all dominions."[64] This is another piece of evidence that Ibn 'Alwān is consistent in his reliance on the guidance of the Qur'ān and the Sunna.

In his analysis of *fanā'/baqā'* as a sign of divine love, Ibn 'Alwān writes:

> You have become the place of myself,
> You have made me pass away.
> There is no hearing except You who are my hearing
> There is no eye except You who are my eye.[65]

In another poem, Ibn 'Alwān describes the state of *fanā'* at which he and his Lover become one:

> My eyes do not sleep and neither do Yours
> My ecstasy (*wajd*) because of You has never disappeared
> and neither has Yours.
> So You are our secrets, but even more so You are our essence.
> And we are Your secrets but even more so we are You.[66]

It is appropriate to note A. J. Arberry's observations on *fanā'*, which are similar to those presented by Ibn 'Alwān. Arberry says: "By passing away from self the mystic does not cease to exist, in the true sense of existence, as an individual, rather his individuality, which is an inalienable gift from God, is perfected, transmuted and eternalized through God and in God."[67] On the one hand, despite the continuity of Sufi claims—especially in their poetry, as seen in verses by Ibn 'Alwān—to have achieved union with God, subsequent theorists of Sufism reached a consensus that such claims do not necessarily presuppose a fusion between human and divine essences, or even a dissolution of the temporal human ego in God. Instead, they developed two acceptable definitions of *fanā'*: first, the annihilation of all things from the consciousness of the mystic, including himself, and the supplanting of this experiential vacuum with a pure consciousness of God; second, the passing away of the creature's imperfect attributes to be replaced by perfect attributes bestowed by God.[68] On the other hand, Sufi theorists describe *baqā'* as an individual's persistence in the new divinely bestowed attributes (*baqā' bi'llāh*), and the mystic's regained consciousness of the created world's plurality. The second complements the first in that being with God entails being with the world, which was created by God and in which God continues to manifest Himself in a variety of forms.[69] Sufis tend to believe that the state of *baqā'* is more perfect than that of *fanā'*. We have already seen Ibn 'Alwān's preference for the state of *baqā'* when he dealt with the episode of *kashf*. He argues that only the select among prophets and friends of God (*awliyā'*) may return to this world with the help of God, after they have been obliterated by the illumination of divine majesty.[70] God selects them to communicate their precious new experiences "to the uninitiated in order to alert them to the beauty of a life that is graced by divine presence."[71] Sufi teachings often distinguish between mystic and prophetic consciousness in the doctrine of *baqā'*. Whereas the ordinary mystic stops at *fanā'*, the prophet lives with both God and the world to implement religio-moral divine truth. This is exemplified by al-Hallāj, who, as discussed in the previous chapter, was tempted to dwell on unified vision and rapture while Ibn 'Alwān went beyond this state—as a paradigmatic mystic, not as a prophet—to enter the state of *baqā'*.

Ibn 'Alwān reached a rare state among Sufi masters in that he experienced the duality of *fanā'/baqā'* simultaneously. Normally, the mystic experiences *fanā'* first and if he is successful, God transfers him to the state of *baqā'*. Ibn 'Alwān's consciousness was supplanted with a pure one of God while he remained an ordinary human being who lived a normal life with his disciples and family. This duality let him avoid being trapped in the state of *fanā'* like al-Hallāj.

Ḥulūl and *Ittiḥād*

Two additional concepts found in Sufi literature—mystical union (*ittiḥād*) and incarnation (*ḥulūl*)—also were considered by Ibn 'Alwān. In Sufi terminology, *ittiḥād* denotes the theory of mystical union between creature and Creator or the theory that holds such a union possible. The parallel doctrine is *ḥulūl,* according to which the Creator is incarnated in the creature. Some scholars (*'ulamā'*) consider these doctrines, which put God on an equal footing with His servant, heretical because they are inconsistent with the notion of divine transcendence.[72] Ibn 'Alwān addressed these two concepts in his literary works. In a poem about mystical union (*ittiḥād*) he says:

> How excellent the lovers are!
> How glorious and proud their ways and doctrines are!
> If one sleeps, the other stays awake to guard him;
> If one does not fast, the other will fast for him.
> If one becomes weak, the other carries his burden.
> If a concern (*hamm*) has seized one, the other will assuage it.
> How astonishing for two to become one!
> If they are described as two, nothing will change.
> They both have affinity with each other.
> Each one sees by the eye of the other.
> Each one hears what is said by the other's hearing.
> So that each will accept what is acceptable and reject what is wrong.
> If one says something, the other says the same thing
> And implies the same meaning, whether speaking or reading.
> If this one strikes with a hand, the other follows suit with the same hand.
> If this one walks, the other walks; and if this one runs, the other runs.[73]

Although this poem seems identical to the Sufi concept of mystical union (*ittiḥād*), Ibn 'Alwān should be understood in the context of his overall position vis-à-vis heretical doctrines. We saw earlier his reaction against Sufi excess, especially against those who despised paradise.[74] In his view, they were not only disrespecting heaven, but also desiring companionship with the Lord of worshippers, and demanding mystical union (*ittiḥād*) with God by a different approach and through different mediators (*zumra ghayr zumratih*). In his censure against such Sufis, Ibn 'Alwān strongly refuted their ridiculing of the joy of heaven by reminding them that the Prophet used to say to his companions: "Ask God to grant me the *wasīla.*" They said: "Oh messenger of God, what is the *wasīla*?" The Prophet replied, "It is a house at the zenith of Heaven; none will live in it except one man, and I hope that I will be that man."[75]

Another version of this *ḥadīth* is reported in *Nayl al-awṭār* by Muhammad ash-Shawkānī (d. 1834/1250), an expert on *ḥadīth*, on the authority of 'Abd Allāh b. 'Amr who heard the Prophet, may God grant him and his family peace and blessings, say: "If you hear the call for prayer (*al-mū'adhdhin*), then say as he says and ask God to pray for me. For whoever prays for me, God will pray ten times for him. Then, ask of God the *wasīla* for me because it is a rank in heaven that it is not obliged except for one of the servants of God, and I hope to be that one. So whoever asks of God the *wasīla* for me, the intercession is granted to him."[76] Furthermore, Ibn 'Alwān pointed out that heaven is the ultimate realm and the highest order of existence. There is no ascension above it except for the majesty of God, Who has neither companion nor friend because He is Alone and the Only One. He spoke so about Himself in the Qur'ān: "Say: He is God the One and Only; God the Eternal Absolute. He begets not, nor is He begotten; and there is none like unto Him."[77]

Nevertheless, Ibn 'Alwān's critical attack is based on his perception that the only way to attain mystical union with God is through the rites and injunctions of Islam, and drawing near to God through supererogatory acts of piety. When God loves the servant, he hears by God's hearing, sees by God's eye, strikes by God's hand, and walks by God's foot. This is the type of divine-human transformation Ibn 'Alwān constantly refers to. The implication is that the Sufi concept of "unified fusion" with God is possible, but not in just any manner. Rather, it has to be by the right path: the path of the Prophet, his companions, and the friends of God. This encompasses the repetition of *dhikr*, constant meditation, and keeping company with Sufis and scholars of revealed law until one reaches mystical union with God (*al-ḥadd al-muttaḥid bi'l-wāḥid*). In this state, the mystic's human attributes pass away, his heart becomes tranquil in God's presence, his eye fixed on His face, his ears attuned to His speech, and his spirit happy to meet Him.[78]

In the following poem Ibn 'Alwān discusses incarnation (*ḥulūl*):

Oh the people of our love
We have enjoyed your company and so have you.
What you say is narrated to us
What we say is narrated to you.
The exhaustion here is that exhaustion
And the tiredness is that tiredness
You and we, through love, have become
[As] water and wine in a vessel

So your water is from our sea
And your wine is from our grape
We are not other than You
You are not other than us.
A lover called his beloved
Who is living inside him.
So listen to the astonishing summons
Two twigs have become one
If this says: "Oh I," the other says: "Oh I"
This is a sign of two spirits that reside in a single body.[79]

This poem echoes the ecstatic outbursts of al-Hallāj, particularly when he said: "Thy spirit has mingled itself with my spirit as amber mixes with fragrant musk"; "We are two spirits that reside (*ḥalalnā*) in a single body."[80] However, does Ibn 'Alwān mean the union of the two substances, the human (*nāsūt*) and the divine (*lāhūt*)? On the contrary, he means the union of human will and divine will. For him this union is an act of faith and love, in which the lover and the beloved remain intensely aware of both themselves and the other. Here is another example of ecstatic outbursts in Ibn 'Alwān's poetry:

Taste oh my lover the love of the beloved
From the wine of my glass [which] is hidden and untouched
Wine is my gaze and intoxication is my word
I rule over people with the *kāf* and *nūn* [be].[81]

The last line portrays the state of spiritual union Ibn 'Alwān experienced in which God witnesses Himself in his heart, for God is far too exalted to dwell within the corporeal body of Ibn 'Alwān or anyone else. Again, the Qur'ān and the Sunna are the sources for his mystical inspiration. He reached the highest stage of mystical love with God not only because he fulfilled his religious duties, but also because he paid close attention to the underlying motives of his actions. He accomplished this goal through meticulous meditation on the Qur'ān, thorough imitation of the Prophet's piety, and the performance of obedience to God in excess of what is obligatory.

Conclusion

It is almost impossible to trace every complex aspect of Ibn 'Alwān's intellectual universe, but this chapter has dealt with the most important keynotes of his Sufi thought. Like many Sufi masters and practitioners, Ibn 'Alwān places himself squarely in the mainstream of Islam by basing all his teachings upon the Qur'ān and the Sunna. His *at-Tawḥīd* and other works are, in fact, nothing but commentaries upon the Qur'ān and the Sunna. It is unquestionable that Ibn 'Alwān read Sufi literature before him but occasionally left the reader uninformed of his sources. This conformed with generic Sufi practices of his time, for all he said was "in the air," that is, circulating in the intellectual climate of his day. That said, he quoted the Sufi practitioners of early Islamic mysticism such as al-Bisṭāmī (d. 234/848 or 261/875), al-Ḥallāj (d. 309/922), an-Niffarī (d. 367/977), and reached as far as al-Ghazālī (d. 505/1111), but no one beyond. It may also have been true that Ibn 'Alwān's vision was a mixture of earlier Sufi literature and his own personal mystical experience. Nonetheless, he helped shape a distinctive Yemeni Sufi tradition. For all this, he should be regarded as an original thinker who developed Sufi literature and presented concepts in a pure image to premodern Yemeni society.

As I have shown throughout this chapter, the doctrine of "union with God" in Ibn 'Alwān's work took different shapes due to the diversity of the mystic path. Ibn 'Alwān admitted the possibility of mystical union with God, but with some restrictions: if the path seeker followed the teachings of the Qur'ān, assimilated the exemplary piety of the Prophet, pursued the practice of the companions, and followed in the footsteps of the friends of God, then, he would be more likely to attain mystical union with God.

When the traveler to God reaches this stage of union, he becomes a friend of God or a "saint" in Christian terminology.[82] The concept of friendship with God (*walāya*) is a central theme in the Sufi tradition, and in the following chapter we move from our in-depth reading of Ibn 'Alwān's thought to shed some light on the concept of *walāya* and its relevance to the popular beliefs that spring from tomb venerations and miracles (*karāmāt*). In so doing, we shift our focus to explore Ibn 'Alwān's place in Yemeni tradition after his death, the veneration of his miracles in Yemeni literature, and the debates on Islamic practice that continued into the twentieth century.

Image 2. Ibn 'Alwān's tomb renovated and covered by a cloth. The disputed date of his birth is given in A.H.

7

THE ISLAMIC CONCEPT OF SAINTHOOD AND IBN 'ALWĀN AS A SAINT

In the following chapter I provide a brief description of the Islamic concept of "*walī*" and a critical analysis of its images as constructed by hagiographical works. I approach the debate surrounding saintly miracles (*karāmāt*) through the works of two Yemeni scholars from two different periods in history. Medieval scholar ash-Sharjī (d. 893/1487) wrote particularly on Yemen's saints and Sufis, including Ibn 'Alwān, arguing for the acceptance of *karāmāt* and the reinterpretation of early Islamic figures as proto-Sufis. Nineteenth-century scholar ash-Shawkānī (d. 1250/1834) likewise argued for *karāmāt* if they do not contradict revealed law, emphasizing God's presence behind all acts. After a review of Ibn 'Alwān's sainthood in Yemeni literature I turn to the controversy surrounding his tomb and the cult of saints in general.

This controversy came to a head at the turn of the nineteenth century when a newly powerful Wahhābīst movement condemned the cult of saints as polytheism and called for the destruction of saints' tombs. Yemeni scholars including ash-Shawkānī and Ibn al-Amīr aṣ-Ṣan'ānī first supported this movement but later opposed it. I explore the reasons for these changing alliances, and in so doing come to grips with a formative debate for Yemeni Islam in the modern period. Finally, I examine the reasons for and eventual responses to the destruction of Ibn 'Alwān's tomb in 1942, an act that polarized Yemeni society between reformists and traditionalists.

Walāya as Muslim Sainthood

The term "*walī*" derives from the Arabic root *walā',* to be near or close, and the verb *waliya* means to govern and protect someone. Therefore, *walī* means protector, benefactor, companion, near relative, and friend. In the Qur'ān, the term *walī* has several meanings: that of a near relative whose murder demands vengeance (17:33), that of a friend or ally of God (10:62); and God Himself ("God is the friend of those who believe" [2:257]). The same title was given to the Prophet and it is one of the names of God in the Muslim rosary.[1] Al-Jurjānī (d. 816/1413) defines *walī* in his *at-Ta'rīfāt* as equivalent to *'ārif bi'llāh* (he who possesses knowledge, he who knows God).[2] Other writers, such as the great Egyptian biographer and *ḥadith* scholar Ibn Ḥajar al-'Asqalānī (d. 852/1449), give the same definition. In the Islamic Middle Period, grammarians and Sufis debated the question of whether *walāya* or *wilāya* was the "correct" verbal noun of *walī.* The prevailing opinion was that "*wilāya*" connotes authority, whereas "*walāya*" connotes closeness to God. Suffice it to say that these terms are semantic twins that coexist, and each relies on the other for its meaning. I use *walāya* to express "Muslim sainthood."[3]

Attitudes toward *Karāmāt*

No discussion of Islamic sainthood is complete without a full understanding of saintly miracles (*karāmāt*), which, according to Maribel Fierro, are treated in four predominant ways in Islam: (1) The Mu'tazilites deny the reality of the *karāmāt* on the basis of Qur'ān (72:26–27) where it says that only God knows the unknown (*al-ghayb*) and that He grants such knowledge only to those whom he chooses as His messenger (*rasūl*). The problem was first raised by al-Jubbā'ī: if the *awliyā'* had the power of performing miracles, how could they be distinguished from the prophets? (2) The philosophers (*falāsifa*) do not see the miracles as gifts freely granted by God: the power of performing miracles is the outcome of the perfection that the soul achieves by virtue of its own nature. (3) The Ash'arites, in general, admitted the authenticity of the *karāmāt.* Miracles can be granted to people other than the prophets, as in the case of Maryam in the Qur'ānic verse (27:40). While for the prophets miracles are proof of their mission, miracles are granted to saints to honor them and confirm their piety. (4) The Sufis who do not fall into "extravagance" (*ghuluww*) adopt the same position as the Ash'arites, stressing that the saint who performs miracles must not be mistaken for a prophet and must submit himself to the religious law given to Muḥammad. Moreover, the saint who flaunts his miracles, such as al-Ḥallāj, can be suspected of making claims to prophethood. Some Sufi miracles are not proof of prophecy, for such proof is solely the mission given to the Prophet by God.[4]

Ash-Sharjī and *karāmāt*

In his *Ṭabaqāt al-khawāṣṣ*, the medieval hagiographer Aḥmad b. Aḥmad ash-Sharjī (d. 893/1487) provided a number of insights into the nature of saintly miracles (*karāmāt al-awliyā'*), supporting his argument with evidence from the Qur'ān and the Sunna. For instance, the Qur'ān informs us about the miracle of Mary with the following verse: "Whenever Zakariyā' came to see her in the chamber, he found her provided with sustenance. He said: 'O Mary, where has this come from?' And she said: 'From God'"(3:37). Ash-Sharjī elaborates on the meaning of this verse by relating the narrated account of the Prophet's interpretation: "Zakariyā' found in the chamber of Mary the fruits of winter in the summertime, and the fruits of the summer in the wintertime."[5] In a different *sura,* God talks directly to Mary: "And shake towards yourself the trunk of the palm-tree, it will drop ripe dates upon you" (19:25). Commenting on this verse, Muslim exegetes say that the dates were not ripe, but when they fell upon Mary they immediately became ripe. This explanation shows that Mary, though not a prophet, performed a saintly miracle (*karāma* pl. *karāmāt*). Ash-Sharjī adds that she received another miracle when she saw the angel Gabriel in the form of a human being.

Moreover, ash-Sharjī tried to locate a basis for the meaning of *karāmāt* in the transportation of Bilqīs's throne from Yemen to Jerusalem by a companion of Solomon, Āṣaf b. Barkhīyā, who, according to the Qur'ān, said: "I will bring it to you in the twinkling of an eye" (27:40). Ash-Sharjī and other Muslim scholars argued that neither Āṣaf b. Barkhīyā's nor Mary's miracles could be considered *mu'jizāt* because these can only be performed by prophets. *Mu'jizāt* are evidentiary miracles granted by God to the prophets as proof of their mission, accompanied by a claim of prophethood and a challenge (*taḥaddī*) to the audience. Whereas the miracles of the prophets should be known as widely as possible, saints should try earnestly to conceal their *karāmāt.*[6]

In the devotional language of Islam, *karāma* has come to mean an exhibition of God's generosity, favor, protection, and assistance toward anyone. In a special sense, *karāmāt* are the miraculous gifts and graces with which God surrounds, protects, and aids his saints.[7] Technically, *karāma* is the act of breaking an established custom. The general term for anything extraordinary is *kharq al-'āda.* According to Schimmel, "When God wants to disrupt the chain of cause and result to which we are accustomed, since He usually acts in this or that way, a *khāriqa* may be performed and change the course of life."[8] The difference between *karāma* and *ma'ūna* is that the latter may be granted by God to any

Muslim, including one who is devoid of special religious experience. *Karāma,* also, differs from *irhāṣ*, an anticipatory miracle worked for a prophet before his call, and from *istidrāj* and *iḥāna,* which lead unbelievers astray and bring them to shame.[9]

Ash-Sharjī provides a fair amount of evidence from the Sunna concerning *karāmāt al-awliyā'*. For instance, he cites the famous *ḥadīth* narrated in *aṣ-Ṣaḥīḥayn,* the two major Sunnī *ḥadīth* collections by al-Bukhārī (d. 257/870) and Muslim (d. 262/875), about those who spoke when they were only infants. Among them was Jurayj, who asked an infant about the name of his father. The infant in the cradle replied, "So and so, the shepherd." To speak as an infant from a cradle is considered a miraculous act (*karāma*), and Jurayj was endowed with the ability to recognize the infant and talk to him. Another example taken from the Sunna is the story of the people of a cave. A rock blocked the entrance of the cave so they could not get out, and so they made a supplication to God. God moved the rock, and they were rescued. Moreover, in the *ḥadīth* of the cow, the cow's owner put a burden on its back and the cow said, "I was not created for this."[10] Furthermore, the story of Usayd b. Ḥuḍayr reported in *Ṣaḥīḥ al-Bukhārī* is another proof of *karāmāt.* While he was reciting the *sura* of the cave, he saw a dark cloud (*ẓulla*) that drove his horse wild. He reported what happened to the Prophet, who explained the incident: "That was Divine Presence (*as-sakīna*) that came down upon you."[11]

Ash-Sharjī provided numerous instances of *karāmāt* to sustain the argument that *walāya* has its roots in the Qur'ān and the Sunna. He concluded that the Sunnī view advocates the concept of *karāmāt,* and the four Sunnī schools of law recognize it. The exceptions, ash-Sharjī argues, are the Mu'tazilites who rejected *karāmāt* as well as some other "heretics." One may add that despite the challenge of Aḥmad b. Taymiyya (d. 728/1328) against Sufi excesses, he admitted the existence of *karāmāt* as part of Sunnī doctrine. In *al-'Aqīda al-wāsiṭiyya,* he says:

> Belief in the miracles of saints (*karāmāt al-awliyā'*) and the supernatural acts which God achieves through them in all varieties of knowledge, inspirations (*mukāshafāt*), power, and impressions (as it is handed down about the ancient nations in *Surat al-Kahf* [that is, in Qur'ān 18] and in other Qur'ānic chapters, and as it is known about the early men of this community of believers among the companions and followers, and of the rest of the generations of this community of believers) is among the fundamental beliefs of

the people of the Sunna. It will be with them until the day of Resurrection.[12]

In his discussion, ash-Sharjī asks why *karāmāt* were reported about a later generation of Muslim saints (*awliyā'*), and not the companions of the Prophet. He asserts that the question had been answered long ago by Aḥmad b. Ḥanbal (d. 241/855), who argued that the faith of the companions was so solid that they did not need an incentive to increase their faith. However, the faith of the *awliyā'* was weaker than the companions', and consequently it had to be strengthened by *karāmāt.* In addition, the companions did not need *karāmāt* due to the blessings of the Prophet and their witnessing the revelation and angels. Their hearts were illuminated, so they renounced the world and saw by their insight the life to come. According to al-Qushayrī (d. 465/1072), every *karāma* granted to a follower of any prophet is considered a miracle for that prophet. Al-Qushayrī goes on to say that "*Karāmāt* can be an answer to a prayer, bringing food without preparation, finding water at a time of thirst, traveling a far distance in a short time, rescuing someone from an enemy, hearing a voice (*hātif*), or any such act that belongs to the phenomenon of breaking a custom."[13]

Ash-Sharjī's *Ṭabaqāt al-khawāṣṣ* is one of the most significant works of the *Ṭabaqāt* genre that deals with the *awliyā'* of Yemen. According to ash-Sharjī, he wrote his work because few books described the *awliyā'* of Yemen in particular. Ash-Sharjī said that he had read books that discussed the status of the *awliyā'* and their features, *karāmāt,* and virtuous deeds, such as *ar-Risāla* by Abū al-Qāsim al-Qushayrī (d. 465/1072), *'Awārif al-ma'ārif* by Shihāb ad-Dīn 'Umar as-Suhrawardī (d. 632/1234), *Ṭabaqāt aṣ-Ṣūfiyya* by Abū 'Abd ar-Raḥmān as-Sulamī (d. 412/1021), *Manāqib al-abrār* by Ibn Khamīs, and others. Nevertheless, ash-Sharjī did not find any discussion of the Yemeni people. They only mentioned the people of *ash-Shām* (Syria), Iraq, and al-Maghrib, which implied that there was no one in Yemen who deserved the title of *walī.* This, argued ash-Sharjī, is false. According to him, the majority of Yemenis have sincere faith, soft hearts, outward piety, and inward purity. As a proof of their proximity to the concept of *walāya,* the Prophet said: "People have come to you from Yemen. They are the most amiable and gentle-hearted of men. Faith is of Yemen, and wisdom is Yemeni."[14] Ash-Sharjī states that there are many Prophetic traditions glorifying Yemen and its people. Among the authors who compiled them are Abū 'Abd Allāh b. Abī aṣ-Ṣayf al-Yamanī, who collected one volume;

Muḥammad b. ʿAbd al-Ḥamīd, who collected forty *ḥadīths* commending the people of Yemen; and the famous Sufi author, ʿAbd Allāh b. Asʿad al-Yāfiʿī (d. 768/1366), who mentioned many traits of the people of Yemen in his *Nashr al-maḥāsin* and other works.[15]

Moreover, there are many other Yemeni historians who wrote about significant features and commendable qualities in the people of Yemen, such as ʿUmar b. Samura al-Jaʿdī (d. 586/1190), Muḥammad al-Janadī (d. 732/1331) and ʿAlī al-Khazrajī (d. 812/1409). Ash-Sharjī adds that al-Qushayrī, the author of *ar-Risāla,* and the authors of ash-Shām and Iraq did not include the *awliyā'* of Yemen in their books because they were far from Yemen and, hence, unsure of their status. Therefore, ash-Sharjī compiled a book to describe the *awliyā'* of Yemen and elaborate on their conditions, sayings, qualities, and *karāmāt.* He added that his intention was to include both revered Sufis and Yemeni saints in general, because the grace of God is not restricted to a specific case or definite form. In ash-Sharjī's view, there is no contradiction between knowledge and Sufism because there is no Sufism without knowledge and there is no knowledge without pious deeds.[16] Sufi hagiographers tried to lend credibility to their works by including both Sufi and non-Sufi *awliyā'* under the same rubric. They hoped to convince their readers that the paradigmatic figures of early Islam were also the forerunners of Sufism. Such hagiographers include the prominent Iranian hagiographer Abū Nuʿaym al-Iṣfahānī (d. 430/1038), and the influential Yemeni hagiographers al-Jaʿdī (d. 586/1190), al-Janadī (d. 732/1331), ash-Sharjī (d. 893/1487), Ibn al-Ahdal (d. 855/1387), and al-Burayhī (d. ca. 904/1498). In their works, early saints are portrayed as proto-Sufis whose teachings foreshadow later Sufi doctrines.[17] According to ash-Sharjī, most Yemeni scholars were famous for their piety, asceticism, and sainthood. Ibn ʿAlwān was just one example who was given a short biography in ash-Sharjī's *Ṭabaqāt al-khawāṣṣ*. In the following section, I focus on a late period in which these ideas are resurrected with some variations by Muḥammad ash-Shawkānī (d. 1250/1834), the towering intellectual figure of early nineteenth-century Yemen.

Ash-Shawkānī's Views on Sainthood

In his book *Qaṭr al-waly ʿalā aḥādīth al-walī,* Muḥammad b. ʿAlī ash-Shawkānī began his discussion of sainthood (*walāya*) with a literal definition from *aṣ-Ṣiḥāḥ* (lexical dictionaries), which highlight a term's meaning by citing its antonyms. For example, *walī* is the antonym of enemy.[18] Ash-Shawkānī supports Ibn Ḥajar al-ʿAsqalānī's definition in *Fatḥ al-bārī,* according to which *walī* is the one who knows God (*ʿālim bi'llāh*). Ash-Shawkānī discusses the status of saints (*awliyā'*) by giving a classification of their ranking degrees. He prioritizes the select few of each rank, arguing that the best *awliyā'* are the prophets, the best prophets are the messengers, and the best messengers are those who have "determination" (*'azm*). They are Noah, Abraham, Moses, Jesus, and Muḥammad, and the latter is the best of all.

In his discussion of the concept of sainthood, ash-Shawkānī points out that the *awliyā'* are not infallible. He argues that magical acts are not signs of infallibility because they can be performed by anyone. For instance, Hindus can perform such acts due to excessive fasting, mortification of the body, and exercises, but these are not real miracles. Ash-Shawkānī provides some features to identify the *walī.* First, the *walī*'s prayers are likely to be answered by God (*mujāb ad-du'ā'*). Second, the *walī* should observe God's commands by avoiding unlawful acts and renouncing the world. Third, he should not preoccupy himself with the accumulation of wealth: if he gains much, he is grateful but if he is poor, he endures. Fourth, praise and blame, wealth and poverty are all the same in his mind. Finally, he should be highly ethical, friendly, and generous. Ash-Shawkānī's description is similar to Vincent Cornell's portrayal of Abū Madyan's (d. 594/1198) Sufi way. Cornell says, "The true Sufi must be neither jealous, egotistical, nor arrogant with his knowledge nor miserly with his money. Rather, he must act as a guide: not confused, but merciful of heart and compassionate with all of creation. To him, every person is as [useful as] one of his hands. He is an ascetic: everything is equal to him, whether it be praise or blame, receiving or giving, acceptance or rejection, wealth or poverty. He is neither joyful about what comes to him nor sad about what has been lost."[19] This description is also close to Ibn 'Alwān's way of Sufism, which relies on extreme piety, altruism, and sincerity, and which derives its teachings from the Qur'ān and the Sunna. In addition, the similarity between Abū Madyan's approach to Sufism and that of Ibn 'Alwān is evident in their emphasis on social engagement. They both encouraged external action (*'amal*), which must complement and not oppose inner knowledge. Giving too much weight to either might upset the balance for spiritual progress.[20]

Ash-Shawkānī admitted the existence of *karāmāt* if they do not conflict with revealed law (*sharī'a*). He rejects the view of those who deny the miraculous acts of the *awliyā'*. His contention is that nothing is impossible if the *walī* is granted *karāmāt* by God. He enumerates various miracles of the *awliyā',* such as traversing great distances, pointing out that God is the invisible actor in all.

Ibn 'Alwān's *Karāmāt*

I now examine Ibn 'Alwān's *karāmāt* as perceived by premodern hagiographers, followed by a critical analysis. Al-Janadī narrates a story on the authority of an anonymous person who told him that a group of people living in as-Samkar (a village close to al-Janad in the suburb of Ta'izz, the Rasūlid capital of Yemen) often visited Ibn 'Alwān in the village of Yafrus or Dhī al-Janān where he was residing. They brought money as a votive gift (*qurba*) to be donated to Ibn 'Alwān's Sufi lodge (*ribāṭ*). Upon their arrival, they greeted Ibn 'Alwān and submitted their donation to the head of the lodge (*naqīb al-fuqarā'*). They stayed for a couple of days, asked the shaykh for supplication (*du'ā'*), and returned to their village. Yet the next morning, each member of the group found back the exact amount he had donated to Ibn 'Alwān's lodge. They were surprised that their money was returned without being carried by anyone.[21]

A modern writer, Muḥammad b. Aḥmad al-'Aqīlī, interprets this *karāma* by saying that Ibn 'Alwān sent one of his followers to return the money to everyone's home. He adds that the houses at that time had no locks and that Ibn 'Alwān, in al-'Aqīlī's eyes, intended to show off his spiritual power. However, there is no evidence to support al-'Aqīlī's interpretation. He seems to oppose the concept of *karāmāt* simply because his analysis stems from an anti-Sufi position.[22] The relationship between rural sainthood and spiritual authority was most clearly visible in the context of the *ribāṭ*, the institutional center of rural Sufism. From his *ribāṭ*, Ibn 'Alwān taught Islamic doctrine and dispensed justice to local tribes. Since his *ribāṭ* also served as a teaching center of orthodox Islam, it complemented Islamic institutions. In the most general sense, Ibn 'Alwān was a friend of God, whose virtue makes him the object of divine consideration. More narrowly conceived, he is also a member of the spiritual elite whose acts elevate him above other human beings.

Ibn 'Alwān's second *karāma* is narrated in *Ṭabqāt ṣulaḥā' al-Yaman* by 'Abd al-Wahhāb al-Burayhī (d. ca. 904/1498). First, however, I provide a brief definition of the term *ṣulaḥā'* (sing. *ṣāliḥ*). The *ṣāliḥ* is a morally upright and socially active individual who performs visible acts of piety toward his fellow believers. As an example from the Prophet's Sunna, the *ṣālih* stands in direct contrast to the *fāsid,* a careless and irresponsible individualist who jeopardizes the Muslim community by debasing the same standards of faith and virtue that the *ṣāliḥ* seeks to maintain. The principal function of the *ṣāliḥ* was to personify the values of Sunnī Islam.[23] Al-Burayhī's book is similar to ash-Sharjī's in that they both deal with exemplary men of Yemen, the *ṣulaḥā'* and the *awliyā'*.

Their main intention is to typify and commemorate the *awliyā'* in works that arrange them in ranks and categories (*ṭabaqāt*).

The second *karāma* of Ibn 'Alwān, according to al-Burayhī, deals with the judge Jamāl ad-Dīn Muḥammad b. 'Umar al-'Awādī (d. 810/1407), who decided to ban Sufi concerts (*samā'*) in the lodge of Ibn 'Alwān in Ta'izz. At night, in a dream, the judge saw a person telling him: "Attend the *ribāṭ* and say 'amen' after you hear the supplication that was originally established by Ibn 'Alwān." When he awoke, he went immediately to the *ribāṭ* and found them reciting the supplication after the *samā'* session. When everyone said "Amen," the judge said it too and went away. He was perplexed and no longer wanted to prevent the *samā'*.[24] This story shows the spiritual power, emerging from an encounter between the divine and the human, that the friend of God enjoys even after his death. The profundity of this encounter often results in the allegorical use of language, often extravagant and yet elusive. Frequently, the internal structure of these mystical texts defies explanation or systematic ordering.[25]

Furthermore, Ibn ad-Dayba' explains in *al-Faḍl al-mazīd* that, in the year 917/1511, an elephant belonging to Sultan 'Āmir b. 'Abd al-Wahhāb (d. 870/1465) sank into the ground because its driver tried to force it to attack the house of Ibn 'Alwān's followers (*fuqarā'*) and because the driver asked them something they could not provide. The ground was granite stone, yet the elephant sank into it and died.[26] This anecdote is similar to an account narrated by an-Nabhānī in *Jāmi' karāmāt al-awliyā'*, which states that a group of people led an elephant to Ibn 'Alwān's *ribāṭ* in search of fodder. Only his followers' food was available, and the elephant leaders wanted to take it, but Ibn 'Alwān refused. When they tried to take it by force, he pointed at the elephant causing it to sink into the ground.[27] Interestingly enough, an-Nabhānī cites this *karāma* under the entry of Ibn 'Alwān, but claims that he was a different person who shared the same name. An-Nabhānī goes on to say that both personalities were Sufis who had *karāmāt* to their credit and had the same name, nationality, and interests. The only difference between them was in the time they lived: one died in 665/1366, the other in the ninth/sixteenth century.[28] However, an-Nabhānī was mistaken because he used as a source *aṭ-Ṭabaqāt al-kubrā* by 'Abd ar-Ra'ūf al-Munāwī (d. 1031/1621). Al-Munāwī assumed the existence of Ibn 'Alwān in two different historical periods without a shred of evidence from either hagiographical sources or historical ones to support his claim. He might have thought that Ibn 'Alwān was still alive in the ninth/sixteenth century due to the miraculous act of the sinking elephant, but the incident happened almost two centuries after Ibn 'Alwān's death. In any case, the story of this *karāma* represents the type of text that deals with ineffability. In some sense, the truth disclosed in a mystical text can be grasped only if the reader allows the text to evoke a response. This response will entail a changed view of reality and participation in the text, in spite of the fact that it may appear preposterous to others.[29] Medieval hagiography is indeed an authoritative discourse that orchestrates communication between heaven and earth.[30]

The following three *karāmāt* are narrated by 'Abd al-Ilāh al-Wazīr (d. 1735) in *Tārīkh al-Yaman khilāl al-qarn al-ḥādī 'ashar.* Al-Wazīr explains that Ḍiyā' al-Islām Ismā'īl b. al-Imām ordered a group of soldiers to cut down a tree on Ibn 'Alwān's property, where people practiced *dhikr.*[31] Muḥammad b. Aḥmad al-Maḥnakī led the group and was behind the order. However, al-Maḥnakī was afflicted with an incurable disease and the order was never executed.[32] This story shows that God supports His friends and protects their belongings.

The narrative of the next *karāma* describes a grain merchant who went to Lower Yemen. When he reached al-Janad he became hungry, so he stopped at a house to ask for something to eat. He came across armed men from Syria who commanded him to carry something on his shoulder, without telling him what it was. When they reached open country, he discovered that he was carrying the corpse of a murdered man. His companions feared he might tell the authorities and decided to kill him. However, God guided him to appeal for Ibn 'Alwān's protection. Suddenly, they saw a person with a spear, which he pointed at their chests. The armed men fled, and the grain merchant was rescued.[33] This *karāma* shows the importance of God's saints, particularly in times of difficulty. They intervene whenever a person in distress asks for their help.

The third *karāma* narrative, according to al-Wazīr, deals with a later follower of Ibn 'Alwān from Thulā (a town in Ḥajja province, west of Ṣan'ā'), who performed miraculous acts (*khawāriq*). He was arrested and imprisoned in the castle of Thulā by the order of the judge al-Mahdī b. 'Abd al-Hādī. The castle was so high that no one could escape from it, yet he jumped from the top of the castle to the marketplace without harming himself. This event was a lesson to the judge and his like for doubting the miracles of saints.[34] The art of hagiography in which these miracles are recorded requires a special understanding of mystical texts. Often the structure of mystical texts defies the possibility of finding any systematic rationality.[35]

Finally, al-Ḥibshī cites an anecdote in the footnotes of *aṣ-Ṣufiyyawa'l-fuqahā' fī'l-Yaman* (1976:40), stating that the historian Yaḥyā b. al-Ḥusayn mentioned in his manuscript *Bahjat az-zaman* an incident he witnessed in 1048/1638. This anecdote describes one of Ibn 'Alwān's dervishes, who ate a third of a snake while reciting the name of God. Al-Ḥibshī's intention was to show that late Sufism degenerated into magic or sleight of hand (*sha'wadha*).

In conclusion, to make sense of Ibn 'Alwān's *karāmāt* one requires a general understanding of the hagiographical genre. According to Cornell, quoting Thomas Heffernan, the composition of hagiographical genres demanded a continual dialogue between author and audience. This demand, in turn, led to the paradox of the "biographical dualism" of a sacred biography. On the one hand, the hagiographer tends to overemphasize the supernatural, which might cause one to lose sight of the historical person discussed in a hagiography. On the other hand, he tends to overemphasize the ordinary, which might cause one to lose sight of the saint.[36] To arrive at a happy medium, Cornell suggests, the hagiographer has to employ his rhetorical skills to convey how he wants the saint to be perceived. If the resulting image accords with the collective recollection of his community and meets religious expectations, it can be incorporated into the body of tradition. Within this hermeneutical circle, rhetoric, politics, and local opinion all played a significant part in constructing the image of a saint.[37]

Yemeni Literature on Ibn 'Alwān's Sainthood

In addition to this discussion of Ibn 'Alwān's saintly miracles (*karāmāt*), it is worthwhile to examine the views of 'Abd Allāh al-Baradūnī (d. 1999), the great Yemeni poet and critic, on the subject of Ibn 'Alwān's *walāya* and *karāmāt.* Al-Baradūnī considers the Yemeni veneration of Ibn 'Alwān's tomb to result from Ibn 'Alwān's service in his community, including his support of the masses against the tyranny and injustice of rulers. Al-Baradūnī argues that no Yemeni Sufi achieved such an honorable status as Ibn 'Alwān. The reason for Ibn 'Alwān's *karāmāt,* al-Baradūnī asserts, is not Ibn 'Alwān's renunciation of the worldly life, but his struggle with the people against despotic rulers. Al-Baradūnī was partly right because Ibn 'Alwān's prestige sprang from his confronting political power. However, there is evidence that Ibn 'Alwān was also a *walī* because he not only renounced the worldly life but also became a paradigm for pious behavior and reached the rank of perfection in the imitation of the Prophet.

Al-Baradūnī's analysis seems to have been partly in line with the hypothesis laid down by Pierre Delooz in the latter's *Sociologie et Canonisations.* Delooz's hypothesis on canonization considerably advances our awareness of the relationship between sainthood and tomb cults. Rather than assuming that a tomb's occupant is venerated simply because others treat him as a saint, Delooz reminds us that the cult of a holy person is closely linked to the memory of who the saint was during his life. Whether the recollection is true or not is of little weight: rather, the significance lies in the collective memory of a saint's past attributes being based on a living model.[38] Whereas al-Baradūnī's analysis of the cult of Ibn 'Alwān emphasizes one feature of sainthood, namely, Ibn 'Alwān's struggle with the masses against despotic rulers, Delooz uncovers a broader view of the cult of saints as expressed in "sacred biography" or hagiographical literature.[39]

Moving away from al-Baradūnī's views, we find examples of scholars who praised Ibn 'Alwān for his renunciation of the world and for his unique sainthood. The medieval biographer and historian 'Abd Allāh b. As'ad al-Yāfi'ī (d. 768/1366) praised him in a short poem, alluding to Ibn 'Alwān's victory against some *fuqahā'* of Zabīd who opposed *samā'* and Sufi practices:

And how many times did Ibn 'Alwān reach a noble rank,
A man who was clothed in the glory of knowledge.
A walī, whose status was always on the rise
Over the highest honor.
His enemies' status was always sinking
To the bottom of the earth, coastal or plateau.
He had still been happy in the army of victory
He had aid under providence,
Until he has become a shelter for them and a sanctuary,
And a protection from slander and ridicule.[40]

Al-Yāfi'ī wrote these lines after a very brief introduction about Ibn 'Alwān's *karāmāt.* He states that the *fuqahā'* of Zabīd, who used to oppose Ibn 'Alwān, had sons who now seek help at Ibn 'Alwān's tomb, particularly protection from secular authorities. Al-Yāfi'ī's poem glorifies and exalts Ibn 'Alwān's good virtues and excellent qualities during his life and after his death.

Another example is a verse attributed to a female poet, ash-Sharīfa Dahmā' b. Yaḥyā al-Murtaḍā (d. 837/1434), who praised Ibn 'Alwān for his sainthood. Al-Baradūnī quotes two lines from her poem in his book *Funūn al-adab ash-sha'bī* without citing his source.

He was one of the saints, privately and publicly,
And an enemy of everyone who rejects God's rule unjustly.[41]

These lines are unique because they came from a woman who resided in the Zaydī part of Yemen and who was apparently interested in the concept of sainthood. It is known that the Zaydīs rejected sainthood, imitating the rationalist Mu'tazilites. Ash-Sharīfa Dahmā', who was a sister and disciple of Imam Aḥmad b. Yaḥyā al-Murtaḍā (d. 840/1436), was an exception. She was also a jurist and author of juridical texts, including a commentary on *Kitāb al-azhār* in four volumes. She taught and died in the town of Thulā.[42]

Finally, a poem of Sufi eulogy was written to exalt the virtuous qualities of Ibn 'Alwān by the distinguished Yemeni Sufi Muḥammad b. 'Alī, known as 'Abd al-Hādī as-Sūdī (d. 932/1525) who said:

That is Ibn 'Alwān, whose virtues are prevalent,
[He is] the sea of knowledge, the axis of earth from ancient [times].
[He is] the kernel of existence, its meaning, and its happiness.
[He is] the shaykh of shaykhs, the garden of knowledge and wisdom.
He is the highest succor (*ghawth*), and the crown of *awliyā'*.
His noble traits are countless.
[He is like] the rain of the country, unique in his good qualities.
[He is like] a moon, which gives light to the darkness of horizons.
The rising moon may be concealed.
But the glory of the master of vast Yemen (i.e., Ibn 'Alwān) is unconcealed . . .
O my lord, O the meteor of religion, O my protector,
You are our savior from the calamities, which we fear.
You are our shelter at the time of adversity,
You are our support, O the perfect security.
Far be it from you that you prevent the expectant and deprive him
Of what he wants, O you who are most high and honorable.
We have reached you, and the longings affect us,
Thanks be to God, this is the end of graces.
Visitors have rights, and you know that,
And you know the right of the guest and his service.[43]

This poem is one of the longest poems in praise of Ibn ʻAlwān of that era. Its author was a popular Yemeni Sufi who lived in the tenth/sixteenth century, and who was respected by the Yemeni masses. As-Sūdī seems to have been influenced by the hegemonic presence of Ibn ʻAlwān. He portrays Ibn ʻAlwān as an extraordinary persona, above all human beings, whose exemplary traits were countless. Finally, not only does he describe him as *ghawth* (the highest rank in the Sufi literature), but he considers him the crown of *awliyā'*.

The Tombs of Saints

With this understanding of Ibn ʻAlwān's place in Yemen's saintly tradition, I turn to a controversy surrounding sainthood: the question of tomb construction. In his treatise *Sharḥ aṣ-ṣudūr fī taḥrīm rafʻ al-qubūr,* ash-Shawkānī states that scholars have agreed that raising tombs and constructing shrines are blameworthy innovations contrary to the traditions of the Prophet.[44] Ash-Shawkānī launches a sharp attack on those who regularly visit these tombs. He narrates a *ḥadīth* taken from *Ṣaḥīh al-Bukhārī* on the authority of Ibn ʻAbbās that the following individuals, mentioned in the Qur'ān, were pious people of the prophet Noah's clan: Wadda, Suwā', Yaghūth, Yaʻūq, or Nasr. When they died, people constructed statues to commemorate their piety. After a long period of time, their descendants forgot the actual reason for commemoration and began to worship them. Ash-Shawkānī criticizes tomb visitors because, he believes, the dead person cannot help himself or others. He asks: if the Prophet, who was infallible, could not help himself, as the Qur'ān says: "Tell them: I am not master of my own gain or loss but as God may please,"[45] then how could the fallible dead intercede on behalf of others?

Ash-Shawkānī condemns believing in the powers of the dead as polytheism, and he cautions visitors of tombs from being cheated by the *qayyimīn,* who are responsible for protecting shrines, but who also claim to communicate with the dead saint. Ash-Shawkānī explains that the *qayyimīn* impress tomb visitors by performing magical acts and fabricating lies. As a result, tomb visitors donate generously, which explains the multiplicity of endowments (*awqāf*) assigned to the tombs. These come from solemn pledges by the tomb visitors, thereby contradicting the Prophet's *ḥadīth:* "There is no vow to disobey God." Such pledges lead people to depart from the privileges of Islamic religion. Furthermore, ash-Shawkānī critiques those who slaughter their best grazing livestock on tombs in the hope that dead saints may help them in their affairs. He compares this sacrifice with the slaughtering of sheep or camels to idols and calls it a repulsive pre-Islamic act.

Moreover, ash-Shawkānī criticizes the cults surrounding the Sufi figures of Ibn 'Alwān and his disciple Ibn 'Ujayl (d. 690/1290), who is the saint of Bayt al-Faqīh, and Aḥmad b. 'Umar az-Zayla'ī (d. 704/1305), a saint from al-Luḥayya. He asks, "And how much one hears in Yemen [as invocations and appeals to dead saints] such calls as: O Ibn 'Ujayl! O Zayla'ī! O Ibn 'Alwān!"[46] He adds:"Outside Yemen, it is even worse: every village has acquired for itself a dead saint who is invoked and appealed to, and even in the Holy sanctuary [in Mecca] one hears such calls as: O Ibn 'Abbās! O Maḥjūb!"[47] Finally, ash-Shawkānī disagrees with the opinion given by the Zaydī Imam Yaḥyā b. Ḥamza (d. 747/1346) who allowed people to erect edifices over tombs and to build shrines. According to ash-Shawkānī, the construction of shrines is heresy (*bid'a*). He seems to have opposed the idea of constructing tombs or shrines because they lead to polytheism or "associationism" (*shirk*). However, others suggest valid reasons for the veneration of saints' tombs in Yemen, including the tomb of Ibn 'Alwan.

Veneration of Tombs

The motives for visiting saints' shrines are numerous. They can be related to common human ailments, such as barrenness in women or physical and mental illnesses. Others have to do with powers of nature, such as rainmaking, or a family occasion such as the birth of a child. Other reasons include obtaining the blessing (*baraka*) of a saint, asking the holy man's assistance in a risky undertaking, or the official annual celebration of the saint's birthday (*mawlid*), which involves an established ceremony.[48] In the case of Ibn 'Alwān's tomb, the customary practice is that the visitors to the tomb enter the shrine and circumambulate the grave, while repeating a number of ritual formulas and prayers. Often people touch the grave to partake of the *baraka* pervading the grounds on which Ibn 'Alwān was buried.[49] In the old days, they used to take some dust from the tomb and sprinkle it over their clothes as a way of enhancing the effect of *baraka*. Nowadays, the tomb is surrounded by iron bars to protect it from damage.

Outside the tomb there is a pond that served for washing feet before entering the mosque. Gradually, it acquired a reputation for healing all kinds of illnesses.[50]

Popular practices at Ibn 'Alwān's shrine aroused the indignation of puritanically minded scholars, who criticized the rituals as "non-Islamic" and extreme violations of the concept of God's unity (*tawḥīd*).

Furthermore, in Yemen, as in the other parts of the Muslim world, the veneration of holy men and their shrines was aggressively attacked by

Image 3. The pond that used to be for healing is expanded and is now used for ablution.

Muslim scholars of purist tendencies. They denounced it as a type of "idolatry" (*wathaniyya*), contrary to the spirit of Islamic monotheism.[51] In general, Yemeni Sufi institutions have tended to develop into "sacred territories" similar to the Meccan sanctuary (*ḥaram*). According to Ignaz Goldziher, the idea of sanctuaries sprang partly from practical need because not all Muslims can fulfill the sacred obligation of the *ḥajj,* and sanctuaries could provide poorer sections of the population in outlying parts of the Muslim world with a substitute for this important religious requirement.[52] Such holy spaces were known under different names such as *ḥaram, ḥimā, ḥawṭa, hijra,* and *ribāṭ.*[53] The founders of these sanctuaries were thought to be pious holy men (*ṣāliḥūn*) or "friends of God" (*awliyā'*). Such sacred enclaves played significant roles in peace negotiations between feuding tribes in the surrounding lands who acknowledged the spiritual authority (*jāh*) of their founders. The veneration of saints was and still is extremely popular in different parts of Yemen, including Ḥaḍramawt. Practically every village claims to possess its own patron saint. Ibn 'Alwān's tomb is visited by the inhabitants of the neighboring areas as well as people from the nearby Bedouin camps.

Peter Brown describes a holy man as "a man who had conquered his body in spectacular feats or mortification. He had gained power over the demons, and so over the disease, the bad weather, the manifest disorders of the material world ruled by the demons. His prayer alone could open the gates of heaven to the timorous believer."[54] To become a holy man in Yemen and Ḥaḍramawt, "one may be a founder of a village, an ancestor of a number of related local families, a pious man, or a Sufi, known for his miracles, a martyr killed in the war, an ordinary man who met violent death, even if he just drowned in a well or a flood."[55] Yet there are certain rules that persist in most cases: the saint is usually a descendant of one of the *sayyid* families, who, in turn, descended from the Prophet, as in the case of Ibn 'Alwān, or one of the local religious *mashāyikh,* claiming a noble origin.[56]

The controversy surrounding grave visitation was brought to a head in Yemen by the Wahhābī movement, who despised the veneration of saints' graves and called for the destruction of tombs.

The Wahhābīs and Tomb Visitation

The destruction of saints' tombs has been a contentious issue in Yemen for decades. The idea was advanced after the formation of an alliance in Arabia between the founder of the Wahhābī movement, Muḥammad b. 'Abd al-Wahhāb (d. 1206/1792) and the emir of the town of Dir'iyya, Muḥammad b. Sa'ūd (d. 1179/1766). By the turn of the nineteenth century, the Wahhābīsts constituted a powerful military force delivering their restrictive interpretation of the doctrine of God's unity (*tawḥīd*) and attacking all whom they felt had deviated from it. The Wahhābīs focused on attacking the cult of saints and the practices associated with tomb visitation, which they felt were against Islamic teachings. Their message was to purify Islamic religion of what they stigmatized as polytheism (*shirk*), that is, associating persons or things with God.

The Wahhābī movement was influenced by the works of Ibn Taymiyya (d. 728/1328) and his student Ibn Qayyim al-Jawziyya (d. 751/1350), both jurisprudentially and theologically indebted to the school of Aḥmad b. Ḥanbal (d. 241/855).[57] Yemeni scholars such as Ibn al-Amīr aṣ-Ṣan'ānī (d. 1182/1768) and ash-Shawkānī did not reject Wahhābīsm at first. They were ready to embrace the Wahhābīs because they saw conformity between their own traditionist views and those of the Wahhābīs.[58] Thus, one finds the Zaydī-Sunnī scholar Muḥammad b. Ismā'īl al-Amīr al-Ṣan'ānī (1099–1182/1687–1768 [or 1769]) writing the treatise "The Purification of Belief from the Dirt of Atheism" (*Taṭhīr al-i'tiqād min daran al-ilḥād*) and other books.[59] Moreover, they disdained popular Sufism, particularly the cult of saints. (I discuss the intricacies of the conflict between Sufi thought and the Zaydīs in particular at length in the following chapter.) Nevertheless, upon hearing that the Wahhābīs were practicing extremism, in particular the indiscriminate excommunication (*takfīr*) of Muslims, the Yemenis immediately "withdrew their support, leveling severe criticism against the Najd-based movement" and "comparing them to those who revolted against the civil war between 'Alī b. Abī Tālib and Mu'āwiya b. Abī Sufian (Khawārij)."[60]

Yemeni scholars seem to have been aware of the activities of the Wahhābī *da'wa* since its early stages. Ibn al-Amīr (d. 1182/1768) sent a poem praising Wahhābīsm around 1755 but retracted it a year later upon hearing the news that the Wahhābīs were excommunicating Muslims, including the Zaydīs.[61] Similarly, ash-Shawkānī followed in the footsteps of Ibn al-Amīr, first praising Muḥammad b. 'Abd al-Wahhāb for his works and sending a mourning poem when Ibn 'Abd al-Wahhāb died in 1206/1792. However, ash-Shawkānī changed his mind about the Wahhābīs, especially after their military incursions in Yemen. In one of his poems, translated by Bernard Haykel, ash-Shawkānī explicitly criticized the Wahhābīs for their extremism:

> Do you not know that we [Yemeni Traditionists] and you [Wahhābīs]
> have recourse to the correct path . . .
> We both refer to the book [Qur'ān] if we differ
> in our respective doctrines, we cannot deny this
> And to the purest of our Prophet's sayings [ḥadīth]
> we also refer, for the Book attests to such . . .
> How is it said that people [tomb visitors] are unbelievers
> if one sees stones and sticks by their graves
> For if they [the Wahhābīs] say that a sound order was given [in ḥadīth]
> to level graves, I would not deny this
> But this [the actions of the visitors of graves] is a misdeed (*dhanb*) and not unbelief (*kufr*),
> nor is it sinfulness (*fisq*), is there in this any refutation?
> For if there is, it would entail calling the person who disobeys through a misdeed
> an unbeliever, and such an assertion is deviant
> And the Khawārij went toward this [excommunication],
> and why would one partake in the conduct of the Khawārij?
> By doing this they [the Khawārij] had truly violated the *ijmā'*,
> and all who have knowledge are witnesses to this

For if you [the Wahhābīs] say they have believed in the graves,
our land [Yemen] knows it not [this belief]
And whosoever comes to a lowly worshipper
and claims to be the Lord of creation
This is *kufr* which cannot be disguised
nor can there be a defense or denial of this
I am not against the destruction of a grave
if monkeys [believers in the dead] play beside it
And they say the Lord of the grave accomplishes
for us needs, so delegations begin streaming to it [the grave] . . .
Benefit us [O Wahhābīs], or else benefit [from us]
and revert back to us in what can be reverted to.
I [Shawkānī] have a book (*kitāb*) in this matter in which I said
something of worth which even the jealous wouldn't deny . . .
The book of God is our model as are
the words of the Prophet, for they are both the pillars
The guidance of the Companions is the best of all guidance
and the most distinguished, even if it is denied by him who denies
So will you [Wahhābīs] turn back to this [the Qur'ān and Sunna];
for if you do, we will thus return.[62]

Bernard Haykel also studies the question of tomb visitation in ash-Shawkānī's treatise entitled *Kitāb ad-durr an-naḍīd fī ikhlāṣ kalimat at-tawḥīd* (The Book of Well-Strung Pearls Rendering the Word on God's Unity Exclusively to Him).[63] In this treatise, ash-Shawkānī responded to a question by Muḥammad b. Aḥmad Mashḥam (d. 1223/1808), the judge of the Zaydī imamate in the Yemeni port Ḥodeida regarding tomb visitation and its practices. Apparently, ash-Shawkānī's treatise was written to clarify the imamate's views on these issues on the one hand, and to compete with the Wahhābī activities in Tihāmah and 'Asīr on the other. Ash-Shawkānī called those who venerate dead saints and visit their tombs "*qubūriyyūn*" (believers in the dead, or *ahl al-qubūr*). The theme of the treatise is God's unity (*tawḥīd*) and the denunciation of all acts and beliefs that may detract from it. Mashḥam addresses the following question to ash-Shawkānī:

> [The query] is about using the dead and the living who are famous for excellence as a means of approaching God (*tawassul*), and the appeal to them for aid (*istighātha*) when needs arise; the query is also about the glorification (*ta'ẓīm*) of their tombs and the belief

> (*i'tiqād*) that they [the dead] have the power (*qudra*) to accomplish the needs (*ḥawā'ij*) and demands (*ṭalabāt*) of the needy. How is one to judge someone involved in such doings? And is it permissible to go to a tomb for the purposes of visiting (*ziyāra*) and invoking (*du'ā'*) God without appealing for aid (*istighātha*) from the dead, but only to use the dead as a means (*tawassul*) to God?[64]

Ash-Shawkānī begins his response with definitions of *istighātha, isti'āna, tashaffu'* and *tawassul.* His contention is that these are lawful practices with regard to the living but that the dead may not be asked for help or intercession. However, one may implore God by citing the good deeds of the dead. In another section, ash-Shawkānī does not rule out that in the community are those who believe that the dead have powers. He says:

> The calamity of all calamities and the trial of all trials . . . is that many among the laymen (*'awāmm*) and some among the elite (*khawāṣṣ*) have come to believe in the dead (*ahl al-qubūr*) and in the living who are known for righteousness. They believe that the latter have the capacity to accomplish what is uniquely God's prerogative. These folk begin to express with their tongues what their hearts have inclined to: at times they invoke them [the dead] with God and sometimes independently [without God]; they shout their names; they glorify them as if they had power over harm and benefit; and they submit (*khuḍū'*) to them more than they would to God when praying or invoking Him. If such is not *shirk* then we know not what is, and if this is not unbelief (*kufr*) then this world knows it not.[65]

Ash-Shawkānī proceeds to say:

> the *qubūriyyūn* have made of some mortals associates and partners with God. They have asked from these mortals what can only be asked of God, and have sought aid in matters over which only God has sovereignty.[66]

Ash-Shawkānī considers the belief of the *qubūriyyūn* to be a result of blind imitation (*taqlīd*). In his *Sharḥ aṣ-ṣudūr fī taḥrīm raf' al-qubūr,* ash-Shawkānī repeats his severe condemnation of tomb visitation in *ad-Durr an-naḍīd,* showing how it can become institutionalized and misused by a few charlatans and swindlers (*qayyimūn*) who deceive the common people into believing that the dead can fulfill their wishes.

Ash-Shawkānī's verdict against the *qubūriyyūn* is equal to his judgment of idolaters (*wathaniyyūn*): they are outlaws who should not have access to wealth and life. They can be accepted in the society if they pledge to follow the *sharī'a,* but otherwise their fate is the sword.[67] The grounds for this verdict are the *qubūriyyūn*'s failures to realize the fundamental purpose for which God sent the prophets and scriptures: to render exclusively to God His unity (*ikhlāṣ at-tawḥīd*) and to worship God exclusively (*ifrādihi bi'l-'ibāda*). As the Qur'ān reports on the authority of the prophet Noah: "O my people, serve God! You have no god other than He."[68] In spite of his condemnation of grave visitation and all practices associated with the cult of saints, ash-Shawkānī concludes his treatise by exonerating grave visitors as long as they do not set a bad example for the common people. He summarizes his judgment of three types of visitors who invoke God at gravesites:

> He who goes [to a tomb] only to visit (*ziyāra*), and while at the tomb invokes without setting a bad example for others to follow (*taghrīr*); this type of visitation is licit. . . . He who goes to the tomb only with the intention of invoking, or to visit as well, while sharing the belief which we have presented [i.e., the belief of the *qubūriyyūn*] is in danger of falling into *shirk,* aside from already being disobedient. And if he does not share any belief in the dead [but still visits by following the example of others] . . . then he is a disobedient sinner (*'āṣin āthim*) and this is the least of his condition.[69]

The major issue of the concluding paragraph of ash-Shawkānī's treatise is the incitement to *taqlīd,* which deserves "worst castigation." Thus, "ash-Shawkānī allows for the actual practice of visiting grave sites and invoking there, on condition that no incitement to imitation takes place, i.e., no *taqlīd.*"[70] As for the legality of visiting tombs in general, one may refer to the Prophet's saying: "I previously prohibited you from visiting tombs, now visit them for they remind you of the hereafter."[71]

The Condemnation of the Cult of Saints

The condemnation of the cult of saints is a Wahhābī concept echoed in ash-Shawkānī's treatises *Sharḥ aṣ-ṣudūr* and *ad-Durr an-naḍīd.* Wahhābīs say that the *qubūriyyūn* practice heresies by venerating deceased saints, which may lead them to polytheism and abandonment of God's unity. Additionally, Wahhābīs use the same argument against those who make the Prophet or any living person the object of a cult. For ash-Shawkānī, both issues were subsidiary to the condemnation of tomb visitors.[72] As the leading scholar of the Zaydī imamate, ash-Shawkānī was embroiled in the debates against the Wahhābīs. In order to defend the imamate, ash-Shawkānī used Wahhābī terms to attack the cult of saints, suggesting that the imamate position was similar to the Wahhābīs.[73] Ash-Shawkānī—like Muḥammad b. 'Abd al-Wahhāb—was influenced by the ideas of Ibn Taymiyya. For instance, the content and conclusions of the first section of *ad-Durr an-naḍīd* concerning the definitions of *tawassul, istighātha,* and *isti'āna* are almost identical with Ibn Taymiyya's *Majmū' Fatāwā.* In addition, Ibn Taymiyya's conclusion that *tawassul* is licit through other than the Prophet—that is, through the good works (*al-a'māl aṣ-ṣāliḥa*) of a saint or a scholar—is taken up by ash-Shawkānī in *ad-Durr an-naḍīd* in the form of the polemic against Shaykh 'Izz ad-Dīn b 'Abd as-Salām (d. 660/1262).[74] Moreover, ash-Shawkānī explicitly cites Ibn Taymiyya's *Iqtiḍā' aṣ-ṣirāṭ al-mustaqīm mukhālafat aṣḥāb al-jaḥīm* (The Exigency of the Right Path: The Disagreement with the People of Hellfire) since it treats tomb visitation and the cult of saints.[75]

The concept of *shirk* in its various forms in the thought of ash-Shawkānī and Wahhābī theorists seems to have been identical. Ash-Shawkānī discusses the first type of *shirk* by questioning the faith of the *qubūriyyūn* who believe that a being can be associated with God in the knowledge of the transcendental world (*'ālam al-ghayb*). This argument is quite similar to what Wahhābī theorists term as "*shirk al-'ilm.*" The second type of *shirk* is the dissimulation of piety (*riyā'*). This happens when worshippers expect the admiration of fellow Muslims due to their worship of God. Their worship is not pure because they "associate men with God."[76] This type of *shirk* is equally condemned by ash-Shawkānī and the Wahhābīs. The third type of *shirk* is a shared conception found in four forms: *shirk at-taṣarruf, shirk al-'ibāda, shirk al-'āda,* and *shirk al-adab.* The generally accepted meaning for *shirk at-taṣarruf* is the denial that God alone has the power to intercede on behalf of His creatures. *Shirk al-'ibāda* is more comprehensive because it includes the veneration of saints' tombs "through circumambulation, offering sacrifices or money, vows, prayer at the grave."[77] *Shirk al-'āda* comprises the habits and beliefs of the pre-Islamic era that have persisted in Islam such as "the belief in omens or reliance on astrology, amulets and lithomancy."[78] As for *shirk al-adab,* its example is when people swear by the name of someone or something other than God. For instance, they may swear by the name of the Prophet or by the name of a saint.[79]

The concept of *tawḥīd* is applicable not only to Wahhābīs but to all Muslims, with no distinction, but it was the Wahhābīs' radical interpretation that led their opponents to call them Wahhābīs, a term which has gained wide currency in Western scholarship. However, the Wahhābīs dispute this term, referring to themselves as *muwaḥḥidūn* (those who support the unity of God). Ibn Taymiyya's understanding of *tawḥīd*—which had a significant impact upon many scholars including Ibn al-Amīr, ash-Shawkānī, and the Wahhābīs—consists of two elements: the unity of divine Lordship (*tawḥīd ar-rubūbiyya*) and the unity of Divinity (*tawḥīd al-ulūhiyya*). In order to achieve *tawḥīd ar-rubūbiyya,* one should affirm God's Lordship in such matters as creation (*khalq*), sustenance (*rizq*), giving life (*iḥyā'*) and taking it away (*imāta*), provision of rain (*inzāl al-maṭar*), growth of vegetation (*inbāt an-nabāt*), and in the direction of all affairs (*tadbīr al-umūr*). In order to achieve *tawḥīd al-ulūhiyya,* one should affirm God's divinity in worship (*'ibāda*) in all its forms, such as invocation (*du'ā'*), fear (*khawf*), hope (*rajā'*), trust (*tawakkul*), repentance (*ināba* or *tawba*), wish (*raghba*), awe (*rahba*), vows (*nudhūr*), and seeking aid (*isti'āna*). In order to be a full *muwaḥḥid* (one who exclusively renders to God His unity), the Wahhābīs emphasize that both *tawḥīd ar-rubūbiyya* and *tawḥīd al-ulūhiyya* are inseparable aspects of God's unity. If a Muslim fails to accomplish either of these aspects of *tawḥīd,* then he has given partners to God, which ultimately means partaking in *shirk.*

Both Yemeni scholars Ibn al-Amīr and ash-Shawkānī shared the Wahhābī concept of *tawḥīd,* and they condemned the *qubūriyyūn* for failing to render God's unity exclusively to Him.[80] Ash-Shawkānī sums up this argument: "All invocation (*du'ā'*), all cries (*nidā'*), all appeals for aid (*istighātha*), all hope (*rajā'*) and all summons for the good and warding off of evil have to be directed to God and no one else."[81] According to Haykel, "the zeal with which the Wahhābīs attacked the practice of visiting the tombs of saints seems to have exceeded that of Ibn Taymiyya as well as that of ash-Shawkānī. This is reflected in the intensity with which the Wahhābīs razed burial mounds, steles and domes over graves of saints."[82]

Ash-Shawkānī did not consider tomb visitation inconsistent with the *sharī'a,* and even considered the practice of *tawassul* through the dead person's good works and virtuous characteristics—though not through the person himself—to be lawful. Contrary to ash-Shawkānī, the Wahhābīs considered both *tawassul* and *istighātha* unlawful because they lead to *shirk.*[83] Thus, ash-Shawkānī parted ways with Wahhābī doctrine on this point despite his critique of the cult of saints. From the practical side, ash-Shawkānī's treatise *ad-Durr an-naḍīd* did not help to change the political atmosphere, for the imamate lost control over Tihāma to the Sharīfs of Abū 'Arīsh who ruled in the name of Ibn Sa'ūd.[84] However, his work shows how a leading judge of the Zaydī imamate engaged in discussions about the Ḥanbalī tradition. This does not mean that ash-Shawkānī stumbled upon alien concepts; on the contrary, he felt they were part of his own tradition.[85] With this understanding of the intricacies surrounding saints' tombs I discuss the controversy that surrounded, and ultimately led to the destruction of, Ibn 'Alwān's tomb.

Controversy around Ibn 'Alwān's Tomb

According to al-Janadī, Ibn 'Alwān died in Yafrus, a village near the city of Ta'izz in 665/1266. His tomb is adjacent to a mosque in the same village and has remained an object of veneration since his death. It was highly respected during the Ottoman reign in Yemen. Almost all viziers who ruled Yemen visited Ibn 'Alwān's tomb, especially when they entered the country and when they finished their terms of appointment. The first ruler who restored and extended Ibn 'Alwān's tomb and mosque was the governor Murād Pāshā in 983/1575. In 1025/1616 the governor Muḥammad Pāshā made some improvements to the mosque, adding the great dome over Ibn 'Alwān's shrine.[86] To borrow Katherine Pratt Ewing's description of colonial domination: "Cultural domination and the constitution of a 'colonial subject'—in a psychological as well as a political sense—requires an effective critique of the dominated culture, a critique that is convincing to both dominator and dominated."[87] Ewing's critique may be applied to the Ottomans as colonial dominators. However, her psychological analysis of the dominated may be seen in the diffusion of that culture, even before the arrival of the Ottomans.

Ash-Sharjī clarifies the significance of Aḥmad b. 'Alwān's tomb: "His tomb is well-known. People pay visits to it from far places, especially on the last Friday of Rajab." He adds, "The people of nearby areas, such as the people of Ta'izz and others, come to visit it from far and wide. They come with their women and children."[88] Ash-Sharjī's statement does not clarify the purposes behind the visitation (*ziyāra*) of Ibn 'Alwān's tomb. Nevertheless, al-Baradūnī provides an interpretation that is commensurate with a sociological understanding of the concept of sainthood. According to al-Baradūnī, the purposes for women visiting Ibn 'Alwān's tomb are to cure sterility, facilitate the delivery of a baby, protect children from envious people, and to capture the heart of their beloved, whether a husband or lover. Al-Baradūnī goes further to say that the pilgrimage to Ibn 'Alwān's tomb became a sacred symbol for the people in all their affairs.[89] This incited the authorities, who ran out of patience, to end the superstition. In 1942 the Crown Prince Aḥmad b. Yaḥyā Ḥamīd ad-Dīn ordered his soldiers to destroy the tomb. The following poem entitled "The Hero and the Idol" (*al-baṭal wa'ṣ-ṣanam*) by revolutionary poet Muḥammad Maḥmūd az-Zubayrī (1918–1965) praises the crown prince for this act.[90]

He is [the embodiment] of glory when he raises the [victorious]
banner or revives religious communities or destroys idols.
O you who revives the traditions of his community: if his chosen
ancestor [the Prophet] had seen it, he would have smiled
[approvingly].
This was a wound on the heart of Islam; you touched it with the
tip of your sword, and made it whole.
This was a deception for the masses, which believed that their
religion consists in worshipping a delusion.
They say: "He [Ibn 'Alwān] has books inside his tomb by which
he forbids and commands as he wants or sees fit."
I wish I knew whether he does this by sheer magic or he uses
paper and the pen.
Has the tomb, in which he resides, become his throne, from which
he rules the universe as he pleases?
So, O prince, make them history and obliterate his traces
forever.[91]

This poem does not exist in az-Zubayrī's nationalist publications, but it is available in one of his manuscripts. Al-Baradūnī believes that az-Zubayrī did not include this poem in his printed works because he ultimately recognized Ibn 'Alwān's social prestige. Textual evidence suggests that az-Zubayrī was uncertain whether to publish his poem, or that he did not have time to publish it.[92] In his *Min awwal qaṣīda ilā ākhar ṭalqa,* al-Baradūnī criticizes the contemporary poet and critic 'Abd al-'Azīz al-Maqāliḥ for his negligence of Zayd b. 'Alī al-Mawshikī (1914–1947)[93] and az-Zubayrī, and for their eulogies to the destruction of Ibn 'Alwān's tomb.

Despite this critique, al-Baradūnī supported al-Maqāliḥ (when the latter declared the crown prince guilty of destroying the tomb. Aḥmad Muḥammad ash-Shāmī (d. 2005), the great Yemeni writer and literary critic, mentions two lines of az-Zubayrī's poem in his *Ma'a ash-shi'r al-*

mu'āṣir fī'l-Yaman. However, the second line differs from all other sources: "You built what he [the Prophet] used to build for his community and you destroyed with the sword in the same way."[94] According to al-Baradūnī, the line in question reads, "You destroyed the tomb which had a significant influence among the people; it would not have been destroyed if you had not had the strong will."[95] The difference in these two readings of the same line may be attributed to the fact that both writers interpreted the manuscript differently.

The poem praises Crown Prince Aḥmad Yaḥyā Ḥamīd ad-Dīn for his courage in destroying the tomb of Ibn 'Alwān. The prince destroyed the tomb to convince reformists (az-Zubayrī and others) that he was responsive to their aspirations, specifically the purification of Islam from innovations such as shrine visitation. As a leader of the reformist movement, az-Zubayrī was deeply influenced by the religious thought of al-Fuḍayl al-Wirtalānī (1907–1958). Al-Wirtalānī was an Algerian leader who fled to Egypt due to his resistance against the French occupation. According to ash-Shāmī, al-Wirtalānī was the true leader of the Yemeni revolution of 1948 because he unified the national movement under "The National Pact" (*al-mīthāq al-waṭanī*).[96] It is likely that al-Wirtalānī's influence inspired az-Zubayrī to take up the cause of purifying religion. Thus, az-Zubayrī composed his poem, pointing out that Ibn 'Alwān's tomb was a temptation to polytheism.

Another leader of the reformist movement was Zayd b. 'Alī al-Mawshikī (d. 1947), a friend of az-Zubayrī. They both opposed the reign of Imam Aḥmad after they became disappointed by his failure to fulfill his earlier promises. Al-Mawshikī composed a poem expressing his condemnation of the cult of Ibn 'Alwān:

> Behold! This is the great idol; and this is Yafrus with its evil custom.
> This is Ibn 'Alwān and that is his tomb; the whole world worships it unceasingly.
> Behold! This is another Hubal, who is even worse than his predecessor.[97]

Al-Mawshikī addressed Crown Prince Aḥmad and exhorted him to ban the masses from visiting Ibn 'Alwān's tomb. He mentioned the location of the tomb (Yafrus) to remind the ruler of that source of "evil" and "corruption" of faith. It seems that the idea of the tomb's destruction was appealing to al-Mawshikī because people would be rescued from polytheism (*shirk*). At the same time, the poem urges Crown Prince Aḥmad to prevent people from visiting Ibn 'Alwān's tomb because it would lead them astray. Moreover, al-Mawshikī compared the pagan worship of Hubal before Islam to the tomb's visitation in his age. Finally, al-Mawshikī condemned these practices as contrary to the doctrine of divine unity (*tawḥīd*).

Al-Mawshikī's position was countered by the modern poet Ibrāhīm al-Ḥaḍrānī, (1921–2007), who severely attacked Crown Prince Aḥmad for the destruction of Ibn 'Alwān's tomb:

> How dare the hand of the dissolute innovator destroy the tomb of the most honorable ascetic and pious man!
> Of the thousands of tombs, you destroyed this one unjustly and without any justifiable reason.
> Destroying tombs is a sin and scandal, even according to the teaching of Buddhism and the Blacks.
> You destroyed this tomb because he [Ibn 'Alwān] belongs to the Sunnī community.[98]

These lines, however, are not found in the poet's collection, *al-Quṭūf ad-dawānī min shi'r Ibrāhīm al-Ḥaḍrānī,* edited by ash-Shāmī. Ash-Shāmī quotes al-Baradūnī in the latter's book *Riḥla fī ash-shi'r al-Yamanī qadīmihi wa ḥadīthihi* saying that al-Ḥaḍrānī was a spokesman of the Sunnī school who opposed the Zaydī school. Ash-Shāmī, however, refuted al-Baradūnī's statement and claimed that al-Ḥaḍrānī belonged to the Zaydī school and that his poetry was dominated by Shī'ī propensities. However, the position of al-Ḥaḍrānī vis-à-vis saints' tombs is obviously closer to that of the Sunnī school. The poet attributes the destruction of Ibn 'Alwān's tomb to the fact that the latter was a Sunnī scholar and a saint. Additionally, the poet reproaches Crown Prince Aḥmad for the tomb's destruction and considers it a grave sin. He cites the examples of the Buddhists and the Blacks to show that people from different religions have respect for tombs.

Conclusion

The story of Ibn 'Alwān's sainthood and veneration in Yemen since his death is a lens through which to understand the changing face of Yemeni Islam leading into the modern period. We learn, for example, about varying understandings of Islamic sainthood. While some, such as al-Baradūnī, interpret the visitation of Ibn 'Alwān's shrine as appreciation for Ibn 'Alwān's struggle with the authorities during his life, others such as al-Yāfi'ī (d. 763/1366), ash-Sharīfa Dahmā' (d. 837/1434), and as-Sūdī (d. 932/1525) praised Ibn 'Alwān solely for his renunciation of worldly pleasures. It was Ibn 'Alwān's fame and inimitable status in Yemeni tradition that made his grave the focus of bitter debates over grave visitation. Only a widely loved saint would stir up the indignation of puritanically minded scholars, in particular the Yemeni reformist and later nationalist movement under the leadership of az-Zubayrī and al-Mawshikī, which eventually led to the destruction of Ibn 'Alwān's tomb in 1942. It was rebuilt, however, in 1963 by one of Ibn 'Alwān's followers who saw his master through a visionary dream and was instructed to reconstruct it.

Finally, in our close readings of noted Yemeni scholars on the subject of sainthood and Ibn 'Alwān, we see them grappling with crucial and quintessentially modern questions of tradition and reform, and local practice and transnational Islamic movements, such as the influential Wahhābīs. The defense of a specifically Yemeni tradition is exemplified in the changing responses of Yemeni scholars, such as Ibn al-Amīr and ash-Shawkānī, to Wahhābī teachings, which they perceived, upon learning of the indiscriminate excommunication (*takfīr*) of Muslims, as extremist. In the following chapter we leave the twentieth century behind and return to the medieval era to investigate a formative conflict in Yemen's Islamic environment, one that provides significant insight into Yemeni scholars' initial support for the extremist Wahhābī movement against Sufi practices: the conflict between Yemeni Sufis like Ibn 'Alwān and the Zaydī imams of his era.

8

ZAYDĪ IMAMS AND THE SUFI TRADITION IN YEMEN

Of the tensions among Yemen's religious groups, one in particular stands out for the purposes of this study: the conflict between Yemen's Sufi masters and Zaydī imams. This conflict melded doctrinal disputes—over what some Zaydī imams regarded as Sufism's dangerous innovations—with competition for political as well as spiritual hegemony in Yemen. As I made clear in Chapter 1, not one of Yemen's three major religious and political rivals—the Zaydīs, Ismāʿīlīs, and the Sunnīs—could achieve total control of the country, thus creating the diverse, sometimes turbulent, conditions that permitted the emergence of Yemen's charismatic Sufi leaders. The ascetic (*zuhd*) movement in Yemen began as early as the inception of Islam and continued latently until the sixth/twelfth century, when Sufi trends emerged with vengeance, particularly in the region of Taʿizz, the Rasūlid capital. These trends would not be fully formed for another century, until we encounter famous Sufi masters such as Abū al-Ghayth b. Jamīl (d. 651/1253) and Aḥmad b. ʿAlwān (d. 665/1266).

The age of these charismatic Sufi masters coincided with early conflicts between Sufis and Zaydī imams in Yemen. Where did the Sufis fit in Yemen's religio-political struggles? A Sufi like Ibn ʿAlwān, as discussed in Chapter 4, was certainly Sunnī but fused aspects of Yemen's Shīʿī influences into his doctrine. Though Ibn ʿAlwān's theology was squarely in Islam's mainstream, the originality of his Sufi theology made it inassimilable to any one *madhhab*. Thus, there is significant overlap between Zaydī thought and Sufism and an intense reflection on the criticism of Sufi theory and practices in Zaydī circles.[1] Furthermore, the popularity of Sufi masters with the Yemeni populace made them formidable political rivals. This factor motivated the Zaydī imams to try to win the hearts and minds of Sufi masters as strategic allies in their quest for religio-political legitimacy; unfortunately, if Sufis did not oblige the imams sometimes resorted to force. The ongoing relevance of this conflict to modern Yemen is exemplified in Prince Aḥmad b. Yaḥyā Ḥamīd al-Dīn's (1367–1382/1948–1962) decision to destroy Sufi tombs, including that of Ibn 'Alwān.

The Zaydīs are a Shī'ī movement distinct from the Twelvers and the Ismā'īlīs, and the history of this important group in Yemen is laid out in detail in Chapter 1. Often considered the closest to the Sunnī tradition of all the Shī'ī groups, the Zaydīs were a political force vying for both religious and worldly power. This chapter will show the complex ways in which this conflict has branched and shaped formative allegiances in Yemen's history. For example, when the Sufis first sided against the Zaydīs and with the new invaders, the Sunnī Ottomans in 945/1538, they realized afterward that their alliance was based on false hopes as they discovered the immoral behavior of the occupiers. Such a reading of Yemeni history requires us to leave behind oversimplified understandings of religion's role in politics: neither a tool to manipulate the masses nor the sole motivation for either side; doctrine and politics fuse to shape Yemen's religio-political landscape. Like any ideological and political conflict, its intensity varied over time, and not all Zaydī imams were in conflict with Sufi masters. Indeed, I must note a general trend by which Zaydī imams of the Caspian Sea region tended to be less confrontational with Sufis than their Yemeni counterparts.

The Origins of the Conflict

In Yemen, the very early conflict between Zaydī imams and Sufi masters is reported to have begun when Zaydī Imam al-Mahdī li-Dīn Allāh Aḥmad b. al-Ḥusayn (646–656/1249–1258) sent a letter to Abū al-Ghayth b. Jamīl asking him to join forces for the sake of commanding right and forbidding wrong (*al-amr bi-l-ma'rūf wa n-nahyy 'an al-munkar*). Abū al-Ghayth apologized tactfully, showing no weakness or timidity before the ambitions of the Zaydī imam. From this time on, this incident was an example reflecting Sufi attitudes and their desire to avert the ambitions of Zaydī imams; it became a powerful precedent that prompted Sufis to side with Sunnī states.[2] On another occasion, when a certain Zaydī imam—probably Imam al-Manṣūr 'Abd Allāh b. Ḥamza (d. 614/1217)—strengthened his position in highland Yemen, Abū al-Ghayth wrote a letter to the famous Sufi master Muḥammad b. Ismā'īl al-Ḥaḍramī (d. 651/1253) informing him of his decision to leave mountainous Yemen for the adjacent coastal area of Tihāma due to the "surge of trials" (*ẓuhūr al-fitan*). Abū al-Ghayth also extended an invitation to al-Ḥaḍramī to join him in this departure. Al-Ḥaḍramī apologized, giving family reasons for his inability to go with him to Tihāma lowlands. However, he suggested that Abū al-Ghayth should protect the lowlands of the coastal areas with his spiritual influence while al-Ḥaḍramī should protect the highlands similarly.[3] Ash-Sharjī (d. 893/1487) provides the above historical evidence in *Ṭabaqāt al-khawāṣṣ ahl al-ṣidq wa l-ikhlāṣṣ*, quoting al-Yāfiʿī (d. 768/1367) as part of al-Ḥaḍramī's saintly miracles (*karāmāt*). In this regard, it is likely that al-Ḥaḍramī predicted the death of the Zaydī imam and informed Abū al-Ghayth during their correspondence. Afterward, when the Zaydī imam died, Abū al-Ghayth realized how farsighted al-Ḥaḍramī was and said, "The jurist (*faqīh*) was right."[4]

The hostile relationship between the Sufis and Zaydī imams of Yemen was further aggravated when Imam an-Nāṣir Ṣalāḥ ad-Dīn Muḥammad b. ʿAlī (773–793/1371–1391) killed the Sufi-jurist (*al-faqīh al-Ṣūfī*) Aḥmad b. Zayd b. ʿAṭiyya ash-Shāwirī in 793/1391 after the latter wrote a book propagating Sunnī views, warning against innovation (*bidʿa*), and denouncing the imam's creed and actions.[5] In retaliation, Imam an-Nāṣir and his soldiers raided ash-Shāwirī's hometown, and killed him, his son Abū Bakr, and some of his disciples. Since the Sufis did not fight back or resist, the event became a notorious massacre.[6] A month after, the imam fell from his mule and died a few days later. When he was asked about the reason for his mule's stampede, he said: "I saw the jurist Aḥmad b. Zayd stabbing the female mule in the face with his finger, which caused her to stampede."[7] This incident, as reported by Aḥmad ash-Sharjī in *Ṭabaqāt al-khawāṣṣ,* is considered ash-Shāwirī saintly miracle (*karāma*). The latter was elegized by the famous jurist Ismāʿīl b. Abī Bakr, better known as Ibn al-Muqrī (d. 837/1433) who played a significant role in late Rasūlid Yemen, taking the jurists' (*fuqahāʾ*) side against the Sufis in debates over the legacy of Sufi philosopher Muḥyī ad-Dīn Ibn ʿArabī (d. 638/1240).

Ibn al-Muqrī was a prolific writer and a great poet. The most important book of his legacy, which one can unquestionably describe as a miracle of the author's eloquence in the Arabic language, is "The Title of Complete Honor" (*ʿUnwān ash-sharaf al-wāfī*). The miraculous nature of the book lies in the author's ability to weave together five different disciplines in a single context.[8] Ibn al-Muqrī wrote a long poem mourning ash-Shawirī's death and appealing to God to accelerate the imam's death, saying in the opening line: "May God show me your head, oh,

Ṣalāḥ, encircled by swords and lances."[9] Despite Ibn al-Muqrī belonging to the jurist camp and ash-Shāwirī to the Sufi camp, and despite the severe debates and the long struggle between these camps, Ibn al-Muqrī lamented ash-Shāwirī's death. In his dirge-like poem he called ash-Shāwirī a friend of God (*walī*) and predicted Imam an-Nāṣir Ṣalāḥ al-Dīn's immediate punishment, which became reality when God answered Ibn al-Muqrī's call.[10] After this incident, the Sufis grew fearful of the Zaydī imams and warned against coming closer to them. In his manuscript, "Guiding the Seeker to the Most Guided Paths" (*Hidāyat al-sālik ilā ahdā al-masālik*), Muḥammad b. Muḥammad b. Abī al-Qāsim al-Mizjājī (d. 829/1425) reports an account that signifies the extent to which the Sufis feared the Zaydī imams: "The Sufi-jurist (*al-faqīh al-ṣūfī*) Muḥammad b. Mūsā b. [Aḥmad b. Mūsā b.] 'Ujayl (d. 760/1358), who was one of the ascetics of his time, whispered in the ear of shaykh Ismā'īl al-Jabartī (d. 806/1403), saying: 'Ask God to protect this country from the Imam of the east (*Imam al-mashriq*),' and pointed his hand towards the city of Ṣan'ā', Dhamār, and their suburbs—and make up your mind on that, and do not be easy on him."[11]

Moderate Zaydī Imams and Sufism

Again, the Zaydī imams of the Caspian region were not all as indiscriminately hostile to the Sufis. In his "Doctrinal Rules of the Prophet's Family" (*Qawā'id 'aqā'id Āl Muḥammad*) written around 707/1307, the Zaydī scholar 'Izz ad-Dīn Muḥammad b. Aḥmad b. al-Ḥasan al-Daylamī (d. 711/1312) is said to have been unwilling to classify Sufis among heretical sects. Nor did he consider them adversaries of the Prophet's family.[12] Al-Daylamī's other book, entitled "The Righteous Path" (*aṣ-Ṣirāṭ al-mustaqīm*), speaks of Sufi ethical doctrines and ascetic tendencies.[13] Owing to the popularity of al-Ghazālī's (d. 505/1111) "Revival of Religious Sciences" (*Iḥyā' 'ulūm al-dīn*), al-Daylamī was asked about it and some other ascetic books, and he responded metaphorically by saying: "every incorrect perception must be rejected." The implication was to undermine the *Iḥyā'* but not in an outspoken way. His manuscript "The Purification of the Destructive and Devastating Obstacles" (*at-Taṣfiya 'an al-mawāni' al-murdiya al-muhlika*) was probably an emulation of the *Iḥyā'* with respect to its ethical message and religious duties.

The relationship between some Zaydī imams and Sufi masters in Yemen seems to have improved due to the efforts of the celebrated Yemeni Sufi and historian 'Afīf ad-Dīn 'Abd Allāh b. As'ad al-Yāfi'ī (698–768/1298–1367). According to al-Yāfi'ī, the Zaydī Imam al-

Mu'ayyad bi-Allāh Yaḥyā b. Ḥamza (729–749/1328–1349) was a pious man who did not reject the Sufi tradition. As a sign of his piety and admiration of Sufi literature, he did not object to al-Yāfi'ī's poem praising the Sufis. Al-Yāfi'ī argues astonishingly in "The Mirror of Intellect and the Lesson of the Alert" (*Mir'āt al-janān wa 'ibrat al-yaqẓān*) that the rejection of his Sufi poem did not spring from the Zaydī imams, who were supposed to have been, at least in the public eye, opponents of Sufism. Rather, it came from the people of the Sunna themselves. Al-Yāfi'ī, commending Imam Yaḥyā, mentions a story that one of his disciples saw the imam on one of his raids against the Ismā'īlī agents (*dā'īs*) in Ḥarāz. When the imam learned that the disciple was en route to Mecca to perform the pilgrimage (*ḥajj*) and see his shaykh, he asked him respectfully: "Would you bring us some of al-Yāfi'ī's poems?"[14] The significance of those poems for the imam, as it seems, is the fact that he was not only interested in Sufism but also the poems were imbued with Sufi metaphorical allusions (*ishārāt*).

Due to his amiable relationship with the Sufis of his time as well as his fascination with Sufi ethics, Imam Yaḥyā b. Ḥamza wrote a book on ethical duties that was described by a number of scholars as a direct emulation of some of al-Ghazālī's topics in the *Iḥyā'*. Entitled "The Purification of Hearts from the Dirt of Burdens and Sins" (*Taṣfiyat al-qulūb 'an daran al-awzār wa'dh-dhunūb*), it is classified by al-Sayyid Aḥmad al-Ḥusaynī as consisting of ten chapters. The first deals with the spiritual athlete and the rectification of ethics (*ar-ryāḍa wa tahdhīb al-akhlāq*); the second treats the qualities that lead to perdition (*asa-ṣifāt al-muhlika*); the third deals with qualities of salvation; the fourth is about customary issues such as eating, drinking, marriage, and so on; the fifth treats Prophethood and miracles; the sixth speaks about seclusion; the seventh is about avoiding self-delusion; the eighth deals with commanding right and forbidding wrong; the ninth talks about the moments before and after death; and the tenth is about the states of the dead from resurrection to their placement in either paradise or hell.[15] Most of these topics were explained in the books of al-Ghazālī, in "The Nourishment of the Hearts" (*Qūt al-qulūb*) by Abū Ṭālib al-Makkī (d. 386/966), and in the treatise on mystical psychology entitled "The Book of Observance of What Is Due to God" (*Kitāb al-ri'āya li-ḥuqūq Allāh*) by al-Ḥārith al-Muḥāsibī (d. 243/857). In addition to these Sufis, many others from the early period of Islamic mysticism are mentioned extensively in Ibn Ḥamza's *Taṣfiyat al-qulūb,* namely Ibrāhīm b. Adham (d. 160/777), Abū Yazīd al-Bisṭāmī (d. 234/848) or (d. 261/875), Abū Bakr al-Shiblī (d.

334/945), and others.[16] Despite the assertion that Imam Yaḥyā b. Ḥamza patterned his book *Taṣfiyat al-qulūb* on al-Ghazālī's *Iḥyā' 'ulūm al-dīn,* he nonetheless wrote a short book entitled "The Necklace of Pearls in the Refutation of Abū Ḥāmid al-Ghazālī" (*'Iqd al-la'ālī fī al-radd 'alā Abī Ḥāmid al-Ghazālī*)[17] in which he vigorously criticized al-Ghazālī's permission for the Sufi concert (*samā'*) in the *Iḥyā'*. It must be noted that al-Ghazālī was not the only scholar who permitted Sufi concerts and chanting of mystical poetry. There were a number of scholars who supported the permissibility of *samā',* including Ibn 'Alwān.[18] Imam Yaḥyā b. Ḥamza, along with moderate Mu'tazilites from the school of Abū l-Ḥusayn al-Baṣrī (d. 436/1044), adopted the theological doctrine that accepted the saintly miracles (*karāmāt*) of non-Prophets.[19] In contrast to this view, the majority of Mu'tazilites rejected the concept of *karāmāt.*

Imam Yaḥyā b. Ḥamza exemplifies the Zaydīs of the Caspian region who paved the way for the potential acceptance of Sufism and the creation of Sufi orders. Since the Caspian region witnessed various waves of mysticism and espoused moderate views of Sufism, some Zaydīs in Yemen followed in their footsteps. Another such imam was Sayyid Yaḥyā b. al-Mahdī b. Qāsim b. al-Muṭahhar, a scholar from the eighth/fourteenth century, an important Zaydī-Ḥusaynī figure who wrote a book vital to the promotion of Sufism in Zaydī areas. In his manuscript entitled "Joining Brothers in the Decorative Blessing of the People of Time" (*Ṣilat al-ikhwān fī ḥilyat barakat ahl az-zamān*), Yaḥyā b. al-Mahdī introduces us to the spiritual life of his shaykh, Ibrāhīm b. Aḥmad al-Kayna'ī (d. 793/1391) who founded Sufi communities across Yemen, including in Ṣa'da, Ḥūth, Thulā, Ṣan'ā', Ma'bar, Dhamār, Maṣna'at Banī Qays, Khubān and Ẓafār—part of Yarīm in the governorate of Ibb—Wa'ra, Qāra, and others.[20] Yaḥyā b. al-Mahdī also speaks of the link between Yemen, Gilan, and Daylam, stating that Aḥmad b. Amīr [b. an-Nāṣir al-Ḥasanī] al-Jīlānī embarked on a trip to Yemen to extend his friendship to Imam al-Mu'ayyad Yaḥyā b. Ḥamza (d. 749/1349) who, however, had died before his arrival. Learning the bad news, he turned to his successor Imam al-Mahdī 'Alī b. Muḥammad (750–773/1359–1371) who resided in Ṣa'da. Al-Jīlānī had brought from Jīl and Daylam a six-volume manuscript, known as "The Book of Sufficient Collection" (*Kitāb al-jāmi' al-kāfī*), on early Zaydī jurisprudence of Kufa by Abū 'Abd Allāh al-'Alawī. He gave it as a gift to Imam al-Mahdī 'Alī b. Muḥammad. The latter's son and successor, an-Nāṣir Ṣalāḥ ad-Dīn Muḥammad b. 'Alī (d. 793/1391), mentioned above, inherited the book and continued to be friends with al-Jīlānī. It is said that al-Jīlānī wrote a book entitled "The Crème de la Crème Regarding the Asceticism of the Companions" (*Ṣafwat aṣafwa fī zuhd aṣ-ṣaḥāba*).[21]

Ibrāhīm al-Kayna'ī and Sufi Literature

According to Yaḥyā b. al-Mahdī, the first person to introduce Sufi rituals and dress code to the Zaydī lands was al-Ḥasan b. Salmān from Wādī l-Ḥār near Dhamār. The latter was noted for his expertise in religious sciences such as Qur'ān exegesis, *ḥadīth,* and Islamic jurisprudence. Owing to the probable influence of Sayyid Aḥmad b. Amīr al-Jīlānī, al-Ḥasan b. Salmān became a prominent expert in the legal doctrine of the Caspian Zaydī Imam an-Nāṣir li-al-Ḥaqq. He also participated in raising funds for Imam al-Mahdī (d. 773/1371) in his fight against those who opposed the Zaydīs. Al-Ḥasan b. Salmān is reported to have founded in his hometown a school of *hijra* (*pl. hijar*). Like the Sufi orders that clustered around a Sufi lodge, the term "*hijra*" implies a migration of students and scholars to a particular place for the purpose of education.[22] Yaḥyā b. al-Mahdī, the author of *Ṣilat al-ikhwān,* suggests that the piety of al-Ḥasan b. Salmān is a reflection of that of Ibrāhīm b. Aḥmad al-Kayna'ī (d. 793/1391), but Yaḥyā al-Mahdī did not mention that al-Ḥasan was a disciple of al-Kayna'ī like himself. However, al-Kayna'ī had other disciples such as Qāsim b. 'Umar al-Jūbalī or al-Jabalī. This latter was one of his closest disciples and became a significant supporter of al-Kayna'ī's teachings after his death. Another disciple of al-Kayna'ī was Yaḥyā b. Ḥamza al-Bazam aṣ-Ṣan'ānī who, according to Yaḥyā b. al-Mahdī, was an ascetic recluse who imitated his shaykh in dress and eating.

Ḥasan b. Mūsā b. Ḥasan was another companion to al-Kayna'ī whether in travel or residence.[23] It should be noted here that Ibrāhīm al-Kayna'ī received his Sufi cloak (*khirqa*) from Ibn Abī al-Khayr who died sometime in the late eighth/fourteenth century. According to ash-Shawkānī (d. 1250/1834), in his "Rising Moon" (*al-Badr al-ṭāli'*), the descendants of (Banū) al-Kayna'ī were spiritual leaders (*lahum riyāsa*).[24] One of al-Kayna'ī's miracles (*karāmāt*), reported by ash-Shawkānī, is that a pious man saw al-Kayna'ī in a dream after his death as being in a station higher than that of Ibrāhīm b. Adham (d. 160/777). He said: "Glory be to God, the station of Ibrāhīm al-Kayna'ī is higher than the station of Ibrāhīm b. Adham." Then, he heard someone saying, "Had the stations not been for the prophets, allowing no one to reside there except them, then Ibrāhīm al-Kayna'ī would have been in them." In describing another *karāma* ash-Shawkānī states that "while al-

Kayna'ī was on his way back from Mecca, passing by Jāzān, which had experienced a long drought, the people asked him to appeal to God to send them rain. He supplicated for them and the rain fell."[25] However, Yaḥyā b. al-Mahdī speaks of his other Sufi shaykh, who was at the same time one of the shaykhs of al-Kayna'ī, 'Abd Allāh b. Abī l-Khayr of Ṣāyid, a branch of the tribe of Hamdān in North Yemen. Ibn Abī l-Khayr was one of the well-known Zaydī scholars, who mastered most Islamic sciences including law, historiography, philosophy, and speculative theology (*kalām*). A prolific writer, Ibn Abī l-Khayr was famous for his refutations of the theology of determinism (*jabr*) as well the esoteric theology (*bāṭinī*) of the Ismā'īlīs. In addition, he wrote a hagiography on the lives of some prominent Sufis and eventually became a devoted Sufi himself. In 773/1371 he was introduced to the practical side of the Sufi state known as the remembrance of God's name (*dhikr*) by Aḥmad b. Muḥammad al-Nassākh, who in turn received it from the well-known Egyptian Sufi master Yūsuf al-Kūrānī (d. 768/1367).[26] The spiritual path of al-Kūrānī goes back to Abū l-Najīb al-Suhrawardī (d. 563/1168), the uncle of Shihāb ad-Dīn Abū Ḥafṣ 'Umar as-Suhrawardī (539–632/1145–1234).[27]

As a Zaydī scholar, Ibn Abī l-Khayr seems to have remained loyal to the Zaydī doctrines over Sufi teaching, particularly those radical ideas that may suggest it is lawful for a person who has attained a high station in the Sufi path to contravene Islamic legal rules. His treatise entitled "The Introduction and the Duties in the Path of the Disciple and the Circumambulator" (*al-Muqaddima wa l-waẓā'if fī ṭarīq al-murīd wa wa ṭ-ṭā'if*), quoted by Yaḥyā b. al-Mahdī, offers clear evidence of his intention to purify Islamic theology—and particularly Zaydī theology—of its perceived "extreme" Sufi influences. He, however, called for support of the Prophet's family in their holy strife (*jihād*) against infidels and the religious necessity to respond to their summons. He also, like Imam Yaḥyā b. Ḥamza (d. 749/1349), rejected the Sufi concerts (*samā'*) as well as ecstatic utterances (*shaṭaḥāt*) and dancing. It seems so far that there was a fierce hostility between the two camps: the Sufis who advocated a spiritual way of life and were confined mostly to the coastal areas of Tihāma, and the Zaydīs in the mountains who were suspicious of Sufi teachings or practices.

Ibrāhīm al-Kayna'ī (d. 793/1391), the Sufi master who had a significant impact on Zaydī regions, was probably favored because he supported the intentions of Zaydī imams. I do not note any resentment from his side against the massacre of the defenseless Sufi ash-Shāwirī and his sons. On the contrary, Ibn al-Muqrī from the opposing camp of jurists (*fuqahā'*) defended the reputation of ash-Shāwirī. Perhaps al-Kayna'ī wanted to appease the imams and break the stigmatizing notion that imams are unapproachable, as has been described throughout the history of Sufism. Moreover, by associating himself with Imam an-Nāṣir Ṣalāḥ ad-Dīn Muḥammad b. 'Alī (773–793/1371–1391), al-Kayna'ī's intentions were perhaps to take advantage of an-Nāṣir's military power to get rid of another opposing local power, the Ṭayyibī-Ismā'īlīs, despite the fact that they were on good terms with the Imam.[28] The Ṭayyibī-Ismā'īlīs were also on good terms with the Rasūlids, who supported Sufism and were powerful opponents of Zaydī authorities in the highlands. In his manuscript *Ṣilat al-ikhwāṇ* Yaḥyā b. al-Mahdī states that Imam an-Nāṣir supported and funded the Sufi communities of al-Kayna'ī, who in turn praised the imam by saying that he had met no one more knowledgeable of the Sufi disciplines and practices than Imam an-Nāṣir Ṣalāh al-Dīn.

It may have been true, too, that al-Kayna'ī was in dispute with other Sufi rivals in Rasūlid Yemen, who compelled him to found Sufi communities in the Zaydī areas with the financial support of Imam an-Nāṣir. It must be noted, however, that al-Kayna'ī was a charismatic Sufi master whose aura of holiness attracted many local inhabitants to seek his blessings. When he was invited by judge (*qāḍī*) 'Abd Allāh b. Ḥasan al-Dawwārī (d. 800/1397 [or 1398]) to preach in Ṣa'da, large crowds from the surrounding areas came to listen to his sermons and started practicing Sufi rituals such as *dhikr,* asceticism (*zuhd*), in addition to reading mystical books. The inhabitants of Ṣa'da frequently gathered in the mosque of Imam al-Manṣūr, located in the desert. Prayers in the mosque were often led by Caspian scholar Dāwūd b. Muḥammad al-Jīlānī, who migrated to Yemen and was famous for his miracles (*karāmāt*). At the fortress of Muḥṭwar around 736/1335, al-Jīlānī summarized Imam al-Mū'ayyad's book "The Radiant Lights in the Explanation of the Innate Forty" (*al-Anwār al-muḍī'a fī sharḥ al-arba'īn al-salīqiyya*) and named it "The Hereafter Intentions: An Abridgement of the Book of the Radiant Lights" (*al-Maqāṣid al-ukhrawiyya: al-muntaza' min kitāb al-anwār al-muḍī'a*).[29]

Among the Zaydī imams who took interest in Sufism, one finds the overthrown Imam al-Mahdī Aḥmad b. Yaḥyā al-Murtaḍā (d. 840/1437) who wrote the monumental jurisprudential work *al-Baḥr al-zakhkhār.*[30] The eleventh chapter, which can be treated as a separate book, is named "Completing the Rulings and Purifying Inward Sins" (*Takmilat al-aḥkām wa t-taṣfiya min bawāṭin al-āthām*). Al-Murtaḍā later composed a commentary on it entitled "The Fruits of Calyxes in the Explanation of Completing the Rulings" (*Thamarāt al-akmām fī sharḥ takmilat al-ahkām*).[31] This book was the object of discussion in Zaydī circles and received a wide range of commentaries. Two leading Zaydī theologians and literary critics wrote individual commentaries on it in the late eleventh/seventeenth century. The first was "The End of Understandings for the Meaning of Completing the Rulings" (*Nihāyat al-afhām li-ma'ānī takmilat al-aḥkām*) by Ṣalāḥ ad-Dīn al-Jaḥḥāfī (d. 1053/1643)[32] and the second was "The Impregnation of Understandings with the True Theology on Completing the Rulings" (*Talqīḥ al-afhām bi-ṣaḥīḥ al-kalām 'alā takmilat al-aḥkām*) by al-Ḥasan b. Aḥmad al-Jalāl (d. 1084/1673).[33] One should also point out that the Zaydī scholar Aḥmad b. Yaḥyā Ḥābis wrote a commentary known as "Healing the Sicknesses in the Clarification of Completing the Rulings" (*Shifā al-asqām ilā tawḍīḥ takmilat al-aḥkām*), which served as the basis for al-Sayyid Muḥammad b. 'Izz al-Dīn, known as al-Muftī, to write another commentary on it and the original, naming it "The Perfection: The Commentary on Completing the Rulings" (*al-Iḥkām: sharḥ takmilat al-aḥkām*). This manuscript was written in (1102/1690) by al-Sayyid 'Alī b. Muḥammad b. al-Hādī.[34] Imam al-Murtaḍā, however, wrote other treatises redolent of Sufi flavor including "The Life of Hearts in Reviving the Worship of the Most Knowledgeable of the Unseen" (*Ḥayāt al-qulūb fī Iḥyā' 'ibādat 'allām al-ghuyūb*) and "The Shinning Blossom in Ridiculing the Worldly Life and Exalting the Hereafter" (*az-Zahra al-zāhira bi-taḥqīr ad-dunyā wa ta'ẓīm al-ākhira*).

On the other hand, Imam al-Murtaḍā, in line with Zaydī theologians and Imam al-Manṣūr 'Abd Allāh b. Ḥamza (d. 614/1217) in particular, severely condemned Sufi concerts (*samā'*) and the use of any musical instruments. He also denounced scholars who allowed singing, entertainment, and the use of musical instruments. Though such scholars were not mentioned explicitly, one may surmise their names from the Sufi tradition, namely, Abū Ḥāmid al-Ghazālī (d. 505/1111), Ibn 'Alwān (d. 665/1266), Ibn 'Arabī (d. 638/1240), Ibn 'Ujayl (d. 760/1358), al-Yāfi'ī (d. 768/1367), and others. Al-Murtaḍā's book "The Illuminating Moon in the Refutation of Those Who Permit Amusements and the Flute" (*al-Qamar an-nawwār fī r-radd 'alā l-murakhkhiṣīn fī l-malāhī wa l-mizmār*) seems to have been a direct attack on the Sufi authorities of his time. It must be noted that those refutations of Sufi concerts by imams, religious scholars (*'ulamā'*), and some jurists (*fuqahā'*) were nothing more than an expression of opposition to Sufi spiritual authority and popularity with the masses. Perhaps the real reason behind this war of words was the struggle over who would gain the spiritual authority. Often, when one goes to the root of these issues, one finds that controversial disputes occur in order to engage the public in discussions that often lead to fighting.

In addition, Imam ʻIzz ad-Dīn b. al-Ḥasan al-Yaḥyāwī (879–900/1474–1495) wrote "The Treasure of Maturity and the Nourishment of Resurrection" (*Kanz al-rashād wa zād al-maʻād*), which principally deals with the desired ethical qualities to be attained by the worshipper and the reprehensible ethical qualities that he should shun. The book is distinguished from other ethical books by its clear organization. It does not deal with topics of the Sufi school of Ibn ʻArabī. Its overall message is closely patterned on "The Nourishment of Resurrection in the Best Guidance of Servants" (*Zād al-maʻād fī khayr hady al-ʻibād*) by Ibn Qayyim al-Jawziyya (d. 750/1350). Despite the fact that Imam ʻIzz ad-Dīn did not condemn ecstatic outbursts (*shaṭḥāt*), as asserted by al-Ḥibshī, it seems that, in line with the overall Zaydī treatment of Sufism, there was an emphasis on following the path of the legal sciences (*al-ʻulūm ash-sharʻiyya*) and remembrance of God (*dhikr*).

The Climax of the Conflict between Sufis and Zaydī Imams

During the Ottoman military campaign in Yemen, Imam al-Mutawakkil Sharaf ad-Dīn Yaḥyā b. Shams ad-Dīn (912–965/1506–1558) found that some groups of Sufis were not ready to support him against the Ottomans. He presumably believed that these Sufi groups were hostile to the ʻAlids and thus should be classified as practicing enmity (*naṣb*) against the Prophet's family (Āl Muḥammad). At that time, the conflict between the proponents of Sufism and their detractors among the Zaydī imams were further aggravated due to the circulation of a doctrine, which was supported by the Zaydī scholar Nashwān b. Saʻīd al-Ḥimyarī (d. 573/1177). Despite the fact that this doctrine did not address the hostility between Sufi leaders and Zaydī imams directly, it played a significant role in animating the Sufi-Zaydī controversy. In one of his poems al-Ḥimyarī makes the following inflammatory statement:

The family of the Prophet are the followers of his religion
Among Persians, Africans, and Arabs.
If his family were only his relatives
Then, prayers—of the person who prays—
would comprise the despotic Abū Lahab.[35]

When this doctrine, which asserts that the Prophet's family were all those who follow his religion, was disseminated among the populace, Imam Sharaf ad-Dīn held debates with Sufi theologians and eventually imprisoned many of them, including the Zaydī jurist (*qāḍī*) Muḥammad b. 'Aṭf Allāh al-'Absī (d. after 942/1535), and persecuted others such as the jurist Shaykh Ḥasan b. 'Alī al-Jadr (d. 942/1535). According to Aḥmad b. Ṣāliḥ b. Abī al-Rijāl (1029–1092/1619–1681) who quoted Ḥasan b. Muḥammad al-Zurayqī (896–960/1490–1552), a biographer of Imam Sharaf ad-Dīn, the imam summoned both al-'Absī and al-Jadr to a debate regarding Sufi beliefs. He found that al-Jadr was unqualified for scholarly debates, whereas *qāḍī* Muḥammad was a formidable debater. The imam threatened to punish al-'Absī if he did not abandon his belief. The imam learned later that al-'Absī was untruthful in his promise to recant his Sufi doctrine. Thus, Imam Sharaf ad-Dīn waited for a different occasion where many scholars were present and demanded that he abandon his belief, threatening him this time with execution. Qāḍī al-'Absī then abjured his belief in Sufism and repented, sending a long letter in which he declared his repudiation of Sufism. In one part of the letter, he said:[36]

> Because repentance purged what had come before [sin], I call God, His angels, His messengers, His Prophets, all Imams, and our Imam Sharaf ad-Dīn, and whoever heard or listened among Muslims that I seek forgiveness from God and I repent to Him of the belief that validates Sufi doctrine, or anything I interpreted before this time or any action, deed, belief, or intent due to my ignorance. I repent for all I did, relinquishing immediately, and determining that I will not return to anything of that nature in the future and God suffices as a witness. "Whoever offends again, God will take vengeance on him"[37] and God is the best witness.[38]

Qāḍī al-'Absī sent this penitent letter after he had been mentally and physically tortured. He also was forced to ask his companions to announce their repentance. Despite the fact that Imam Sharaf ad-Dīn did not regard the jurist Ḥasan b. 'Alī al-Jadr as a potential threat, he summoned him to court and demanded he relinquish his belief in the ecstatic Sufi utterances (*shaṭaḥāt al-Sufiyya*). Like Qāḍī al-'Absī, al-Jadr sent a repentant letter in which he declared his rejection of Sufi thought and practices. Imam Sharaf ad-Dīn found out later that al-Jadr was not sincere in his letter of repentance, nor did he fear the imam's threats. As a result, he was executed in 942/1535 by order of Imam Sharaf ad-Dīn.[39] The relationship between the Imams and the Sufi leaders during the reign of Imam Sharaf ad-Dīn went from bad to worse, mainly for political reasons fueled by doctrinal views. There was competition to win the hearts and minds of Sufi leaders whose spiritual authority made them important figures for both the populace and intellectuals. When the imams failed to convince Sufi leaders to rally behind their cause, they were often subjected to severe punishments.

Another Zaydī scholar and jurist who was imprisoned by Imam Sharf ad-Dīn was ʻAbd Allāh b. Qāsim b. al-Hādī al-ʻAlawī (889–980/1484–1572). At the beginning, he had a good relationship with the imam, but as soon as the imam learned that al-ʻAlawī was affiliated with a Sufi movement, particularly with the so-called doctrine of incarnation (*naẓarīyat al-ḥulūl*) according to which God is allegedly incarnated inside the body of the Sufi, as well as the doctrine of the unity of being (*waḥdat al-wujūd*), according to which God manifests Himself in the phenomena and objects of the material universe, he admonished him to abandon such heretical beliefs. Such "dangerous doctrines," along with the practice of clapping and singing during Sufi gatherings (*samāʻ*), were presumed in the eyes of the Zaydī imams at variance with the outward practices of Islamic law (*ẓāhir al-sharīʻa*). The imam was thus suspicious of these practices and had them under his watch. He was a staunch advocate of what he believed to be the protection of Muḥammadan law (*ḥifẓ al-sharīʻa al-Muḥammadiyya*).[40] Al-ʻAlawī was influenced by a Sufi shaykh known as ʻAlī al-Jabartī who arrived at al-Ẓahrayn in the region of Ḥajja, where he accompanied al-Sayyid al-ʻAlawī on his travels. According to Ibn Abī al-Rijāl (d. 1092/1681), it is said that al-ʻAlawī did not accompany al-Jabartī for Sufi ideas per se; rather, he thought that al-Jabaritī was expert in alchemy and the divine names. However, when Imam Sharaf ad-Dīn noticed al-ʻAlawī's Sufi tendencies, he imprisoned him in the fortress of al-ʻArūs.[41] Similarly, after reading al-ʻAbsī's and al-Jadr's apologetic letters, al-ʻAlawī sent his own repentant letter to the imam, clarifying his position, asserting that he had dissociated himself from the ecstatic outburst of the Sufis (*shaṭaḥāt al-Sufiyya*), and praising the imam for his kind treatment. When the imam received the letter, he immediately released him from prison and honored him.[42] The imam's strategy, however, did not achieve its goal, and the tension between imams and the Sufis remained on the rise.

Conversely, the first Ottoman invasion of Yemen around 945/1538 was at first welcomed by the Yemeni Sufis, who had suffered fierce hostility from the Zaydī imams. The Sufis seemed supportive to the new colonial power, and thought that the Ottomans , who were Sunnīs like them, would liberate them from the tyranny of the Zaydī imams.[43] An example of the alliance between the Ottomans and Sufis can be found in the story of the Ottoman navy captain Ṣifr Bik, who was known as the "captain of Yemen" (*Qubṭān al-Yaman*). While Ṣifr Bik was thinking how he could enter Aden under the cover of night, he fell asleep. In a dream, he saw the great Sufi Sayyid Abū Bakr al-'Aydarūs who was one of the famous friends of God (*awliyā'*), and who was reported to have performed many saintly miracles (*karāmāt*) in Aden, where he resided. Al-'Aydarūs reportedly took the Turkish captain by the hand and led him to the Shamsān fortress. Quṭbān al-Yaman woke and followed the plan outlined in his dream. The Ottomans took Aden in 976/1568.[44] This alliance between the Sufis and the Ottomans was strengthened due to the political and religious activities of Murād Bāshā, the governor who ruled Yemen during the period 983–989/1575–1581. Besides building colleges and mosques in Ṣan'ā', such as the Murādī school (*al-madrasa al-Murādiyya*) , and removing some taxes (*rusūm*) instituted by his Turkish predecessors, he left behind endowments (*awqāf*) in Ta'izz, but most importantly contributed to the renovation of many Sufi shrines, including the lodge (*turbat*) of Shaykh al-Harrār b. 'Umar, the shrine of Aḥmad al-Sindī in Ta'izz, and the expansion of the mosque of Aḥmad b. 'Alwān.[45]

Nevertheless, as soon as the Sufis saw the magnitude of the Ottoman soldiers' immorality, such as depredation and using excessive force on civilians, in addition to drinking wine and depravity, they withdrew their support.[46] These reprehensible actions were unacceptable to the Sufis; hence, they unified with those who lived in the mountains and revolted against the Ottomans. At that time a Yemeni rebel assumed the title "Manṣūr Ḥimyar," who was believed to appear in the last days (before the day of judgment), and became powerful in the region of Ānis. He had a number of zealous followers and was able to expel the administrator Murād Bāshā.[47] Ultimately, an army was sent to capture him and many people were killed. He hid in the region until Murād Bāshā put a price on his head. He was then seized and brought to Ta'izz, where he was killed by the order of Murād Bāshā.[48]

On a different occasion, the Turkish commander Qānṣuwa al-Ghūrī demanded that the people of Bait al-Faqīh, a town in the area of Tihāma in the western coastal area of Yemen, bring him a large amount of money. The Sufi Aḥmad b. Ja'far objected, giving the reason that people were scattered in the mountains, thereby unable to provide any money to the commander. This answer infuriated the Turkish commander, who killed the Sufi Aḥmad b. Ja'far.[49] Then, al-Ghūrī intended to lead another military campaign in order to subjugate all Sufis to his rule. He was advised to kill the great Sufi Abū Bakr b. Maqbūl az-Zayla'ī (d. 1042/1632) who had spiritual influence over the coastal area of al-Luḥayya. Az-Zayla'ī was brought up, along with his disciple the jurist Maqbūl b. Aḥmad to Qānṣuwa al-Ghūrī, who remained silent for the afternoon. Upon leaving al-Ghūrī's court, the beads of az-Zayla'ī fell to the ground and scattered. Al-Ghūrī and his soldeirs started collecting the beads while the disciple of az-Zayla'ī and the jurist Maqbūl b. Aḥmad called upon God to scatter Qānṣuwa's power and to disperse his throngs, just as this happened to the beads (*allāhumma shattit shamlahu wa farriq jam'ahu*).[50]

The conflict during the second Ottoman invasion between the Ottomans and the Yemeni tribes continued to grow. For instance, in the year of 1290/1873, a Sufi man appeared in Tihāma claiming to know magic as well as alchemy. He rallied the masses behind him, especially from the tribe of Khawlān, against the Ottoman occupation. Yet he was compelled to flee and his followers scattered around the country, thereby subjecting the Tihāma to the Ottoman administration.[51]

Hostility between the Zaydī imams and the Sufis escalated and reached the brink during the reign of Imam al-Manṣūr al-Qāsim b. Muḥammad (1006–1029/1598–1620), the founder of the Qāsimī imamate. This hostility was incited partially by the alliances between the Sufis and the Ottomans. However, the Sufis never carried arms against the imams and their support for the Ottomans was merely ideological, and most of the time nominal. Since Imam al-Qāsim was struggling relentlessly against the Ottoman invasion of Yemen, he reacted fiercely to the alliances between the Sufis and Ottomans. According to al-Ḥibshī, Imam al-Qāsim studied Sufi teachings and found that they were dangerous. He refuted their doctrines in his book titled "Digging the Liar's Grave" (*Ḥatf anf al-āfik*).[52] In some parts of it, he commented on a poem he composed entitled, "The Full Attainment in the Clarification of the Position of the Sufi Doomed to Perdition" (*al-Kāmil al-mutadārik fī bayān ḥāl al-ṣūfī al-hālik*).[53] The beginning of the poem revolves around an exaggerated statement about the repudiation (*rafḍ*) of the Prophet's family by the majority of the Muslim community that goes back to the time of the Prophet's death. As in the work of "The Difference between the Sects" (*al-Farq bayna al-Firaq*) by 'Abd al-Qāhir al-Baghdādī (d.

429/1037), Imam al-Qāsim enumerates the division of Islamic sects, paying attention to the "heresies of the Sufis" and accusing them of "sexual depravity." In a different treatise, Imam al-Qāsim equated the doctrines of the Sufis to the un-Islamic "esoteric doctrines" (*al-'aqā'id al-bāṭiniyya*), whose roots go back to the pre-Islamic Zoroastrian (*majūs*) religion.[54]

During the period of the Ottoman governor Ḥasan Pāshā, most prominent descendants of Imam Sharaf ad-Dīn were deported to Istanbul for their fierce resistance to the Ottoman occupation. A grandson of Imam Sharaf ad-Dīn, Sayyid Muḥammad b. 'Abd Allāh (d. 1008/1599), was one of the best poets and Zaydī scholars left in Yemen. The new Ottoman governor, Sinān Pāshā, who was more powerful than Ḥasan Pāshā, compelled Sayyid Muḥammad to refute the polemic ideas presented in the poem of Imam al-Qāsim. Being fearful of the Ottoman reprisal, Sayyid Muḥammad composed a poem refuting the ideas of *al-Kāmil al-mutadārik,* defending Sufi music (*samā'*) and moderate Sufi doctrines, and praising the Ottoman sultan Mehmet III along with Sinān Pāshā. Imam al-Qāsim responded to the refutation only after the death of both Sayyid Muḥammad and the Ottoman sultan Mehmet III, naming it *Kitāb Ḥatf anf al-āfik fī jawābihi 'alā l-Kāmil al-mutadārik.* He also apologized for Sayyid Muḥammad, giving the reason that Sayyid Muḥammad did not volunteer to write the refutation and was coerced to do so. In his response, Imam al-Qāsim reiterated the ideas of his previous book *Ḥatf* and concluded that Sufism was the product of Zoroastrianism and Mazdakism. In addition, he equated the Sufis to the Ismā'īlīs, a major branch of the Shī'a, who used symbolism in their interpretation of some universal doctrines, thereby implying that members of these two sects should be executed. It must be noted here, however, that at this time the struggle among the three major theological schools, the Sunnīs, the Zaydīs, and the Ismā'īlīs, was fierce and vicious.

Zaydī imams continued to attack Sufi leaders and Sufi teachings. Imam al-Mutawakkil Ismā'īl, who is the son of Imam al-Qāsim b. Muḥamamd, went further than his father and ordered his retinue to burn "The Bezels of Wisdom" (*Fuṣūṣ al-ḥikam*) by Ibn 'Arabī (d. 638/1240) because of the "heretical" ideas it contained. This attitude was the norm among all later Zaydī imams, who were driven by political considerations. Thus, Ṣāliḥ b. Mahdī al-Maqbalī's (d. 1108/1696 [or 1697]) book "The Towering Banner in the Preference of Truth over Fathers and Scholars" (*al-'Alam al-Shāmikh fī īthār al-ḥaqq 'alā l-ābā' wa-l-mashāyikh*) eulogized Zaydī imams for preventing Sufism from spreading in the northern areas of the country. Much later, after the departure of the third occupation of the Ottoman troops from Yemen, Imam Yaḥyā b. Ḥamīd ad-Dīn (1322–1367/1904–1948) took an oppressive stance against all Sufi brotherhoods, particularly the Shādhilyya Sufi order. Unlike the Ottomans, Imam Yaḥyā was short of troops and so he resorted to a different political strategy, such as capturing and holding hostage the sons of tribal leaders and the sons of Sufi masters in his fortresses. This was a disorganized but smart move to avert the reprisals and revolts of these leaders against his reign.[55]

Crown Prince Aḥmad b. Yaḥyā Ḥamīd ad-Dīn (1367–1382/1948–1962) went further by ordering the destruction of Sufi tombs, including the tomb of the celebrated Sufi master Aḥmad b. 'Alwān (d. 665/1266). Interestingly, the lineage of Zaydī imams and Sufi master Aḥmad b. 'Alwān goes back to 'Alī b. Abī Ṭālib, the Prophet's cousin and son-in-law. However, the history of the Prophet's family is full of fighting and rivalry, not only with foreign powers but also with internal tribal leaders and those within the ruling families of the house of the Prophet. As discussed at length in Chapter 7, the responses to the destruction of the tomb were polarized: Muḥammad Maḥmūd az-Zubayrī (1918–1965), before becoming one of the orchestrators of 1962 Republican Revolution, wrote a poem praising the crown prince for this act.[56] On the other side, in an attempt to match al-Zubayrī's zeal, Zayd b. 'Alī al-Mawshikī (d. 1947) composed a poem expressing his condemnation of the cult of Ibn 'Alwān, while the prolific poet and critic Ibrāhīm al-Ḥaḍrānī (d. 2007) rebuked the destruction of the tomb, arguing that this happened only because Ibn 'Alwān belonged to the Sunnī community.[57] It should be emphasized that literary support by az-Zubayrī and al-Mawshikī for Crown Prince Aḥmad b. Yaḥyā Ḥamīd ad-Dīn occurred only before they became disappointed with his failure to fulfill his reform promises.

Conclusion

The discussion of the Zaydī-Sufi conflict should shed considerable light on the controversy over grave visitation and the influence of the Wahhābī movement in Yemen. Their zeal for destroying Sufi tombs was first an attempt to rid religion of associating idols with God; however, their ambitions expanded to include ruling over territory. Thus, the Zaydī-Sunnī scholars Muḥammad b. Ismā'īl al-Amīr al-Ṣan'ānī (1099–1182/1687–1768 [or 1769]) and Muḥammad b. 'Alī ash-Shawkānī (1172–1250/1758–1834) who had been chief judge for several imams was initially in line with Ibn al-Amīr and others in showing their support for the

Image 4. A woman lying outside Ibn 'Alwān's tomb in wait for a cure for her illness.

Wahhābī movement.[58] As we saw in Chapter 7, Imam ash-Shawkānī later rejected Wahhābī teachings, and at the same time desisted from attacking the Sufi party. Although he wrote a treatise with anti-Sufi views entitled "The Sharp Swords that Cut the Straps of the Lords of Unification [with God]" (*al-Ṣawārim al-ḥidād al-qāṭi'a li-'alā'q arbāb al-ittiḥād*),[59] his student Muḥammad b. Ḥsan ash-Shijnī made it clear at the end of the treatise and in his book entitled *at-Tiqṣār* that ash-Shawkānī made an apology, explaining that his anti-Sufi views were only during ash-Shawkānī's youth and young adulthood. In the following chapter I examine the state of Sufism in Yemen following the age of Ibn 'Alwān.

9

SUFISM IN YEMEN AFTER THE AGE OF IBN 'ALWĀN

What were the contours and debates shaping Yemeni Sufism after the age of Ibn 'Alwān (d. 665/1266), and how are they reflected in contemporary Yemen's Sufi practices? The following chapter provides a survey of Sufi orders in Yemen from their inception up to the present day, including those orders that are no longer functional or neglected in scholarship to date. These orders are the Qādriyya, Rifā'iyya, Shādhiliyya, Suhrawardiyya, Naqshabandiyya, Yāfi'iyya, 'Alawiyya, and the rarely studied al-Aḥmadiyya. This allows us to situate the legacy of Ibn 'Alwān and his order in Yemen. Following this I discuss the long struggle between the Sufis and the jurists (*fuqahā'*) who accused them of heresy. For a significant period following the age of Ibn 'Alwān, Yemeni Sufism was dominated by debates over the teachings of Ibn 'Arabī. However, a sea change in thought coincided with the Ottoman invasion of Yemen: no longer overshadowed by the legacy of Ibn 'Arabī, Yemeni Sufism entered a new period. It was shaped by Sufi thinkers such as 'Abd al-Hādī as-Sūdī (d. 932/1525), whose lyrical poetry echoes Ibn 'Alwān, and 'Umar Muḥammad Bā Makhrama (d. 952/1545), whose popular poetry took on philosophical topics with unprecedented ease.

The Rise of the *Ṭarīqa*

Sufism in Yemen after the age of Ibn 'Alwān (d. 665/1266) entered a new organizational stage based on the *ṭarīqa* institution of the 'Alawī brotherhood. Ibn 'Alwān and his peers Ibn Jamīl (d. 651/1253) and al-Faqīh al-Muqaddam (d. 653/1256) enjoyed a wide following. However, their spiritual lineages did not survive institutionally, despite the fact that their influence on various subsequent Sufi brotherhoods was noticeable. Around that time, Sufism in Ḥaḍramawt was widely disseminated under the auspices of al-Faqīh al-Muqaddam, who was as famous as Ibn Jamīl and Ibn ʿAlwān and who is considered to have been the first *sayyid* to turn to Sufism. I discuss him in some detail when I examine the issue of the ʿAlawī brotherhood (*ṭarīqa*).

Sufi orders in Yemen were, at first, imitations of the grand Sufi orders of Iraq, Syria, North Africa, and Egypt. However, the idea of centralized hierarchal authority was not appealing to the Yemeni communities, and so they did not organize as did their counterparts in the central lands of Islam. Nevertheless, they were able to establish Sufi lodges (*arbiṭa;* sing. *ribāṭ* or Sufi communities *zawāyā;* sing. *zāwiya*) or partial lodges (*khāniqās;* sing. *khāniqa*) run by revered masters who were famous for their saintly miracles (*karāmāt*) and who "used their spiritual authority (*jāh*) to mediate frequent conflicts between rulers and tribes and to protect the peasants from the exactions of both."[1] Such lodges or communities were funded by the rich and pious, who donated generously in the form of land grants or endowments (*awqāf*). The main purpose of the *awqāf* was to support students or disciples who studied Islamic sciences. A significant share of *awqāf* was spent on building religious colleges and mosques under the auspices of some revered Sufi masters. Although these lands were usually exempt from taxation for political and other reasons, Sufi shaykhs generally abstained from using such *awqāf* for personal or family goals.[2]

In all Sufi orders, a central practice was particularly pervasive. It consisted of gatherings, known as "remembering God," or *dhikr.* The founder of the order was a Sufi spiritual guide, who received oaths of obedience from his disciples (*murīdūn*) and was believed to have been the last person in a formal chain of spiritual descent (*silsila*) pertaining to a *ṭarīqah.* Such a chain usually went back to the Prophet Muḥammad.[3] Unfortunately, studies about Sufi orders in Yemen today are rare, and it is assumed that they share the features of other Sufi orders in the Islamic world except for the absence of centralized authority. They share the doctrines of spiritual states and stations (*al-aḥwāl wa'l-maqāmāt*), annihilation (*fanā'*) and subsistence in God (*baqā'*), the doctrine of unveiling (*kashf*), spiritual retreat (*khalwa*), remembrance of God or recitation of His names (*dhikr*), contentment (*riḍā*), trust (*tawakkul*), asceticism (*zuhd*), intuitive knowledge (*maʿrifa*), and finally Sufi concerts (*samāʿ*). The last feature became predominant in Yemeni society, especially in the coastal areas. Before turning to the Yemeni links to the major Sufi orders and their representatives, I provide a brief description of the now extinct ʿAlwāniyya order in Yemen.

'Alwāniyya Order

This order is named after its founder Aḥmad b. 'Alwān (d. 665/1266). Scholarship to date has wrongly classified this order and its origins under the influence of various other Sufis. However, I contend that the essential and distinguishing characteristics of Ibn 'Alwān's order are independent of any another *ṭarīqa* order.

In his *The Sufi Orders in Islam,* J. Spencer Trimingham cites the 'Alwāniyya order among the orders of Badawiyya, Dasūqiyya, Shādhiliyya, which were founded as offshoots of the main Rifā'ī *ṭarīqa,* named after its founder Aḥmad b. 'Alī ar-Rifā'ī (d. 578/1182).[4] Trimingham's source is al-Wāsiṭī's *Tiryāq al-muḥibbīn,* which tells us that Ibn 'Alwān took his *ṭarīqa* from Aḥmad al-Badawī (d. 675/1276) and Aḥmad aṣ-Ṣayyād (d. 579/1183); the latter being a successor (*khalīfa*) of the founder of the Rifā'ī *ṭarīqa,* Aḥmad ar-Rifā'ī. It seems that historians of celebrated saints tend to tie the most prominent Sufi masters to the person whom they are writing about. This is evident from the works of Massignon who ties Ibn 'Alwān to the Ḥallājī tradition simply because Ibn 'Alwān wrote an apologetic treatise about the state of "annihilation" in al-Ḥallāj's mystical experience. Another example is *al-Jawāhir as-saniyya wa'l-karāmāt al-Aḥmadiyya* by 'Abd aṣ-Ṣamad al-Aḥmadī, who mentioned Ibn 'Alwān as one of the successors of al-Badawī. Contemporary Yemeni writers such as al-Ḥibshī and al-Maqāliḥ have attempted to link Ibn 'Alwān to the well-known Sufi master Ibn 'Arabī. As established in Chapter 5, Ibn 'Alwān devised his own Sufism, which is evident throughout all of his works. In spite of the fact that his teachings call for respect and reverence for Sufi masters, he clearly argues that disciples can manage without masters provided they follow the teachings of the Qur'ān and Sunna. Ibn 'Alwān's multitude of supplications and litanies (*awrād; sing. wird*) are scattered throughout his writings and particularly in *at-Tawḥīd al-a'ẓam.* Here I provide an important example of the litanies to be read individually after each prayer (five times a day).

Du'ā' *after the Dawn Prayer* (ṣalāt aṣ-ṣubḥ)

O Allāh, I woke up in the morning [as] a captive at your door, and in need of your mercy. I do not have control over myself, nor harm or benefit, nor death or life, nor resurrection. "And say: 'My Lord, lead me in with a just ingoing, and lead me out with a just outgoing; grant me authority from You'" (17:80). O Allāh, support me with Your spirit, guide me to Your proximity (*sawḥika*), enable me to obey You and preserve me from falling into disobedience; make me among Your party and among those whom You love. Do not allow my soul to control me nor any human being. Take care of all my affairs; confirm my strength with certitude and knowledge, and set me free from the shackles of desires. Elevate my honor in both worlds, the world of empirical appearances (*mulk*) and that of divine sovereignty (*malakūt*). Expand my breast with the certainties of faith. Be my intimate when I am alone in my grave and resurrect me in the company of Your Prophet. Send Your abundant blessings and peace upon our master, the Prophet, and his family and Companions.

Du'ā' ***after the Noon Prayer (*****ṣalāt aẓ-ẓuhr*****)***

Oh God, the sun has passed the midday, and after being high has begun to descend. You are the King, the Compeller, the Proud, the Dominator. You make things perish, while You Yourself persists, and You transform things, while You Yourself are not subject to transformation. I ask for Your forgiveness for what I hear and say, and for wherever I move and roam. Oh You Who always answers [the prayers of the] seekers, accept my deeds with Your favor and generosity. Erase my evil-doings from the record of Your angels. Grant me Your promise and save me from Your punishment. Add me to the elect of Your faithful and humble worshippers, for You are the Grace-Giver. Send Your abundant blessings and peace upon our master, the Prophet, and his family and Companions.

Du'ā' ***after the Afternoon Prayer (*****ṣalāt al-'aṣr*****)***

Oh God, your sun is approaching its setting and it is about to go down and disappear [while] your knowledge encompasses sins I committed and wrong doings I did. I seek your forgiveness to my sins, the effacement of my defects, and paying no attention to my evil-deeds. I ask You to conclude my day with forgiveness, beneficence, kindness, and gratitude. Oh Whose giving is kindness, and Whose rule is justice, save me from [the court of] Your justice to [the court of] Your favor, and from Your judgment to Your forbearance. Oh the Best Benefactor and the Best Grace-Giver. Send Your abundant blessings and peace upon our master, the Prophet, and his family and Companions.

Du'ā' ***after the Sunset Prayer (*****ṣalāt al-maghrib*****)***

Oh God, by Your power the sun set and disappeared from the recognizable sight and touch. What we describe as "today" has become yesterday. The night comes with its darkness, the daylight has passed with its brightness and roses. The moving [objects] have stopped [their motion] and what was motionless has started to move. Whoever was frightened becomes secure, and whoever was secure becomes frightened. I ask You, Oh God, to accept what the angels lift to You of my good deeds and to efface what the angels lift [to You] of my evil deeds, [committed] by my hand, tongue, hearing, sight, or my intellect. [I also ask You] to fix my affairs in this world and the hereafter, and to make the pious people my fellows and brothers, for You are the Generous, the Bestower, the Tremendous, and the Giver without counting. Send Your abundant blessings and peace upon our master, the Prophet, and his family and Companions.

Du'ā' ***after the Night Prayer*** **(ṣalāt al-'ishā')**

Oh God, the night has darkened and displayed its darkness, and Your worshippers have laid the hands of hope and have asked You to rescue them. I ask You to include me among those who called You and You answered them, among those who asked Your help and You helped them, among those who feared You and You rescued them. Oh God, I ask you to make my prayers acceptable, my sins disregarded. I [seek] to connect my means with Your means, to transform myself to the presence of Your holiness. [I ask] that You preserve me during my sleep as You did during my day; and that You preserve my faith in You, my Islam upon You, my trust on You, and my dependence on You. I seek refuge from the temptation of Satan, from his seduction, from his exposure, and from his jealousy. "Oh Lord, in You we trust, and to You we turn, and to You is the homecoming. Oh Lord, make us not a temptation to those who disbelieve, and forgive us. Oh Lord, You are All-mighty and All-wise." (60:4–5).[5] Send Your abundant blessings and peace upon our master, the Prophet, and his family and Companions.

These types of prayers are devotional and esoteric. Their underlying message invites devotees to understand the mystical dimension of Islam. Moreover, they enrich Islamic literature by their simple style and didactic teaching. Most important, they develop in their practitioners contentment, thankfulness, and purity of soul and heart. Of course, there are many other *awrād* and supplications scattered throughout Ibn 'Alwān's works, particularly in *at-Tawḥīd al-'aẓam and Kitāb wa Dīwān al-*

Futūḥ, and are sufficient to be published as a separate book. Although the 'Alwāniyya order no longer exists, its presence in Yemeni intellectual and popular culture is still noticeable. The followers of other Sufi orders frequently use Ibn 'Alwān's *awrād* and lyrical poems during their *samā'* sessions and local gatherings that one may not rule out the possibility of a revival of the 'Alwānī brotherhood in the future. In the following sections, I provide an overview of the major Sufi orders and their representatives in Yemen.

Sufi Orders in Yemen

According to Knysh, the Qādirī, and, to some extent, the Rifā'ī orders were active in the preservation of Ibn 'Arabī's ideas in Yemen. However, while the Qādirī order still enjoys some scattered followers, the Rifā'ī order has faded away. Likewise, the Suhrawardī and Naqshabandī orders are, like the 'Alwāniyya order, no longer active. There is no major difference between the Shādhilī and 'Alawī orders in Yemen, and both continue to have Sufi communities. Whereas the Shādhilī order has spread in the rural areas near the two cities, Ta'izz and Ibb, the 'Alawī order has been active in Ḥaḍramawt. It has been reported by some *sāda* historians that there was a spiritual link between the mystical lineage going back to Abū Madyan (d. 594/1191), a famous Sufi from al-Maghrib, and the 'Alawī *ṭarīqa.* The Yāfi'īyya and the Aḥmadiyya Sufi orders are not as prominent in Yemeni culture as the other Sufi orders, but are represented in two important geographical regions, Yāfi' and Aden, which is a testimony to Sufism's wide range in Yemen.[6]

Qādiriyya Order

The Qādirī order in Yemen traces back its Sufi practices to 'Abd al-Qādir al-Jīlānī (d. 561/1166) who came from a family of *sayyids,* descendants of 'Alī b. Abī Ṭālib, the Prophet's cousin and son-in-law. According to Hodgson, al-Jīlānī neither intentionally founded an order, nor appointed a successor. "But he had bestowed the *khirqa* cloak, in recognition of spiritual maturity, on many disciples."[7] Among the Yemeni disciples who took the *khirqa* directly from 'Abd al-Qādir at Mecca in 561/1166 was shaykh 'Alī b. 'Abd ar-Raḥmān al-Ḥaddād. He was sent by 'Abd al-Qādir to propagate the Qādirī order in Yemen.[8]

According to ash-Sharjī (d. 893/1487), the majority of Yemeni Sufi shaykhs received their Qādirī *khirqas* from al-Ḥaddād.[9] One of these Sufis was 'Abd Allāh b. 'Alī al-Asdī (d. 620/1223) who first took the Sufi *khirqa* from al-Ḥaddād and later obtained another from 'Abd al-Qādir himself while on pilgrimage.[10] Another Qādirī Sufi is Ibrāhīm b.

Bashshār al-'Adanī, who received the *khirqa* from 'Abd al-Qādir himself and was a disciple of the famous Yemenī Sufi, Aḥmad b. Abī al-Khayr, known as aṣ-Ṣayyād (d. 579/1183). Al-'Adanī benefited from the companionship of aṣ-Ṣayyād and eventually compiled an account of aṣ-Ṣayyād's biography and miracles. It appears that numerous Yemeni Sufis were influenced by the Qādirī brotherhood, such as Ibrāhīm b. Muḥammad Bā Hurmuz; Aḥmad b. Yaḥyā al-Musāwā (d. 841/1437), the leader of the Sufi community in Zabīd; Ismā'īl al-Jabartī (d. 806/1403), who will be discussed below; Abū Bakr b. Ḥarba; 'Abd Allāh b. 'Aqīl Bā 'Abbād; Aḥmad b. al-Ja'd; and others.[11] But the fervent advocate of the Qādiriyya Sufi brotherhood is 'Abd Allāh b. As'ad al-Yāfi'ī (d. 768/1367).[12] He wrote a hagiographical book titled "The Most Brilliant Glory in the Virtues of 'Abd al-Qādir" (*Asnā al-mafākhir fī manāqib 'Abd al-Qādir*) in which he praises the excellent qualities of 'Abd al-Qādir al-Jīlānī (d. 561/1166) and shows his deep love and tremendous respect for him. The Qādirī order shares with other Sufi brotherhoods major characteristics such as the practice of *samā'*, remembrance of God (*dhikr*), and supplications for the Prophet (*ṣalāt 'alā an-nabī*). Finally, the Qādirī order in Yemen was especially active in the preservation and diffusion of Ibn 'Arabī's ideas in Yemen.[13]

Rifā'iyya Order

The Rifā'ī order of Yemen can be traced back to the middle of the sixth/thirteenth century. It was named after its founder, Aḥmad b. 'Alī ar-Rifā'ī (d. 578/1182). Ar-Rifā'ī is the grandfather of Najm ad-Dīn al-Akhḍar who inherited ar-Rifā'ī's teachings and was the primary teacher of 'Uthmān b. 'Abd ar-Raḥmān al-Qudsī (d. 688/1289), a native of Jerusalem. According to ash-Sharjī (d. 893/1487), al-Akhḍar bestowed the Sufi *khirqa* upon al-Qudsī and sent him to Yemen to propagate the Rifā'ī teaching.[14] Al-Qudsī stayed for a while with the Sufi shaykh 'Umar b. Sa'īd al-Hamdānī (d. 663/1264) in Dhī 'Uqayb, a village near the town of Jibla. Then, he traveled to other places in Yemen where he established Sufi lodges (*arbiṭa;* sing. *ribāṭ*), the last of which was at adh-Dhahūb, a village below the town of Ibb, where he stayed until his death. His tomb is still in adh-Dhahūb and used to be an object of occasional visitation (*ziyāra*). *Ribāṭ* adh-Dhahūb was, like many other *arbiṭa* in the Ibb province, a major center of religious and Sufi studies, although it is no longer functional today.

One characteristic of the Rifā'ī order in Yemen is its loud *dhikr.* This feature has an impact on the other Sufi orders, particularly the late-arriving Shādhiliyya. The Rifā'iyya is notorious for engaging in strange activities, such as eating live snakes, cutting themselves with swords and lances without being hurt, and taking out their own eyes. In his manuscript *Bahjat az-zaman,* Yaḥyā b. al-Ḥusayn mentioned an incident which he himself saw in 1048/1638. According to him, one of Ibn ʻAlwān's spiritually affiliated dervishes had eaten a third of a snake while reciting the name of God. The contemporary writer and critic, al-Ḥibshī comments on this act as being notorious, which provided evidence that later Sufism declined into magic and sleight of hand (*sha'wadha*).[15] Jāmī (d. 898/1492) excused Aḥmad ar-Rifā'ī from such "aberrations" by saying that "this is something the shaykh did not know, nor did his companions."[16] However, it is worth noting that eating snakes in Yemen by some followers of unidentified Sufi orders came to an end after the revolution of 1962 against the Imams of Ḥamīd ad-Dīn's family because of the spread of progressive ideas. Finally, alongside the Qādirī order, the Rifā'ī was active in the preservation and diffusion of Ibn ʻArabī's ideas in Yemen.

Shādhiliyya Order

The Shādhilī order is named after its founder Abū al-Ḥasan ʻAlī b. ʻAbd Allāh ash-Shādhilī (d. 656/1258). The order seems to have arrived in Yemen at the beginning of the ninth/fifteenth century, though some have suggested that it arrived in Ḥaḍramawt around the thirteenth century via the disciples of Abū Madyan, who is considered to have been the spiritual father of the Shādhiliyya order. According to some sources, the Yemeni national ʻAlī b. ʻUmar b. Da'sayn (d. 821/1418) left Yemen for Mecca to perform the pilgrimage and then traveled as an itinerant ascetic to Syria and Egypt. There he met shaykh Nāṣir ad-Dīn b. Bint al-Maylaq ash-Shādhilī in 797/1394 who exposed him to Shādhilī teachings and sent him to Yemen to propagate the Shādhilī cause.[17] On his return trip to Yemen, he stopped in Ethiopia and made friends with Sultan Sa'd ad-Dīn al-Mujāhid, who, according to ash-Sharjī (d. 893/1487), put his trust in him and eventually had him marry his sister. Then, he finally reached Yemen and settled in al-Makhā' where he established a Sufi lodge (*zāwiya*) and disseminated Shādhilī teachings.[18] It is said that he was the first to discover coffee and qat but al-Ḥibshī refutes this claim by saying that this cannot be proved.[19] The Shādhilī order is still active in some regions, especially in the suburbs of the towns of Ta'izz and Ibb. They practice their rituals on certain days of the year, such as the night of the middle of the lunar month Sha'bān. Yemeni Shādhilīs believed that night to be the night of God's determination of events (*laylat al-qadr*). They also celebrate the whole night of the Prophet's birthday (*al-mawlid an-nabawī*) in which they recite the chapter of *Yāsīn* from the Qur'ān as well as various *dhikr* formulas.

It has been the custom of the Shādhilyya order in Yemen to practice the prayers (*awrād*) of its founder, Abū al-Ḥasan ash-Shādhilī, until the present day. The most prominent and widely circulated is the Great Prayer (*al-Hizb al-Kabīr*), which is also called the prayer of piety (*Ḥizb al-Birr*). Other prayers are known as the prayers of Abū al-Ḥasan. These prayers were put together by Ibn 'Atā' Allāh as-Sakandarī (d. 1309) without a name. It is evident that they belong to Abū al-Ḥasan due to their similarity with his other prayers.[20] They consist of some selected verses from selected chapters of the Qur'ān, starting with the whole opening chapter and followed by the following prayer:

> O God, we ask you the accompaniment of fear [of you], the overwhelming longing, the stability of knowledge, and the permanence of thought. We ask you the greatest of secrets (*sirr al-asrār*) which would prevent [us] from the persistence [of committing sin] so that we will have no tranquility with the sin or defect. Purify and guide us to practice these words which You provided through Your Messenger and You tempted with them Your friend Ibrāhīm, who passed the test.

At the very end of these prayers, and after citing many verses of the Qur'ān, Abū al-Ḥasan continues to say:

> O God, connect me with your Great Name, with which no harm may happen in earth or Heaven. By it, grant me a secret in which sins would not count; and by it provide me with an authority to furnish the needs for the heart, mind, inner soul, spirit, and flesh; and an authority to remove the needs of the heart, mind, inner soul, spirit, flesh, and place my names under your names, my attributes under your attributes, and my actions under your actions in a peaceful manner not a faulty way.[21]

In a different prayer Abū al-Ḥasan says:

> O Allāh, O Giver, O Benevolent, O Possessor of Grace, to whom the disobedient servant should turn except to you. Indeed, he was unable to rise to Your satisfaction, for caprice prevented him from

> entering Your obedience. He has no support to rely on except Your Unity. How does one dare to ask while he is turning away from you? Or how one does not ask while he is in need of You![22]

These few prayers are only examples of the hundreds of prayers that the Shādhiliyya order employs in its rituals. Their litanies are divided into daily, weekly, monthly, and yearly uses.The characteristics that unify the Shādhilī followers are their gatherings on special occasions for purely constant remembrance of God (*dhikr*) or other occasions such as celebrating the Prophet's birthdays or keeping vigil on certain nights for the glorification of God.

One of the major representatives of the Shādhilī order in modern times is Sayyid Aḥmad al-Ghurbānī (d. 1980), who was a Sufi recluse from the province of Ibb in central Yemen, and a spiritual leader. Al-Ghurbānī was a muezzin at the Great Mosque of the old city. He left behind a collection of prayers, most dealing with the Prophet's birthday; Sufi poems describing the concept of annihilation (*fanā'*); and various supplications.[23] When he died, his son Muḥammad took charge of the calls to prayers, and he went further than his father by chanting the poetic praises of the Prophet every Thursday after the night prayers at the mosque. His sons in the twenty-first century are among the spiritual leaders of the Shādhilī order around the Great Mosque. Another representative of the Shādhilī order from the same province was Muḥammad b. Qāyid al-'Awāḍī (d. 2005), who had a Sufi gathering community in his house known as *zāwiya.* Many followers flocked to his *zāwiya* from around the country but mainly from the surrounding areas of Ibb, particularly from some villages around Ba'dān and al-'Udayn. Al-'Awāḍī used to attend the physical tomb of the great Sufi Aḥmad b. 'Alwān every year on the first Friday of the month of Rajab, where an annual pilgrimage is held to celebrate the sainthood and the good deeds of Aḥmad b. Alwān.[24] The last of the representatives whom I must mention is our contemporary shaykh of the Shādhilī order, 'Abd as-Salām b. Muḥammad al-Qāḍī. His *zāwiya* is attended by numerous residents of Ibb and those of the surrounding villages of al-'Udayn where he was born and became a celebrated Sufi of our present time. He always celebrates the Prophet's birthday and is extremely knowledgeable of Sufi literature.[25] The most recurrent feature that dominates his *zāwiya* is the session of *dhikr.* Those who were extravagant in committing sins always find relief at his *zāwiya* and their hearts become purified, especially after uninterrupted spiritual exercise. It is safe to say that 'Alawiyya and Shādhiliyya Sufi orders are at the top of other Sufi orders due to their pure reputation and the hundreds of followers.

Suhrawardiyya Order

The Suhrawardī order in Yemen is an extinct order, which dates back to its founder, ʻUmar b. Muḥammad as-Suhrawardī (d. 632/1234), the nephew of Abū'n-Najīb as-Suhrawardī (d. 563/1168). Al-Ḥibshī quotes al-ʻAydarūs (d. 917/1511) in *al-Juz' al-laṭīf* that the only remnant of this order is its "Sufi robe" (*khirqa*).[26] According to as-Suhrawardī, the *khirqa* is of two types: (1) the "robe of discipleship" (*khirqat al-irāda*) and (2) the "robe of seeking blessing" (*khirqat at-tabarruk*). The former is intended only for the true disciple (*murīd ḥaqīqī*), which is an outward emblem of his inner loyalty. The latter, however, is "an imitation of the" former "and as such is acquired only by the imitator (*mutashabbih*)."[27] According to al-Ḥibshī, al-ʻAydarūs mentioned some Yemeni representatives of this order, including Ibrāhīm al-ʻAlawī (d. 752/1351) and Ismāʻīl al-Jabartī (d. 806/1403).[28] However, al-ʻAydarūs also includes al-Jabartī as a famous representative of the three major brotherhoods, Qādiriyya, Rifāʻiyya, and Suhrawardiyya. Perhaps al-ʻAydarūs was referring to the early life of al-Jabartī, who might have been influenced by these orders, but he was the mastermind of an independent Sufi brotherhood known as al-Jabartiyya in Zabīd. The significance of as-Suhrawardiyya lies in the wide circulation in Yemen of Suhrawardī's Sufi manual "Gifts of Divine Knowledge" (*ʻAwārif al-maʻārif*), which became a common text not only for al-Jabartī's circle in Zabīd, but also for the study of Sufism in general.

Naqshabandiyya Order

The Naqshabandī order is one of the late Sufi orders, which was brought to Yemen by Tāj ad-Dīn b. Zakariyā al-Hindī an-Naqshabandī (d. 1050/1640). According to Muhammad Amīn b. Fadl allāh al-Muhibbī (d. 1089/1699), this order was embraced by Aḥmad b. Muḥammad b. ʻUjayl (d. 1074/1663), known as al-ʻAjil, a grandson of the famous friend of God (*walī*) Ahmad b. Mūsā b. ʻUjayl (d. 690/1291) (see Chapter 3).[29] Al-ʻAjil's son was also a prominent member of this order. Al-Ḥibshī quotes al-Muḥibbī in *Khulāṣat al-athar* saying that ʻAbd al-Bāqī b. az-Zayn al-Mizjājī (d. 1074/1663) accompanied shaykh Tāj ad-Dīn al-Hindī and inherited Naqshabandī teachings from him to become his successor in Yemen.[30] In *Tārīkh Ḥadramawt,* Sālim b. Muḥammad al-Kindī, quoted by ʻAbd al-Karīm Saʻīd, states that Muḥammad b.ʻAlā ad-

Dīn al-Mizjājī (d. 1180/1766) was one of the famous followers of this brotherhood who traveled to as-Sind (present-day Pakistan) and disseminated its teachings there.[31]

It appears that the Yemeni branch of this order is now inactive. In some parts of the country, there remain a few abandoned lodges. Many contemporary Sufi teachers and some of their disciples have links to the Naqshabandī order but not as an independent brotherhood. These Sufi learners may even have litanies (*awrād*), which are obviously known and practiced in all major Sufi orders, during which they silently recite the names of God and observe the typical Sufi remembrance of God (*dhikr*). The main characteristic that sets the Naqshabandī order apart from other Sufi orders is their insistence on the devotional type of piety and, to some extent, the mortification of the body, which can be found with Sufis of the early period or mystics from other religious backgrounds, particularly the Indian and Asian religions. The difference between the Naqshabandī brotherhood and the Shādhilī order is insignificant. Whereas the Shādhilīs emphasize *dhikr,* the Naqshabandīs give more weight to austerity, self-imposed strictures, seclusion, and a "silent" *dhikr.*

Yāfi'iyya Order

This order goes back to its founder Abū's-Sa'āda 'Afīf ad-Dīn 'Abd Allāh b. As'ad al-Yāfi'ī (698–768/1298–1367), a well-known scholar, historian, poet, and Sufi of Yemeni background.[32] Due to his intellectual and spiritual abilities at the age of eleven, his father sent him to Aden to further his religious education. After one year of study, al-Yāfi'ī performed the pilgrimage to Mecca and, upon returning to his homeland, joined the circle of the Sufi master, 'Alī b. 'Abd Allāh aṭ-Ṭawāshī (d. 748/1347), announcing his decision to embrace asceticism. In 718/1319, after a period of hesitancy between taking up a life as an ascetic or pursuing knowledge (*'ilm*), he finally decided to continue his religious learning. He then moved to Mecca to study the major collections of Prophetic *ḥadīth* in addition to the Sufi manual *'Awārif al-Ma'ārif* of as-Suhrawardī (d. 632/1234), at the feet of Ibrāhīm Muḥammad b. Abī Bakr known as Raḍiyy ad-Dīn aṭ-Ṭabarī (d. 822/1419). Simultaneously, he studied Islamic jurisprudence with the judge Muḥammad b. Aḥmad, known as Najm ad-din aṭ-Ṭabarī (d. 765/1363).[33] While there he married, but his marriage was unsuccessful; perhaps because he favored an ascetic life. His life as an ascetic lasted for ten years in Madina. In 734/1335 al-Yāfi'ī made a trip to Syria (ash-Shām), visited Jerusalem, remained in al-Khalīl for a hundred days, then left for Egypt where he met a number of celebrated local Sufis.

As mentioned above, al-Yāfi'ī wrote a hagiographical book titled "The Most Brilliant Glory in the Virtues of 'Abd al-Qādir" (*Asnā al-mafākhir fī manāqib 'Abd al-Qādir*) in which he shed light on the exceptional qualities of 'Abd al-Qādir al-Jīlānī (d. 561/1166), the founder of the Qādiriyya Sufi brotherhood.[34] Al-Yāfi'ī was aware of the Sufi brotherhoods of his time and was in friendly relations with all of them. He founded his own Sufi brotherhood, known in premodern Yemen as al-Yāfi'iyya and which has some followers today.[35] One of his most distinguished disciples was Shāh Ni'matullāhī Walī (731–834/1330–1431), who spent seven years with him for spiritual training that allowed him to achieve an advanced level of mystical awareness. Subsequently, Shāh Ni'matullāhī became the founder of the popular Ni'matullāhī Sufi order.[36] Influenced by his master, al-Yāfi'ī, Ni'matullāhī also distinguished himself as an interpreter and disseminator of the teachings of Ibn 'Arabī (d. 638/1242). In his *Abū al-Ḥasan ash-Shādhilī,* 'Ali Sālem 'Ammār argues that despite the fact that the masters of the Shādhiliyya order had entrusted no one other than al-Yāfi'ī with their mystical secrets, his name was not circulated among their masters and had not appeared in their chain of transmitters.[37] This was sufficient evidence for E. Geoffroy to consider al-Yāfi'ī's relations with the Shādhiliyya to be problematic.[38] However, the disappearance of al-Yāfi'ī's name from the Shādhiliyya *silsila* (a chain of Sufi transmitters of knowledge) should not undermine his cordial relationship with them.

After completing his journeys, al-Yāfi'ī returned to Mecca and remarried. He divided his time between teaching, writing, and occasionally mediating disputes among tribal leaders. He was sought out for his knowledge, spiritual guidance, and above all his blessings (*baraka*). Influenced by the Ash'arite speculative theology, al-Yāfi'ī opposed the rationalistic dialectics of the Mu'tazilites. He even wrote a polemical work: *Marham al-'ilal al-mu'ḍila fī 'r-radd 'alā a'immat al-mu'tazila.*[39] Ibn Ḥajar al-'Asqalānī (d. 852/1448) reported on the authority of Taqiyy al-Dīn b. Rāfi' that al-Yāfi'ī took sides with the Ash'arites and attacked Ibn Taymiyya (d. 728/1328) but added that al-Yāfi'ī in turn was attacked by the Ḥanbalites who supported Ibn Taymiyya, such as aḍ-Ḍiyā' al-Ḥamawī.[40] Al-Yāfi'ī wrote on a wide range of topics from history to hagiography. His most celebrated books include *Mir'āt al-janān wa 'ibrat al-yaqẓān,*[41] *ad-Durr an-naẓīm, Rawḍ ar-rayāḥīn fī ḥikāyāt aṣ-ṣāliḥīn,*[42] and *Nashr al-maḥāsin al-ghāliya fī faḍl al-mashāyikh aṣ-ṣūfiyya.*[43]

These books seem apologetic, polemical, and above all enlighten the stories of friends of God (*awliyā'*). Like Ibn 'Alwān (d. 665/1266), al-Yāfi'ī defended the sainthood of al-Ḥallāj (d. 309/922) and years later was embroiled in the debate over the sainthood of Ibn 'Arabī (d. 638/1240). Of course, he was an advocate of Ibn 'Arabī's status as a great "friend of God."

Ash-Sharjī (d. 893/1487) considered al-Yāfi'ī not only a master of the two ways, that is, exoteric and esoteric, but also an accomplished mystical poet and miracle worker.[44] Owing to al-Yāfi'ī's excellent quality of holiness, Jamāl ad-Dīn al-Asnawī (d. 772/1370) in his *Ṭabaqāt ash-shāfi'iyya* reports that al-Yāfi'ī's unimportant belongings were sold at high prices because people wanted to keep them as relics and because they were thought to be holy.[45] The Yemeni followers of al-Yāfi'ī's Sufi order rely on his books mentioned above and read them during their spiritual gatherings in the afternoons. They do not have specific prayers like the other Sufi orders. They feel proud not because of al-Yāfi'ī mystical legacy, but because he descended from their same geographical region. Although, the Yāfi'īyya order is now almost extinct, there are a few followers who are scattered around the tribal regions of Yāfi' who still recite some of the private prayers composed by al-Yāfi'ī and gather on certain occasions for spiritual learning or blessings.

'Alawiyya Order

In 1289/1872 Aḥmad b. Muḥammad b. Ḥusayn al-Ḥibshī finished copying the draft of his father's book titled *al-'Uqūd al-lu'lu'iyya fī bayān ṭarīqat as-sāda al-'Alawiyya.* This manuscript was printed with four other treatises in a collection called *al-Majmū' al-laṭīf* by Sayyid Shaykh b. Muḥammad b. Ḥusayn al-Ḥibshī in 1328/1910. According to the author of *al-'Uqūd,* the famous Sufi scholar 'Abd Allāh b. 'Alawī al-Ḥaddād (d. 1044/1634) provided a description of the nature of the 'Alawī order and its development. Al-Ḥaddād argues that the path of the Banū 'Alawī Sayyids is inherited from al-Ḥusayn b. 'Alī (d. 61/680), 'Alī Zayn al-'Ābidīn (d. 96/714), Muḥammad al-Bāqir (d. 115/733), Ja'far aṣ-Ṣādiq (d. 148/795), and other Ḥusaynid imams. He also states that it is the "Right Path," which is based on the Qur'ān, the Prophet's sayings (*aqwāl*), acts (*af'āl*), and his tacit approval (*taqrīr*) of certain actions. Al-Ḥaddād adds that it is the path of the companions, the Prophet's family, and the orthodox members of his community who followed in their footsteps.[46] According to al-Ḥaddād, the tenets of this *ṭarīqa* were laid down by Abū Ṭālib al-Makkī (d. 386/996) in his "The Nourishment for the Hearts" (*Qūt al-qulūb*), and by 'Abd al-Karīm al-Qushayrī (d. 465/1072) in his "Epistle on Sufism" (*ar-Risāla fī at-taṣawwuf*), then detailed and refined by Abū Ḥāmid al-Ghazālī (d. 505/1111) in his "The Revival of the Religious Sciences" (*Iḥyā' 'ulūm ad-Dīn*).

Al-Ḥaddād quotes 'Abd Allāh Bā Sudān in *Fayḍ al-asrār wa'qtibās al-anwār* saying that the 'Alawī *ṭarīqa* is distinct from other Sufi orders due to its features, pious characteristics, and above all its direct spiritual transmission from the Prophet. Bā Sudān argues that there was a consensus regarding the importance (*faḍl*) and distinctiveness (*khuṣūṣiyya*) of Āl Bā 'Alawī over all the other members of the Prophet's family.[47] When al-Ḥabīb 'Abd ar-Raḥmān b. 'Abd Allāh Balfaqīh was asked about the 'Alawī order and whether it is sufficient to describe it as "following the Qur'ān and Sunna," he answered by saying that it is one of the Sufi orders that adheres to the principle of "following the Texts" (i.e., the Qur'ān and Sunna), but in a special way (*'alā wajh makhṣūṣ*). He elaborates by saying that the order has a feature, which is more than just following the Book and Sunna in a general way (*'alā wajh al-'umūm*). He adds that since people differ in their understanding of religion, there has to be a special knowledge limited to a special people (i.e., the elect members of the Muslim community, specifically the *sāda* of the Bā 'Alawī clan).[48]

Like many other Sufi orders, the 'Alawī order supports the doctrine of outward (*ẓāhir*) and inward (*bāṭin*). The outward aspect of the *ṭarīqa* consists of pursuing religious sciences and ritual practices while its inward aspect is the attainment of Sufi stations (*maqāmāt*) and states (*aḥwāl*). The virtues of the order lie in the fact that its adherents never disclose its secrets (*ṣawn al-asrār*) and that they preserve them from the uninitiated. The outward aspect of the order can be found in al-Ghazālī's *Iḥyā'* whereas the inward is what the Shādhiliyya describe as the attainment of the ultimate reality (*taḥqīq al-ḥaqā'iq*) and divesting God's unity (*tajrīd at-tawḥīd*) of any traces of polytheism. Some other characteristics that the 'Alawī order share with other orders are the solemn pledge between the master and his disciple (*akhdh al-'ahd*), instruction (*talqīn*), wearing the Sufi robe (*lubs al-khirqa*), entering the spiritual retreat (*dukhūl al-khalwa*), spiritual exercise (*riyāda*), spiritual struggle (*mujāhada*), and living in a community (*ṣuḥba* and *mukhālaṭa*).

The 'Alawī *ṭarīqa,* according to historians of *sāda* extraction, is linked to the Madyaniyyah order, which goes back to its great mystic and founder Abū Madyan Shu'ayb al-Maghribī (d. 594/1191), who was also the preceptor of Abū al-Ḥasan ash-Shādhilī (d. 656/1258), the founder of the Shādhiliyya brotherhood. In addition, the 'Alawī order is linked to 'Abd al-Qādir al-Jīlānī (d. 561/1166), through the spiritual transmission of poleship (*al-quṭbiyya*). According to al-Ḥabīb 'Abd Allāh b. 'Alawī al-Ḥaddād (d. 1044/1634), the poleship transferred from 'Abd al-Qādir, a great preacher of Baghdad; to Abū Madyan, a mystic of the Maghrib; to Muḥammad b. 'Alī al-'Alawī, known as al-Faqīh al-Muqaddam (d. 653/1256), a renowned Sufi master of Ḥaḍramawt. This transmission of *quṭbiyya* was through rank, not succession. The life of al-Faqīh al-Muqaddam was very important not only for the political history of Ḥaḍramawt but also to the 'Alawī family in general. His significance springs from his status as a charismatic leader at a time when Ḥaḍramawt was torn by constant tribal fights. He advised the descendants of the Sayyid clans to abandon arms, which they used to carry all the time and to join him in the pursuit of religious and moral values.[49] Al-Faqīh al-Muqaddam was the founding father of the first Sufi order in Ḥaḍramawt and, thus, the pole (*quṭb*) of the 'Alawī *ṭarīqa,* which continues to exist to the present day.[50] Based on *al-'Uqūd al-lu'lu'iyya fī bayān ṭarīqat as-sāda al-'Alawiyya* by Muḥammad al-Ḥibshī, R. B. Serjeant summarizes the main points of the 'Alawī *ṭarīqa:*

> The Sayyids affirm it is the best *ṭarīqa,* based on the Qur'ān, the Sunna, and the beliefs of the Pious Ancestors (*al-aslāf*). No 'Alawī may go counter to the way of those Pious Ancestors, but act with humility, piety, and lofty motive, with the Prophet for his model. The 'Alawī Sufi must love obscurity, dislike manifestation, withdraw from the madding crowd, but he must warn against neglect of religious duties. He must show kindness to wife, children, neighbors, relations, to the tribes, and all Muslims. A 19th century writer advises the Sayyids not to mix with the people of that evil age when rulers are prone to injure those of religious rank. Silence and restraint, he says, are best; if perforce you meet evil persons, speak little and leave as soon as possible.[51] The famous blind 18th century saint 'Abd Allāh al-Ḥaddād avers that Bā 'Alawī *ṭarīqa* is acknowledged the best by Yemenis despite their heresy (*bid'a*), and the Sharīfs of Mecca despite their own honorable rank. Arguments are adduced by 19th century writers to show that an 'Alawī should join no other *ṭarīqa* such as, for example, the Sanūsī. The 'Alawī *dhikr* is not accompanied by the practices so distasteful to contemporary Muslims in many other countries, but *ḥaḍras* are held in the mosques, and the Saqqāf mosque has musicians, the Servants of the Saqqāf, who sing Sufi songs to pipe and drum.[52]

In general, the 'Alawī *ṭarīqa* was based on oral transmission in its first generation because there was no need for written texts. Later on, writing about the *ṭarīqa* became a necessity in order to clarify some obscurities, especially with regard to spiritual behavior. Books such *al-Kibrīt al-aḥmar, al-Juz' al-laṭīf, al-Ma'ārij, al-Burqa,* and others were written to forestall the gradual disappearance of mystical knowledge. In other words, the 'Alawī *ṭarīqa* seems to have experienced a gradual transmission of knowledge similar to that of the historical process of knowledge transmission of Islam itself. That is to say, Islamic knowledge was transmitted orally during the time of the Prophet and his companions. But at the time of the successors, compilation started to take place. The same may be true about the transmission of Sufi literature. According to al-Qushayrī (d. 465/1072), at the beginning, Sufi wisdom was transmitted orally. Then, at a later age, and more precisely, after heresies had sprung out and people began to fear the spread of delusion, compilation of Sufi manuals became indispensable.[53] Accordingly, the evolution of the 'Alawī *ṭarīqa* can be compared with the history of Islam itself or the history of Sufism in general.

Al-Aḥmadiyya Sufi Order

The research on the al-Aḥmadiyya Sufi order in Yemen is extremely rare and its history is yet to be written. In what follows, I will provide a cursory overview of its presence in Yemeni society since a more detailed discussion is impossible at this stage due to the scarcity of sources. The Aḥmadiyya is a Sufi order that confined itself to the port of Aden. Its origin must have derived from the Sufi teachings of Aḥmad Ibn Idrīs (1164–1253/1750–1837) whose legacy spread in Africa and Arabia as a response to the challenges advanced by the Wahhābī movement in the late nineteenth century.[54] A distinction must be made here, however, to clarify the confusion that sprang from the coexistence of a more recent but totally different group known as the Aḥmadiyya, which derived its teachings from the Qadyāniyya, a new religion in India founded by Ghulām Aḥmad (d. 1908) of Qadian, a village in Punjab. The latter group does not seem to be possible because of the mixed messages that Ghulām Aḥmad had in his teachings. He claimed to have been the Promised Messiah of the Christians and a prophet and the guided one (*Mahdī*) for the Muslims, in addition to his assertion of being the return of Krishna. These doctrines are surely in contradiction to pure Islamic teachings. After the death of his successor, Nūr ad-Dīn in 1914, the community split and the majority followed Ghulām Aḥmad's son Maḥmaūd Aḥmad while the minority withdrew to Lahore.[55]

According to Trimingham, the Aḥmadiyya sent their missionaries to many coastal areas, especially west Africa.[56] Since Aden was one of the coastal areas, and closer to India than west Africa, it became one of the major centers for the intellectual activities of the Aḥmadiyya missionaries, even though its influence remained marginalized. The intellectual activities of these missionaries was likely strengthened by the constant cultural exchange and activities of businessmen who were residing in Aden under British rule (1839–1963). Interestingly, agents from the Lahore branch came to Aden to propagate for their cause headed by Ghulām Aḥmad Mubashshir in 1947. He remained in Aden for two years, trying to call for the new religion but never succeeded in developing it further. In 1949, he returned to Lahore after he had passed his teaching to a few confidants whereupon the new religion completely disappeared. However, our research is meant only to clarify the confusion between the two names of the Aḥmadiyya and will not focus on the Qadyāniyya since it is not a Sufi order and certainly un-Islamic. Rather, I provide a cursory glance at the Aḥmadiyya Sufi order.

The Idrīsī tradition that was popular in Sudan, 'Asīr of Saudi Arabia, and Tihāma and Zabīd of Yemen began to compete for spiritual leadership and made significant progress. Three distinguished branches diverged early from the original Sufi order of Ibn Idrīs. These are the Sanūsiyya, the Khatmiyya, and the Aḥmadiyya.[57] All of these Sufi orders have one thing in common, namely, the allegiance to the house of the Prophet and his descendants. The former two developed very sophisticated rituals that Ibn Idrīs, himself, had rejected.[58] Unlike the Sanūsiyya and the Khatmiyya, the Aḥmadiyya remained closer to the teachings of Ibn Idrīs. Its founder is Ibrahim Ibn Sālih Ibn 'Abd ar-Rahmān ad-Duwayhi, who was later known as ar-Rashīd. At the time of Ameen Fares Rihani (1876–1940), this Sufi order was called the Rashīdiyya.[59]

According to Rihani, the circle (*halaqa*) of the Rashīdiyya-Aḥmadiyya "makes certain pretensions to art, but has nothing spiritual in it. Among the devotees are boys, who stand in rows facing the men; they sing together amatory verses from the Sufi[c] poets; they sway towards each other, the boys looking swooningly at the stars, the men casting sheep's-eyes upon the boys; while the sheikh, sitting on a chair set upon a platform, looks on with supreme satisfaction. The performance, otherwise, is theatrical, and, unlike the *halaqa* at Hodeida, without casualties. How different is the devotion of the Master!"[60] This important piece by Rihani reveals mysteries and differences among Sufi orders even when they have branched out of the same spiritual source. According to Rihani, the rituals of the Aḥmadiyya Sufi order are similar to those of the Shādhiliyya.[61] Rihani points out that "there are four or five *tariqahs* (Sufi cults) in Hodeida, chief among which is the Marghaniyah, whose founder Muhammad al-Marghani was a student of Ahmad ibn Idris."[62] Although the shaykh had died, his followers experienced a wild ecstasy during their rituals to the extent of harming themselves in a violent way, such as by knocking their heads against pillars and causing fatal wounds.[63] Thus, the rituals of the Aḥmadiyya Sufi order is harmless when compared to other Sufi orders. While the Aḥmadiyya continued to propagate their teachings in Aden, especially around some mosques including the famous mosque of Al-'Aaydarūs, the Yemeni revolution in the north of the country against the Ḥamīd ad-Dīn family took place in 1962 and was followed by another revolution in the south against the British in 1963. With the coming of new ideas and progressive movements, the Sufi orders were suppressed and prohibited from public appearances and the Aḥmadiyya disappeared and went into hiding.

The Long Struggle between aṣ-Ṣūfiyya and the Fuqahā'

The history of Sufism in Yemen from the middle of the seventh/twelfth century onward can be classified into three major stages of struggle between *aṣ-ṣūfiyya* and the *fuqahā'* (jurists).[64] While the Sufis promulgated the teachings of Ibn 'Arabī, the *fuqahā'* aggressively tried to discredit them. First, al-Yaḥyāwī (d. 709/1309) and al-Jabartī (d. 806/1403) provoked the *fuqahā'* by founding a circle that skillfully spread his teachings. Among the major figures of al-Jabartī's circle was the head of Zabīd's Sufi community, Ibn ar-Raddād (d. 821/1418) and the well-known Sufi scholar al-Jīlī (d. 832/1428). The second stage was marked by the triumph of the Sufis over their detractors. The major characters of this period were al-Mizjājī (d. 829/1425) who supported the Sufi party, and Ibn al-Muqrī (d. 837/1444) who advocated the position of the anti-Sufi *fuqahā'*. The third stage was marked by debates between Ibn Rawbak (d. 835/1431) and his counterpart Ibn al-Muqrī. There is no doubt that Ibn al-Muqrī played an important part in rallying the *fuqahā'* against the Sufi party in the last two stages. Without the efforts of Ibn al-Muqrī, the *fuqahā'* would not have gained the upper hand over the Sufis. I should note that this long struggle has been critically investigated by Alexander Knysh, and I agree with his analysis—that is, the struggle in question deals with "tension within the Yemeni scholarly community and not a conflict between the 'orthodox' *fuqahā'* and the 'heterodox'

Sufis."[65] Before examining these three stages in detail, I examine the historical conditions that led to their emergence.

Everything began with the discussions between 'Umar b.'Abd ar-Raḥmān b. Ḥasan al-Qudsī (d. 688/1289), a native of Jerusalem, who was sent to Yemen as an emissary by his teacher Najm ad-Dīn al-Akhḍar to propagate Rifā'ī teaching, and his Yemeni disciple and companion, Muḥammad b. Sālim, known as Ibn al-Bāna (d. 677/1278).[66] These discussions took place at the famous religious college Umm as-Sultan in Ta'izz, where al-Qudsī was appointed as professor of speculative theology by the Rasūlid prince al-Ashraf 'Umar (d. 696/1297), who later became the ruler of Yemen.[67] This post is similar in its significance to that of al-Ghazālī (d. 505/1111) when Niẓām al-Mulk appointed him to teach at the Niẓẓāmiyya college (*madrasa*) in Baghdad. The debates over speculative theology (*'ilm al-kalām*) and the philosophical and theosophical ideas discussed by al-Qudsī and his disciple and intimate friend Ibn al-Bāna led some students to accuse them of heresy and unbelief (*kufr*).[68] One of these students, Aḥmad b. 'Abd ad-Dā'im aṣ-Ṣafī (d. 707/1307), reported to his fellow jurisprudents (*fuqahā'*) that al-Qudsī and Ibn al-Bāna "denied the Qur'ān (*yunkirān al-Qur'ān*)" and claimed that "the Qur'ān was not the speech of God (*laysa kalām Al-lāh*)."[69] The *fuqahā'* went to the city's chief religious authority (*ra's al-muftīn*), Abū Bakr Ibn Adam (d. 676/1277) to inform him about what had happened and to gain his support in preventing this heresy from dissemination. Ibn Adam suggested that they kill al-Qudsī and Ibn al-Bāna after the congregational prayer on Friday. They all agreed and pledged to do it.

However, al-Qudsī and Ibn al-Bāna were informed about the plan. When the time of prayer came, al-Qudsī entered the mosque with armed guards and Ibn al-Bāna chose not to attend. The *fuqahā'* inquired about the reason for his absence. They were told, "When Ibn al-Bāna came to know that you had concocted this plan, he warned al-Qudsī . . . and fled to Zabīd to meet al-Muẓaffar and his son al-Ashraf."[70] Al-Janadī (d. 732/1331) states that when al-Ashraf heard Ibn al-Bāna's story about the plot of the *fuqahā',* he wrote to his father al-Muẓaffar about what had happened. When al-Muẓaffar learned of the conspiracy, he immediately sent a letter of reprimand to the *fuqahā'*. He threatened them with severe punishment if they did not cease their bigotry and stirring up unrest in the Rasūlid state.[71] The letter was sent to the governor of Ta'izz to be read during the Friday sermon (*khuṭba*) so that the *fuqahā'* would hear it. When the *fuqahā'* listened to the threatening letter, they were frightened and dispersed. With the dispersal of the *fuqahā',* the initial struggle between the Ṣūfiyya and the *fuqahā'* came to an end.

Upon the death of Ibn al-Bāna, who had succeeded al-Qudsī in teaching speculative theology at the Umm as-Sultan college, his disciple and the active exponent of Ibn 'Arabī's works in Yemen, Abū'l-'Atīq Abū Bakr Ibn al-Hazzāz al-Yaḥyāwī (d. 709/1309), became known. During his pilgrimage to Mecca and Madina, he befriended some scholars (*akābir*), and while there he copied many of Ibn 'Arabī's books.[72] Upon his return, he was received with respect by rulers such as al-Mu'ayyad (d. 721/1322) and others. Biographers such as al-Khazrajī and Ibn al-Ahdal reiterated al-Janadī's description of the intimate friendship between al-Yaḥyāwī and Sultan al-Mu'ayyad. When the latter was put in prison by al-Ashraf (d. 696/1297), al-Yaḥyāwī fled to Wuṣāb where he cultivated Sukhmul, one of the famous irrigated valleys of Yemen.[73] According to Ba'kar, a modern writer, al-Yaḥyāwī sent a poem to al-Ashraf warning him that his reign would not last more than twenty months—a prediction that came true. Ba'kar explains that this was due to divine knowledge (*'ilm ladunnī*).[74] According to al-Janadī, people held different opinions regarding al-Yaḥyāwī's character. Some said he was a saint (*walī*), while the majority attributed to him delusion (*talbīs*), vainglorious pretensions (*ar-raghba fī'd-dunyā'*), and fascination with magic properties of the divine names and alchemy (*kimiyā'*).[75]

Although al-Yaḥyāwī supported the doctrine of commanding the right and forbidding the evil (*al-amr bi'l-ma'rūf wa'n-nahy 'an al-munkar*), a doctrine which all *fuqahā'* advocated, his opponents among the *fuqahā'* were still not satisfied. It was reported that they were hostile to him while he was humble and respectful toward them. On his advice, charitable funds and endowments (*awqāf*) were transferred to the state. According to Ibn al-Ahdal, al-Yaḥyāwī's advice was not given because he was a pious man but because of his desire to curry favor with the rulers. The biases of Ibn al-Ahdal and before him his teacher Aḥmad b. Abū Bakr an-Nāshirī (d. 815/1412) are obvious. The latter, upon the demise of al-Yaḥyāwī, claimed that "Ibn 'Arabī's teaching here [in Yemen] came to an end."[76] An-Nāshirī, however, warned that Ibn 'Arabī's books would reappear in the last quarter of the eighth/fourteenth century.

During the reign of al-Mujāhid, which lasted from 721/1322 to 764/1362, the Yemeni Sufis started to form large communities, similar to the Sufi orders in the rest of the Islamic world. They began to practice Sufi rituals and musical sessions (*samā'*) in the mosques of Zabīd. It was reported that al-Mujāhid (d. 764/1362) cultivated a friendship with the charismatic Sufi leader Ismāʿīl al-Jabartī (d. 806/1403) and gave him numerous gifts. Al-Jabartī enjoyed royal patronage and was on friendly terms with al-Mujāhid and his successors. He gained their respect not only because he was famous for sainthood and miracles but also due to his astute leadership of the Sufi community in Zabīd. One dominant feature of his teachings was the recitation of the Yāsīn chapter of the Qur'ān; he and his circle even came to be known as the people of Yāsīn (*ahl Yāsīn*).[77] Ibn Ḥajar al-ʿAsqalānī (d. 852/1448) emphasized in *Inbāʾ al-ghumr bi anbāʾ al-ʿumr* that al-Jabartī cited a false *ḥadīth* that reciting Yāsīn was a panacea for all misfortunes.[78] However, major experts in *ḥadīth,* including as-Sakhāwī (d. 902/1496) and ash-Shawkānī (d. 1250/1834) did not comment on the *ḥadīth* in question.[79]

According to ash-Sharjī (893/1487), one of al-Jabartī's *karāmāt* was that "while al-Jabartī was attending a Sufi concert (*samāʿ*), he was screaming and running back and forth, saying twice with a loud voice: 'whirlpool' (*al-jalaba*). He stood for a while, pointing with his hands as though he was holding something. Then, he returned to the *samāʿ*. A few days later, shaykh Yaʿqūb al-Mukhāwī arrived from his journey and informed [the people] that on that same night he and his companions were exposed to a strong wind and the sea was rough and they thought they were about to perish. Al-Mukhāwī cried: 'Oh shaykh Ismāʿīl, Oh ahl Yāsīn'. Then, al-Mukhāwī said: 'I saw al-Jabartī coming to the surface of water like a bird and holding the whirlpool by his hands until it stopped. Due to his blessing, God rescued us.'"[80] His biographers mention that al-Jabartī's fame and wide popularity began with his prediction to Sultan al-Ashraf Ismāʿīl b. al-ʿAbbās (d. 803/1400) that the siege of Zabīd by the powerful Zaydī imam Ṣalāḥ ad-Dīn Muḥammad Ibn al-Mahdī (d. 773/1371 or 793/1390) would end in failure.[81] Although ash-Shawkānī gave the same version, he did not mention the name of the imam. According to ash-Shawkānī, al-Jabartī informed Sultan al-Ashraf of the latter's victory against the "mercenaries," who would attack him.[82]

Ibn al-Ahdal, on the other hand, portrays al-Jabartī as an illiterate Sufi.[83] This judgment, however, springs from his bias against the Sufi party, which is obvious from his *Kashf al-ghiṭāʾ*. Al-Jabartī's insistence on teaching Ibn ʿArabī's books to his disciples exonerates him from accusations of ignorance and illiteracy. Paying no attention to the envious *fuqahāʾ* who fiercely attacked his teachings, al-Jabartī successfully legitimized Ibn ʿArabī's Sufi doctrines and disseminated them among his numerous followers.[84] Knysh observes: "His [al-Jabartī's] tireless efforts to promote the ideals of mystical Islam led to the rise of a Sufi school that derived its identity from an enthusiastic allegiance to the teaching of Ibn 'Arabī and his later interpreters."[85] Although the introduction of the Sufi *samā'* to the community of Zabīd at the hands of Ibn Jamīl and others had been known before the establishment of al-Jabartī's circle, the latter helped in regulating *samā'* and in making it a dominant feature of Yemeni Sufism.

Alongside the *samā'* and the recitation of the *Yāsīn* chapter of the Qur'ān, al-Jabartī instructed his numerous disciples to embrace Ibn 'Arabī's doctrine to the extent that if a student did not have a copy of Ibn 'Arabī's *Fuṣūs al-ḥikam*, he "would turn his back on him" (*lā yaltafitu ilayhi*).[86] In al-Jabartī's circle, other books were also taught, including al-Qushayrī's *Risāla,* as-Suhrawardī's *'Awārif al-ma'ārif,* and the two main books of Ibn 'Arabī, *al-Futūḥāt* and *al-Fuṣūṣ*. The latter, according to Ibn al-Ahdal, was taught with its several commentaries by 'Abd ar-Razzāq al-Qāshānī (d. 730/1329 or 887/1482), Dawūd al-Qayṣarī (d. 751/1350), and al-Mu'ayyad al-Janadī (d. 690/1291).[87] These three authors were, according to Knysh, "prominent representatives of the rationalist interpretation of Ibn 'Arabī's legacy that became closely entwined with the Islamicized new-Platonic philosophy of Avicenna."[88]

First Stage: Polarization around Ibn 'Arabī

Al-Jabartī's contribution to the development of Sufism in Yemen was outstanding. Although his admiration for Ibn 'Arabī's teaching infuriated the *fuqahā',* he was aware that most of his disciples were amateurs. Therefore, he used to prohibit some disciples from attending *samā'* sessions since they were not able to understand its implications and hidden meaning.[89] In order to understand the nature of the long struggle between the Sufis and the *fuqahā'* and the state's involvement therein, I consider the question posed by Sultan an-Nāṣir Aḥmad (d. 827/1423) before Majd ad-Dīn al-Fayrūzabādī (d. 817/1415) with regard to the followers of Ibn 'Arabī. He asked: "What do the revered *'ulamā',* may God sustain religion and unify the scattered Muslims (by them), say about Shaykh Muḥyī ad-Dīn Ibn al-'Arabī, may God be pleased with him, and his books such as *al-Futūḥāt, al-Fuṣūṣ* and others; is it permitted to read and teach them? Are they among the books [that are assigned] for reading and listening or not?"[90] When Sultan an-Nāṣir received a long answer from Majd ad-Dīn al-Fayrūzabādī in favor of Ibn 'Arabī's doctrine and his books, he sent the same question to Ibn al-Khayyāṭ in order to weigh other views of the scholarly community. Ibn al-Khayyāṭ's answer was that it was not lawful to obtain Ibn 'Arabī's books, nor to read or teach them.[91]

Ibn al-Ahdal reports that Ibn ar-Raddād (d. 821/1418) wrote a book on the Sufi robe (*fī ḥukm khirqat aṣ-ṣūfiyya*), praising his teacher Shaykh Ismā'īl al-Jabartī, who asked him [Ibn ar-Raddād] whether it was permissible for a servant of God (*'abd*) to identify himself with the attributes of the Divine Essence. Al-Jabartī answered that the people of knowledge (*ahl al-'ilm*) had disagreed over this issue; while some admitted it, others denied it. Then, al-Jabartī told his disciple: "Now I have become eternal self-subsisting (*qā'im qayyūm*)."[92] This suggests that al-Jabartī adhered to the doctrine that it is possible for the servant of God (*'abd*) or, be it may, the Sufi saint to identify himself with the attributes of the Divine Essence. But, assuming the attributes of the Divine Essence is not a violation of the *sharī'a.* In fact it was supported by the Prophet's saying: "Assume the character traits of God" (*takhallaqū bi akhlāqi Allāh*). Although Ibn 'Arabī does not attribute this saying to the Prophet,[93] it is reported in the normative *ḥadīth* literature as being sound. Finally, Ibn al-Ahdal conceded that al-Jabartī and Ibn ar-Raddād were saints and that their knowledge was useful to Muslims,[94] a fact that he had earlier vigorously denied.

However, before moving to the second stage of the long struggle between the *fuqahā'* and the *ṣūfiyya,* I discuss al-Jabartī's associate 'Abd al-Karīm al-Jīlī (d. 832/1428), who was famous for his elaboration of Ibn 'Arabī's concept of the perfect man (*al-Insān al-kāmil*). Al-Jīlī was born in the suburb of Baghdad and grew up in Persia. His biography is ignored by Muslim biographers, including Yemenis. Al-Jīlī tells us that he had traveled in India in order to study under the auspices of Shaykh al-Jabartī before he came to Zabīd.[95] Al-Jīlī wrote about thirty books and treatises, of which *al-Insān al-kāmil fī ma'rifat al-awākhir wa'l-awā'il* (The Perfect Human Being through the Understanding of the Endings and the Beginnings) and *al-Manāẓir al-'ayniyya* (The Immutable Scenes) are the best known. Twenty books were reported to have been lost.[96] Little information regarding al-Jīlī's exists. However, in his *Kashf al-ghiṭā',* Ibn al-Ahdal (d. 815/1412) provides a cursory glimpse of al-Jīlī's character and theological beliefs as seen by his detractors. Alexander Knysh mentions the following passage, which shows that al-Jīlī blended smoothly into the landscape of Yemeni Sufism:

> Among those doomed to be lost in this sea more than anyone else is 'Abd al-Karīm al-Jīlī, the Persian. A reliable and honest scholar

> told me about him that he had accompanied him [i.e., al-Jīlī] in one of his travels, during which he heard him praising profusely Ibn 'Arabī's books and teachings. This person [i.e., the informant] also heard him overtly ascribing lordship (*rubūbiyya*) to every human being, bird, or tree, which he happened to see on his way.[97]

On another occasion, Ibn al-Ahdal, who was the chief *muftī* of Zabīd, tells us that he met al-Jīlī in Abyāt Husayn, a town near Zabīd. During that time, Ibn al-Ahdal was not aware of al-Jīlī's affiliation with the Ibn 'Arabī's school of monistic theology. For this reason, Ibn al-Ahdal did not engage him in the discussion of Ibn 'Arabī's theosophical ideas. Although al-Jīlī made friends, as he remarks, with all the major Sufi authorities in al-Jabartī's circle—such as Muḥammad al-Mukdish (d. 778/1376), Ibn ar-Raddād (d. 821/1418), al-Mizjājī (d. 829/1425), and his own shaykh, al-Jabartī (d. 806/1403)—his contribution to the local Sufi community is not clear. Al-Jīlī never settled for a long period in one place. It is known that he made trips—in addition to his previous stay in Persia and India—to San'ā', Mecca, and Cairo.[98] The decline of the Sufi community in Zabīd was partly caused by the activities of the famous Yemeni scholar and poet, Ibn al-Muqrī (d. 837/1444), which coincided with the death of al-Jīlī at Abyāt Ḥusayn in 826/1421 or 832/1428.

Learning Ibn 'Arabī's works, particularly *al-Futūḥāt al-makkiyya* and *Fuṣūṣ al-ḥikam,* were the main requirements of mystical wisdom in the Sufi community of Zabīd, where al-Jīlī and his shaykh taught. If a disciple were confused about the mysteries of the path and preferred to wait for the grace of God to reveal these mysteries through mystical unveiling, al-Jabartī's response was: "What you search for is exactly what the shaykh [i.e., Ibn 'Arabī] tells you in his books."[99] According to Knysh, this story helps us understand the teaching methods employed by the Sufi masters of al-Jabartī's school. They tended to overemphasize the importance of Ibn 'Arabī's writings, arguing that the latter should be treated as a source of identity for the local Sufi community.

Al-Jīlī divided his book *al-Insān al-kāmil* into sixty-four chapters in two volumes. It is only in chapter sixty that he explicitly addressed the idea of the perfect man (*al-Insān al-kāmil*) and argued that the whole book is nothing but a commentary on that chapter. In *al-Insān al-kāmil,* al-Jīlī speaks of the Muḥammadan image as an archetype or paradigm for all humankind. When the Muslim saint is transformed into the perfect human being, he reaches the sublime station of sanctity, which is the beginning of prophecy. Al-Jīlī says:

> Know, may God preserve you, that the Perfect Human Being is the axis (*quṭb*) around which revolve the spheres of existence (*aflāk al-wujūd*) from the beginning to the end. . . . He has other names with respect to other images and in every age possesses a name associated with his image at that particular time. It is thus that I discovered [Muḥammad] in the form of my master, shaykh Sharaf ad-Dīn Ismā'īl al-Jabartī. At that time, I did not know that he actually was [a manifestation] of the Prophet [Muḥammad], and I thought him to be my master. This is one of the visions that I was granted . . . in Zabīd in the year 796/1393. . . . Beware, lest you imagine my statements to be based on the doctrine of metempsychosis (*tanāsukh*)! May God and the Messenger of God forbid that this was my intention! Rather, the Messenger of God is latent in every human image until he becomes manifest in that image, and his tradition (Sunna) is to be depicted in every age in the image of [humanity's] most perfect forms so that he may exalt them and cause others to be attracted to them. They are his successors (*khulafā'uhu*) on the outside and he is their reality on the inside.[100]

Al-Jīlī's theory of the "Perfect Human Being" is founded on several premises. The most significant of these is the notion that the Prophet Muḥammad is not only the deceased founder of the Islamic religion, but also a living reality who reappears to guide Muslims toward the pinnacle of human achievement. Muḥammad is the Most Perfect Man to whom all the saints and the rest of the prophets are subordinate. In every age, Muḥammad assumes the form of a living saint and in that guise makes himself known to select mystics.[101] However, this involves neither the transmigration of souls nor the resurrection of Muḥammad as a flesh-and-blood human being. The reappearance of Muḥammadan Reality occurs on the level of analogy, which is the "secret" (*sirr*) of the perfect man (*al-Insān al-kāmil*). According to al-Jīlī, this secret is latent in all human beings, but it is only actualized in the person whose qualities best match those of the Prophet himself. This "perfect human being," whose image is reconfigured by the Muḥammadan attributes he has taken on, is revealed in his true form as the paradigmatic saint and the successor (*khalīfa*) to the Prophet in his time.[102] Al-Jīlī also divides the attributes of God into four classes: attributes of the essence, attributes of beauty, attributes of majesty, and attributes of perfection. The perfect man alone displays the sum total of divine attributes because he is a copy of God.

He combines the aspects of the ultimate truth (*al-ḥaqq*) and human nature (*al-khalq*). Finally, he is the mirror of the names of God.

Second Stage: Ibn ar-Raddād and Sufi Hegemony

The struggle between *aṣ-ṣūfiyya* and the *fuqahā'* grew even more severe when Ibn ar-Raddād (d. 821/1418) was appointed grand *qāḍī* of the state (*al-qaḍā' al-'āmm*).[103] The post was held vacant for Ibn Ḥajar al-'Asqalānī (d. 852/1448), who mentions that Sultan an-Nāṣir was waiting for him to assume this post, but when Ibn Ḥajar declined an-Nāṣir gave it to Ibn ar-Raddād. Ibn Ḥajar adds that the *fuqahā'* wanted an-Nāshirī to take the office but that Sultan an-Nāṣir still decided to award it to Ibn ar-Raddād.[104] The latter was not unqualified for it (*muzjan al-biḍā'a*) as Ibn Ḥajar stated. In fact, he was praised by al-Burayhī (d. 904/1498) in *Ṭabaqāt ṣulaḥā' al-Yaman* for his efforts to take back the endowments that the sultans had seized and to spend them as required by the *sharī'a*.[105]

Unlike al-Yaḥyāwī, who had helped the Rasūlid sultans gain control over charitable funds and endowments, Ibn ar-Raddād abolished the percentage of income that Rasūlid sultans could take from any given endowment (*waqf*). Those who were in office before Ibn ar-Raddād's appointment would not have dared to take action against the sultans. At any rate, the *fuqahā'* demanded that Ibn ar-Raddād be removed from office. Their protests, however, fell on deaf ears. Ibn ar-Raddād retaliated and was reported to have imposed severe punishments on those who had objected to Sufi *samā'* and his predilection for Ibn 'Arabī's teaching.

During the second stage of the long struggle between the Sufis and the *'ulamā',* the former gained the upper hand. For example, al-Jabartī ordered some of his followers to beat up Ṣāliḥ al-Makkī (or al-Maṣrī) who was also exiled to India due to his criticism of al-Jabartī.[106] Another example of Sufi hegemony under the judgeship of Ibn ar-Raddād, according to al-Burayhī, is that "when Muḥammad b. Nūr ad-Dīn al-Khaṭīb al-Mawza'ī (d. after 810/1407) protested against allowing people to read Ibn 'Arabī's books, Ibn ar-Raddād brought al-Mawza'ī from his town to Zabīd for a debate in the presence of some of the two parties, the *ṣūfiyya* and the *fuqahā'*. After al-Mawza'ī established his proof against Ibn 'Arabī's books, the Sufis intended to attack him but he was protected by prince Muḥammad b. Ziyād. When al-Mawza'ī returned to his town, he wrote *Kitāb kashf aḍ-ḍulma 'an hadhihi al-'umma,* refuting Ibn 'Arabī's doctrine"[107]

After the death of an-Nāshirī (d. 815/1412), Ibn al-Muqrī (d. 837/1444), a brilliant Yemeni scholar and poet, assumed the leadership of the *'ulamā'* party to refute the Sufi teachings of Ibn 'Arabī. Ibn al-Muqrī kept silent during the first stage of the long struggle because, as he mentioned in an apologetic poem sent to the family of an-Nāshirī, he had not read the *Fuṣūṣ* before that time and, thus, was unaware of Ibn 'Arabī's heresies. Ibn al-Muqrī's attack on the teachings of Ibn 'Arabī intensified not only because Ibn ar-Raddād advocated them, but also because Ibn ar-Raddād was appointed for the supreme judgeship in Rasūlid Yemen—a position Ibn al-Muqrī was seeking to attain.

With the demise of Ibn ar-Raddād, Sufi leadership was transferred to Shaykh Muḥammad b. Muḥammad al-Mizjājī (d. 829/1425) who was trained by al-Jabartī and Ibn ar-Raddād. The importance of al-Mizjājī to the Sufi community in Zabīd lies not only in his financial support but also in his commitment to disseminating the *Fuṣūṣ* and the *Futūḥāt* of Ibn 'Arabī among the Yemeni masses. According to al-Ḥibshī, al-Mizjājī's manuscript *Hidāyat as-sālik ilā asnā al-masālik* was the last attempt to support the Sufis in their long struggle. According to al-Ḥibshī, this treatise was significant for its intellectual as well as its historical value.[108] Although al-Mizjājī and Ibn al-Muqrī were friends for a long time, they eventually parted ways over Ibn 'Arabī's teachings. However, their poetic polemic was not as hostile as the rivalry between Ibn al-Muqrī and Ibn ar-Raddād and, later on, between Ibn al-Muqrī and al-Kirmānī (d. 845/1441).

Third Stage: The Decline of the Sufi Party

In the final episode of the long struggle between the *fuqahā'* and the *ṣūfiyya,* the Sufis actively sought an-Nāṣir's support. The stage for the battle began when Ibn Rawbak (d. 835/1431) sent a poem to Sultan an-Nāṣir, explaining the intentions of Ibn al-Muqrī who wrote a poem of complaint about the adverse circumstances. Ibn Rawbak and some other Sufi fellows interpreted Ibn al-Muqrī's complaint as a direct indictment of the sultan's rule.[109] In addition, an-Nāṣir listened to Aḥmad al-Kirmānī (d. 845/1441), a native of Persia who came to join the Sufi circle in Zabīd and whose intimate relationship with Ibn ar-Raddād and al-Mizjājī earned him the sultan's trust. Al-Kirmānī advised Sultan an-Nāṣir to be on his guard against a possible uprising by the anti-Sufi party led by Ibn al-Muqrī.[110] The sultan sent some soldiers to capture Ibn al-Muqrī who had already fled to Bayt al-Faqīh, seeking protection from the respected "holy" clan of Banū 'Ujayl.[111] Later on, Ibn al-Muqrī sent several flattering poems to an-Nāṣir seeking his pardon. Within a year, an-Nāṣir granted him forgiveness "and generously compensated him for the tribulations he had suffered,"[112] bearing in mind that Ibn al-Muqrī might seek political asylum with 'Alī b. Ṣalāḥ, the Zaydī imam of Ṣan'ā',[113] "the principal political rival to the Rasūlids."[114]

With the death of an-Nāṣir in 827/1424, the Sufi party lost the necessary political support for their cause to endure. His successor was his son al-Manṣūr 'Abd Allāh (d. 830/1427) who was familiar with the controversy and who, unlike his father, sided with the anti-Sufi party.[115] Ibn al-Muqrī took advantage of the situation and collected *fatwas* from the majority of the *'ulamā'* to prohibit the study of Ibn 'Arabī's works and submitted them to the sultan. Additionally, Ibn al-Muqrī found it convenient to avenge himself on the Sufis, represented by their leader al-Kirmānī who had lost two strong supporters, Sultan an-Nāṣir and al-Mizjājī. Al-Manṣūr responded to Ibn al-Muqrī's demands and ordered his soldiers to capture al-Kirmānī and to confiscate his house and belongings.[116] Al-Kirmānī took refuge in Bayt al-Faqīh, the same place where Ibn al-Muqrī found his protection. However, al-Kirmānī could not stay for long in Bayt al-Faqīh as his opponent did; he decided to return to Ta'izz where he was arrested and tried. The reason for his trial was due to Ibn al-Muqrī's second strenuous efforts to collect *fatwas* from local Yemeni *'ulamā'* and from Ibn al-Jazarī (d. 834/1430) who was invited to Yemen by the sultan.[117] The latter declared al-Kirmānī to be an apostate. Then, he was asked to declare his repentance on the condition that he must abandon Ibn 'Arabī's works. This was documented and announced in the mosques of Zabīd and al-Mahjam. Moreover, he was exiled to Jīzān (Jayzān or Jāzān) where he remained until the death of al-Manṣūr in 830/1427.[118]

With the ascension of the young sultan, al-Ashraf Ismā'īl to the Rasūlid throne, the political and economic situation deteriorated. Sultan al-Ashraf's rule was marked by rampant corruption and chaos. According to al-Ḥibshī, despite al-Ashraf's short period on the Rasūlid throne, al-Kirmānī (d. 845/1441) managed to enter Zabīd secretly and met with the young sultan, who was easily influenced.[119] Al-Kirmānī exploited the new chaotic atmosphere, nullified his previous "repentance," and wrote an epistle refuting Ibn al-Muqrī and restating his previous beliefs. In return, Ibn al-Muqrī wrote some poems reminding al-Kirmānī of his previous "repentance" under the fear of the sword.[120] With the imprisonment of al-Ashraf and the ascension of aẓ-Ẓāhir Yaḥyā b. Ismā'īl (r. 831–842/1428–1438), the *fuqahā'* gained the upper hand. Al-Kirmānī was exiled for the second time to Bayt al-Faqīh where he freely disseminated his teachings until his followers reached over fifty. One year after his banishment, al-Kirmānī decided to attend the Ramaḍān banquet held by the sultan for his entourage and the *'ulamā'*. Ibn al-Muqrī was furious and vehemently asked the sultan how an infidel (*kāfir*) (i.e., al-Kirmānī) could stay among the Muslims. Ibn al-Muqrī brought to the sultan's attention the old debate regarding al-Kirmānī's doctrine and demanded that he be executed. He said in a poem translated by Knysh:

> Had you cut off his [al-Kirmānī] head the other day,
> God's religion would have been delivered from at least one minor ailment.
> No sacrifice in the eyes of God is more preferable than spilling the blood of al-Kirmānī.
> It is an insult to God that he walked away safe and sound on his own feet for was he not the one who blasphemed?!
> By God, oh, the best kings, that was a grave mistake, but it will no doubt be redressed.
> With the sword, after the men of learning have concluded that the likes of him must not be spared![121]

After the agitation of Ibn al-Muqrī who was supported by many *'ulamā'*, al-Kirmānī was summoned to Zabīd. He was tried by the *fuqahā'* and was forced to choose between repentance and execution. Because al-Kirmānī was also accused of political intrigues—by making alliance with Prince al-'Abbās b. Ismā'īl who had revolted in 839/1435 among other claimants to the Rasūlid throne—he chose repentance and fled again to Jayzān, where he stayed until his death in 841/1437.

Yemeni Sufism during the Ottoman Empire

After the long struggle between the *ṣūfiyya* and the *fuqahā'*, the focus of Sufi thought in Yemen began to drift away from the debates over Ibn 'Arabī's ideas. Like all debates, it abated as ideas found their way to the hearts of people and events no longer exacerbated the same tensions. Notably, Yemen faced new threats from the incursion of European and Ottoman colonial powers. I have already discussed the fierce tensions in the previous chapter between the Zaydī imams and the Sufis and how the Sufis first supported the Ottomans, believing that they would liberate them from the tyranny of the Zaydīs, but later turned against them due to the un-Islamic practices of the new colonial power. New priorities and ideas emerged with Sufi masters who sought to render more accessible, often through popular verse, the theology and imagery of Sufi thought. To understand the transformation of ideas in Yemen, the literary achievements of the celebrated Sufi, Muḥammad b. 'Alī, known as 'Abd al-Hādī as-Sūdī (d. 932/1525) and the famous Sufi of Ḥaḍramawt 'Umar Muḥammad Bā Makhrama (d. 952/1545) should be highlighted.

As-Sūdī was born after 870/1465, which coincided with Portuguese explorations off the Cape of Good Hope, along the coastal areas of Africa, and in the Indian Ocean. Around that time, Yemen witnessed the transfer of power from the powerful Rasūlid dynasty to the new state of Banū Ṭāhir. Ṭāhirid rule began in 858/1454 and reached its apogee during the reign of Sultan 'Āmir b. 'Abd al-Wahhāb, who was killed in 923/1517. The Ṭāhirids faced constant threats both internally and externally. The internal threat was caused by dissension within the ruling family. Externally they were subject to the militant campaigns of the imams, especially those of Muḥammad b. 'Alī as-Surājī (d. 910/1504) and of Sharaf ad-Dīn b. Mahdī and his son al-Muṭahhar, who captured most of Yemen after the death of Sultan 'Āmir b. 'Abd al-Wahhāb. Another external threat was the continuing Portuguese expansion.[122]

As-Sūdī received his primary education in the Qur'ān, *ḥadīth,* rhetoric, grammar, jurisprudence (*fiqh*), inheritance, and Sufism. He traveled to Mecca and Medina and to Yemeni cities such as Ḥaraḍ, Ṣan'ā', Ibb, and finally Ta'izz, where he stayed until his death in 932/1525. Although it is said that as-Sūdī received the Qādirī *khirqa* in Mecca, no information remains about his master. However, he received the same Qādirī *khirqa* in the Sufi lodge (*ribāṭ*) of al-Ma'āyin in the suburb of Ibb from 'Umar b. Dā'ūd al-Bishrī al-Ghaythī.[123] Among the disciples who received the Qādirī *khirqa* from as-Sūdī were Imam al-Washaliyy Muḥammad b. 'Alī as-Surājī and Ḥusayn b. 'Abd Allāh al-'Aydarūs (d. 917/1511). A manuscript written by as-Sūdī's grandson mentions four hundred of his disciples. As-Sūdī was given a short biography in *al-Badr aṭ-Ṭāli'* by ash-Shawkānī (d. 1250/1834) and in *an-Nūr as-Sāfir* by 'Abd al-Qādir al-'Aydarūs.[124] Ash-Shawkānī reports that as-Sūdī experienced a "divine attraction" (*jadhba*) that caused him to leave Ṣan'ā' and settle in Ta'izz. Al-'Aydarūs reports that as-Sūdī began to write his Sufi poetry sometime after his "divine attraction." It was said that his poetry was a product of a Sufi state that resembles, to some extent, that of Ibn al-Fāriḍ (d. 632/1235).[125] While falling into a spiritual trance, as-Sūdī used to write his poems with a piece of charcoal on the walls. When he came back to his senses, he erased them. His students, however, after realizing this state, hastened to write down his spontaneous poetry before he woke up.[126] Because as-Sūdī was a famous scholar, Sultan ʿĀmir b. ʿAbd al-Wahhāb invited him to assume the post of the grand judge of Taʿizz. However, as-Sūdī did not accept that offer. As-Sūdī felt the suffering of his community, which prompted him to intercede with the sultan's court for the release of some prisoners. This intercession fell on deaf ears. As a result, as-Sūdī uttered his famous warning prediction: "We have permitted '*ar-Rūm*' to enter Yemen."[127] Soon, indeed, the Ottomans invaded Yemen and killed the sultan.

As-Sūdī left two poetic *dīwāns, Bulbul al-afrāḥ* and *Nusaymāt as-saḥar,* and a number of treatises including one in praise of the Prophet's family. The following poem is taken from *Bulbul al-afrāh.* It is usually recited at death rituals and often in Sufi gatherings.

If it had not been for you, oh the adornment of existence,
My living and existence would not have been pleasant,
Nor [even] a flash of lightning had grieved me,
Nor a beat of the tambourine, nor a sound of a thunder
You are the one whom I have fallen in love with
And the night of union with you is my celebration
By God, visit me; my spirit is for you
Stop Your abandonment and turning away
How difficult is it for a lover to be abandoned
Especially for a longing one!
And what a pleasant Laylā's union
At night on the top of a mountain near *Zarūd*
Oh the nights of pleasure for us,
Please return so that my bone may again become fresh.[128]

The next poem is recited during celebrations of the Prophet's birthday (*mawlid*). It is taken from *Nusaymāt as-saḥar.* As-Sūdī reinterpreted classical themes—the love of Laylā and Majnūn—to intimate a Sufi view of life, which he shared with many thinkers before him such as Ibn al-Fāriḍ (d. 632/1235) and Ibn ʿAlwān (d. 665/1266).[129]

Oh the moon of highness, what is my fault?
[Why did] You prolong the abandonment?
Stop putting off my [meeting with You]
Indeed, you have embarrassed me in front of the jealous [people].
Have a look at my condition

So that the nights of *Zarūd* may return.
Oh the shining beauty
Do not untie the knots of promises.
Make a union with a lover, who is madly in love
By God, he never sleeps because he misses You
Always crying, he does not hear a word from a censurer.[130]

These poems are similar to Ibn 'Alwān's poems in their lyrical quality and in the effect that they have upon their listeners. The poet expresses feelings of grief and loss amid the joyous nights spent with the beloved at Zarūd, which is mentioned in the sixth line. He is deeply longing for mystical union. His painful condition may entitle him to a spiritual meeting with his lover. It is important to note that this poem belongs to the *dīwān* of *Nusaymāt as-saḥar,* which, according to 'Abd al-'Azīz al-Maqāliḥ, is written in the vernacular language (*al-lugha al-'āmmiyya*). The other poem, which belongs to the *dīwān* of *Bulbul al-afrāḥ*, al-Maqāliḥ argues, is written in classical Arabic (*fuṣḥā*). Al-Maqāliḥ emphasized that the language of the two *dīwāns* is the language of common use (*mutadāwal*). Al-Maqāliḥ thereby rejects the thesis of several Orientalists and Arab scholars who attempted to show a divergence between the two levels of the Arabic language. Al-Maqāliḥ concludes his argument by saying that the *dīwān* of *Nusaymāt as-saḥar* is not different from *Bulbul al-afrāh* except in that it omitted the case endings.[131]

In any case, as-Sūdī was one of the best representatives of Yemeni Sufism during the tenth/sixteenth century. He was well versed in the Sufi tradition of his age.[132] As-Sūdī's literary contribution is not related to the major debates over Ibn 'Arabī's ideas, for although one may see in his poetry traces of the fierce debates over Ibn 'Arabī's legacy, his main intention was reviving some images of Sufism based on previous historical periods of Sufism—i.e., before the establishment of Sufi orders.

Another representative of the Sufi movement of the tenth/sixteenth century was 'Umar b. 'Abd Allāh Bā Makhrama. He was born in the city of Hajarayn in Ḥaḍramawt in 884/1479. When he reached adulthood, he joined his father (d. 903/1497), who was the judge of Aden. While there, Bā Makhrama studied jurisprudence (*fiqh*), Qur'ānic exegesis, *ḥadīth,* syntax, morphology, linguistics, and rhetoric at the hands of Abū Bakr al-'Aydarūs and Muḥammad ad-Daw'anī. Later, when he came back to Ḥaḍramawt, he became a disciple of such spiritual masters as Sahl b. 'Abd Allāh b. Isḥāq and 'Abd ar-Raḥmān Bā Hurmuz. Bā Makhrama visited Zabīd, Socotra, Mecca, and Madina. A contemporary Yemeni writer, 'Abd ar-Raḥmān Ja'far b. 'Aqīl, who edited Bā Makhrama's *diwān* of popular poetry, states that Bā Makhrama was deeply influenced by the major Sufi works, specifically, *ar-Risāla* by al-Qushayrī (d. 466/1073), *'Awārif al-ma'ārif* by as-Suhrawardī (d. 632/1234), the Sufi poetry of Ibn al-Fāriḍ (d. 632/1235), and *Iḥyā' 'ulūm ad-dīn* by al-Ghazālī (d. 505/1111). Bā Makhrama referred to these works in a poem as containing "divine knowledge" (*'ilm ladunnī*).[133] In addition to the *diwān,* Bā Makhrama wrote the following books, which are still in manuscript: *al-Wārid fī sharḥ āyat al-kursī, Sharḥ asmā' Allāh al-Ḥusnā, al-Maṭlab al-yasīr min as-sālik al-faqīr,* and a number of sermons and treatises.[134]

Bā Makhrama is the first poet to introduce philosophical topics into the Ḥaḍramī vernacular language. He also emphasized the feature of *ad-dān,* a musical sentence, which helps in constructing the melody of various popular songs. The sounds of *ad-dān* were often associated with Sufi *samā'* sessions and *dhikr.* Bā Makhrama says in a poem:

> "*Dān,*" oh singer, for I am enraptured due to your "*dān*"
> Repeat in it: "Let us drink from the pure [spring]"
> For I have a different taste than people.
> My way is not similar to any other way.[135]

Almost all of Bā Makhrama's poetry is vernacular or "popular" (*ḥumaynī*), but it has all the characteristics of regular poetry. It is very simple and perhaps Bā Makhrama intended to make it simple so that the ordinary people would understand it with ease. What distinguishes Bā Makhrama's poetry from other popular poetry is the fact that he was able to convey sophisticated philosophical ideas in a very accessible manner. To illustrate this, I show how he dealt with the concept of Ibn 'Arabī's unity of being (*waḥdat al-wujūd*) in the following poem:

> After you, oh He Who takes the shape of all forms
> And Whose attributes bewilder thoughts.
> You have left me residing between the desert and the city
> Hesitating between ascending and descending.[136]

This is just a cursory glance at the well-known Sufi of Ḥaḍramawt, Bā Makhrama. He was contemporary to the famous Yemeni Sufi as-Sūdī. Both of them wrote their poems in a colloquial language, which could be understood by the intellectuals as well as the ordinary people. Their Sufi literature, which they left behind, played a major role in the development of the Sufi movement of the tenth/sixteenth century.

Conclusion

Sufism in Yemen after the age of Ibn 'Alwān and Abū al-Ghayth Ibn Jamīl witnessed the rise of the *ṭarīqa* institution, which was distinguished from its counterparts across the Islamic world by its lack of centralized hierarchy. These Sufi lodges (*arbiṭa* or *zawāyā*) were formed under the auspices of revered masters who, like Ibn 'Alwān, were famous for mediating frequent conflicts between rulers and tribes. Ibn 'Alwān's Sufism, which was marked by permitting a similar movement away from centralized authority, had and still has a significant impact upon Sufi *ṭarīqas* in Yemen. Furthermore, the recitation of his lyrical poems at some Sufi gatherings is proof of his ongoing relevance to popular Yemeni culture.

As we saw, the Sufis ultimately lost their foothold in the struggle against the *fuqahā',* and the last Sufi attempt to gain the sultan's support was made by Aḥmad al-Kirmānī (d. 845/1441). However, secular rulers made their own decisions, and some supported the *fuqahā'* against the Sufis. Thus, Sufism after the Rasūlid dynasty (632–837/1234–1424) declined. The ruling classes were no longer as interested in participating in debates over Ibn 'Arabī's legacy as their predecessors. However, by the tenth/sixteenth century we notice Yemeni Sufism witnessing a return to the Sufi concepts of al-Ḥallāj (d. 309/922) and al-Ghazālī (d. 505/1111). The major Yemeni representatives of the tenth/sixteenth century were as-Sūdī in Ta'izz and Bā Makhrama in Ḥaḍramawt whose literary output was characterized by their extensive use of vernacular language, in an attempt to popularize Sufi experience among the masses. In this historical moment of Yemeni Sufism we note a return to the lyricism that marked Ibn 'Alwān's Sufi poetry.

In conclusion, I underscore Ibn 'Alwān's exceptional status in contemporary Yemen with a gesture toward the research of David Buchman, who provides a critical analysis of the link between the Shādhiliyya and the 'Alawiyya Sufi orders.[137] The Shādhiliyya/'Alawiyya Sufi order legitimizes and interprets their current situation as a return to the pure age when Sufism was inconspicuous and sincere.[138] This Sufi order considers politics a corrupting factor, but they believe that great masters can survive the corrupting influences of politics and keep their orders away from involvement in politics. It is notable that the current Shādhiliyya/'Alawiyya Sufi order considers Ibn 'Alwān "to be among the greatest sheikhs to have lived in Yemen and, out of all the sheikhs in the past, see[s] his involvement with politics as incorruptible, thus indicating that perhaps the Sufis will now read their past differently as their current situation changes to pro-Sufi political leanings."[139]

CONCLUSION

Medieval hagiographers discussed the conversion of Ibn ʿAlwān (d. 665/1266) to Sufism, citing a mysterious incident that prompted Ibn ʿAlwān to change the entire course of his life. This incident, widely cited in medieval sources, had a profound impact on Ibn ʿAlwān's religious attitude, and thereby on the face of Yemeni Sufism at a critical moment in its historical development. Ibn ʿAlwān formulated a remarkably original Sufi theology that partook of the diversity of his religious environment but which nevertheless was marked both by his allegiance to Sunnī Islam and his unwavering adherence to the letter of Islamic scriptures. However, Ibn ʿAlwān's life is also distinguished for his close interaction with the ruling elites of the two dynasties, the Egyptian Ayyūbids (569–626/1173–1228) and their lieutenants, the powerful Rasūlids (632–827/1234–1424). This commitment to justice was one of the major features of his political and social thought. Like many Sufi masters, he frequently mediated conflicts between rulers and tribal leaders and protected the peasants from the exactions of both. For this, Ibn ʿAlwān was rightly praised in medieval as well as contemporary sources.

It is hoped that this study has helped to rectify one of the common mistakes in Western scholarship about Yemen's religious and political climate in the early Islamic centuries, which emphasizes its lack of central authority, rugged terrain, inhospitable climate, and political instability. Far from being a static backwater of Islamic civilization, Yemen became a dramatic scene of political as well as theological struggles between the two major Shīʿī sects, the Zaydīs and the Ismāʿīlīs on the one hand, and their Sunnī counterparts on the other. When the Ayyūbids invaded Yemen in 569/1173, they promoted Sunnī learning and encouraged the diffusion of Sufi lodges and generously funded their construction. The Rasūlids, following in the footsteps of the Ayyūbids, promoted Sunnī scholarship, built colleges, encouraged intellectual activities, and advanced religious studies. The age of the Rasūlids was unprecedented and was viewed by some investigators as the most brilliant one in the entire history of Yemen.

Unlike many Sufi masters whose works tend to be ambiguous or elusive, Ibn 'Alwān's doctrine is clear and straightforward. His theological views revolve around the concept of unity of God, the exemplary behavior of the Prophet, and the respective status of the Rightly Guided Caliphs. Overall, his theological views are informed by Ash'arite theology. His semi-indebtedness to the well-known Ash'arite theologian, al-Ghazālī (d. 505/1111), in both theology and Sufism, is unquestionable, though the distinctive styles and originality of each scholar is beyond doubt. I have also disproven recent studies claiming that Sufi masters such as al-Ḥallāj (d. 309/922), al-Badawī (d. 675/1276), and Ibn 'Arabī (d. 638/1242) influenced the theology and Sufi thought of Ibn 'Alwān. Ibn 'Alwān's Sufism was clearly a product of his native Yemeni environment, the tensions between him and Ibn Jamīl (d. 651/1253) notwithstanding. While it is impossible to summarize a body of work as extensive and complex as Ibn 'Alwān's Sufism, this study provides an ample beginning by emphasizing the most significant and dominant feature of his Sufi thought, his extensive use of the Qur'ān and the Sunna. Another unique aspect of his thought was his position that while Sufi masters ought to be respected and honored, they should not be sanctified as other Sufi thinkers claimed. Rather, he strongly advocated the notion that the Qur'ān and the Sunna are sufficient for the seekers of the Sufi path and that they need look no further.

Among other Sufi topics Ibn 'Alwān discussed was the doctrine of the "union with God." This union can be achieved through various mystical states such as annihilation (*fanā'*) and its opposite *baqā'* (subsisting in God) or through *ittiḥād* (union) and its opposite *ḥulūl* (incarnation). Mystical union with God takes on these different forms as well as many other states on account of the diversity of the mystic paths and their followers. However, Ibn 'Alwān restricted the possibility of attaining mystical union to the condition that the seeker commits himself to the teachings of the Qur'ān, the Sunna, and the practice of the companions and "friends of God." When the traveler to God reaches the stage of union with God, he or she becomes a saint (*walī*).

Studies of the characteristic features of friends of God (*awliyā'*) in medieval Yemen are unfortunately extremely rare, a lack which this study has taken a step to remedy. As we have seen, following the death of Ibn 'Alwān he occupied a central place in Yemeni intellectuals' debates over the meaning of sainthood and miracles. The premodern hagiographer ash-Sharjī (d. 893/1487) wrote his famous book *Ṭabaqāt al-khawāṣṣ* to fill that gap, and its significance lies in its providing a short account of Ibn 'Alwān's life within the framework of the *ṭabaqāt* genre of Sufi literature. Later, by the turn of the nineteenth century, we witness Ibn 'Alwān and other Sufi saints once again rising to the forefront of debates when the Wahhābī movement expanded its domains to 'Asīr and Tihāma at the expense of the Yemeni lands. As the Wahhābīs sought to expand their doctrine of God's unity (*tawḥīd*) and purify Islam of the reprehensible practices associated with the cult of saints, Yemeni scholars such as Ibn al-Amīr (d. 1182/1768) and ash-Shawkānī (d. 1250/1834) first welcomed their teachings. However, upon hearing about the Wahhābīs' indiscriminate excommunication (*takfīr*) of Muslims, they withdrew their support.

In my treatment of Ibn 'Alwān's sainthood and saintly miracles (*karāmāt*), I did not deal with hagiographies as accounts of "real" people and phenomena because rhetoric, politics, and local opinion played a central role in constructing the image of a saint. In line with this approach, I presented Ibn 'Alwān's *karāmāt* in the form I found them in an attempt to let our sources speak for themselves. Yemeni studies of Ibn 'Alwān's sainthood seem to have taken two main directions: While sociological approaches, as exemplified by the great Yemeni poet al-Baradūnī (d. 1999), valorize Ibn 'Alwān's struggle against despotic rulers, more traditional hagiographical approaches exemplified by al-Yāfi'ī (d. 763/1366), ash-Sharīfah Dahmā' (d. 837/1434), and as-Sūdī (d. 932/1525) support the ascetic and devotional interpretation of his sainthood. Their argument springs from their understanding of sainthood as a pious way of life, which strives to achieve spiritual closeness to God. Consequently, the veneration of Ibn 'Alwān's tomb was due to people's conviction that Ibn 'Alwān was a friend of God, Who endowed him with supernatural powers and the ability to perform saintly miracles (*karāmāt*).

Despite the fact that Ibn 'Alwān's Sufi order did not survive, his influence on the local Sufi orders and later Yemeni Sufism was considerable. Sufism after the age of Ibn 'Alwān entered a new phase, which was marked by the spread of *ṭarīqa* networks. Although Sufi orders in Yemen resembled the grand Sufi orders in the major lands of Islam, they never adopted their rigid hierarchical system of authority. Sufi masters in Yemen preferred to form Sufi lodges (*arbiṭa* or *zawāya*) and to mediate frequent conflicts between rulers and tribal leaders. Beyond this institutional influence, Ibn 'Alwān's thought, expounded in his major works,[1] had a significant impact on the development of Yemeni Sufism. The recitation of his lyrical poems during Sufi "concerts" is evidence of his continuing relevance to popular Yemeni culture. The study of Sufi orders in Yemen was not the main goal of this book because they would need a separate study. I have provided a look at the link between the major Sufi orders in Islamic lands and their representatives in Yemen. Many Sufi orders in Yemen, including the 'Alwāniyya, Suhrawardiyya, Jabartiyya, Ghythiyya, Naqshabandiyya, and Rifā'iyya are now extinct. The Yāfi'ī and the Aḥmadī Sufi orders are not as prominent in Yemeni culture as the other Sufi orders. However, they certainly represented two important geographical regions, Yāfi' and Aden, which serves as a testimony that Sufism in Yemen is not limited to certain areas but includes a number of cultural centers all over Yemen. There are three Sufi orders not included within this book, such as al-'Aydarūsiyya in Hadramawt and al-Ahdaliyya and al-Marghaniya in Tihāma, but these are only branches of the 'Alawī and Shādhilī orders that do not require a separate study. Other minor Sufi communities, whose doctrines and teachings are not new but fall under one or a combination of the major Sufi orders, include al-Jabartiyya, al-Ḥadādiyya, al-Maghribiyya, al-Asadiyya, al-Bajaliyya, al-Ghaythiyya, az-Zayla'iyya, al-Ḥakamiyya, al-'Ujayliyya, an-Nūriyya, and al-Ṭūshiyya. However, the Qādiriyya, Shādhiliyya, and 'Alawiyya Sufi orders have survived due to the efforts of their followers.

A significant portion of this study has been dedicated to the intricacies of religious and political struggles in Yemen from the earliest days of Islam up to the tenth/sixteenth century, and even beyond into the modern period. Most notable among these tensions were the tensions between Yemen's triad of theological schools (*madhhabs*)—the Zaydī, the Ismā'īlī, and the Sunnī; the conflict between the Zaydī imams and the Sufi masters; and finally the conflict 'Abd Allāh al-Hibshī termed "the long struggle: the *Ṣūfiyya* versus the *fuqahā*." Ibn 'Alwān's life and legacy certainly played a pivotal role in these conflicts and debates, though he was not the only Sufi master to mark Yemen's religious landscape. With the rise of Sufi orders in Yemen, the jurists (*fuqahā'*) felt threatened and hastened to defend their status as "heirs to the Prophet." The dominant feature of this struggle was the fierce debate over Ibn 'Arabī's monistic ideas. Thus, at times I have departed from my focus on Ibn 'Alwān to tell the broader story of Sufism, and more broadly the history of Islamic movements in medieval Yemen.

Following the passing away of the charismatic age of Sufi leaders, Yemeni Sufism after the second half of the eighth/fourteenth century experienced a relative decline. However, the tenth/sixteenth century witnessed a revival of interest in the Sufi concepts of al-Ḥallāj (d. 309/922) and al-Ghazālī (d. 505/1111). Echoes of Ibn 'Alwān's lyrical poetry are heard in the major representatives of this new Sufi movement, 'Abd al-Hādī as-Sūdī (d. 932/1525) in Ta'izz and 'Umar Bā Makhrama (d. 952/1545) in Ḥaḍramawt. The literary output of these two prominent Sufis was characterized by their extensive usage of vernacular language. This age also represents a new set of priorities in Yemeni Sufism, notably an emphasis on accessibility for the common people. Sufism after the tenth/sixteenth century up to the present requires a thorough investigation of the historical and rare sources and thus requires different settings.

NOTES

Introduction

1. All the dates are given according to the Muslim lunar calendar (*hijra*), which are followed by a backslash and the Common Era equivalent.

Chapter 1

1. Aḥmad, Muḥammad 'Abd al-'Āl, *Banū Rasūl wa banū Ṭāhir*, al-Hay'ah al-'Āmmah li'l-Kutub, Cairo (1980), p. 19.
2. Al-Ashā'ir is a Yemeni tribe residing in Zabīd. The famous theologian Abū al-Ḥasan al-Ash'arī belonged to this tribe. The term "al-Jazzār" literally means "the butcher." See Aḥmad, *Banū Rasūl wa banū Ṭāhir*, p. 20.
3. Aḥmad, *Banū Rasūl wa banū Ṭāhir*, pp. 23–24.
4. Aḥmad, *Banū Rasūl wa banū Ṭāhir*, p. 24.
5. Cf. Al-Hamdānī, Ḥusayn b. Faiḍ Allāh with al-Juhanī, Ḥasan Sulaymān Maḥmūd, *aṣ-Ṣulayḥiyyūn wa'l-ḥarkah al-fāṭimiyya fī al-Yaman*, Wizārat al-I'lām wa'th-Thaqāfa, Yemen, reprinted at Dār al-Mukhtār, Damascus (1955), pp. 47–48.
6. Other motives include pressure on Turānshāh from 'Umārah, the Yemeni poet; the desire to find a place of refuge for the Ayyūbid house; economic motives; the desire to find a territory for Turānshāh; and the disturbed state of Yemen.
7. The non-Yemenite medieval sources cited by G. Rex Smith are Ibn Shaddād, *Nawādir*; Abū Shāma, *Rawḍatayn*, quoting Ibn Abī Ṭayy'; Ibn al-Athīr, *Kāmil*; Ibn al-Jawzī, *Mir'āt*; Ibn Wāṣil, *Mufarrij*; Ibn Khallikān, *Wafayāt*; al-Maqrīzī, *Khiṭaṭ*. The Yemeni sources are Ismā'īl b. al-'Abbās, *Fākihat*; al-Khazrajī, *Kifāyah* and *Ṭirāz*; al-Ahdal, *Tuḥfat*; Ibn ad-Dayba', *Bughyat* and *Qurrat*; Abū Makhrama, *Tārīkh*, Yaḥyā b. al-Ḥusayn, *Ghāyat*. For a full citation, see the bibliography. Cf. Smith, *The Ayyūbids*, v. 2, pp. 32–33.
8. The detailed rules of Islamic law in its various branches.
9. The doctrinal principles of faith.
10. Yaḥyā b. al-Ḥusayn, *Ghāyat al-amānī fī akhbār al-quṭr al-Yamānī*, ed. Sa'īd 'Abd al-Fattāḥ 'Āshūr, revised by Muḥammad Muṣṭafā Ziyāda, v. 1, Dār al-Kātib al-'Arabī, Cairo (1388/1968), pp. 322–323, n. 3. However, 'Āshūr, the editor of *Ghāyat al-amānī*, misinterprets the Arabic personal pronoun in the

quote "their *madhhab.*" He assumes it refers to the Ayyūbids and argues that these opinions were exaggerated, if not incorrect. But the fact of the matter is that the author Yaḥyā b. al-Ḥusayn was referring to B. Mahdī, the rulers of Zabīd and Tihāma. Smith does not comment on this.

11. Smith describes the expeditionary force: "When Tūrānshāh arrived in Yemen from Egypt in 569/1173, he marched down through Tihāma, passing by Ḥaraḍ, as far as Zabīd. From there he crossed to the Ta'izz area before turning southwards to Aden. Having dealt with Aden, he turned north and halted for a while in ad-Dumluwah and Dhū Jibla. Continuing his way northward, he took over the important town of Dhamār and afterwards stood at the gates of Ṣan'ā'. This is, in essence, the sum total of the achievements of Tūrānshāh in Yemen. He returned to Egypt in 571/1176." Smith, *The Ayyūbids*, v. 2, pp. 46–51.
12. Stookey, R. W., *Yemen: The Politics of the Yemen Arab Republic,* Westview Press, Boulder, Colo. (1978), p. 295.
13. Ibn Ḥātim, Badr ad-Dīn Muḥammad, *Kitāb as-simṭ al-ghālī ath-thaman fī akhbār al-mulūk min al-ghuzz bi'l-Yaman* (henceforth *as-Simṭ*), ed. G. Rex Smith, v. 1 *The Ayyūbids and Early Rasūlids in the Yemen*, Luzac, London (1974), p. 39.
14. Aḥmad, Muḥammad 'Abd al-'Āl, *Banū Rasūl wa banū Ṭāhir*, al-Hay'a al-Miṣriyya al-'Āmma li'l-Kitāb, Cairo (1980), p. 35.
15. Al-Khazrajī says that Nūr ad-Dīn 'Umar was appointed as *atābek* "commander of his [al-Mas'ūd's] forces and of all his affairs" and *nā'ib*. The account of Ibn Ḥātim in *as-Simṭ* is slightly different. He says that al-Mas'ūd asked his *mamlūk*, Ḥusām ad-Dīn Lu'lu', to be the deputy (*nā'ib*). The latter showed reluctance to stay in Yemen. Then, al-Mas'ūd asked Nūr ad-Dīn to be *nā'ib* until a later notice to hand in the country to whomever will be appointed and, then, to join al-Mas'ūd in Egypt. See Smith, *The Ayyūbids and Early Rasūlids in the Yemen*, v. 2, p. 89.
16. Knysh, Alexander, *Ibn 'Arabī in the Later Islamic Tradition*, State University of New York Press (1999), p. 230.
17. Al-Khazrajī, 'Alī b. al-Ḥasan, *Kitāb al-'uqūd al-lu'lu'iyya* (henceforth *al-'Uqūd*), ed. Muḥammad Basyūnī 'Asal, v. 1, Maṭba'at al-Hilāl, Cairo (1911), p. 46; Smith, G. Rex, "The Ayyūbids and Rasūlids: The Transference of Power in 7th/13th Century Yemen," in *Studies in the Medieval History of the Yemen and South Arabia*, Variorum (1997), p. 10.
18. Aḥmad, *Banū Rasūl wa banū Ṭāhir*, pp. 97–99.
19. Knysh, *Ibn 'Arabī in the Later Islamic Tradition*, p. 230.
20. Al-Khazrajī, *al-'Uqūd*, v. 1, p. 82; Aḥmad, *Banū Rasūl wa banū Ṭāhir*, p. 116; Knysh, *Ibn 'Arabī in the Later Islamic Tradition*, p. 230.
21. Al-Ḥibshī, 'Abd Allāh, *Mu'allafāt ḥukkām al-Yaman*, ed. Elke Niewohner-Eberhard, Otto Harrassowitz, Wiesbaden (1979), p. 54; Knysh, *Ibn 'Arabī in the Later Islamic Tradition*, p. 230.
22. Stookey, *Yemen,* pp. 105–108.
23. Smith, *The Ayyūbids and Early Rasūlids in the Yemen*, v. 2, p. 85.
24. Knysh, *Ibn 'Arabī in the Later Islamic Tradition*, p. 230.
25. Varisco, Daniel, "Texts and Pretexts: The Unity of the Rasūlid State Under al-Malik al-Muẓaffar," in *La Revu du Musulman et de la Méditerranée* (*REMMM*), v. 67/1 (1993), p. 13.

26. Knysh, *Ibn 'Arabī in the Later Islamic Tradition*, p. 230.
27. Smith, "The Political History of Islamic Yemen," *in Studies in the Medieval History of the Yemen and South Arabia*, Variorum (1997), p. 137. Cf. Knysh, *Ibn 'Arabī in the Later Islamic Tradition*, p. 231.
28. Aḥmad, Muḥammad 'Abd al-'Āl, *Banū Rasūl wa banū Ṭāhir* (1980), p. 547.
29. El-Shami, A., and Serjeant, Robert, "Regional Literature: The Yemen," in *'Abbasid Belles-Lettres*, Cambridge University Press (1990), p. 461.
30. Varisco, "Texts and Pretexts," p. 21; al-Ḥibshī, *Ḥayāt al-adab al-Yamanī*, pp. 50–51.
31. Al-Ḥibshī, *Ḥayāt al-adab al-Yamanī*, pp. 50–51.
32. Ash-Sharjī, *Ṭabaqāt al-khawāṣṣ*, p. 62; Knysh, *Ibn 'Arabī in the Later Islamic Tradition*, p. 228; al-Ḥibshī, *Ḥayāt al-adab al-Yamanī*, pp. 50–51.
33. Knysh, *Ibn 'Arabī in the Later Islamic Tradition*, p. 232.
34. Al-Burayhī, *Ṭabaqāt ṣulaḥā' al-Yaman*, pp. 349–350. Cf. Knysh, *Ibn 'Arabī in the Later Islamic Tradition*, p. 232.
35. Knysh, *Ibn 'Arabī in the Later Islamic Tradition*, p. 232.
36. Al-Burayhī, *Ṭabaqāt ṣulaḥā' al-Yaman*, pp. 349–350. Cf. Knysh, *Ibn 'Arabī in the Later Islamic Tradition*, pp. 232, 370; Varisco, "Texts and Pretexts," p. 21; al-Ḥibshī, *aṣ-Ṣufiyyah wa'l-fuqahā'*, passim.
37. *EI2*, art. "Ismā'īliyya." Cf. Daftary, Farhad, *The Ismā'īlīs: Their History and Doctrine*, Cambridge University Press, reprinted (1994), p. 91.
38. Halm, Heinz, *The Empire of the Mahdī: The Rise of the Fāṭimids*, trans. Michael Bonner, E. J. Brill (1996), p. 36. Cf. *EI2*, art. "Ismā'īliyya."
39. Stookey, *Yemen*, p. 56.
40. Ash-Shamāḥī, 'Abd Allāh, *al-Yaman: al-insān wa'l-ḥaḍāra*, Dār al-Kutub, Cairo (1972), p. 109.
41. *EI2*, art. "Ismā'īliyya."
42. Daftary, *The Ismā'īlīs*, p. 208.
43. El-Shami and Serjeant, "Regional Literature: The Yemen," p. 455.
44. *EI2*, art. "Ismā'īliyya."
45. *EI2*, art. "Ismā'īliyya." Cf. Daftary, *The Ismā'īlīs*, p. 208.
46. *EI2*, art. "Ismā'īliyya." Cf. Fayzee, A. A. A., "Three Sulaymānī Dā'īs: 1936–1939," in *Journal of the Bombay Branch of the Royal Asiatic Society*, Bombay, 14 (1940), pp. 101–104.
47. See, for instance, Chapter 4.
48. *Shorter Encyclopedia of Islam*, art. "Ismā'īliyya," E. J. Brill, fourth impression (1995), p. 181 (henceforth, *SEI4*).
49. *EI2*, art. "Ismā'īliyya."
50. *EI2*, art. "Ismā'īliyya."
51. Al-Hamdānī, Ḥ. F., "Fāṭimid History and Historians," in *Religion, Learning and Science in the 'Abbāsid Period*, ed. M. J. L. Young, J. D. Latham, and R. B. Serjeant, Cambridge University Press, Cambridge (1990), pp. 243–244.
52. Knysh, *Ibn 'Arabī in the Later Islamic Tradition*, p. 226.
53. Knysh, *Ibn 'Arabī in the Later Islamic Tradition*, p. 226.
54. Knysh, *Ibn 'Arabī in the Later Islamic Tradition*, p. 226.
55. See Chapter 3.
56. *EI2*, art. "Al-Zaidīya."
57. *SIE4*, art. "Al-Zaidīya."

58. *EI2*, art. "Al-Zaidīya".
59. Momen, Moojan, *An Introduction to Shī'ī Islam*, Yale University Press, New Haven and London (1983), p. 49. Cf. ash-Shahrastānī, Muḥammad, *al-Milal wa'n-niḥal*, ed. William Cureton, Otto Horrassowitz, Leipzig (1923), p. 116.
60. Al-'Amrī, Ḥusayn b. 'Abdullah, *The Yemen in 18th & 19th Centuries: A Political & Intellectual History*, Ithaca Press, London (1983), p. 124.
61. Watt, W. M., *Islamic Philosophy and Theology*, reprinted, Edinburgh University Press (1995), p. 129.
62. Al-Jārūdiyya, named after Abū al-Jārūd, was opposed to the approval of the companions of the Prophet. They considered the companions sinful in failing to recognize 'Alī. Moreover, they denied the legitimacy of Abū Bakr and 'Umar. This sect was active during the late Umayyad and early 'Abbāsid period and its views predominated among the later Zaydīs. See Momen, *An Introduction to Shī'ī Islam*, pp. 50–51.
63. These are the followers of Sulaymān b. Jarīr. They claim that the Imamate is consultative. According to the account of Zurqān, al-Ash'arī says, Sulaymān b. Jarīr claimed that the pledge of allegiance (*bay'a*) to Abū Bakr and 'Umar was an error that does not amount to sin and that the community abandoned the better (*al-aṣlaḥ*) in favor of that which is less excellent. See al-Ash'arī, Abū al-Ḥasan, *Maqālāt al-islāmiyyīn*, ed. Hellmut Ritter, Franz Steiner, Wiesbaden (1963), p. 68.
64. This group, named after Kathīr an-Nawa, known as al-Abtar, and the followers of al-Ḥasan b. Ṣāliḥ held the same view as as-Sulaymāniyya but suspended judgment with respect to 'Uthmān. See ash-Shahrastānī, *al-Milal*, p. 120.
65. These are the followers of Nu'aym b. al-Yamān. They claim that 'Alī was the best man after the Prophet. They also held that the community was not erroneous when they allowed Abū Bakr and 'Umar to assume power but they were in error in abandoning the better. See al-Ash'arī, *Maqālāt al-islāmiyyīn*, p. 69.
66. Al-Ash'arī, *Maqālāt al-islāmiyyīn*, pp. 66–69.
67. Messick, Brinkley, *The Calligraphic State*, University of California Press, Berkeley (1993), p. 39.
68. Messick, *The Calligraphic State*, p. 39.
69. Al-'Amrī, *The Yemen*, p. 124.
70. *EI2*, art. "Al-Zaidīya."
71. Abū Zahra, Muḥammad, *al-Imām Zayd*, Dār al-Fikr al-'Arabī, Cairo (1378/1959), p. 507.
72. This is not definitely true because one can normally find studies about Shī'a and its branch az-Zaydiyya, but scholarship is extremely rare in mainstream Sunnīsm.
73. Al-Akwa', Ismā'īl, *az-Zaydiyya: nash'atuhā wa mu'taqadātuhā*, name of publisher is not found (1421/2000), p. 5.
74. Al-Akwa', *az-Zaydiyya*, p. 7.
75. Ṣubḥī, Aḥmad Maḥmūd, *az-Zaydiyya*, az-Zahrā' lil-I'lām al-'Arabī, Cairo (1984).
76. Al-Akwa', Ismā'īl, *az-Zaydiyya*, p. 9.

77. Al-Akwa‘, *az-Zaydiyya*, p. 35.
78. Al-Akwa‘, *az-Zaydiyya*, p. 35.
79. Ash-Shawkānī, *Adab aṭ-ṭalab wa muntahā al-irab*, ed. ‘Abd Allāh Yaḥyā as-Surayḥī, Dār Ibn Ḥazm, Beirut (1998), p. 122.
80. Ash-Shawkānī, *Adab aṭ-ṭalab wa muntahā al-irab*, p. 122.
81. Hallaq, Wael, *A History of Islamic Legal Theories*, Cambridge University Press, Cambridge (1997), p. 121.
82. Ash-Shawkānī, *Adab aṭ-ṭalab*, pp.123–124.
83. Ash-Shawkānī, *Adab aṭ-ṭalab*, pp.123–124.
84. Ash-Shāmī, Aḥmad Muḥammad, *Tārīkh al-Yaman al-fikrī fī al-‘aṣr al-‘Abbāsī*, v. 1, Manshūrāt al-‘Aṣr al-Ḥadīth (1987), p. 114.
85. Ash-Shamāḥī, ‘Abd Allāh, *al-Yaman: al-insān wa’l-ḥaḍāra*, Dār ‘Ālam al-Kutub, Cairo (1972), p. 100.
86. Ash-Shamāḥī, *al-Yaman: al-insān wa’l-ḥaḍāra*, p. 101.
87. Ash-Shamāḥī, *al-Yaman: al-insān wa’l-ḥaḍāra*, pp. 107–108.
88. Ash-Shamāḥī, ‘Abd Allāh, *al-Yaman: al-insān wa’l-ḥaḍāra*, Dār al-Kutub, Cairo (1972), pp. 101–102.
89. Ash-Shāmī, *Tārīkh al-Yaman al-fikrī fī al-‘aṣr al-‘Abbāsī*, pp. 115116. For the dates of their reign, see Chapter 2.
90. Ash-Shāmī, *Tārīkh al-Yaman al-fikrī fī al-‘aṣr al-‘Abbāsī*, pp. 118–119.
91. For instance, in his *The Venture of Islam* (I, 278), Marshall G. S. Hodgson summarizes three ways in which the term “Sunnī” has been most used: to mean Jamā‘ī vs. Shī‘ī; to mean Ḥadīthī vs. Kalāmī (including Mu‘tazilīs and Ash‘arīs); to mean Shar‘ī vs. Sufi. He adds that the term has been extended to those ‘Alid loyalists, kalām men, and Sufis who accepted key positions of their respective opponents.
92. Qur’ān (8:38); (15:13); (18:55); (35:43).
93. Qur’ān (17:77); (33:62); (35:43); (48:23).
94. Al-Aẓsmī, Muḥammad, *On Shacht's Origin of Muḥammadan Jurisprudence*, King Saud University (1985), p. 30.
95. Hodgson, M. G. S. *The Venture of Islam*, v. 1, University of Chicago Press (1977), pp. 276–278.
96. Watt, *The Formative Period of Islamic Thought*, pp. 256–260.
97. Abrahamov, Binyamin, *Islamic Theology: Traditionalism and Rationalism*, Edinburgh University Press (1998), pp. viii, ix.
98. Hodgson, *The Venture of Islam*, pp. 388–389.
99. Kennedy, H. N., “The ‘Abbāsid Caliphate: A Historical Introduction,” in *‘Abbāsid Belles-lettres*, Cambridge University Press (1990), p. 5.
100. From the Sunnī point of view, Shī‘īsm is 9 percent, Kharijite is 1 percent, and Sunnīsm is 90 percent. See Makdisi, George, “Ash‘arī and the Ash‘arites in Islamic Religious History,” in *Studia Islamica*, v. 17 (1962), pp. 44–45.
101. Ibn Samurah, ‘Umar b. ‘Alī, *Ṭabaqāt fuqahā’ al-Yaman*, ed. Fū’ād Sayyid, Cairo (1957), p. 74.
102. El-Shami and Serjeant, “Regional Literature: The Yemen,” p. 445.
103. Al-Ḥibshī, ‘Abd Allāh, *Ḥayāt al-adab al-Yamanī fī ‘aṣr banī Rasūl* (henceforth, *Ḥayāt*), Manshūrāt Wizārat al-I‘lām wa’th-Thaqāfah, Yemen Arab Republic (1980), pp. 52–53.

104. Ibn Samurah, *Ṭabaqāt*, p. 80.
105. Al-Janadī, *as-Sulūk*, v. 1, p. 264; Ibn Samurah, *Ṭabaqāt*, p. 87; al-Ḥibshī, *Ḥayāt*, p. 52.
106. Al-Ḥibshī, *Ḥayāt*, p. 53; cf. Varisco, "Texts and Pretexts," p. 21.
107. Al-Ḥibshī, *Ḥayāt*, p. 53.
108. Ibn Samurah, *Ṭabaqāt*, p. 118; al-Ḥibshī, *Ḥayāt*, p. 53.
109. Al-Ḥibshī, *Ḥayāt*, p. 54.
110. El-Shamī and Serjeant, "Regional Literature," p. 454.
111. Ar-Rāzī, Aḥmad b. ʻAbd Allāh, *Tārīkh Madīnat Sanaa*, 3rd ed., ed. Ḥusayn ʻAbd Allāh al-ʻAmrī, Dār al-Fikr, Damascus (1409/1989), pp. 287, 530, and passim.
112. El-Shamī and Serjeant, "Regional Literature," p. 458. See Chapter 2 for further discussion of *al-Bayān*.
113. El-Shamī and Serjeant, "Regional Literature," p. 458.
114. Al-Ḥibshī, *Ḥayāt*, p. 96.
115. Al-Janadī, *as-Sulūk*, p. 367.
116. Al-Janadī, *as-Sulūk*, p. 367.
117. Al-Janadī, *as-Sulūk*, p. 367.
118. Al-Janadī, *as-Sulūk*, p. 368; al-Ḥibshī, *Ḥayāt*, p. 55.
119. Al-Ḥibshī, *Ḥayāt*, p. 55.
120. Al-Akwaʻ, Ismāʻīl, *al-Madāris al-islāmiyya fī al-Yaman*, Manshūrāt Jāmiʻat Sanaa (1980), p. 7.
121. Knysh, *Ibn ʻArabī in the Later Islamic Tradition*, p. 231.
122. Knysh, *Ibn ʻArabī in the Later Islamic Tradition*, p. 232.
123. Al-Hamdānī, Ḥusayn b. Faiḍ Allāh with al-Juhanī, Ḥasan Sulaymān Maḥmūd, *aṣ-Ṣulayḥiyyūn wa'l-ḥarka al-fāṭimiyya fī al-Yaman*, Wizārat al-Iʻlām wa'th-Thaqāfa, Yemen, reprinted at Dār al-Mukhtār, Damascus (n.d.), p. 29.
124. Evidence of this competition lies in the fact that when the Isamāʻīlī, ʻAlī Muḥammad aṣ-Ṣulayḥī (d. 473/1080 or 459/1066), captured Ṣanʻā', the Zaydī imam Abū al-Fatḥ ad-Daylamī hastened to form a military and political alliance with the Sunnī dynasty of the black slaves in Tihāma. Al-Hamdānī, *aṣ-Ṣulayḥiyyūn*, p. 236.
125. El-Shami and Searjeant, "Regional Literature," p. 460.
126. In the late eighth/fourteenth centuries the powerful Rasūlid dynasty reduced their Zaydī rivals to a handful of strongholds in the mountainous region of Ṣaʻdahh, which did not play a significant role in the political life of the rest of Yemen. In the early ninth/fifteenth century, the Rasūlids continued to fight the Zaydīs bitterly, sometimes with the help of the Ismāʻīlī community. The latter, however, went into a steep decline and never regained its former power. Knysh, *Ibn ʻArabī in the Later Islamic Tradition*, p. 227.

Chapter 2

1. A previous version of this chapter was published as "A Short Survey of Yemeni Sufism from Its Inception up to the Thirteenth Century," *American Journal of Islamic Social Sciences* (*AJISS*), 2/1 (Winter 2009).
2. Knysh, Alexander, *Islamic Mysticism: A Short History*, E. J. Brill (2000), p. 5. Note that dates are given according to the Muslim lunar calendar (*hijra*), which are followed by a backslash and the Common Era equivalent.

3. Melchert, Christopher, "The Transition from Asceticism to Mysticism at the Middle of the Ninth Century C.E.," *Studia Islamica*, 83 (1996), p. 57. See also Knysh, *Islamic Mysticism*, p. 5.
4. Knysh, *Islamic Mysticism*, p. 6.
5. Al-Ja'dī, Ibn Samurah, *Ṭabaqāt fuqahā' al-Yaman*, ed. Fu'ād Sayyid, Maṭba'at as-Sunna al-Muḥammadiyyah, Cairo (1957), p. 5. Cf. Stookey, Robert, *Yemen*, Westview Press, Boulder, Colo. (1978), p. 29.
6. *Shorter Encyclopaedia of Islam*, art. "Abū Mūsā al-Ash'arī," fourth impression, E. J. Brill, Leiden (1995).
7. Ash-Sha'rānī, 'Abd al-Wahhāb, *aṭ-Ṭabaqāt al-Kubrā*, v. 1, ed. Aḥmad Abd ar-Raḥīm al-Sā'iḥ and Tawfīq Ali Wahbah, Maktabat ath-Thaqāfa ad-Dīniyya, Cairo (2005), p. 49. Cf. Khaled, Muḥammad Khaled, *Rijāl ḥawl ar-rasūl*, v. 4, Dār al-Kutub al-Ḥadītha, Cairo (1965), pp. 38–39.
8. Schimmel, Annemarie, *Mystical Dimension of Islam*, University of North Carolina Press (1975), p. 28.
9. Shimmmel, *Mystical Dimension of Islam*, p. 29.
10. Al-Janadī, Muḥammad b. Yūsuf, *as-Sulūk fī ṭabaqāt al-'ulamā' wa-l-mulūk*, ed. Muḥammad 'Alī al-Akwa', vol. 1, Wizārat al-I'lām wa'th-Thaqāfah, Ṣan'ā' (1983), p. 98.
11. Al-Janadī, *as-Sulūk*, v. 1, p. 98.
12. Trimingham, Spencer, *The Sufi Orders in Islam*, Oxford University Press, New York (1998), pp. 12–13.
13. Al-Janadī, *as-Sulūk*, v. 1, p. 98.
14. Al-Jawzī, Abū al-Faraj 'Abd ar-Raḥmān, *Ṣifat aṣ-ṣafwa*, v. 2, Dār al-Jīl, Beirut (1992), pp. 24–32. See also ash-Sharjī, Aḥmad, *Ṭabaqāt al-khawāṣṣ ahl aṣ-ṣidq wa'l-ikhlāṣs,* ad-Dār al-Yamaniyyah l'n-nashr wat-tawzī' (1986), pp. 109–114.
15. Al-Ṭabarī, Ibn Jarīr, *The History of al-Ṭabarī*, v. 39, trans. Ella Landau-Tasseron, State University of New York Press, pp. 207–208, 266.
16. Goldziher, Ignaz, *Introduction to Islamic Theology and Law*, trans. Andras and Ruth Hamori, Princeton University Press, Princeton (1981), p. 131.
17. At-Taftazānī, Abū l-Wafā, *Madkhal ilā at-tṣawwuf al-Islamī,* Dār ath-Thaqāfa, Cairo (1976), pp. 50–58.
18. At-Taftazānī, *Madkhal ilā at-tṣawwuf al-Islamī*, pp. 58–64.
19. Ibn al-Jawzī, *Ṣifat aṣ-ṣafwa*, v. 1, p. 506. Cf. Aḥmad b. 'Abd Allāh ar-Rāzī, *Tārīkh Madīnat Ṣan'ā'*, ed. Ḥusayn 'Abd Allāh al-'Amrī, 3rd ed., Dār al-Fikr, Damascus (1989), p. 359.
20. See their biographies in Ar-Rāzī, *Tārīkh Madīnat Ṣan'ā'*.
21. Ad-Dujaylī, Muḥammad Riḍā Ḥasan, *al-Ḥayā al-fikrīya fī al-Yaman fī al-qarn as-sādis al-hijrī,* Markaz Dirāsāt al-Khalīj al-'Arabī, University of Basra (1985), pp. 215–217. Cf. Muṣṭafā, Shākir, *at-Tārīkh al-'arabī wa'l-mu'arrikhūn*, v. 2, Dār al-'Ilm Li'l-Malāyyīn, Beirut (1979), pp. 318–322. See also v. 1, p. 135. Cf. Sa'īd, 'Abd al-Karīm, *Qaḍayā wa ishkāliyyāt at-taṣawwuf 'ind Aḥmad b. 'Alwān*, Maktabat Murād, Ṣan'ā' (1997), pp. 34–35.
23. For further discussion on the transmission of Greek thought into Arabic, see the invaluable work of Dimitri Gutas, *Greek Thought, Arabic Culture,* Routledge (1999).
24. Sa'īd, *Qaḍāyā*, p. 44. Cf. al-Yāfi'ī, 'Abd Allāh b. As'ad, *Rawḍ ar-rayāḥīn fī*

ḥikāyāt aṣ-ṣāliḥīn, 2nd ed., Maṭba'at Muṣṭafā al-Bābī al-Ḥalābī, Cairo (1955), pp. 43–45. The last sentence concerning the man's death was not quoted by Sa'īd's, but can be found in al-Yāfi'ī's *Rawḍ ar-rayāḥīn,* p. 45.
25. Al-Madanī, as-Sayyid Abū Ḍayf, *Dhū 'n-Nūn al-Miṣirī*, Dār ash-Shrūq, Cairo (1973), p. 53; Sa'īd, 'Abd al-Karīm, *Qaḍayā wa ishkāliyyāt at-taṣawwuf 'ind Aḥmad b. 'Alwān*, Maktabat Murād, Ṣan'ā' (1997), p. 44. See also Sharaf, Muḥammad Jalāl, *at-Taṣawwuf al-islāmī: madārisuh wa naẓariyyātuh*, Dār al-'Ulūm al-'Arabiyya, Beirut (1990), p. 61.
26. Ar-Rāzī, *Tārīkh madīnat Ṣan'ā'*, p. 343. Cf. al-Ḥibshī, *aṣ-Ṣūfiyya wa'l-fuqahā' fī al-Yaman,* p. 12.
27. Ash-Sharjī, Aḥmad b. Aḥmad, *Ṭabaqāt al-khawāṣṣ: ahl aṣ-ṣidq wa'l-ikhlāṣ*, Ad-Dār al-Yamaniyya, Beirut (1986), p. 150.
28. See Al-Janadī, Muḥammad b. Yūsuf, *as-Sulūk fī ṭabaqāt al-'ulamā' wa-l-mulūk*, ed. Muḥammad 'Alī al-Akwa', v. 1., Wizārat al-I'lām wa'th-Thaqāfah, Ṣan'ā' (1983); cf. ash-Sharjī, *Ṭabaqāt al-khawāṣs.*
29. He is different from al-Yāfi'ī, the author of *Rawḍ ar-Rayāḥīn.*
30. Al-Janadī, *as-Sulūk fī ṭabaqāt al-'ulamā' wa-l-mulūk*, p. 310.
31. Just like the modern electric doors that sense someone coming and open automatically.
32. Ash-Sharjī, *Ṭabaqāt al-khawāṣṣ*, p. 138.
33. Al-Janadī, *as-Sulūk*, p. 310.
34. Ash-Sharjī, *Ṭabaqāt al-khawāṣṣ*, p. 188.
35. *Qur'ān* (97:1–5).
36. Ash-Sharjī, *Ṭabaqāt al-khawāṣṣ*, p. 64.
37. Ash-Sharjī, *Ṭabaqāt al-khawāṣṣ*, p. 65.
38. Ash-Sharjī, *Ṭabaqāt al-khawāṣṣ*, p. 66.
39. Ash-Sharjī, *Ṭabaqāt al-khawāṣṣ*, p. 68.
40. Sa'īd, *Qaḍāyā*, p. 35.
41. For further discussion on the Sayyid history see Knysh, Alexander, "The Sāda in History: A Critical Essay on Ḥaḍramī Historiography," in *Journal of the Royal Asiatic Society,* 9/2 (July 1999). Cf. R. B. Serjeant, *The Sayyids of Ḥaḍramawt* (London 1957). See also al-Shillī, Muḥammad b. Abū Bakr, *al-Mashra' al-rawī fī manāqib al-sāda al-kirām Āl Abī 'Alawī* Cairo (1319/1901).
42. Ash-Sharjī, *Ṭabaqāt al-khawāṣṣ*, p. 250.

Chapter 3

1. In *as-Sulūk fī ṭabaqāt al-'ulamā' wa-l-mulūk* by Muḥammad al-Janadī (d. 732/1331) and in *al-'Uqūd al-lu'lu'iyya* by 'Alī b. al-Ḥaṣan al-Khazrajī (d. 812/1409), Ibn 'Alwān is called "Abū al-Ḥaṣan," whereas in *Ṭabaqāt al-khawāṣṣ* by Aḥmad b. Aḥmad ash-Sharjī (d. 893/1487) and in *Jāmi' karāmāt al-awliyā'* by Yūsuf an-Nabhānī (d. 1932), Ibn 'Alwān is called "Abū al-'Abbās."
2. Ibn 'Alwān, Aḥmad, *at-Tawḥīd al-a'ẓam*, ed. 'Abd al-'Azīz al-Manṣūb, Dār al-Fikr al-Mu'āṣir, Beirut (1990), p. 22. All the dates are given according to the Muslim lunar calendar (*hijra*), which are followed by a backslash and the Common Era equivalent.
3. The manuscript's call number is 1513.

4. Ibn 'Alwān, *at-Tawḥīd,* p. 20.
5. Al-Barzanjī, Ja'far b. al-Ḥaṣan, *Fatḥ al-karīm al-jawād al-mannān bi-wāsiṭat 'iqd sayyid az-zamān fī ba'ḍ manāqib Aḥmad ibn 'Alwān*, Die Handschriften-Verzeichnisse der königlichen Bibliothek zu Berlin. Bd.21, Verzeichniss der Arabischen Hanschriften von W. Ahlwardt, 9. Bd., Berlin: A. Asher, 1897 # 10064, pp. 465–467.
6. The name of Ibn 'Alwān's father is misspelled. The correct spelling is 'Aṭṭāf.
7. Ibn 'Alwān, *al-Mahrajān wa l—baḥr al-mushakkal al-gharīb*, ed. al-Manṣūb, Dār al-Fikr al-Mu'āṣir, Beirut (1992), footnote, p. 5.
8. The function of the royal scribe was to read all letters that came to the sultan and to compose replies. The royal scribe could also receive royal mandates and implement them. If the sultan needed to send a letter, he asked one of his scribes to do so. When he finished, he could send it to the sultan to be signed. See 'Umarī, Shihāb ad-Dīn Aḥmad b. Yaḥyā b. Faḍl Allāh, *Masālik abṣār fī mamālik al-amṣār,* ed. Ayman Fu'ād Sayyid, Publications de L'institut Français d'Archiologie Orientale du Caire (1985), p. 160.
9. Aḥmad, Muḥammad 'Abd al-'Āl, *Banū Rasūl wa banū Ṭāhir*, al-Hay'ah al-Miṣriyyah, Alexandria (1980), p. 36.
10. Al-Janadī, Muḥammad, *as-Sulūk*, v.1, Dār at-Tanwīr, Beirut (1989), p. 349.
11. Al-Janadī, *as-Sulūk*, p. 456. Cf. Messick, Brinkley, *The Calligraphic State*, University of California Press, Berkeley (1993), p. 276.
12. Al-Janadī, *as-Sulūk*, p. 456. Al-Khazrajī, 'Alī b. al-Ḥaṣan, *al-'Uqūd al-lū' lū'iyya*, Maṭba'at al-Hilāl, Cairo (1911), p. 161. Cf. Messick, *The Calligraphic State*, p. 276.
13. Jarāda, Muḥammad Sa'īd, *al-Adab wath-thaqāfah fī al-Yaman 'abr al-'uṣūr*, Dār al-Fārābī, Beirut (1977), p. 213.
14. Al-Khazrajī, 'Alī b. al-Ḥaṣan, *al-'Uqūd al-lū' lū'iyya*, Maṭba'at al-Hilāl, Cairo (1911), p. 162.
15. Ibn al-Jawzī, *Talbīs iblīs*, 2nd ed. Dār al-Kutub al-'Ilmiyya, Beirut (1368/1948), p. 168.
16. Giffen, Lois, *Theory of Profane Love Among the Arabs*, New York University Press, New York (1971), p. 28.
17. Ibn 'Alwān, *at-Tawḥīd al-a'ẓam*, ed. Al-Manṣūb, Markaz ad-Dirāsāt wa l—Buḥūth al-Yamanī, San'a (1990), pp. 29–30. Al-Manṣūb argues that there was no textual evidence that Ibn Jamīl was Ibn 'Alwān's teacher. However, al-Manṣūb thinks that Ibn Jamīl was Ibn 'Alwān's teacher by methods of inference. The relationship between Ibn Jamīl and Ibn 'Alwān will be discussed further on.
18. Al-Janadī, *as-Sulūk*, v. 2, p. 107.
19. As-Samkar is a village near al-Janad in Ta'izz, see Muḥammad Aḥmad al-Ḥajrī, *Mu'jam al-buldān al-Yamaniyya*, ed. al-Akwa', Isma'īl, v. 3, p. 432.
20. Al-Janadī, *as-Sulūk*, v.1, pp. 457–458.
21. Al-Jandī, *as-Sulūk*, v. 1, p. 457.
22. Ibn al-Ahdal, *Tuḥfat az-zaman fī ta'rīkh al-Yaman*, ed. al-Ḥibshī, Dār at-Tanwīr, Beirut (1986), p. 355.
23. Ibn 'Alwān, *al-Futūḥ,* p. 223.
24. Al-Barzanjī did not give any details about the relationship between Ibn 'Alwān and Ibn 'Ujayl except the fact that the latter was a disciple of the former.

25. Qur'ān (10:59).
26. Ash-Sharjī, *Ṭabaqāt al-khawāṣṣ*, p. 62.
27. In *Ḥayāt al-adab al-Yamanī fī 'asr banī Rasūl*, 2nd ed. (1980), p. 34, al-Ḥibshī thought the letter and the poem were addressed to al-Muẓaffar, who was the son of al-Manṣūr, and Muḥammad Yaḥyā al-Ḥaddād followed him in *at-Tārīkh al-'āmm lil-Yaman*, v. 3, Dār at-Tanwīr, Beirut (1986), p. 208. But in *al-Futūḥ* by Ibn 'Alwān, ed. al-Manṣūb, the letter and the poem were addressed to the father Imām al-Manṣūr 'Ûmar b. 'Alī b. Rasūl. Also, this can be found in a previous edition of the same book titled *Kitāb al-futūḥ al-maṣūna al-maknūna wa-l-'ulūm al-makhzūna*, which was printed electronically, without edition by al-Hājj Ḥasan 'Abd al-Jalīl Muḥammad al-Abyaḍ, Maṭba'at Kamāl as-Suways (1990), pp. 217–222.
28. *Encyclopedia of Islam*, 2nd ed. (henceforth, *EI2*), art. "Rāfiḍa," v. 3., E. J. Brill, Leiden (1994).
29. Momen, Moojan, *An Introduction to Shī'ī Islam*, Yale University Press, London (1985), p. 73. See also, Watt, W. Montgomery, *The Formative Period of Islamic Thought*, Oneworld, Oxford (1998), p. 157.
30. Perhaps the author is referring to the second caliph of Islam, 'Umar b. al-Khaṭṭāb (d. 24/644) and the Umayyad caliph 'Umar b. 'Abd al-'Azīz (d. 101/720), who were known for their justice and moral rectitude.
31. Ibn 'Alwān, Aḥmad, *al-Futūḥ,* ed. al-Manṣūb, Dār al-Fikr al-Mu'āṣir, Beirut (1991), pp. 505–507.
32. Ibn 'Alwān, *al-Futūḥ*, pp. 505–507.
33. Ibn 'Alwān, *al-Futūḥ,* p. 56. However, Carl Brockelmann, in his *Geschichte der Arabischen Litteratur*, E. J. Brill, Leiden (1996), p. 806, mentioned the following: *Dīwān, al-Futūḥ aṣ-ṣāfī li-kull qalb majrūḥ, Qasīda, al-Futūḥ al-maṣūna wa-l-asrār al-maknūna*, and a book called *Fatḥ al-Karīm al-jawād al-mannān bi-wāsiṭat 'iqd saiyid az-zamān fī ba'ḍ manāqib A. b. 'Alwān* by Ja'far b. H. al-Barzanjī (d. 1079/1765). In volume 1 (p. 584), Brockelmann added *at-Tawḥīd and Fawā'id*. Those mentioned by Brockelmann are now combined in one book called *Dīwān wa kitāb al-Futūḥ*. The *Fawā'id* is not a separate book but had been added as an attachment to *at-Tawḥīd*.
34. Ibn 'Alwān, *at-Tawḥīd,* p. 84.
35. The division was made by the editor, al-Manṣūb.
36. I discuss this later when I talk about Ibn 'Alwān's Sufi order.
37. Ibn 'Alwān, *at-Tawḥīd,* p. 256.
38. Perhaps the author is referring to Rābi'a al-'Adawiyya (d. 185/801). See 39. I talk about Ibn 'Alwān's theological views in Chapter 4.
40. Ibn 'Alwān, *at-Tawḥīd,* p. 300.
41. This will elaborated in Chapter 5.
42. Al-Qiyarī, Hamūd, "Edition of *Dīwān al-futūḥ*," unpublished M.A. thesis, Cairo University (1988), p. 10.
43. Brockelmann, *Geschichte der Arabischen Litteratur*, p. 806.
44. The word *mawlid* refers to the celebration of the Prophet's birth or a Sufi saint, while *tahlīl* refers to any death rituals. The literal meaning of *tahlīl* is *lā ilāha illā Allāh* (there is no God, but God), and the main function of it in Yemen, and specifically in my native town of Ibb, is to attract attention to

the process of death rituals. There are two kinds of death rituals. The first one is called *tashyī' al-janāza* (the procession of the funeral), which differs from place to place, according to traditions and customs. It is said that during the Prophet's time, people used to walk after the funeral contemplating the transition of human beings. Then, in later times, people started to talk about worldly affairs during the funeral procession. After that, some scholars (*'ulamā'*) suggested that it might be a good idea to preoccupy the people with *dhikr*, which consists of remembering the names of God and the name of His Prophet and reciting some pious poems. Some of the famous poems belong to al-Ḥallāj (d. 309/922), 'Abd ar-Raḥīm al-Bura'ī (d. 803/1400), Ibn 'Alwān, and others. The second kind of death rituals is called *tahlīl*. It can be performed either at the deceased person's house or at a mosque. Usually, poor people make their *tahlīl* at a mosque because of the high cost of mourners; they recite some *sūras* from the Qur'ān, especially chapter 36 (*Yā Sīn*), which is described in a *ḥadīth* as the heart of the Qur'ān (*qalb al-Qur'ān*). They also recite Sufi poems and *dhikr* aloud.

45. Browne, E. G., *A Literary History of Persia*, v. 1, Iranbooks (1997), p. 473.
46. Arberry, A. J., *The Rubā'iyyāt of Jalāl ad-Dīn Rumī*, Emery Walker, London (1949), p. v.
47. Arberry, *The Rubā'iyyāt*, p. v.
48. Al-Maqāliḥ, "Introduction," to *al-Futūḥ*, 2nd ed., ed. al-Manṣūb, Dār al-Fikr al-Mu'āṣir, Beirut (1995), pp. 21–23.
49. Al-Janadī, *as-Sulūk*, v. 1, pp. 456–457; Ibn al-Ahdal, *Tuḥfat az-zaman*, pp. 354–355; ash-Sharjī, *Ṭabaqāt al-khawāṣṣ*, p. 69; Knysh, *Ibn 'Arabī in the later Islamic Tradition*, p. 237.
50. Al-Ḥibshī, *aṣ-Ṣufiyya wa l—fuqahā'*, Maktabat al-Jīl al-Jadīd, San'a (1976), p. 72.
51. They are as follows: *iṭbāṭūn, isṭāsūn, arusṭā, ardashīr, istimdār, asbāsāṭ, iṣfihsilāra, izmakhshalīl, izmakhshalūs, irbikhshināshūt, irmsāhūn, ursṭā'īl, bārqūsh, bānūn min yānūn, barahūt,bārhūj, bārūj, bāqūsh, biyrqīmush, biraḥmūt, birḥmūt, birahbūt, tadalkashī, tabarkashī, thābūt, jayrūn, khaylikhān, khandarīs, dustukān, dustumān, dustūn, ruzdukāsh, rustāf, raghabūt, zubruqān, zamardakūsh, zamkhatrūsh, zamakhtarūsh, zaynhatrūsh, sibsihān, sibinstak, sirbās, sibāhshatūt, saylāhāsūn, sirnār, sharqishānī, shimikhshāl, shimrākh, shibrishaq, shārqūsh, shibihshāhūn, ṭayrasūn, ṭastūn, qahrimān, kardakūsh, mamūt, marmūt, mihtār, māsūk, nafth, nāfūth, nāfrūt, nāyūsh, nāsūk,* and *warshān*. See Sa'īd, Abd al-Karīm, *Qaḍāyā wa ishkāliyyāt at-taṣawwuf 'ind Aḥmad bin 'Alwān*, Maktabat Murād (1997), pp. 22–23. There are some other terms in *al-Futūḥ* that have been overlooked from this list, such as *shāhīn, rustāq, fayrūz, jullunār, arjawān, jawānī*.
52. Ibn 'Alwān, *al-Futūḥ*, p. 117.
54. Literally, it means to "hew" or "carve." In linguistics it means combining two syllables to form one word to carry the meaning of a common expression, e.g., *dam'aza* is a verb taken from the expression "*adāma Allāhu 'izzak*" (may God continue your glory).
54. Ba'kar, 'Abd ar-Raḥmān, *at-Turjumān al-mujaddid Aḥmad bin 'Alwān*, published in articles in the *ath-Thaqāfiyya*'s newspaper, which was then an

appendix of *al-Jumhuriyya*'s newspaper, now is independent; see the issue of 31 August 1999.

55. Ba'kar, *at-Turjumān al-mujaddid Aḥmad bin 'Alwān*, see the issue of 16 September 1999. I am familiar with the basics of Persian languages, but there is no indication of a single Persian sentence. There is neither structure nor verb system that might be regarded as a proof of Ibn 'Alwān's knowledge of Persian. Those were isolated words; some of them carry Persian meaning while others do not. Moreover, I discussed the list of foreign terms with an educated native speaker and instructor of Persian language, who was visiting the Department of Near Eastern Studies at the University of Michigan, Ann Arbor, around 2001, who argued that only very few words out of the long list are of Persian origin.
56. Line 11 of the poem on pp. 125–126.
57. *EI2*, art. "Ramz" by Alexander Knysh.
58. Qur'ān (5:54).
29. Knysh, *Islamic Mysticism,* p. 151.
60. Hodgson, Marshall, *The Venture of Islam*, v. 2, University of Chicago Press (1977), pp. 201–244.
61. Rahman, Fazlur, *Islam*, 2nd ed., University of Chicago Press (1979), p. 148.
62. Ibn 'Alwān, *al-Mahrajān wa l—baḥr al-mushakkal al-gharīb*, ed. 'Abd al-'Azīz Sulṭān Ṭāhir al-Manṣūb, Markaz ad-Dirāsāt wa l—Buḥūth al-Yamanī, Dār al-Fikr al-Mu'āṣir, Beirut (1992), p. 59.
63. Ibn 'Alwān, *al-Mahrajān*, p. 32.
64. Ibn 'Alwān, *al-Mahrajān*, p. 30.
65. Ibn 'Alwān, *al-Mahrajān*, pp. 77–78.
66. An M.A. thesis titled *al-Ma'rifa wa l-wujūd fī falsafat Aḥmad Ibn 'Alwān aṣ-ṣūfiyya* presented to the University of Kufa (1996) by 'Abd Allāh Muḥammad al-Falāḥī used this manuscript as one of its chief sources.
67. In Yemen whoever has the family name or the last name of "al-'Ajamī" is considered Persian or a descendant from a Persian lineage.

Chapter 4

1. Knysh, Alexander, *Ibn 'Arabī in the Later Islamic Tradition*, State University of New York Press (1999).
2. Qur'ān (51:56).
3. Ibn 'Alwān, Aḥmad, *at-Tawḥīd al-a'ẓam*, ed. 'Abd al-'Azīz al-Manṣūb, Dār al-Fikr al-Mu'āṣir, Beirut (1990), p. 350.
4. Watt, W. Montgomery, *The Formative Period of Islamic Thought,* Oneworld (1998), pp. 246–247.
5. Qur'ān (42:11) and (6:103).
6. Ibn 'Alwān, *at-Tawḥīd al-a'ẓam*, p. 352.
7. Qur'ān (47:17).
8. Qur'ān (9:115).
9. Qur'ān (4:78–79).
10. Ibn 'Alwān, *at-Tawḥīd al-a'ẓam*, p. 356.
11. During my visit to Yemen in 1999, I met Shaykh Aḥmad b. Qāyid in his lodge (*zāwiya*) in Ibb during a session of God's remembrance (*dhikr*). He told me that he had traveled to Sanaa, trying to convince the editor of Ibn 'Alwān's books, al-Manṣūb, to correct this mistake, but the editor said it was "too late

to fix the problem since the printed editions had been distributed." The shaykh answered, "I did my duty."

12. Qur'ān (76:30).
13. Qur'ān (15:21).
14. Ibn 'Alwān, *at-Tawḥīd,* p. 362.
15. Ibn 'Alwān, *at-Tawḥīd,* p. 353.
16. Gutas, Dimitri, *Greek Thought, Arabic Culture*, Routledge (2005), p. 2.
17. Gutas, *Greek Thought, Arabic Culture*, p. 2.
18. Gutas, *Greek Thought, Arabic Culture*, p. 2.
19. Watt, *Islamic Philosophy and Theology*, pp. 42–43.
20. Sa'īd, 'Abd al-Karīm, *Qaḍāyā wa ishkāliyyāt at-taṣawwuf 'ind Ibn 'Alwān*, Maktabat Murād, Ṣan'ā' (1997), pp. 88–89.
21. "Mu'tazilites" is an anglicized form representing the Arabic term "Mu'tazila," which may be described as a plural and a collective noun respectively; a single person is a Mu'tazilī.
22. Ash-Shahrastānī, Muḥammad, *Kitāb al-milal wa–n-niḥal*, ed. William Cureton, Gorgias Press (2002), p. 33.
23. Ash-Shahrastānī, *Kitāb al-milal wa–n-niḥal*, p. 33. Cf. Watt, W. Montgomery, *Islamic Philosophy and Theology*, Edinburgh University Press (1995), p. 47.
24. Watt, *Islamic Philosophy and Theology*, p. 47.
25. Watt, *Islamic Philosophy and Theology*, p. 47.
26. Ibn 'Alwān, *al-Futūḥ,* p. 315.
27. Fakhrī, Majid, *A History of Islamic Philosophy*, 2nd ed., Columbia University Press, New York (1983), p. 221.
28. Al-Ghazālī, Abū Hāmid, *The Incoherence of the Philosophers*, translated, introduced and annotated by Michael E. Marmura, Brigham Young University Press, Provo, Utah (2000).
29. Buchman, David, "Translator's Introduction" of *al-Ghazālī's The Niche of Lights*, Brigham Young University Press, Provo, Utah (1998), p. xxii.
30. Ibn 'Alwān, *al-Futūḥ,* pp. 543–546.
31. For the struggle among the Zaydī, Ismā'īlī, and Sunnī school see Chapter 1.
32. The Ḥanafites, the Shāfi'ites, the Mālikites, and the Ḥanbalites are the four Sunnī schools of law.
33. Armstrong, Karen, *Islam: A Short History*, Phoenix Press, London (2005), p. 54.
34. Sa'īd, *Qaḍāyā*, pp. 110–113.
35. Ibn 'Alwān, *at-Tawḥīd al-a'ẓam*, p. 353.
36. Ibn 'Alwān, *al-Futūḥ,* p. 283.
37. Ibn Ḥazm, Abū Muḥammad,'Alī b. Aḥmad, *al-Fiṣal fī-l-milal wa-l-ahwā' wa-n-niḥal*, v. 3, ed. Muḥammad Ibrāhīm Nasr and 'Abd ar-Raḥmān 'Umayra, Dār al-Jīl, Beirut (1405/1985), p. 8.
38. Ibn Ḥazm, *al-Fiṣal*, p. 9.
39. Watt, *The Formative Period of Islamic Thought*, pp. 280–281.
40. Ibn 'Alwān, *at-Tawḥīd al-a'ẓam*, pp. 349–353.
41. See Chapter 1 for further details.
42. Daftary, Farhad, "Ismā'īlī-Sufi Relations in Early Post-Alamūt and Safavid Persia" in *The Heritage of Sufism*, ed. Leonard Lewisohn and David Morgan, v. 3, Oneworld, Oxford (1999), p. 279.
43. Ibn 'Alwān, *al-Futūḥ,* p. 151.

44. Ibn 'Alwān, *al-Futūḥ,* p. 161.
45. Netton, Ian, Richard, "The Brethren of Purity (Ikhwān al-Ṣafā')," *in History of Islamic Philosophy,* ed. Seyyed Hossein Hasr and Oliver Leaman, Routledge (2001), pp. 228–229.
46. This view is supported by Jamīl 'Uthmān'Uthmān, Jamīl Muḥammad Sulṭān, "The Poetry of Mysticism of Aḥmad b. 'Alwān," M.A. thesis, University of Āl al-Bayt, Amman, Jordan (no. 9920301006) (2002), p. 14.
47. Ibn 'Alwān, *al-Mahrajān wa 'l-baḥr al-mushakkal al-gharīb*, ed. al-Manṣūb, Dār al-Fikral-Mu'āṣir, Beirut (1992), pp. 26–27.
48. Ibn 'Alwān, *al-Mahrajān*, pp. 26–27.
49. Ibn 'Alwān, *al-Mahrajān*, p. 30.
50. Ibn 'Alwān, *at-Tawḥīd,* p. 270.
51. Sachedina, Abdulaziz Abdulhussein, *Islamic Messianism*, State University of New York Press (1981), p.10.
52. Ibn 'Alwān, *al-Futūḥ,* p. 208. See also Ibn 'Alwān, *at-Tawḥīd,* p. 270.
53. Ibn 'Alwān, *al-Mahrajān*, p. 117.
54. 1Ibn 'Alwān, *at-Tawḥīd,* p. 278.
55. Qur'ān (68:4).
56. Ibn 'Alwān, *at-Tawḥīd,* p. 276.
57. Ibn 'Alwān, *at-Tawḥīd,* pp. 275–257.
58. Sa'īd, *Qaḍāyā wa ishkāliyyāt*, p. 121.
59. Sa'īd, *Qaḍāyā wa ishkāliyyāt*, p. 121.
60. Ibn 'Alwān, *al-Futūḥ,* p. 480.
61. Sa'īd, *Qaḍāyā wa ishkāliyyāt*, p. 121.

Chapter 5

1. Ash-Sharjī, Aḥmad Ibn Aḥmad, *Ṭabaqāt al-khawāṣṣ,* ad-Dār al-Yamaniyya li 'n-Nashr wa't-Tawzi' (1986), p. 406.
2. Hammoudi, Abdellah, *Master and Disciple,* University of Chicago Press, Chicago (1997), pp. 81–97.
3. Al-Janadī, Muḥammad, *as-Sulūk fī ṭabaqāt al-'ulamā' wa-l-mulūk,* ed. Al-Akwa', v. 1, Markaz ad-Dirāsāt wa-l-buḥūth al-Yamanī, Sanaa (1983), p. 384.
4. Bayt 'Aṭā' is a village in Surdud valley in Tihāma, near Zabīd where Shaykh Ibn Jamīl lived.
5. Al-'Aqīlī, Muḥammad b. Aḥmad, *at-Taṣawwuf fī tihāma,* 2nd ed., Dār al-Bilād l'ṭ-Ṭibā'ah wan-Nashr, Jeddah (n. d.), p. 152.
6. The term "*dustūr*" literally means constitution, but here it refers to the authority (*taḥkīm*), which is symbolized by granting the *khirqa*.
7. The word "*jabalī*" means mountaineer, but here it refers to Ibn 'Alwān because he came from a mountainous area. The word "*qumāsh*" literally means cloth and technically refers to the *khirqa*. See al-Janadī, as-Sulūk, v. 1, p. 456.
8. In another version "knew."
9. Al-Janadi, *as-Sulūk*, ed. al-Akwa', v. 1, p. 385.
10. The term "Laylā" has been associated, in the Arabic literature, with an imaginary character, "Majnūn Banī 'Āmir." In some versions, the name was misspelled as Lubnā.

11. "The name given to the hero of a romantic love story, the original form of which could date back as far as the second half of the 1st/7th century." However, "Majnūn's unrequited love is interpreted as a metaphorical means to divine reality." Also, "Majnūn appears as the symbol for the religious ideology of love." See *EI2*, art. "Madjnūn Laylā," v. 5 (1986).
12. Al-Janadi, *as-Sulūk*, p. 385.
13. Chittick, William C., *The Sufi Path of Knowledge,* State University of New York Press (1989), p. 376.
14. Al-Janadī, *As-Sulūk*, p. 456.
15. Al-Janadī, *As-Sulūk,* p. 456.
16. Ibn al-Ahdal, Ḥusayn Ibn 'Abd ar-Raḥmān, *Tuḥfat az-zaman,* ed. al-Ḥibshī, Manshurāt al-Madīnah, Beirut (1986), p. 286.
17. Ibn al-Ahdal, *Tuḥfat az-zaman*, p. 286. Cf. Ash-Sharjī, *Ṭabaqāt al-khawāṣṣ,* p. 409.
18. Ibn al-Ahdal, *Tuḥfat az-zaman,* p. 286.
19. Ash-Sharjī, *Ṭabaqāt al-khawāṣṣ,* p. 173.
20. Ibn al-Ahdal, *Tuḥfat az-zaman,* p. 286.
21. Al-Ḥibshī, *aṣ-Ṣūfiyya wa'l-fuqahā',* p. 73.
22. Al-Yāfi'ī, *Nashr al-maḥāsin al-ghāliya* in the margin of *Jāmi' karāmāt al-awliyā'* by *an-Nabhānī*, v. 2, Dār Ṣādir, Beirut (not dated), p. 305.
23. Knysh, Alexander, *Ibn 'Arabī in the Later Islamic Tradition,* State University of New York Press (1999), p. 237.
24. An-Nawawī, Yaḥyā b. Sharf ad-Dīn, *An-Nawawī's Forty Ḥadīth,* 2nd ed., trans. Ezzedin Ibrahim and Dennys Johnson-Davies, Dār al-Qur'ān al-Karīm, Damascus (1977), p. 118.
25. Ibn al-Ahdal, Ḥusayn b. 'Abd ar-Raḥman, *Tuḥfat az-zaman,* ed. al-Ḥibshī, Manshūrāt al-Madīnah (1986), p. 287.
26. Al-Ḥibshī, 'Abd Allah, *aṣ-Ṣūfiyya wa'l-fuqahā' fī l-Yaman*, Maktabat al-Jīl al-Jadīd, Sanaa (1976), p. 71. See al-Janadī, *as-Sulūk*, p. 385.
27. Al-'Aqīlī, *at-Taṣawwuf fī Tihāma,* p. 155.
28. The Zaydīs are known as supreme rulers of the Yemeni community who may be considered as caliphs and who must be descendants of the Prophet's cousin, 'Alī b. Abī Ṭālib (d. 40/661) through the Prophet's daughter Fāṭima.
29. Qur'ān (3:64).
30. Al-Janadī, *as-Sulūk*, p. 384.
31. Qur'ān (3.160).
32. Ḥibshī, 'Abd Allāh, *aṣ-Ṣūfiyyah wa'l-fuqahā' fī'l-Yaman,* Maktabat al-Jīl al-Jadīd, Ṣan'ā' (1976), pp. 53–54; the whole letter was quoted from different sources, see al-Janadī, *as-Sulūk,* p. 385. Cf. Wilferd Madelung, "Zaydī Attitudes to Sufism," in *Islamic Mysticism Contested: Thirteen Centuries of Controversies and Polemics,* ed. Frederick De Jong and Bernd Radtke, Brill, Leiden (1999), p. 128.
33. See Chapter 8 for further discussion.
34. Al-Janadī, *as-Sulūk,* v. 1, p. 456.
35. Al-Aḥmadī, Abd aṣ-Ṣamad, *al-Jawāhir as-saniyya fī'n-nisba wa'l-karāmāt al-Aḥmadiyya,* no publisher (1277/1860), p. 39.
36. Al-Barzanjī, Ja'far b. Ḥasan, Fatḥ al-karīm al-jawwād al-mannān biwāsiṭ at 'iqd saiyid az zamān fī ba'ḍ manāqib A. b. 'Alwān (manuscript), Berlin.

37. An M.A thesis presented to University of Cairo in 1988 titled "Taḥqīq wa Dirāsat Ibn 'Alwān's Dīwān al-Futīḥ."
38. Sa'īd, 'Abd al-Karīm, *Qaḍāyā wa ishkāliyyāt at-taṣawwuf 'ind Ibn 'Alwān,* Maktabat Murād, Sanaa (1997), p. 129.
39. Ibn 'Alwān, *al-Mahrajān wa'l-baḥr al-mushakkal al-gharīb,* ed. al-Manṣūb, Dār al-Fikral-Mu'āṣir, Beirut (1992), p. 50.
40. Ibn 'Alwān, *al-Futūḥ,* ed. al-Manṣūb, Dār al-Fikr al-Mu'āṣir, Beirut (1991), pp. 543–546.
41. Watt, W. M., *Islamic Philosophy and Theology,* reprinted, Edinburgh University Press (1995), p. 92.
42. Knysh, *Islamic Mysticism,* p. 146; Schimmel, Annemarie, *Mystical Dimensions of Islam,* The University of North Carolina Press (1975), pp. 94–95. See also al-Ghazālī, Abū Ḥāmid, *Iḥyā' 'ulūm ad-dīn,* 5 vols., Dār al-Wa'y bi-Ḥalab, Syria (1998).
43. Jackson, Sherman, *On the Boundaries of Theological Tolerance in Islam: Abū Ḥāmid al-Ghazālī's Fayṣal at-tafriqa,* Oxford University Press (2002), p. 94.
44. Ibn 'Alwan, *at-Tawḥīd,* pp. 290–291.
45. See Chapter 1 for further discussion of the Ismā'īlī thought and literature.
46. Knysh, *Islamic Mysticism,* p. 143. "The works whose authenticity has been doubted are mostly ones expressing advanced theosophical and philosophical views that appear to be at variance with the teaching of al-Ghazālī in the works generally accepted as authentic."
47. Massignon, Louis, *The Passion of al-Ḥallāj,* v. 2, trans. Herbert Mason, Princeton University Press (1982). Massignon was quoting Carl Brockelmann's *Geschichte der Arabischen Litteratur.*
48. Al-Ḥibshī, *aṣ-Ṣūfiyya wa l-fuqahā' fī l-Yaman,* p. 72.
49. Massignon, *The Passion of al-Ḥallāj,* p. 293.
50. Massignon, *The Passion of al-Ḥallāj,* p. 293. "I" refers to al-Ḥallāj's historic statement that means "the Truth, i.e., God."
51. Massignon, *The Passion of al-Ḥallāj,* v. 2, p. 294.
52. Qur'ān (28:19); although the interpretation of this verse is beyond Ibn 'Alwān's purpose, he applies it to his condition for the sake of discussion. He was alluding to the crucifixion of al-Ḥallāj.
53. Ibn 'Alwān, *al-Futūḥ,* pp. 479–480.
54. Al-Ghazālī, Abū Hāmid, *Mishkāt al-anwār,* ed. Abū al-'Alā 'Afīfī, ad-Dār al-Qawmiyya, Cairo (1964), p. 57. See also al-Ghazālī, *Mishkāt al-anwār,* trans. W.H.T. Gairdner, Ashraf Press, Lahore (1952), pp. 106–107.
55. Massignon, *The Passions of al-Ḥallāj,* p. 294.
56. Al-Baradūnī, 'Abd Allāh, *Funūn al-adab ash-sha'bī fī'l-Yaman,* 3rd ed., Dār al-Fikr, Damascus (1995), pp. 73–75.
57. See Chapter 6 for further discussion on the categories of knowledge (*ma'rifa*).
58. Al-Ḥibshī, 'Abd Allāh, *aṣ-Ṣūfiyya wa'l-fuqahā' fī'l-Yaman* (1976:72), quoting *al-Mawrid* magazine (*Majallat al-Mawrid*), v. 3 (1392/1972:62).
59. Ibn Alwān, *al-Futūḥ,* pp. 472–480.
60. Sa'īd, Abd al-Karīm Qāsim, *Qaḍāyā wa ishkāliyyāt at-taṣawwuf 'ind Aḥmad b. 'Alwān,* Dār ash-Shawkānī, Sanaa (1997), p. 25.

61. Massignon, *The Passion of al-Ḥallāj,* p. 41.
62. Jarāda, *al-Adab wath-thaqāfa fī al-Yaman ʻabr al-ʻuṣūr* (1977), p. 214.
63. Al-Maqāliḥ, "Introduction," *al-Futūḥ* of Ibn ʻAlwān, ed. al-Manṣūb, pp. 11–12.
64. Al-Barzanjī, *Fatḥ al-karīm al-jawād al-mannān* (manuscript).
65. Knysh, Ibn *ʻArabī in the Later Islamic Tradition,* p. 41.
66. Al-Ḥibshī, *aṣ-Ṣūfiyya wa'l-fuqahā',* pp. 69–70.
67. Al-Ḥibshī, *aṣ-Ṣūfiyya wa'l-fuqahā',* p. 73.
68. Al-Ḥibshī, *aṣ-Ṣūfiyya wa'l-fuqahā',* p. 70.
69. Knysh, *Islamic Mysticism,* p. 164. Cf. Chapter 2 of this study.

Chapter 6

1. Saʻīd, ʻAbd al-Karīm, *Qaḍāyā wa ishkāliyyāt at-taṣawwuf ʻind Ibn ʻAlwān*, Maktabat Murād, Ṣanʻā' (1997), p. 72.
2. Qur'ān (15:29).
3. Ibn ʻAlwān, Aḥmad, *at-Tawḥīd al-aʻẓam*, ed. ʻAbd al-ʻAzīz al-Manṣūb, Dār al-Fikr al-Muʻāṣir, Beirut (1990), p. 131.
4. Qur'ān (2:31).
5. Qur'ān (40:67), Ibn ʻAlwān's interpretation, in every line, follows immediately after the inverted commas.
6. Ibn ʻAlwān, *al-Futūḥ,* p. 344; Chittick, William C., *The Sufi Path of Knowledge*, State University of New York Press (1989), p. 15; Saʻīd, *Qaḍāyā*, p. 75.
7. Qur'ān (3:26–27). The translation is taken from A. J. Arberry, *The Koran Interpreted*, Touchstone (1996) and compared with Aḥmad ʻAlī, *Al-Qur'ān: A Contemporary Translation*, Princeton University Press (1994). In addition, the translation of Abdullah Yusuf ʻAlī was consulted occasionally. The latter's version was abridged by Sayed Asgar A. Razwy, who got rid of the Biblical style, published by Tahike Tarsile Qur'ān, Elmhurst, New York (1955). Finally, I consulted *The Qur'ān*, ed. Ṣaḥeeḥ International, Abulqasim Publication House (1997). See also Ibn ʻAlwān, *al-Mahrajān wa'l-baḥr*, pp. 23–25, *at-Tawḥīd,* p. 132.
8. An-Nawawī, Yaḥyā b. Sharf ad-Dīn, *An-Nawawī's Forty Hadīth*, 2nd ed., trans. Ezzedin Ibrahim and Dennys Johnson-Davies, Dār al-Qur'ān al-Karīm, Damascus (1977), p. 118.
9. See, for instance, Ibn ʻAlwān, *al-Futūḥ,* pp. 272, 336, 383. Cf. Ibn ʻAlwān, *at-Tawḥīd,* pp. 254, 316.
10. Chittick, William, *The Self-Disclosure of God*, State University of New York Press (1998), p. xv.
11. *EI*, art. "Samāʻ." Cf. Knysh, Alexander, *Islamic Mysticism: A Short History*, Brill, Leiden (2000), p. 323.
12. *EI*, art. "Samāʻ." Cf. Knysh, *Islamic Mysticism: A Short History*, p. 323.
13. Ibn ʻAlwān, *al-Futūḥ,* pp. 441–442.
14. *EI*, art. "Samāʻ." Cf. Knysh, *Islamic Mysticism: A Short History*, p. 323.
15. Ibn ʻAlwān, *at-Tawḥīd,* p. 133.
16. Ibn ʻAlwān, an appendix to *al-Mahrajān wa'l-baḥr al-mushakkal al-gharīb*, p. 118.
17. Ibn ʻAlwān, *at-Tawḥīd,* pp. 133–134.

18. *Qur'ān* (38:72).
19. Ibn 'Alwān, *al-Futūḥ,* p. 382.
20. *Qur'ān* (18:28).
21. *Qur'ān* (2:33).
22. Ibn 'Alwān, *at-Tawḥīd,* p. 314.
23. Ibn 'Alwān, *at-Tawḥīd,* pp. 314–315.
24. Ibn 'Alwān, *at-Tawḥīd,* p. 316.
25. *Qur'ān* (4:65).
26. *Qur'ān* (3:31).
27. *Qur'ān* (5:77).
28. Ibn 'Alwān, *at-Tawḥīd,* pp. 317.
29. *Qur'ān* (12:108).
30. Ibn 'Alwān, *at-Tawḥīd,* p. 318. According to al-'Irāqī, who has *ḥadīth* commentary on Ghazālī's *Iḥyā',* this *ḥadīth* can also be found in the famous four *Sunnas.*
31. Here, Ibn 'Alwān refers to the book that he wrote about the *khirqa* ritual (*'ilm at-tahkīm*). This book is one of his missing works.
32. Ibn 'Alwān, *at-Tawḥīd,* p. 318.
33. Ibn 'Alwān, *at-Tawḥīd,* p. 318.
34. Ibn 'Alwān, *at-Tawḥīd,* p. 319.
35. Qur'ān (11:46). This verse comes as a response to Noah's invocation summed up in the verse: "Noah called on his Lord and said: "O Lord, my son is surely a member of my family, and verily Your promise is true," Qur'ān (11:45).
36. Ibn 'Alwān, *al-Ajwibah* (manuscript), p. 3.
37. Ibn 'Alwān, *al-Ajwibah* (manuscript), p. 3.
38. Ibn 'Alwān, *al-Ajwibah* (manuscript), p. 3.
39. Ibn 'Alwān, *al-Ajwiba* (manuscript), p. 4.
40. Ibn 'Alwān, *al-Ajwiba* (manuscript), p. 4.
41. Ibn 'Alwān, *al-Mahrajān wa'l-baḥr al-mushakkal al-gharīb*, ed. 'Abd al-'Azīz Sulṭān Ṭāhir al-Manṣūb, first edition, Markaz ad-Dirāsāt wa'l-Buḥūth al-Yamanī, Ṣan'ā', Dār al-Fikr al-Mu'āṣir, Beirut (1992), pp. 58–59.
42. Ibn 'Alwān, *al-Mahrajān wa'l-baḥr*, pp. 59–60.
43. Ibn 'Alwān, *al-Mahrajān wa'l-baḥr*, p. 62.
44. Al-Jurjānī, *at-Ta'rīfāt*, p. 162. Cf. *Encyclopedia of Islam*, 2nd ed. (*EI2*), E. J. Brill (1994), art. "Kashf."
45. *EI2*, art. "Kashf." Cf. Knysh, *Islamic Mysticism*, pp. 311–312.
46. Al-Kalābādhī, Abū Bakr b. Muḥammad, *at-Ta'arruf li-madhhab ahl at-tasawwuf*, ed. Maḥmūd Amīn an-Nawāwī, 1st ed., Maktabat al-Kulliyyāt al-Azhariyya, Cairo (1389/1969), p. 145. Cf. Arberry, Arthur, *The Doctrines of the Sufis*, Ashraf Press, Lahore (1966), p. 128. See *EI2*, art. "Kashf." Cf. Knysh, *Islamic Mysticism*, pp. 311–312.
47. Al-Qushayrī, *ar-Risāla al-qushayriyy*, with its commentary by Abū Zakariyā Al-Anṣārī, in the margins of *Natā'ij al-afkār al-qudsiyya fī bayān ma'ānī sharḥ ar-risāla al-qushayriyy* by as-Sayyid Muṣṭafā al-'Arūsī, v. 2, published by 'Abd al-Wakīl ad-Darūbī and Yāsīn 'Arafah, Damascus (1290/1873), pp. 77–79; *EI2*, art. "Kashf," p. 697. Cf. Knysh, *Islamic Mysticism*, p. 312.

48. Al-Jurjānī, 'Alī b. Muḥammad, *at-Ta'rīfāt*, Maṭba'at Muṣṭafā al-Bābī al-Ḥalabī, Cairo (1357/1938), p. 203.
49. *EI2*, art. "Kashf," p. 697. Cf. Knysh, *Islamic Mysticism*, p. 313.
50. Al-Ghazālī, *Iḥyā' 'ulūm ad-Dīn*, v. 1, Dār al-Wa'y bi-Ḥalab (1998), p. 48; *EI2*, art. "Kashf," p. 698. Cf. Knysh, *Islamic Mysticism*, p. 314. Cf. Farid Jabre, *La notion de certitude selon Ghazali*, Paris (1958).
51. Al-Ghazālī, *Iḥyā'*, p. 48; *EI2*, art. "Kashf," p. 698. Cf. Knysh, *Islamic Mysticism*, p. 314.
52. Qur'ān (62:4).
53. Ibn 'Alwān, *at-Tawḥīd,* p. 322.
54. Ibn 'Alwān, *al-Ajwiba*, p. 6.
55. Ibn 'Alwān, *al-Futūḥ,* p. 197.
56. Ibn 'Alwān, *al-Ajwiba*, p. 7.
57. Ibn 'Alwān, *al-Futūḥ,* p. 450.
58. Qur'ān (55:26–27).
59. Arberry, A. J., *Sufism*, Dover Publications, Mineola, New York (2002), p. 55.
60. Arberry, *Sufism*, p. 56.
61. *EI2*, art. "Baqā' wa-Fanā'"; cf. Knysh, *Islamic Mysticism*, p. 309.
62. Ibn 'Alwān, *al-Mahrajān wa'l-baḥr*, pp. 22–23.
63. Schimmel, Annemarie, "Man and His Perfection in Islam," in *The World Treasury of Modern Religious Thought*, ed. Jaroslav Pelikan, Little Brown, Boston (1990), p. 444.
64. Qur'ān (3:26–27).
65. Ibn 'Alwān, *al-Futūḥ,* p. 381.
66. Ibn 'Alwān, *al-Futūḥ,* p. 105.
67. Arberry, *Sufism*, p. 58.
68. *EI2*, art. "Baqā' wa-Fanā'"; cf. Knysh, *Islamic Mysticism*, p. 310.
69. *EI2*, art. "Baqā' wa-Fanā'"; cf. Knysh, *Islamic Mysticism*, p. 310.
70. Ibn 'Alwān, *al-Ajwiba*, pp. 7, 15.
71. Knysh, *Islamic Mysticism*, p. 310.
72. *SIE4*, art. "ittiḥād".
73. Ibn 'Alwān, *al-Futīh*, p. 458.
74. See Chapter 3.
75. Ibn 'Alwān, *at-Tawḥīd,* p. 252.
76. Ash-Shawkānī, *Nayl al-awṭār min aḥādīth sayyid al-akhyār sharḥ muntaqā al-akhbār,* ed. Muḥammad Sālim Hāshim, v. 2, Dār al-Kutub al-'Ilmiyyah, Beirut (1995), p. 56.
77. Qur'ān (112:1–4).
78. Ibn 'Alwān, *at-Tawḥīd,* p. 131.
79. Ibn 'Alwān, *al-Futūḥ,* pp. 111–112.
80. Knysh, *Islamic Mysticism*, p. 79.
81. Ibn 'Alwān, *al-Futūḥ,* p. 109.
82. This is equivalent to the Islamic term *walī*, except that a *walī* is neither canonized nor appointed by religious authorities. Rather, the people recognize him for his miraculous deeds and charisma. A *wali* might even remain hidden from the world, covered by the divine mystery, and only become visible to perform a miracle or rescue someone by God's permission.

Chapter 7

1. *Shorter Encyclopedia of Islam* (*SEI4*), art. "Walī" (1953), p. 629.
2. Al-Jurjānī, *at-Ta'rīfāt*, Maṭba'at Muṣṭafā al-Ḥalabī, Cairo (1938), pp. 227–228. See also *SEI4*, art. "Walī."
3. For more details on this topic, see Cornell, Vincent, *Realm of the Saint: Power and Authority in Moroccan Sufism*, University of Texas Press (1998), pp. 17–21. For my purpose, substantial differences between the Muslim *walī* and the Christian saint are not of primary significance and thus are disregarded.
4. Fierro, Maribel, quoting L. Gardet, "The Polemic about *karāmāt al-awliyā'* and the Development of Sufism in al-Andalus (fourth/tenth–fifth/eleventh centuries)," *Bulletin of the School of Oriental and African Studies* (*BSOAS*), University of London, 55, part 2 (1992), p. 240.
5. Ash-Sharjī, Aḥmad, *Ṭabaqāt al-khawāṣṣ*, p. 37.
6. Fierro, Maribel, "The Polemic about *karāmāt al-awliyā'*," p. 240.
7. *SIE4*, art. "Karāma."
8. Schimmel, Annemarie, *Mystical Dimensions of Islam*, University of North Carolina Press (1975), p. 206.
9. *SIE4*, art. "Karāma."
10. Ash-Sharjī, Aḥmad b. Muḥammad, *Ṭabaqāt al-khawāṣṣ: ahl aṣ-ṣidq wa'l-ikhlāṣ*, ad-Dār al-Yamaniyyah li'n-Nashr wa't-Tawzī' (1986), p. 38.
11. Ash-Sharjī, Aḥmad, *Ṭabaqāt al-khawāṣṣ*, pp. 37–39.
12. Laoust, Henri, *La Profession de Foi d'Ibn Taymiyyah: Texte, traduction et commentaire de la Wāsitiyyah*, Librairie Orientaliste Pau Geuthner, Paris (1986), pp. 82–83. See also the Arabic text in the same book, p. 25. The English translation is taken from Josef W. Meri's "The Etiquette of Devotion in the Islamic Cult of Saints," in *The Cult of Saints in Late Antiquity and the Early Middle Ages: Essays on the Contribution of Peter Brown*, ed. James Howard-Johnston and Paul Antony Hayward, Oxford University Press (2002), pp. 267–268.
13. Ash-Sharjī, Aḥmad, *Ṭabaqāt al-khawāṣṣ*, pp. 39–40.
14. Ash-Sharjī, Aḥmad, *Ṭabaqāt al-khawāṣṣ*, p. 36.
15. Ash-Sharjī, Aḥmad, *Ṭabaqāt al-khawāṣṣ*, p. 36.
16. Ash-Sharjī, Aḥmad, *Ṭabaqāt al-khawāṣṣ*, pp. 40–41.
17. Cornell, Vincent J., *Realm of the Saint: Power and Authority in Moroccan Sufism*, University of Texas Press (1998), p. 7.
18. Ash-Shawkānī, Muḥammad b. 'Alī, *Qatr al-waly 'alā aḥādīth al-walī*, ed. Ibrāhīm Hilāl, Dār al-Kutub al-Ḥadīthah, Cairo (1969), p. 223. The term "*waly*" is different from "*walī*." *Waly* is a synonym for rain.
19. Cornell, *Realm of the Saint*, p. 138. See also Cornell, Vincent, *The Way of Abū Madyan: Doctrinal and Poetic Works of Abū Madyan Shu'ayb ibn ibn al-Ḥusayn al-Anṣārī*, Cambridge (1996), p. 96.
20. Cornell, *Realm of the Saint*, p. 135.
21. Al-Janadī, Muḥammad, *as-Sulūk fī ṭabaqāt al-'ulamā' wa-l-mulūk*, ed. Al-Akwa', 2 vols., Markaz ad-Dirāsāt wa-l-buḥūth al-Yamanī, Sanaa (1994?), p. 458.
22. Al-'Aqīlī, Muḥammad b. Aḥmad, *at-Taṣawwuf fī Tihāma*, 2nd ed., Dār al-Bilād Li'tibā'ah wa'n-Nashr, Jeddah (n.d.), pp. 55–61.

23. Cornell, *Realm of the Saint*, p. 6.
24. Al-Burayhī, 'Abd al-Wahhāb b. 'Abd ar-Raḥmān, *Ṭabqāt ṣulaḥā' al-Yaman*, ed. Al-Ḥibshī, Dār al-Ādāb, Beirut (1983), p. 199.
25. Ruffing, Janet, "An Introduction," in *Mysticism and Social Transformation*, ed. Janet Ruffing, Syracuse University Press (2001), p. 15.
26. Ibn ad-Dayba', 'Abd ar-Raḥmān b. 'Alī, *al-Fadl al-mazīd 'alā bughyat al-mustafīd fī akhbār madīnat Zabīd*, ed. Yūsuf Shulhud, Markaz ad-Dirāsāt wa'l-Buḥūth al-Yamanī, Ṣan'ā' (1983), p. 334. See also Ibn 'Alwān, *al-Futūḥ*, p. 71.
27. An-Nabhānī, Yūsuf, *Jāmi' karāmāt al-awliyā'*, v. 1, Dār Sādir, Beirut (1911), p. 318.
28. An-Nabhānī, *Jāmi' karāmāt al-awliyā'*, p. 318.
29. Ruffing, "Introduction," p. 15.
30. Cazelles, Brigitte, "Introduction," in *Images of Sainthood in Medieval Europe*, ed. Renate Blumenfeld-Kosinski and Timea Szell, Cornell University Press, Ithaca (1991), p. 2.
31. Imām al-Mutawakkil Ismā'īl b. al-Qāsim b. Muḥammad (1610–1676) ruled Yemen after his brother's death. During his reign, he managed to unify Yemen. He was also a jurist (*faqīh*) who wrote many books including *al-'Aqīda aṣ-ṣaḥīḥa, al-Masā'il al-murtaḍā 'alā jamī' al-quḍā,* and others. See al-Wazīr, 'Abd al-Ilāh, *Tārīkh al-Yaman khilāl al-qarn al-ḥādī 'ashar*, ed. Muḥammad 'Abd ar-Raḥmān Jāzim, Dār al-Masīrah, Beirut (1985), p. 56.
32. Al-Wazīr, *Tārīkh al-Yaman,* p. 311.
33. Al-Wazīr, *Tārīkh al-Yaman,* p. 313.
34. Al-Wazīr, *Tārīkh al-Yaman,* p. 314.
35. Ruffing, Janet, "An Introduction," p. 15.
36. Cornell, *Realm of the Saint,* p. 65.
37. Cornell, *Realm of the Saint,* p. 65.
38. Delooz, Pierre, *Sociologie et Canonisations*, Liege (1969); cf. Cornell, *Realm of the Saint*, p. xxxii.
39. Cornell, *Realm of the Saint*, p. xxxi.
40. Al-Yāfi'ī, 'Abd Allāh b. As'ad, *Mir'āt al-janān wa 'ibrat al-yaqẓān*, v. 4, 2nd ed., Manshūrāt Mu'ssasat al-A'lamī lil-Matbū'āt, Beirut (1390/1970), pp. 357–358. Cf. Chapter 3.
41. Al-Baradūnī, 'Abd Allāh, *Funūn al-adab ash-sha'bī fī'l-Yaman*, 3rd ed., Dār al-Fikr, Damascus (1995), pp. 83–84.
42. Ash-Shawkānī, *al-Badr aṭ-Ṭāli' bi maḥāsin man ba'd al-qarn as-sābi'*, v. 1, Dār al-Ma'rifah, Beirut (1348/1929), p. 248.
43. 'Abd al-Hādī as-Sūdī, *Shi'ruh- rasā'iluh- manāqibuh*, ed. 'Abd al-'Azīz Sulṭān al-Manṣūb, Dar al-Fikr al-Mu'āṣir, Beirut (1995), pp. 141–143.
44. Ash-Shawkānī, *Sharḥ aṣ-ṣudūr fī taḥrīm raf' al-qubūr*, in *Majmū'at rasā'il fī 'ilm at-tawḥīd*, ed. 'Abd ar-Raḥmān b. Yaḥyā al-Iryānī, one of the former presidents of Yemen, Wizārat al-I'lām wa'th-Thaqāfah, Dār al-Fikr, Damascus (1983), pp. 69–80.
45. Qur'ān (7:188).
46. Ash-Shawkānī, Muḥammad, *ad-Durr an-naḍīd fī ikhlāṣ kalimat at-tawḥīd*, ed. Abū 'Abd Allāh al-Ḥalabī, Dār Ibn Khuzaymah (1414/1993), p. 73. Cf.

Haykel, Bernard, *Revival and Reform in Islam: The Legacy of Muḥammad al-Shawkānī*, Cambridge University Press (2003), p. 132.

47. Ash-Shawkānī, Muḥammad, *ad-Durr an-naḍīd*, p. 73. Cf. Haykel, *Revival and Reform in Islam*, p. 132.
48. Knysh, Alexander, "The Cult of Saints in Ḥaḍramawt: An Overview," in *New Arabian Studies*, v. 1, ed. R. B. Serjeant, R. L. Bidwell, and G. Rex. Smith, University of Exeter Press (1993), pp. 141–143.
49. Knysh, "The Cult of Saints," p. 143.
50. Fayṣal al-Mikhlāfī and 'Abduh b. Murshid al-Maghribī, "Yafrus and *ḥujāj* Ibn 'Alwān!!" *al-Jumhūriyya ath-Thaqāfiyya*, 6 October 1999, pp. 4–5.
51. Knysh, "The Cult of Saints," p. 145.
52. Goldziher, Ignaz, "The Veneration of Saints in Islam," in his *Muslim Studies*, translated from German by C. R. Barber and S. M. Stern, v. 2, Chicago (1971), p. 288.
53. Knysh, "The Cult of Saints," p. 138.
54. Brown, Peter, "The Rise and Function of the Holy Man in Late Antiquity," *Journal of Roman Studies* (*JRS*), 61, London (1971), p. 81.
55. Knysh, "The Cult of Saints," p. 139. See also the translation of this article in *al-Yaman kamā yarāhu al-ākhar*, ed. Lucine Taminian, with the assistance of Abd Al-Karim Al-Aug, American Institute for Yemeni Studies, v. 2 (n.d), p. 308 and passim.
56. Knysh, "The Cult of Saints," p. 139.
57. For studies on Ibn Taymiyyah, see Laoust, Henri, *Essai sur les doctrines sociales et politiques de Taki-D-Din Aḥmad b. Taimiya* Imprimerie de l'Institut Francais d'Archeologie Orientale, Cairo (1939). On the early history of the Wahhābī movement see Peskes, Esther, *Muḥammad b. 'Abdalwahhābim Widerstreit*, Orient-Institut, Beirut (1993).
58. Haykel, *Revival and Reform in Islam,* p. 14.
59. For this treatise, see *Majmū'at rasā'il fī 'ilm at-tawḥīd*, ed. al-Qāḍī 'Abd ar-Raḥmān b. Yaḥyā al-Iryānī, Dār al-Fikr, Damascus (1983).
60. Haykel, *Revival and Reform in Islam*, pp. 14, 128. Cf. ash-Shawkānī, *Dīwān ash-Shawkānī aslāk al-Jawhar wa'l-ḥayāt al-fikriyya wa'l-sīyāsiyya fī 'aṣrih*, 2nd ed., ed. Husayn al-'Amrī, Dār al-Fikr, Damascus (1986), pp. 160–164.
61. Haykel, *Revival and Reform in Islam*, pp. 128–129. See also the following: Cook, Michael, "On the Origins of Wahhābism," *Journal of the Royal Asiatic Society*, 2.2 (1992): 200–201; Ḥamad al-Jāsir, aṣ-Ṣilāt bayn Ṣan'ā' wa'd-Dir'iyya, *al-'Arab*, 22 (1987): 433–435; Muḥammad Ṣiddīq Ḥasan Khān, *Abjad al-'ulūm*, 3 vols., Dār al-Kutub al-'Ilmiyya, Damascus, (1978), v. 3, pp. 196f. Cf. Muḥammad b. Ismā'īl al-Amīr, *Risāla ḥawl madhhab Ibn 'Abd al-Wahhāb*, ms., Ṣan'ā', Sharqiyyah Library, *majmū'* no. 1; idem, *Irshād dhawī al-albāb ilā ḥaqīqat aqwāl Muḥammad b. 'Abd al-Wahhāb*, ms., Ṣan'ā', Gharbiyya Library, majmū' no. 107, fols. 131–142.
62. Haykel, *Revival and Reform in Islam*, pp. 129–130. Cf. ash-Shawkānī, *Dīwān*, pp. 161–164. For a view of a reconciliation between ash-Shawkānī and the Wahhābī movement, see Ḥamad al-Jāsir, "al-Imām Muḥammad b. 'Alī al-Shawkānī wa mawqifuhu min al-da'wa al-salafiyya al-iṣlāḥiyya," *al-Dir'iyya* 8 and 10 (2000), 9–16 and 13–19.

63. The following segment is indebted to the excellent study advanced in *Revival and Reform in Islam* by Haykel. See Ash-Shawkānī, Muḥammad, *ad-Durr an-naḍīd fī ikhlāṣ kalimat at-tawḥīd*, ed. Abū 'Abd Allāh al-Ḥalabī, Dār Ibn Khuzayma (1414/1993).
64. Ash-Shawkānī, *ad-Durr an-naḍīd*, p. 8; Haykel, *Revival and Reform in Islam*, p. 131.
65. Haykel, *Revival and Reform in Islam*, p. 131.
66. Haykel, *Revival and Reform in Islam*, p. 131.
67. Ash-Shawkānī, *ad-Durr an-naḍīd*, p. 83; Haykel, *Revival and Reform in Islam*, pp. 132–133.
68. Ash-Shawkānī, *ad-Durr an-naḍīd*, pp. 66–67. Cf. Qur'ān (7:59), trans. A. J. Arberry. Cf. Haykel, *Revival and Reform in Islam*, p. 133.
69. Haykel, *Revival and Reform in Islam*, p. 133.
70. Haykel, *Revival and Reform in Islam*, p. 133. On the question of *taqlīd* see Chapter 1.
71. Meri, "The Etiquette of Cult," p. 274. Cf. *Jāmi' as-Ṣaḥīh, by Muslim ibn al-Hajjāj al-Qushayrī*, iii, p. 65.
72. Haykel, *Revival and Reform in Islam*, p. 134.
73. Haykel, *Revival and Reform in Islam*, p. 137.
74. Ibn Taymiyya, *Majmū' fatāwā Shaykh al-Islam Aḥmad b. Taymiyya*, ed. 'Abd ar-Raḥmān b. Muḥammad b. Qāsim, 27 vols., al-Maktab at-Ta'līmī as-Sa'ūdī bi'l-Maghrib, Rabat (n.d.), v. 1, pp. 102–107, 309, 347.
75. Ibn Taymiyyah, *Iqtiḍā' aṣ-ṣirāṭ al-mustaqīm mukhālafat aṣḥāb al-jaḥīm*, ed. Aḥmad Hamadī, Maktabat al-Madanī, Jedda (n.d.), pp. 408–412. Cf. Ash-Shawkānī, *ad-Durr an-naḍīd*, passim.
76. Ash-Shawkānī, *ad-Durr an-naḍīd*, pp. 56–60. See also Muḥammad b. 'Abd al-Wahhāb, *Kitāb at-tawḥīd*, Maktab al-Islāmī, Beirut (1408/1988), pp. 80–81.
77. Haykel, *Revival and Reform in Islam*, p. 135.
78. Haykel, *Revival and Reform in Islam*, p. 135.
79. For a detailed discussion of the Wahhābī understanding of types of *shirk*, see Ibn 'Abd al-Wahhāb, *Kitāb at-tawḥīd*, pp. 32–46, 62–71.
80. Haykel, *Revival and Reform in Islam*, p. 136.
81. Haykel, *Revival and Reform in Islam*, p. 136.
82. Haykel, *Revival and Reform in Islam*, p. 136. Cf. Laoust, *Essai les Doctrines*, pp. 529–530.
83. Sulayman b. Sahmān (ed.), *al-Hadiyya as-saniyya*, pp. 47–48.
84. Haykel, *Revival and Reform in Islam*, p. 137.
85. Haykel, *Revival and Reform in Islam*, p. 138.
86. Al-Mūza'ī, 'Abd aṣ-Ṣamad, *al-Iḥsān*, ed. Al-Ḥibshī, pp. 56, 151–152. See also Ibn 'Alwān, *al-Futūḥ*, pp. 72–73.
87. Ewing, Katherine, *Arguing Sainthood*, Duke University Press (1997), p. 44.
88. Ash-Sharjī, Aḥmad, *Ṭabaqāt al-khawāṣṣ*, p. 71.
89. Al-Baradūnī, *Funūn al-adab ash-sha'bī fī'l-Yaman*, p. 82.
90. For the correct date of az-Zubayrī's birth, see ash-Shāmī, Aḥmad b. Muḥammad, *Ma'a ash-shi'r al-mu'āsir fī'l-Yaman*, Dār an-Nafā'is, Beirut (1980), 149.
91. Al-Baradūnī, *Funūn al-adab ash-sha'bī fī'l-Yaman*, pp. 82–83.

92. The first source to mention this extract is Jarāda, Muḥammad Sa'īd, *al-Adab wath-thaqāfa fī'l-Yaman 'abr al-'uṣūr*, Dār al-Fārābī, Beirut (1977), p. 217. It is also cited in al-Baradūnī's *Funūn al-adab ash-sha'bī fī'l-Yaman,* pp. 82–83, and Baradūnī, 'Abd Allāh, *Min awwal qaṣīdah ilā ākhir ṭalqah*, Dār al-Ḥadāthah, Beirut, (1993), p. 185.
93. For his biography, see Zabārah, Muḥammad b. Muḥammad Yaḥyā, *Nuzhat an-nazar fī rijāl al-qarn ar-rābi' 'ashar*, Markaz ad-Dirāsāt wa'l-Buḥūth al-Yamannī, Ṣan'ā' (1979), p. 306.
94. Ash-Shāmī, Aḥmad b. Muḥammad, *Ma'ash-shi'r al-mu'āṣir fī'l-Yaman*, Dār an-Nafā'is, Beirut (1980), 70.
95. Al-Baradūnī, *Min awwal qaṣīda ilā ākhar ṭalqa*, p. 185. However, in *Funūn al-adab*, al-Baradūnī kept the poem unchanged.
96. Ash-Shāmī, Aḥmad b. Muḥammad, *Riyāḥ at-taghyyīr fī'l-Yaman* (1948), 194.
97. Al-Baradūnī, *Funūn al-adab*, p. 83. Hubal is the chief idol of the Meccan Sanctuary (Haram) before Islam.
98. Ibn 'Alwān*, al-Futūḥ,* footnote, p. 81.

Chapter 8

1. A prominent example was Zaydī Imam Aḥmad b. al-Ḥusayn al-Mu'yyad bi-Allāh (333–411/944–1021), who wrote a Sufi treatise entitled "A Treatise on the Management of Disciples" (*Risālat siyāsat al-murīdin*). Imam al-Mu'ayyad wrote other books, including "The Book of Prophethoods" (*Kitāb al-nubuwāt*) and "Neutrality in the Jurisprudence of Imam al-Hādī" (*at-Tajrīd fī fiqh al-Imam al-Hādī*), but his *Risālat* is an indication of his profound knowledge of, if not his affiliation with, Sufism. This *Risālat* was quoted at length in "The Flowery Gardens" (*al-Ḥadā'iq al-wardiyya*) by Ḥumayd al-Muḥallī whose book was a major biographical collection of the early Zaydī imams. This study has relied on the chapter by Wilferd Madelung, "Zaydī Attitudes to Sufism," in *Islamic Mysticism Contested*, ed. Frederick De Jong and Bernd Radtke, Leiden, Brill (1999), pp. 124–144; and Abd Allāh al-Ḥibshī, *al-Ṣūfiyya wa-l-fuqahā' fī-l-Yaman*, Maktabat al-Jīl al-Jadīd, Ṣan'ā' (1976); and others. See also Wilferd Madelung, *Arabic Texts Concerning the History of the Zaydī Imams of Ṭabaristān, Daylamān and Gilān*, Beirut (1987), pp. 293–305; Muhallī, Abū l-Ḥasan, Ḥusām d-Dīn, Ḥumayd b. Aḥmad, *al-Ḥadā'iq al-wardiyya*, vol. 2, magnetic print by Preservation Technologies (2007), pp. 65–87.
2. Al-Ḥibshī, *al-Ṣūfiyya wa-l-fuqahā' fī-l-Yaman*, p. 55.
3. Ash-Sharjī, Aḥmad b. Muḥammad, *Ṭabaqāt al-khawāṣṣ: ahl aṣ-ṣidq wa'l-ikhlāṣ*, ad-Dār al-Yamaniyyah li'n-Nashr wa't-Tawzī' (1986), p. 280.
4. Al-Ḥibshī, *al-Ṣūfiyya wa-l-fuqahā' fī-l-Yaman*, p. 55.
5. Al-Ḥibshī however, argues that this book was refuted by Muḥammad b. Yūsuf al-Faḍlī in his *al-Inṣāf fī al-radd 'alā ahl al-zaygh wa l-i'tisāf*. Al-Ḥibshī, *al-Ṣūfiyya wa-l-fuqahā' fī-l-Yaman*, p. 55.
6. Al-Ḥibshī, *al-Ṣūfiyya wa-l-fuqahā' fī-l-Yaman*, p. 55.
7. Al-Sharjī, *Ṭabaqāt al-khawāṣṣ*, pp. 77–78.
8. It is divided like a newspaper into columns with uneven length. If you read the first column, you find a short history of the Rasūlid dynasty until the

death of al-Ashraf Ismā'īl (842–845/1438–1441). If you read the second column, you find an introduction to Arabic syntax (*naḥw*). Then, if you read the last letter of each word at the end of each line by adding letters as you go down the lines, you will find an introduction to the science of prosody (*'ilm al-'arūḍ*). After that, if you read the first letter of each line in the same way, you will come up with what is known as the science of rhyme scheme (*'ilm al-qawāfī*). Most important, when you try to make sense of the whole thing by reading each line from each column horizontally before going to the second line of each column, you will find another totally different branch of knowledge, namely, jurisprudence (*fiqh*). The interwoven integration is done so skillfully that some people described it as a miracle. Although this has nothing to do with Sufism directly, I have decided to mention it due to its significance and importance, and as a very brief way to identify the design of this miraculous book.

9. Ibn al-Muqrī, *Dīwān Ibn al-Muqrī*, revised by 'Abd Allāh b. Ibrāhīm al-Ansārī, Idārat Iḥyā' al-Turāth al-Islāmī, Qatar (1988), p. 454.
10. Al-Sharjī, *Ṭabaqāt al-khawāṣṣ*, pp. 77–78; Al-Ḥibshī, *al-Ṣūfiyya wa-l-fuqahā' fī-l-Yaman*, p. 56. Cf. Madelung, "Zaydī Attitudes to Sufism," p. 134. The zealous attitude of Ibn al-Muqrī can be explained first by the fact that this happened when he was still young—before he became a major critic and eventually a threat to Sufism. Second, it could also be the fact that both al-Muqrī and ash-Shāwirī had come from the same geographical area. Third, ash-Shāwirī was not only a Sufi but a jurist as well and, hence, Ibn al-Muqrī's supportive position can be understood. Otherwise, it would have been strange for someone who severely criticized the Sufis and their teachings and simultaneously defended their leaders.
11. Mizjājī, Muhamamd b. Muḥammad, *Hidāyat al-sālik ilā ahdā al-masālik* (manuscript); Cf. al-Ḥibshī, *al-Ṣūfiyya wa-l-fuqahā' fī-l-Yaman*, pp. 56–57.
12. Ms. Ṣan'ā', Great Mosque; see al-Ḥusaynī, as-Sayyid Aḥmad, *Mu'allafāt al-Zaydiyya*, v. 2, Manshūrāt Maktabat Āyat Allāh al-'Uzmā al-Mar'ashiyy an-Najafiyy, Qumm (1413/1993), p. 357. Cf. Madelung, "Zaydī Attitudes to Sufism," pp. 128, 129 (n11).
13. However, al-Ḥusaynī in *Mu'allafāt al-Zaydiyya* in the same volume called the author of *aṣ-ṣirāṭ al-mustaqīm* Badr ad-Dīn Muḥammad b. al-Ḥasan ad-Daylamī, which raises some doubts that he could be a different author than 'Izz al-Dīn Muḥammad b. Aḥmad b. al-Ḥasan al-Daylamī. In volume 1 when he talks about *al-Taṣfiya* he provided the same name as Badr ad-Dīn Muḥammad b. al-Ḥasan. In the indexes of volume 3, the author is called Muḥammad b. al-Ḥasan, Badr al-Dīn and listed the three books under his name: *at-Taṣfiya*, *al-Ṣirāṭ,* and *'Aqā'id ahl al-bayt* in addition to *al-Mishkā*, which can also be found in the same volume, p. 20. But, also in the index of volume 3, p. 40, the author of *qawā'id 'aqā'id Āl Muḥammad* is named Muḥammad b. Aḥmad b. al-Ḥasan al-Daylamī. Al-Ḥusaynī apologized in his introduction to *Mu'llafāt* for any repetition due to the difficulty of reading various manuscripts.
14. Al-Yāfi'ī, 'Abd Allāh b. As'ad, *Mir'āt al-janān wa 'ibrat al-yaqẓān,* v. 4, Dā'irat al-Ma'ārif an-Niẓāmiyyah, Ḥayderabad (1349/1921), p. 315; al-Ḥibshī, *al-Ṣūfiyya wa-l-fuqahā' fī-l-Yaman*, pp. 63–64.

15. Al-Ḥusaynī, *Mu'allafāt al-Zaydiyya*, v. 1, pp. 290–291. See also al-Ḥibshī who omits chapter 2, combines chapters 3 and 4, and has chapter 7 instead of 8. For al-Ḥibshī, chapter 8 is about asceticism, while chapter 9 instead of 7 and finally chapter 10 is about the mention of death. Cf. Al-Ḥibshī, *al-Ṣūfiyya wa-l-fuqahā' fī-l-Yaman*, pp. 64–65.
16. Madelung, "Zaydī Attitudes to Sufism," pp. 129–130.
17. Ms. Great Mosque, no. 10; al-Ḥibshī, *al-Ṣūfiyya wa-l-fuqahā' fī-l-Yaman*, p. 65.
18. Aziz, Muḥammad, *Medieval Sufism in Yemen: The Case of Aḥmad b. 'Alwān*, unpublished Ph.D. thesis, University of Michigan, Ann Arbor (2004), pp. 136–139. For a full treatment of *sama'* in this volume, see Chapter 6.
19. For further study on this topic, consult Madelung, Wilferd, *Der Imam al-Qāsim ibn Ibrāhīm und die Glaubenslehre der Zaiditen*, Berlin (1965), p. 222 and note 456; see also *Abū l-Ḥasan al-Baṣrī: Taṣaffuḥ al-adilla*, the extant parts introduced and edited by Wilferd Madelung and Sabine Schmidtke, Deutsche Morgenlandische Gesellschaft, Harrassowitz Verlag, Wiesbaden (2006).
20. Al-Ḥasanī, Yaḥya Ibn al-Mahdī b. al-Qāsim, *Ṣilat al-Ikhwān fī ḥilyat barakat ahl az-zamān*, Mu'ssasat al-Imam Zayd b. 'Alī, San'a (manuscript). Cf. Al-Ḥibshī, *al-Ṣūfiyya wa-l-fuqahā' fī-l-Yaman*, p. 22.
21. Yaḥyā b. Mahdī, *Ṣilat al-Ikhwān*, pp. 19b–20a. Cf. Madelung, "Zaydī Attitudes to Sufism," p. 131.
22. For further discussion on this topic, see Ismā'īl b. 'Alī al-Akwa', *Hijar al-'ilm wa ma'āqilihi fī l-Yaman*, 5 vols., Dar al-Fikr al-Mu'aṣir, Beirut (1995–1996). The major difference between the *hijra* and a Sufi lodge, be it a *khāniqa* or a *zāwiya*, is that Sufi lodges and by extension Sufi orders tend to found their teachings around mystical knowledge that sustain the spiritual path to God while *hijar* tend to focus mainly on preparing scholars to become erudite and experts in all kinds of disciplines, such as Arabic language, syntax, rhetoric, Mu'tazilite commentaries on the Qur'ān such as *al-Kashshāf 'an ḥaqāi q al-tanzīl wa-'uyūn al-aqāwīl fī wujūh at-law īl* by Abū l-Qāsim az-Zamakhsharī (468–539/1075–1144), Zaydī jurisprudence, and others.
23. Al-Ḥibshī, *al-Ṣūfiyya wa-l-fuqahā' fī-l-Yaman*, pp. 22–23.
24. Some of the descendants of Banū al-Kayna'ī are now living in the province of Ibb and hold some important offices with the government. When ash-Shawkānī spoke of their residence by saying it is one day's journey (*barīd*) west of Dhamār, he probably meant Ibb or Khubān of Yarīm, which both used to be administratively part of the governorate of Ibb. Some of them are still in charge of the remaining endowments (*awqāf*) of al-Ghaythī, which was known before and after the Yemeni revolution of 1962 as *waqf al-Ghaythī*. Perhaps this goes back to the founder of the al-Ghaythiyya Sufi order, Abū al-Ghayth b. Jamīl (d. 651/1253). See ash-Shawkānī, Muḥammad b. 'Alī, *al-Badr al-ṭāli' bi-maḥāsin man ba'd al-qarn as-sābi'*, v. 1, Dār al-Ma'rifa, Beirut (n.d.), p. 4.
25. Ash-Shawkānī, *al-Badr aṭ-ṭāli'*, p. 6.
26. Madelung, "Zaydī Attitudes to Sufism," p. 132.
27. For further study on as-Suhrawardī, see Ohlander, Erik, *Sufism in an Age of*

Transition: 'Umar al-Suhrawardī and the Rise of the Islamic Mystical Brotherhoods, Leiden, Brill (2008).
28. Cf. Yahya b. al-Mahdī, *Ṣilat al-ikhwān* (manuscript).
29. Al-Ḥusaynī, *Mu'allafāt al-Zaydiyya*, v. 3, p. 44.
30. Al-Ḥusaynī, *Mu'allafāt al-Zaydiyya*, v. 1, p. 193.
31. Al-Ḥusaynī, *Mu'allafāt al-Zaydiyya*, v. 1, p. 350.
32. Al-Ḥusaynī, *Mu'allafāt al-Zaydiyya*, v. 3, p. 132.
33. Al-Ḥusaynī, *Mu'allafāt al-Zaydiyya*, v. 1, p. 135.
34. Mss. 664, Landberg, Bienecke Library, Yale University.
35. Abū Lahab is the Prophet's uncle who did not submit to the message of the Prophet. The Qur'ān has a whole chapter by the name of Al-Lahb (i.e., the Fire) after his name. See Ibn Abī l-Rijāl, Aḥmad b. Ṣāliḥ, *Maṭla' al-budūr wa majma'al-buḥūr fī trājim rijāl al-Zaydiyya*, v. 4, ed. 'Abd al-Raqīb Mutahhar Muḥammad Ḥajar, Markaz Ahl al-Bait lil-Dirāsāt al-Islāmiyya, Ṣa'da, Yemen (2004), p. 443. For further study on this topic, see *Darr al-saḥāba fī manāqib al-qarāba wa-l-saḥāba* by Muḥammad ash-Shawkānī (d. 1250/1834).
36. For the full letter, see Ibn Abī al-Rijāl, Aḥmad b. Ṣāliḥ, *Maṭla' al-budūr wa majma'al-buḥūr fī trājim rijāl al-Zaydiyya*, v. 4, ed. 'Abd al-Raqīb Muṭahhar Muḥammad Ḥajar, Markaz Ahl al-Bait lil-Dirāsāt al-Islāmiyya, Ṣa'da, Yemen (2004), pp. 339–343.
37. Qur'ān (5:95).
38. Ibn Abī al-Rijāl, *Maṭla' al-budūr* v. 4, pp. 339–342.
39. Yaḥyā b. al-Ḥusayn, *Ghāyat al-amānī fī akhbār al-qṭr al-Yamānī*, 2 vols., ed. Sa'īd 'Abd al-Fattāḥ 'Āshūr, revised by Muḥammad Muṣṭafā Ziyāda, Dār al-Kātib al-'aArabī (1388/1968), pp. 680–681.
40. Ibn Abī al-Rijāl, *Maṭla' al-budūr* v. 3, p. 113.
41. Ibn Abī al-Rijāl, *Maṭla' al-budūr* v. 3, p. 113. See also al-Ḥibshī, *al-Ṣūfiyya wa-l-fuqahā' fī al-Yaman*, p. 58.
42. Ibn Abī al-Rijāl, *Maṭla' al-budūr* v. 3, pp. 114–117.
43. Al-Ḥibshī, *al-Ṣūfiyya wa-l-fuqahā' fī al-Yaman*, p. 53.
44. It must be noted that there is no need to mention the occupation of the British or the Soviet Union of Aden since we are dealing only with a certain period of history relevant to the Sufi movement in Yemen. For the full story of the Ottoman occupation see Qutb al-Dīn Muḥammad b. Aḥmad al-Nahrawālī, *al-Barq al-Yamānī fī-l-Fatḥ al-'Uthmānī*, 2nd ed., Manshūrāt al-Madīna, Beirut (1407/1986), pp. 251–253.
45. Yaḥyā b. al-Ḥusayn, *Ghāyat al-amānī,* p. 756. By the way, al-Ḥibshī thought the renovator was Ḥasan Bāshā. Perhaps the confusion stems from the fact that Ḥasan Bāshā replaced Murād Bāshā in Yemen. See al-Ḥibshī, *al-Ṣūfiyya wa-l-fuqahā' fī al-Yaman*, p. 53.
46. Al-Maqbalī, Ṣāliḥ, *al-'Alam al-Shāmikh*, 2nd ed., al-Maktaba al-Yamaniyya lil-Nashr wa-l-Tawzī', Ṣan'ā' (1985), p. 258.
47. Al-Ḥibshī calls him "Manṣūr al-Yaman." Cf. *al-Ṣūfiyya wa-l-fuqahā' fī al-Yaman*, p. 52.
48. Yaḥyā b. al-Ḥusayn, *Ghāyat al-amānī,* p. 749.
49. Al-Ḥibshī, *al-Ṣūfiyya wa-l-fuqahā' fī al-Yaman*, p. 52.
50. Al-Muḥibbī, Muḥammad Amīn, *Khulāṣat al-athar fī a'yān al-qar n al-ḥādī*

'ashar, v. 1, Egypt (1284/1867), p. 98. Al-Ḥibshī, however, thought that the person who asked God to scatter Qānsuwa's power was the Sufī al-Zayla'ī, not his disciple the jurist Maqbūl b. Aḥmad. Cf. al-Ḥibshī, *al-Ṣūfiyya wa-l-fuqahā' fī al-Yaman*, p. 53.

51. Al-Wāsi'ī, Abd al-Wāsi' b. Yaḥyā, *Tārīkh al-Yaman*, 2nd ed., Maktabat al-Yaman al-Kubrā Ṣan'ā', (1991), p. 262. Cf. Abāẓa, Fārūq 'Uthmān, *al-Ḥukm al-'Uthmānī fī-l-Yaman,* al-Hay'a al-Misriyya al-'Āmma lil-Kitāb, Cairo (1975), p. 119. Al-Ḥibshī depended on the former books, see his *al-Ṣūfiyya wa-l-fuqahā' fī al-Yaman*, p. 52.
52. Ms. no. 130, Great Mosque, Ṣan'ā', Yemen, under the category of "speculative theology" (*'ilm al-kalām*).
53. The first two words of the title may also refer to the two famous Arabic poetic meters known as "*al-kāmil*" and "*al-mutadārik.*"
54. Al-Jurmūzī, al-Ḥaṣan b. Muḥammad, *al-Nubdha al-mushīra,* facsimile edition, Ṣan'ā' (ca. 1981?), pp. 31–32. Cf. Madelung, "Zaydī Attitudes to Sufism," p. 139.
55. For details on how hostages are treated in the fortresses of Imam, see the Arabic novel *Ar-Rahina* by Zayd Mutī' Dammaj (Dār al-Ādāb, Beirut, 1984). Its translation is entitled *The Hostage*, by May Jayyusi and Christopher Tingley (Interlink Books, New York, 1994).
56. This poem is quoted in full in Chapter 7.
57. These poems are quoted in full in Chapter 7.
58. He wrote several treatises, such as "Satisfying the Hearts in Forbidding the Elevation of Graves" (*Sharḥ al-Ṣudūr fī taḥrīm raf' al-qubūr*).
59. Ash-Shawkānī, Muḥammad b. 'Alī, *al-Ṣawārim al-ḥidād al-qāṭi'a li-'alā'q arbāb al-ittiḥād in Majmū'at rasā'il fī 'ilm at-tawḥīd*, ed. al-Qāḍī 'Abd ar-Raḥmān b. Yaḥyā al-Iryānī, Dār al-Fikr, Damascus (1983). Ash-Shawkānī, however, apologized for writing such a treatise giving the reason that it was written during young adulthood, but after getting old and gaining more experience, he stopped judging the doctrinal views of the followers of Ibn 'Arabī. One letter to be added to the previous treatises is entitled "The Cutting Sword for the Nicks of Grave Worshippers" (*al-Sayf al-bātir li-a'nāq 'ubbād al-maqābir*) by 'Aqīl b. Yaḥyā al-Iryānī (1324–1346/1906–1927 [or 1928]). All these treatises were published in a collection of articles edited by Qādī 'Abd al-Rahmān al-Iryānī entitled "The Collection of Treatises in the Knowledge of [God's] Union" (*Majmū'at rasā'il fī 'ilm at-tawḥīd*).

Chapter 9

1. Knysh, Alexander, *Ibn 'Arabī in the Later Islamic Tradition*, State University of New York Press (1999), p. 249.
2. Hodgson, Marshal G. S., *The Venture of Islam*, v. 2, University of Chicago Press, Chicago and London (1977), p. 216.
3. Voll, John O, "Sufi Orders," in *The Oxford Encyclopedia of Modern Islamic World*, v. 4, Oxford University Press (1995), p. 10.
4. Trimingham, J. Spencer, *The Sufi Orders in Islam*, Oxford University Press (1998), p. 38.
5. Ibn 'Alwān, Aḥmad, *at-Tawḥīd al-a'ẓam,* ed. 'Abd al-'Azīz al-Manṣūb, Dār al-Fikr al-Mu'āṣir, Beirut (1990), pp. 199–202.

6. There are many other Sufi orders that we have not included in this book such as al-'Aydarūsiyya in Ḥaḍramawt and al-Ahdaliyya in the Tihama but these are only branches of the 'Alawiyya and Shādhiliyya orders that do not require a separate study. There are many other minor Sufi communities whose doctrines and teachings are not new and fall under one or a combination of the major Sufi orders. These minor Sufi orders include al-Jabartiyya, al-Ḥaddādiyya, al-Maghribiyya, al-Asadiyya, al-Bajaliyya, al-Ghaythiyya, az-Zayla'iyya, al-Ḥakamiyya, al-'Ujayliyya, an-Nūriyya, and al-Ṭūshiyya.
7. Hodgson, *The Venture of Islam*, v. 2, p. 217.
8. Ash-Sharjī, Aḥmad b. Muḥammad, *Ṭabaqāt al-khawāṣṣ: ahl aṣ-ṣidq wa'l-ikhlāṣ*, ad-Dār al-Yamaniyyah li'n-Nashr wa't-Tawzī' (1986), p. 204. For further study on al-Jīlānī, see Knysh, Alexander, *Islamic Mysticism: A Short History*, Brill, Leiden (2000), pp. 179–192. See also Qādirī, Muḥammad Riaz, *The Sultan of the Saints,* Abbasi Publications, Pakistan (2000).
9. Ash-Sharjī, *Ṭabaqāt al-khawāṣṣ*, p. 204.
10. According to ash-Sharjī, al-Asdī lived 100 years while some sources claim that he had lived 180 years. Cf. Ash-Sharjī, *Ṭabaqāt al-khawāṣṣ*, p. 179.
11. Al-Ḥibshī, 'Abd Allāh, *aṣ-Ṣūfiyya wa'l-fuqahā' fī'l-Yaman*, Maktabat al-Jīl al-Jadīd, Ṣan'ā' (1976), p. 34.
12. He will be discussed when we talk about his Sufi order, i.e., al-Yāfi'iyya.
13. Zaydān, Yūsuf, *al-Fikr aṣ-ṣūfī 'ind 'Abd al-Karīm al-Jīlī*, Dār an-Nahdah al-'Arabiyyah, Beirut (1988), p. 39. Cf. Knysh, *Ibn 'Arabī in the Later Islamic Tradition*, p. 250.
14. Ash-Sharjī, *Ṭabaqāt al-khawāṣṣ*, p. 204. Cf. Knysh, *Ibn 'Arabī in the Later Islamic Tradition*, p. 238.
15. Al-Ḥibshī, 'Abd Allāh, *aṣ-Sūfiyya wa'l-fuqahā'*, p. 40.
16. Schimmel, Annemarie, *Mystical Dimensions of Islam*, University of North Carolina Press (1975), p. 249.
17. The name "Bint al-Maylaq" is according to al-Ḥibshī. But in *Ṭabaqāt al-khawāṣṣ* his name is read "Ibn al-Maylaq or al-Muylaq."
18. Ash-Sharjī, *Ṭabaqāt al-khawāṣṣ*, p. 233.
19. Al-Ḥibshī, 'Abd Allāh, *aṣ-Ṣūfiyya wa'l-fuqahā'*, p. 35.
20. Maḥmūd, Abd al-Halīm, *Abū l-Ḥasan ash-Shādhilī,* Dār al-Islam, Cairo (1967), p. 193.
21. Ibn 'Atā' Allāh as-Sakandarī, *Latāif al-minan,* Al-Maktaba al-Sa'diyya, Cairo (1972), p. 190. Cf. Maḥmūd , *Abū l-Ḥasan ash-Shādhilī*, p. 197.
22. Maḥmūd, *Abū l-Ḥasan ash-Shādhilī*, p. 163.
23. I have in my possession a tape cassette of some of his beautiful collections that deal with a Prophet's birthday celebration along with his recorded voice of God's Glorification before dawn prayers.
24. We mentioned his opinion with regard to the difference between Ash'arite and Mu'tazilite theology and how he made an effort to correct the mistake that crept into the edited book of the Supreme Union (*at-Tawḥīd al-a'zam*) and was not successful since the book was already published and circulated.
25. I have known him for a long time and attended his *zāwiyah* on numerous occasions.
26. Al-Ḥibshī, 'Abd Allāh, *aṣ-Ṣūfiyya wa'l-fuqahā'*, p. 36.

27. Ohlander, Erik, *Sufism in an Age of Transition: 'Umar al-Suhrawardī and the Rise of the Islamic Mystical Brotherhoods,* Brill, Leiden (2008), p. 212.
28. Al-Ḥibshī, 'Abd Allāh, *aṣ-Ṣūfiyya wa'l-fuqahā'*, p. 37.
29. Al-Muḥibbī, Muḥammad Amīn, *Khulāsat al-athar*, v. 1 (n.d.), pp. 346–347.
30. Al-Ḥibshī, 'Abd Allāh, *aṣ-Ṣūfiyya wa'l-fuqahā'*, p. 37.
31. Sa'īd 'Abd al-Karīm, *Qaḍāyā wa ishkāliyyāt at-taṣawwuf 'ind Ibn 'Alwān*, Maktabat Murād, Ṣan'ā' (1997), p. 52.
32. This episode is a modified version of an article I wrote for the *I. B. Tauris Biographical Dictionary of Islamic Civilization*, ed. Mustafa Shah and Muḥammad Abdel Haleem, London.
33. al-Fāsī, Taqiyy ad-Dīn, *al-'Iqd ath-thamīn fī tārīkh al-balad al-amīn*, v. 5, ed. Fou'ād Sayyid, Cairo (1966), p. 104.
34. Al-Asnawī, Jamāl ad-Dīn, *Ṭabaqāt ash-shāfi'iyya,* v. 2, ed. 'Abd Allāh al-Jubūr, Dār al-'Ulūm (1981).
35. Trimingham, *The Sufi Orders*, p. 273.
36. Graham, T., "Shāh Ni'matullāhī Walī: Founder of the Ni'matullāhī Sufi Order," in *The Legacy of Mediaeval Persian Sufism,* ed. Leonard Lewisohn, London, (1992), pp. 173–190; see also:"Ni'matullāhiyya," in the *Encyclopedia of Islam*, 2nd ed (1984).
37. Ammār, 'Alī Sālim, *Abū al-Ḥaṣan ash-Shādhilī*, v. 2, Cairo (1952), pp. 186–187.
38. Geoffroy, E., "Al-Yāfi'ī," in *Encyclopedia of Islam,* 2nd ed. (1984).
39. al-Yāfi'ī 'Abd Allāh b. As'ad, *Marham al-'ilal al-mu'dila fī 'r-radd 'alā a'immat al-mu'tazila,* Calcutta (1910).
40. al-'Asqalānī Ibn Ḥajar, *ad-Durar al-kāmina fī a'yān al-mi'a ath-thāmina,* v. 2, Dār al-Jīl, Beirut (1993), p. 249.
41. Ḥaydarābād, 1339/1920.
42. Many editions, i.e., Cairo, 1989.
43. Cairo, 1961.
44. ash-Sharjī, *Ṭabqāt al-khawāṣṣ,* pp. 172–176.
45. Asnawī, Jamāl ad-Dīn, *Ṭabaqāt ash-shāfi'iyya,* ed. 'Abd Allāh al-Jubūr, v. 2, Dār al-'Ulūm (1981), pp. 579–583.
46. Al-Ḥibshī, Muḥammad b. Husayn, *al-'Uqūd al-lu'lu'iyya fī bayān tarīqat as-sāda al-'Alawiyya*, al-Matba'ah ash-Sharafiyyah, Egypt (1328/1910), p. 5.
47. Al-Ḥibshī, Muḥammad, *al-'Uqūd*, p. 10.
48. Al-Ḥibshī, Muḥammad, *al-'Uqūd*, p. 11.
49. Ibn 'Aqīl, 'Abd ar-Raḥmān b. Ja'far, *'Umar Bā Makhramah as-Saybānī: ḥayātuhu wa tasawwufuhu wa shi'ruhu*, Dār al-Fikr, Damascus (2002), p. 38. Henceforth (*Bā Makhramah*).
50. Knysh, Alexander, "The Sāda in History: A Critical Essay on Ḥaḍramī Historiography," *Journal of the Royal Asiatic Society*, 9/2 (July 1999), p. 215. Cf. Serjeant, R. B., *The Sayyids of Ḥaḍramawt*, London (1957), p. 19.
51. 'Alawī b. Aḥmad as-Saqqāf, *Majmū'at Kutub Mufīda* (no date or place), p. 178, says, "Ṣuḥbat al-Ashrār tūrith aẓ-ẓann bi-'l-akhyār'." (Accompanying evil people bequeaths ill manners on good-people.)
52. Serjeant, *The Sayyids of Ḥaḍramawt*, pp. 19–20.
53. Al-Ḥibshī, Muḥammad, *al-'Uqūd*, p. 13.

54. Sedgwick, Mark, *Saints and Sons: The Making and Remaking of the Rashīdī Aḥmadī Sufi Order, 1799–2000*, Brill, Leiden (2005), pp. 10–26. For a comprehensive study of Aḥmad b. Idris and his influence see O'Fahey, R. S., *Engimatic Saint: Aḥmad Ibn Idris and the Idrisi Tradition,* Northwestern University Press, Evanston, Illinois (1990).
55. Fisher, Humphrey J., *Aḥmadiyyah: A Study in Contemporary Islam on the West African Coast,* Oxford University Press (1963), p. ix.
56. Trimingham, J. Spencer, *A History of Islam in West Africa,* reprint ed., Oxford University Press, Oxford (1982), p. 226.
57. Sedgwick, *Saints and Sons*, p. 65.
58. Sedgwick, *Saints and Sons*, p. 65.
59. Rihani, Ameen, *Around the Coasts of Arabia,* Constable, London (1930), p. 157. Cf. Sedgwick, *Saints and Sons*, p. 65.
60. Rihani, *Around the Coasts of Arabia*, p. 157.
61. Rihani, *Around the Coasts of Arabia*, p. 154.
62. Rihani, *Around the Coasts of Arabia*, pp. 143–144.
63. Rihani, *Around the Coasts of Arabia*, p. 147.
64. Al-Ḥibshī, 'Abd Allāh, *aṣ-Ṣūfiyya wa'l-fuqahā'*, p. 119.
65. Knysh, *Ibn 'Arabī in the Later Islamic Tradition*, p. 229.
66. Al-Ḥibshī, 'Abd Allāh, aṣ-Ṣūfiyya wa'l-fuqahā', p. 73. Cf. Knysh, Ibn 'Arabī in the Later Islamic Tradition, p. 238. Cf. Ibn al-Ahdal, Kashf al-ghiṭā' 'an ḥaqā'q at-tawḥīd wa'r-radd 'alā Ibn 'Arabī al-faylasūf aṣ-ṣūfī, ed. Aḥmad Bukar Muḥammad, Tunis (1964), p. 217.
67. Knysh, *Ibn 'Arabī in the Later Islamic Tradition*, pp. 238–239.
68. Knysh, *Ibn 'Arabī in the Later Islamic Tradition*, p. 239.
69. Al-Janadī, *as-Sulūk*, p. 112. However, this is the account of al-Janadī, which all biographers depended on. The account did not state that they were referring to the typical Mu'tazilite doctrine "the createdness of the Qur'ān." The Mu'tazilites never denied that the Qur'ān was the word of God. Their argument was that the Qur'ān was the word of God, which was created. The main dispute between Mu'tazilites and their opponents was whether the Qur'ān was created or not. Here, we have a completely different issue. Ibn al-Bāna and his teacher al-Qudsī were accused of denying the truthfulness of the Qur'ān as well as of saying that it is not the word of God. Whether this accusation was due to an exaggeration by their opponents, while in fact they adhered to the Mu'tazilite doctrine, is unclear.
70. Al-Ḥibshī, 'Abd Allāh, *aṣ-Ṣūfiyya wa'l-fuqahā'*, pp. 111–114. Cf. Knysh, *Ibn 'Arabī in the Later Islamic Tradition*, p. 219.
71. Al-Janadī, *as-Sulūk*, p. 112; al-Ḥibshī, 'Abd Allāh, *aṣ-Ṣūfiyya wa'l-fuqahā'*, pp. 111–114. Cf. Knysh, *Ibn 'Arabī in the Later Islamic Tradition*, p. 239. Cf. Ibn al-Ahdal, *Kashf al-ghiṭā'*, p. 219.
72. Al-Janadī, *as-Sulūk*, v. 2, p. 120.
73. Al-Janadī, *as-Sulūk*, v. 2, p. 120.
74. Ba'kar, 'Abd ar-Raḥmān, *Kawākib yamaniyyah fī samā' al-Islām*, Dār al-Fikr al-Mu'āṣir, Beirut (1990), p. 544.
75. Al-Janadī, *as-Sulūk*, v. 2, p. 120. Cf. Knysh, *Ibn 'Arabī in the Later Islamic Tradition*, pp. 240–241.

76. Ibn al-Ahdal, *Kashf al-ghiṭā'*, pp. 217–218; al-Ḥibshī, 'Abd Allāh, *aṣ-Ṣūfiyya*, pp. 74–75. Cf. Knysh, *Ibn 'Arabī in the Later Islamic Tradition*, p. 241.
77. Probably al-Jabartī's insistence on recommending the recitation of Yasīn to everyone as a means of healing or even as a panacea to attain all purposes springs from the Prophet's report that "Yāsīn is the heart of the Qur'ān." And since the Qur'ān is asserting this fact: "What we have sent down of the Qur'ān is a healing and a grace for the faithful" (17:82), al-Jabartī chose the chapter of Yāsīn for permanent recitation for the obvious two reasons. First, because it is part of the Qur'ān and, second, because it is the essence of the Qur'ān, as recommended by the Prophet.
78. Ibn Ḥajar, *Inbā' al-ghumr bi anbā' al-'umr*, ed. Ḥasan Ḥabashī, v. 2, Cairo (1971), p. 272.
79. Ash-Shawkānī, Muḥammad b. 'Alī, *al-Badr aṭ-ṭāli' bi-maḥāsin man ba'd al-qarn as-sābi'*, v. 1, Dār al-Ma'rifah, Beirut, p. 139; as-Sakhāwī, Muḥammad b. 'Abd ar-Raḥmān, *aḍ-Ḍaw' al-lāmi' li-ahl al-qarn at-tāsi'*, v. 2, Manshūrāt Dār Maktabat al-Ḥayāh, Beirut (n.d.), p. 282.
80. Ash-Sharjī, *Ṭabaqāt al-khawass*, p. 102.
81. Ash-Shawkānī, *al-Badr*, v. 1, p. 139; as-Sakhāwī, *aḍ-Ḍaw' al-lāmi',* v. 2, p. 282; Ibn Ḥajar, *Inbā' al-ghumr*, v. 2, p. 272.
82. Ash-Shawkānī, *al-Badr*, p. 139.
83. Ibn al-Ahdal, *Kashf al-ghiṭā'*, p. 215.
84. Knysh, *Ibn 'Arabī*, p. 242.
85. Knysh, *Ibn 'Arabī*, p. 242. See also al-Ḥibshī, *aṣ-Ṣūfiyya*, p. 48.
86. As-Sakhāwī, *aḍ-Ḍaw' al-lāmi'*v., pp. 282–283.
87. Ibn al-Ahdal, *Kashf al-ghiṭā'*, p. 214.
88. Knysh, *Ibn 'Arabī*, p. 244.
89. Ash-Sharjī, *Ṭabqāt al-khawāṣṣ*, pp. 104–105.
90. Al-Qāri' al-Baghdādī, Abū al-Ḥaṣan 'Alī, *Manāqib Ibn 'Arabī,* ed. by Ṣalāḥ ad-Dīn al-Munajjid, Mu'ssasat at-Turāth al-'Arabī, Beirut (1959), p. 64.
91. Al-Qāri'*, Manāqib Ibn 'Arabī*, p. 68.
92. Ibn al-Ahdal, *Kashf al-ghiṭā'*, p. 215.
93. Chittick, William C., *The Sufi Path of Knowledge*, State University of New York Press (1989), p. 283.
94. Ibn al-Ahdal, *Kashf al-ghiṭā'*, p. 216.
95. Nicholson, Reynold Alleyne, *Studies in Islamic Mysticism*, reprint ed., Curzon Press, London (1994), p. 81. Cf. Knysh, *Ibn 'Arabī in the Later Islamic Tradition*, p. 248. See also *EI2* art. "al-Djīlī."
96. Nicholson, *Studies in Islamic Mysticism*, p. 81.
97. Knysh, *Ibn 'Arab in the Later Islamic Tradition*, p. 249.
98. Zaydān, Yūsuf, *al-Fikr as-Sūfī 'ind 'Abd al-Karīm al-Jīlī*, pp. 23–26. Cf. Knysh, *Ibn 'Arabī*, p. 249.
99. Knysh, *Ibn 'Arabī*, p. 250.
100. Al-Jīlī, 'Abd al-Karīm, *al-Insān al-kāmil fī ma'rifat al-awākhir wa'l awā'il*, v. 2, Maktabat wa Maṭba'at Muḥammad 'Alī Ṣabīḥ, Cairo (1963), pp. 46–47. Cf. Cornell, Vincent, *Realm of the Saint*, pp. 210–211. Cf. Knysh, *Islamic Mysticism*, p. 251.
101. *Shorter Encyclopedia of Islam* (*SEI4*), art. "al-Insān al-kamil."

102. Cornell, *Realm of the Saint*, p. 211.
103. Al-Burayhī, 'Abd al-Wahhāb b. 'Abd ar-Raḥmān, *Ṭabqāt ṣulaḥā' al-Yaman*, ed. al-Ḥibshī, Markaz ad-Dirāsāt wa'l-Buḥūth al-Yamanī, Sanaa, Dār al-Adāb, Beirut (1983), p. 299. Al-Ḥibshī, *aṣ-Ṣūfiyya*, p. 132. Ibn Ḥajar, *Inbā' al-ghumr*, v. 3, p. 178.
104. Ibn Ḥajar, *Inbā' al-ghumr*, v. 3, p. 178.
105. Al-Burayhī, *Ṭabqāt ṣulaḥā' al-Yaman*, p. 299.
106. Al-Khazrajī, *al-'Uqūd*, v. 2, p. 273; ash-Shawkānī, *al-Badr*, v. 1, p. 139; al-Ḥibshī, *aṣ-Ṣūfiyya*, p. 118.
107. Al-Burayhī, *Ṭabqāt*, p. 269.
108. Al-Ḥibshī, *aṣ-Ṣūfiyya*, p. 107.
109. Al-Ḥibshī, *aṣ-Ṣūfiyya*, p. 149.
110. Knysh, *Ibn 'Arabī*, p. 264.
111. Ibn al-Ahdal, *Kashf al-ghiṭā'*, p. 222. Cf. Knysh, *Ibn 'Arabī*, p. 264; al-Ḥibshī, *aṣ-Ṣūfiyya*, p. 150.
112. Knysh, *Ibn 'Arabī*, p. 264.
113. Ibn al-Ahdal, *Kashf al-ghiṭā'*, p. 222; al-Ḥibshī, *aṣ-Ṣūfiyya*, pp. 151–152.
114. Knysh, *Ibn 'Arabī*, p. 264.
115. Al-Ḥibshī, *aṣ-Ṣūfiyya*, pp. 154–155.
116. Al-Ḥibshī, *aṣ-Ṣūfiyya*, p. 159.
117. Knysh, *Ibn 'Arabī*, p. 265.
118. Al-Ḥibshī, *aṣ-Ṣūfiyya*, p. 161.
119. Al-Ḥibshī, *aṣ-Ṣūfiyya*, pp. 161–162.
120. Ibn al-Muqrī, Ismā'īl, *Majmū' diwān Ibn al-Muqrī*, p. 38. See also, al-Ḥibshī, *aṣ-Ṣūfiyya*, p. 162.
121. Knysh, *Ibn 'Arabī*, pp. 265–266.
122. Al-Manṣūb, *'Abd al-Hādī as-Sūdī: Shi'ruh, Rasā'iluh, Manāqibuh*, Dār al-Fikr al-'Arabī, Beirut (1995), pp. 37–90.
123. Al-Manṣūb, *as-Sūdī*, pp. 57, 145–147, 193–195.
124. Ash-Shawkānī, *al-Badr at-Tāli'*, v. 1, p. 408; al-'Aydarūs, *an-Nūr as-Sāfir* (n. d.), p. 155.
125. Al-Manṣūb, *as-Sūdī*, p. 65.
126. Al-Maqāliḥ, 'Abd al-'Azīz, "Qirā'ah fī dīwān shā'ir aṣ-ṣūfiyya al-akbar fī al-Yaman ash-Shayh 'Abd al-Hādī as-Sūdī" in *Dirāsāt Yamaniyya*, Markaz ad-Dirāsāt wa'l-Buḥūth al-Yamanī, v. 43 (1411/1991), p. 15.
127. Perhaps as-Sūdī meant the Ottomans. Cf. al-Manṣūb, *as-Sūdī*, p. 55.
128. Al-Manṣūb, *as-Sūdī*, p. 135.
129. Cf. Homerin, Emil, *From Arab Poet to Muslim Saint*, American University in Cairo Press (2001), pp. 4–14. Cf. Chapter 4 of this study.
130. Al-Manṣūb, *as-Sūdī*, pp. 227–228.
131. Al-Maqāliḥ, "Qirā'ah" in *Dirāsāt*, p. 19.
132. See Chapter 6 for an excerpt from his laudatory poem about Ibn 'Alwān.
133. 'Aqīl, 'Abd ar-Raḥmān b. Ja'far, *'Umar Bā Makhramh as-Saybānī: : ḥayātuh wa taṣawwufuh wa shi'ruh*, Dār al-Fikr, Damascus (2002), pp. 95–100.
134. 'Aqīl, *Bā Makhrama*, p. 109.
135. 'Aqīl, *Bā Makhrama*, p. 89.
136. 'Aqīl, *Bā Makhrama*, p. 225.
137. Buchman, David, *The Pedagogy of Perfection: Levels of Complementarity*

within and between the Beliefs and Practices of the Shādhiliyya/'Alawiyya Sufi Order of Ṣan'ā' Yemen, Ph.D. thesis in anthropology, State University of New York (1998) p. 25. According to Buchman, the Shādhiliyya/'Alawiyya Sufi order presently consists of about fifty Shāfi'ī males, who were born in Ta'izz or its environs. However, the shaykh of this order claims to have 100,000 males who are dispersed throughout the Shāfi'ī regions of Yemen.

138. Buchman, *The Pedagogy of Perfection*, pp. 123, 142.

139. Buchman, *The Pedagogy of Perfection*, p. 143.

Conclusion

1. See Chapter 3.

BIBLIOGRAPHY

Manuscripts

Ḥasanī, Yaḥya Ibn al-Mahdī b. al-Qāsim, *Ṣilat al-Ikhwān fī ḥilyat barakat ahl az-zamān* , Mu'ssasat al-Imam Zayd b. 'Alī, San'a (manuscript).

Barzanjī, Ja'far b. Ḥasan, *Fatḥ al-karīm al-gawād al-mannān biwāsiṭ at 'iqd saiyid az zamān fī ba'ḍ manāqib A. b. 'Alwān*, Die Handschriften-Verzeichnisse der königlichen Bibliothek zu Berlin. Bd. 21, Verzeichniss der Arabischen Hanschriften von W. Ahlwardt, 9. Bd., Berlin: A. Asher, 1897 no. 10064 (pp. 465–467) (manuscript).

Ibn al-Amīr, Muḥammad b. Ismā'īl, *Risāla ḥawl madhhab Ibn 'Abd al-Wahhāb,* ms. Ṣan'ā', Sharqiyya library, *majmū'* no. 1 (manuscript).

Ibn al-Amīr, Muḥammad b. Ismā'īl, *Irshād dhawī al-albāb ilā ḥaqā'iq Muḥammad b. 'Abd al-Wahhāb*, ms. Ṣan'ā', Gharbiyya library, *majmū'* no. 107, vols. 131–142 (manuscript).

Ibn 'Alwān, Aḥmad, *al-Ajwiba al-lā'īqa 'alā al-as'īla al-fā'īqa* (manuscript).

'Izz al-Dīn, Sayyid Muḥammad, al-Muftī, *al-Iḥkām: sharḥ takmilat al-aḥkām,* Mss 664, Landberg, Bienecke Library, Yale University, New Haven.

Ibn 'Alwān's Edited Books

Ibn 'Alwān, Aḥmad, *al-Futūḥ*, ed. al-Manṣūb, Dār al-Fikr al-Mu'āṣir, Beirut (1991).

Ibn 'Alwān, Aḥmad, *al-Mahrajān wa'l-baḥr al-mushakkal al-gharīb*, ed. 'Abd al-'Azīz Sultān Tāhir al-Mansūb, Markaz ad-Dirāsāt wa l—Buhūth al-Yamanī, Dār al-Fikral-Mu'āṣir, Beirut (1992).

Ibn 'Alwān, Aḥmad, *at-Tawḥīd al-a'ẓam*, ed. 'Abd al-'Azīz al-Manṣūb, Dār al-Fikr al-Mu'āṣir, Beirut (1990).

References in Arabic

Abāẓa, Fārūq 'Uthmān, *al-Ḥukm al-'Uthmānī fī-l-Yaman,* al-Hay'a al-Miṣriyya al-'Āmma lil-Kitāb, Cairo (1975).

'Abd al-'Āl, Aḥmad, Muḥammad, *Banū rasūl wa banū ṭāhir*, al-Hay'ah al-'Āmmah li'l-Kutub al-Maṣriyya, Alexandria (1980).

'Abd al-Bāqī, Muḥammad, Fouad, *al-Mu'jam al-mufahras l'al-fāḍ al-qur'ān al-karīm*, Dar al-Fikr, Beirut (1987).

Abū Shāma, 'Abd ar-Raḥmān b. Ismā'īl, *Kitāb ar-Rawḍatayn fī akhbār ad-dawlatayn: an-Nūrīya wa-ṣ-Ṣalāḥīya*, ed. Ibrahīm az-Zabaq, 5 vols., Mu'assassat ar-Risāla, Beirut (1997).

Abū Zahra, Muḥammad *Tārīkh al-madhāhib al-islāmiyyah*, vol.1, Dār al-Fikr al-'Arabī (n.d.).

Abū Zahra, Muḥammad, *al-Imām Zayd*, Dār al-Fikr al-'Arabī, Cairo (1378/1959).

Abū Zayd, Ṭaha Aḥmad, *Ismā'īl al-Muqrī: ḥayātuh wa shi'ruh*, Markaz ad-Dirāsāt wa'l-Buḥūth al-Yamanī and Dār al-Adab, Ṣan'ā' (1986).

Abyad, al-Hājj Ḥasan 'Abd al-Jalīl Muḥammad, *Kitāb al-futūḥ al-maṣūna al-maknūna wa'l-'ulūm al-makhzūna*, Maṭba'at Kamāl as-Suways (1990).

Aḥmad 'Alī, trans., *Qur'ān*, Princeton University Press (1994).

Aḥmadī, Abd aṣ-Ṣamad, *al-Jawāhir as-saniyya fī'n-nisba wa'l-karāmāt al-Aḥmadiyya*, no publisher (1277/1860).

Akwa', Ismā'īl, *Al-Madāris al-islāmiyya fī'l-Yaman*, Maktabat al-Jīl al-Jadīd, San'a (1986).

Akwa', Ismā'īl, *Hijar al-'ilm wa ma'āqilihi fī l-Yaman*, 5 vols., Dār al-Fikr al-Mu'āṣir, Beirut (1995–1996).

Akwa', Ismā'īl, *az-Zaydiyya: nash'atuhā wa mu'taqadātuhā*, no publisher (1421/2000).

'Alawī, Aḥmad as-Saqqāf, *Majmū'at Kutub Mufīda* (n.d.).

'Alawī, Ṣāliḥ al-Ḥāmid, *Ta'rīkh Ḥaḍramawt*, 2 vols., Maktabat al-Irshād, Jedda (1968).

'Alī, 'Abdaullah Yusuf, *The Qur'ān Translation*, Tahrike Tarsile Qur'ān, New York (2002).

'Ammār, 'Alī Sālim, *Abū al-Hasan ash-Shādhilī*, vol. 2, Cairo (1952).

'Aqīlī, Muḥammad b. Aḥmad, *At-Taṣawwuf fī Tihāmah*, Maktabat al-Irshād, Jeddah (1964).

'Aqīlī, Muḥammad b. Aḥmad, *Tārikh al-mikhlāf al-sulaymānī,* Dār al-Yamāmah, Riyad (1982).

Arberry, A. J., *The Qur'ān Interpreted,* trans. Touchstone (1955).

Ash'arī, Abū al-Ḥasan, *Maqālāt al-islāmiyyīn*, ed. Hellmut Ritter, Franz Steiner, Wiesbaden (1963).

Asnawī, Jamāl ad-Dīn, *Tabaqāt ash-shāfi'iyya,* vol. 2, ed. 'Abd Allāh al-Jubūr, Dār al-'Ulūm (1981).

'Aṭṭār Farīd ad-Dīn, *Muslim Saints and Mystics*, trans. A. J. Arberry, Arkana (1990).

Badawī, 'Abd ar-Raḥman, *Tārikh at-taṣawwuf al-Islāmī*, 2nd ed., Wikālāt al-Maṭbū'āt, Kuwait (1978).

Baghdādī, 'Abd al-Qāhir, *Al-Farq bayn al-firaq*, ed. Muḥammad Muḥyī ad-Dīn 'Abd al-Ḥamīd, Maṭba'at al-Madanī, Cairo (1964).

Ba'kar, 'Abd ar-Raḥmān, *Kawākib yamaniyya fī samā' al-Islām*, Dār al-Fikr al-Mu'āṣir, Beirut (1990).

Ba'kar, 'Abd ar-Raḥmān, "At-Turjumān al-Mujadid Aḥmad b. 'Alwān," *Al-Jumhūriyya ath-Thaqāfiyya,* Ta'izz (1999).

Ba'labkī, Munīr, *Al-Mawrid: A Modern English-Arabic Dictionary*, Dār El-'Ilm Lil-Malāyen (1982).

Ba'labkī, Roḥī, *Al-Mawrid: A Modern Arabic-English Dictionary*, Dār El-'Ilm Lil-Malāyen (2002).

Baradūnī, 'Abd Allāh, *Funūn al-adab ash-sha'bī fī al-Yaman*, 3rd ed., Dār al-Fikr, Damascus (1995).

Baradūnī, 'Abd Allāh, *Min awwal qaṣīda ilā ākhir ṭalqa*, Dār al-Ḥadāthah, Beirut (1993).

Baradūnī, 'Abd Allāh, *Riḥla fī'sh shi'r al-Yamanī*, 3rd ed., Dār al-'Awdah, Beirut (1978).

Baṣrī, Abū l-Ḥasan: Taṣaffuḥ al-adilla, the extant parts introduced and edited by Wilferd Madelung and Sabine Schmidtke, Deutsche Morgenlandische Gesellschaft, Harrassowitz Verlag, Wiesbaden (2006).

Burayhī, 'Abd al-Wahhāb b. 'Abd ar-Raḥmān, *Ṭabaqāt ṣulaḥā' al-Yaman*, ed. Al-Ḥibshī, Dār al-Ādāb, Beirut (1983).

Dammaj, Zayd Muṭī', *Ar-Rahina,* Dār al-Ādāb, Beirut (1984).

Dammaj, Zayd Muṭī', *The Hostage*, trans. May Jayyusi and Christopher Tingley, Interlink Books, New York (1994).

Dayba', 'Abd ar-Raḥman b. 'Alī, *al-Faḍl al-mazīd 'alā bughyat al-mustafīd fī akhbār madīnat Zabīd*, ed. Yūsuf Shulḥud, Markaz ad-Dirāsāt wa'l-Buḥūth al-Yamanī, Ṣan'ā' (1983).

Dhahabī, Muḥammad b. Aḥmad, *Siyar a'lām an-nubalā'*, 23 vols., ed. Shu'ayb al-Arnā'ūṭ and Ḥusayn al-Asad, Mu'assat ar-Risāla, Beirut (1985).

Dujaylī, Muḥammad Riḍā Ḥasan, *al-Ḥayā al-fikrīya fī al-Yaman fī al-qarn as-sādis al-hijrī,* Markaz Dirāsāt al-Khalīj al-'Arabī, University of Basra (1985).

Falāḥī, 'Abd Allāh, Muḥammad, "Al-Ma'rifah wa'l-wjūd fī falsafat Aḥmad b. 'Alwān aṣ-ṣūfiyya," unpublished M.A. thesis, University of Kufa (1996).

Faqī, 'Iṣām ad-Dīn, *al-Yaman fī ẓill al-Islam*, Dār al-fikr al-'Arabī (1982).

Fayṣal al-Mikhlāfī and 'Abduh Murshid al-Maghribī, "Yafrus and ḥujāj Ibn 'Alwān," *al-Jumhūriyyah ath-Thaqāfiyyah*, 6 October 1999.

Ghazālī, Abū Ḥāmid, *Iḥyā' 'ulūm ad-dīn*, Ḥalab Dar al-Wa'y (1998).

Ghazālī, Abū Ḥāmid, *Mishkāt al-anwār*, ed. Abū al-'Alā 'Afīfī, ad-Dār al-Qawmiyya, Cairo (1964).

Ghazālī, Abū Ḥāmid, *Mukāshafat al-Qulūb*, Egypt, al-Maṭba'ah al-'Uthmāniyyah al-Miṣriyyah (1882–1883).

Ghazālī, Abū Ḥāmid, *al-Munqidh min aḍ-ḍalāl*, 2nd ed., Maṭba'at Ibn Zaydūn, Damascus (1934).

Ḥaddād, Muḥammaad Yaḥyā, *at-Tārīkh al-'āmm li'l-Yaman*, 5 vols., Dār at-Tanwīr, Beirut (1986).

Ḥadīthī, Nizār, 'Abd al-Laṭīf, *Ahl al-Yaman fī ṣadr al-Islām*, al-Mu'assasah al-Miṣriyyah li'd-Dirāsāt wan-Nashr, Beirut (n.d.).

Hamdānī, al-Ḥasan, b. Aḥmad, *Ṣifat jazīrat al-'Arab*, ed. Muḥammad b. 'Alī al-Akwa', Markaz ad-Dirāsāt wa'l-Buḥūth al-Yamanī, Ṣan'ā' (1403/1983).

Hamdānī, Ḥusayn b. Faiḍ Allāh with al-Juhanī, Ḥusayn Maḥmūd, *aṣ-Ṣulayḥiyyūn wa'l-ḥarakah al-fāṭimiyyah fī al-Yaman*, Wizārat al-I'lām wa'th-Thaqāfa, Yemen, reprint ed., Dār al-Mukhtār, Damascus (n.d.).

Ḥāmid, Ṣāliḥ, *Tārīkh Ḥaḍramwt*, 2 vols., Maktabat al-Irshād, Jeddah (1366/1946).

Ḥibshī, 'Abd Allāh, *Ḥayāt al-adab al-Yamanī fī 'aṣr banī Rasūl*, 2nd ed., Manshūrāt Wizārat al-I'lām wa'th-Thaqāfa, Ṣan'ā', Yemen Arab Republic (1980).

Ḥibshī, ʻAbd Allāh, *Maṣādir al-Fikr al-Islāmī fī'l-Yaman*, al-Maktabah al-ʻAṣriyyah, Beirut (1988).

Ḥibshī, ʻAbd Allāh, *Mu'allafāt ḥukkām al-Yaman*, ed. Elke Niewohner-Eberhard, Otto Harrassowitz, Wiesbaden (1979).

Ḥibshī, ʻAbd Allāh, *aṣ-Ṣūfiyya wa'l-fuqahā' fī'l-Yaman*, Maktabat al-Jīl al-Jadīd, Ṣanʻā' (1976).

Ḥibshī, Muḥammad, b. Ḥusayn, *al-ʻUqūd al-lu' lu'iyya fī bayān ṭarīqat as-sāda al-ʻAlawiyya*, al-Maṭbaʻah ash-Sharafiyyah, Egypt (1328/1910).

Ḥimyarī, Nashwān, *al-Ḥūr al-ʻīn*, ed. Kamāl Muṣṭafā, Dār Azāl li'ṭ-Ṭibāʻah wa'n-Nashr wa't-Tawzī, Beirut (1985).

Ibn ʻAbd al-Wahhāb, Muḥammad, *Kitāb at-tawḥīd*, Maktab al-Islāmī, Beirut (1408/1988).

Ibn Abī l-Rijāl, Aḥmad b. Ṣāliḥ, *Maṭla' al-budūr wa majmaʻal-buḥūr fī trājim rijāl al-Zaydiyya*, 4 vols., ed. ʻAbd al-Raqīb Muṭahhar Muḥammad Ḥajar, Markaz Ahl al-Bait lil-Dirāsāt al-Islāmiyya, Ṣaʻda, Yemen, 2004.

Ibn al-Ahdal, *Kashf al-ghiṭā ʻan ḥaqā'q at-tawḥīd wa'r-radd ʻalā Ibn ʻArabī al-faylasūf aṣ-ṣūfī*, ed. Aḥmad Bukar Muḥammad, Tunis (1964).

Ibn al-Ahdal, Ḥusayn, Ibn ʻAbd ar-Raḥmān, *Tuḥfat az-zaman fī Tārīkh al-Yaman*, ed. Al-Ḥibshī, Manshurāt al-Madīnah (1986).

Ibn al-Athīr, ʻIzz ad-Dīn, *al-Kāmil fī't-tārīkh*, 13 vols., Dār Ṣādir, Beirut (1995).

Ibn al-Athīr, ʻIzz ad-Dīn, *al-Kāmil fī't-tārīkh*, vol. 2, ed. ʻUmar b. ʻAbd as-Salām Tadmurī, Dār al-Kitāb al-ʻArabī, Beirut (1999).

Ibn ʻAqīl, ʻAbd ar-Raḥmān b. Jaʻfar, *ʻUmar Bā Makhrama as-Saybānī: ḥayātuhu wa taṣawwufuhu wa shiʻruhu*, Dār al-Fikr, Damascus (2002).

Ibn ʻAtā' Allāh as-Sakandarī, *Latā'f al-minan,* Al-Maktaba as-Sa'īdiyya, Cairo (1972).

Ibn ad-Daybaʻ, ʻAbd ar-Raḥmān, *Qurrat al-ʻuyūn fī akhbār al-Yaman al-maymūn*: 2 vols., ed. Muḥammad b. ʻAlī al-Akwaʻ,al-Maṭbaʻa as-Salafiyya, Cairo (1977).

Ibn ad-Daybaʻ, ʻAbd ar-Raḥmān, *al-Faḍl al-mazīd ʻalā bughyat al-mustafīd fī akhbār madīnat zabīd*, ed. Yūsuf Shulḥud, Markaz ad-Dirāsāt wa'l-Buḥūth al-Yamanī, Ṣanʻā' (1983).

Ibn Ḥajar al-ʻAsqalānī, Aḥmad b. Alī, *Inbā al-ghumr bi-anbā' al-ʻumr*, 3 vols., ed. Ḥasan Ḥabashī, Lajnat Ihiyā at-Turāth al-Islāmī, Cairo (1968–1972).

Ibn Ḥātim, Badr ad-Dīn Muḥammad, *Kitāb as-simṭ al-ghālī ath-thaman fī akhbār al-mulūk min al-ghuzz bi'l-Yaman*, ed. G. Rex Smith, vol. 1 of *The Ayyūbids and Early Rasūlids in the Yemen*, Luzac, London (1974).

Ibn Ḥazm, Abū Muḥammad,ʻAlī b. Aḥmad, *al-Fiṣal fī-l-milal wa-l-ahwā' wa-n-niḥal*, vol. 3, ed. Muḥammad Ibrāhīm Naṣr and ʻAbd ar-Raḥmān ʻUmayra, Dār al-Jīl, Beirut (1405/1985).

Ibn al-Jawzī, Abū al-Faraj, ʻAbd ar-Raḥmān b. ʻAlī, *Talbīs Iblīs*, Dār al-Kutub al-ʻIlmiyyah, Beirut (1368/1948).

Ibn al-Jawzī, Abū al-Faraj ʻAbd ar-Raḥmān, *Ṣifat aṣ-ṣafwa*, vol. 2, Dār al-Jīl, Beirut (1992).

Ibn Khaldūn, ʻAbd ar-Raḥmān, *al-Muqaddimah*, 2 vols., Dār al-Qalam, Beirut (1981).

Ibn al-Mulaqqin, ʻUmar b. ʻAlī, *Ṭabaqāt al-awliyā'*, ed. Muṣṭafā ʻAbd al-Qādir ʻAṭā, Dār al-Kutub al-ʻIlmiyya, Beirut (1999).

Ibn al-Muqrī, Ismā'īl, *Majmū' al-qāḍī al-fāḍil . . . Sharf ad-dīn Ismā'īl Ibn Abū Bakr al-Muqrī*, Maṭba'at Nukhbat al-Akhbār, Bombay (1305/1887).

Ibn Samura, 'Umar b. 'Alī al-Ja'dī, *Ṭabaqāt fuqahā' al-Yaman*, ed. Fu'ad Sayyid, Maṭba'at as-Sunna al-Muḥammadiyya, Cairo (1957).

Ibn Shaddād, Bahā' ad-Dīn, *an-Nawādir as-Sulṭānīya wa-l-maḥāsin al-Yūsufīyah, aw, Sīrat Ṣalāḥ ad-Dīn*, ed. Jamāl ad-Dīn ash-Shayāl, ad-Dār al-Miṣrīyah lil-Ta'līf wa-l-Tarjamah, Cairo (1964).

Ibn Taymiyya, Aḥmad b. 'Abd al-Ḥalīm, *Iqtiḍā' aṣ-ṣirāṭ al-mustaqīm mukhālafat aṣḥāb al-jaḥīm*, ed. Aḥmad Ḥamadī, Maktabat al-Madanī, Jedda (n.d.).

Ibn Taymiyya, Aḥmad b. 'Abd al-Ḥalīm, *Majmū'at ar-rasā'il wa'l-masā'il*, 4 vols., ed. Muḥammad Rashīd Riḍā, Maṭba'at al-Manār, Cairo (1341/1922).

Ibn Taymiyya, Aḥmad b. 'Abd al-Ḥalīm, *Majmū' fatawā Shaykh al-Islam Aḥmad b. Taymiyya*, ed. 'Abd ar-Raḥmān b. Muḥammad b. Qāsim, 27 vols., al-Maktab at-Ta'līmī as-Sa'ūdī bi'l-Maghrib, Rabāṭ (n.d.).

Ibn az-Zayyāt, Yūsuf b. Yaḥyā, *at-Tashawwuf ilā rijāl at-taṣawwuf*, ed. A. Faure, Maṭbū'āt Ifrīqiyya ash-Shamāliyya al-Fanniyya, Rabat (1958).

Janadī, Muhammad, *as-Sulūk fī ṭabaqāt al-'ulamā' wa-l-mulūk*, ed. Al-Akwa', 2 vols., Markaz ad-Dirāsāt wa-l-buḥūth al-Yamanī, Sanaa (1983, 1989).

Jarāda, Muḥammad Sa'īd, *al-Adab wath-thaqāfah fī al-Yaman 'abr al-'uṣūr*, Dār al-Fārābī, Beirut (1977).

Jāsir, Ḥamad, "al-Imām Muḥammad b. 'Alī ash-Shawkānī wa mawāqifuhu min ad-da'wa as-salafiyya al-iṣlāḥiyya," *al-Dir'iyya*, 8 and 10 (2000).

Jāsir, Ḥamad, aṣ-Ṣilāt bayn Ṣan'ā' wa'd-Dir'iyya, *al-'Arab*, 22 (1987).

Jawzī, Abū al-Faraj 'Abd ar-Raḥmān, *Ṣifat aṣ-ṣafwa*, 2 vols., Dār al-Jīl, Beirut (1992).

Jīlī, 'Abd al-Karīm, *al-Insān al-kāmil fī ma'rifat l-awākhir wa'l-awā'il*, 2 vols., Maktabat wa Maṭba'at Muḥammad 'Alī Ṣabīḥ, Cairo (1963).

Jīlī, 'Abd al-Karīm, *al-Manāẓir al-ilāhiyya*, ed. Najāḥ al-Ghanīmī, Dār al-Manār (1407/1987).

Jurjānī, 'Alī b. Muḥammad, *at-Ta'rīfāt*, Maṭba'at Muṣṭafā al-Bābī al-Ḥalabī, Cairo (1357/1938).

Kaḥḥāla, 'Umar Riḍā, *Mu'jam al-mu'allifīn*, 15 vols., al-Maktabah al-'Arabiyyah, Damascus (1957–1961).

Kalābādhī, Abū Bakr b. Muḥammad, *at-Ta'arruf li-madhhab ahl at-taṣawwuf*, ed. Maḥmūd Amīn an-Nawāwī, Matabat al-Kulliyyāt al-Azhariyyah, Cairo (1389/1969).

Khaled, Muhammad Khaled, *Rijāl ḥawl ar-rasūl*, 4 vols., Dār al-Kutub al-Ḥadīthah, Cairo (1965).

Khān, Muḥammad Ṣiddīq Ḥasan, *Abjad al-'ulūm*, 3 vols., Dār al-Kutub al-'Ilmiyyah, Damascus (1978).

Khaṭīb al-Baghdādī, *Tārīkh Baghdād*, 14 vols., Cairo (1931).

Khazrajī, 'Alī b. al-Ḥasan, *Kitāb al-'uqūd al-lu'lu'iyya*, ed. Muḥammad Basyūnī 'Asal, vol. 1, Maṭba'at al-Hilāl, Cairo (1911).

Madanī, as-Sayyid Abū Ḍayf, *Dhū 'n-Nūn al-Miṣirī*, Dār ash-Shrūq, Cairo (1973).

Mahmūd, Abd al-Halīm, *Abū l-Hasan ash-Shādhilī,* Dār al-Islam, Cairo (1967).

Maḥmūd, Ḥasan Sulaymān, *Tārīkh al-Yaman as-siyāsī fī'l-'aṣr al-Islāmī*, al-Majma' al-'Ilmī al-'Irāqī (1969).

Maqāliḥ, 'Abd al-'Azīz, "Introduction," to *al-Futūḥ* by Ibn 'Alwān, ed. al-Manṣūb, Beirut (1991).

Maqālih, 'Abd al-'Azīz, "Introduction," to *al-Futūh*, 2nd ed., ed. al-Mansūb, Dār al-Fikr al-Mu'āsir, Beirut (1995).

Maqāliḥ, 'Abd al-'Azīz, "Qirā'ah fī shā'ir aṣ-ṣūfiyya al-akbar fī al-Yaman ash-Shaykh 'Abd al-Hādī as-Sūdī," in *Dirāsāt Yamaniyya*, Markaz ad-Dirāsāt wa'l-Buḥūth al-Yamanī, vol. 43 (1411/1991).

Maqbalī, Ṣāliḥ, *al-'Alam al-Shāmikh*, 2nd ed., al-Maktaba al-Yamaniyya lil-Nashr wa-l-Tawzī', Ṣan'ā' (1985).

Maqḥafi, Ibrahim Aḥmad, *Mu'jam al-buldan wa-al-qaba'il al-Yamaniya,* Ṣan'ā': Dar al-Kalimah (2002).

Muḥibbī, Muḥammad Amīn, *Khulāṣat al-athar fī a'yān al-qar n al-ḥādī 'ashar*, vol. 1, Egypt (1284/1867).

Munāwī, Muḥammad 'Abd ar-Ra'ūf, *al-Kawākib ad-durriyya fī tarājim as-sāda aṣ-ṣūfiyya*, Maṭba'at al-Anwār, Cairo (1938).

Munjid fī al-lughah wa'l-a'lām, Dār al-Mashriq, Beirut (1986).

Muqrī, Ismā'īl b. Abī Bakr, *'Unwān ash-sharaf al-wāfī*, Maktabat al-Ma'ārif, at-Tāif, Saudi Arabia, (n.d.).

Mūza'ī, 'Abd aṣ-Ṣamad, *al-Iḥsān*, ed. Al-Ḥibshī (n.d.).

Nabhānī, Yūsuf, *Jāmi' karāmāt al-awliyā'*, 2 vols., Dār Ṣādir, Beirut (1911).

Nahrawālī, Quṭb al-Dīn Muḥammad b. Aḥmad, *al-Barq al-Yamānī fī-l-Fatḥ al-'Uthmānī*, 2nd ed., Manshūrāt al-Madīna, Beirut (1407/1986).

Nawawī, Yaḥyā b. Sharf ad-Dīn, *an-Nawawī's Forty Ḥadīth*, 2nd ed., trans. Ezzedin Ibrāhīm and Dennys Johnson-Savies, Dār al-Qur'ān al-Karīm, Damascus (1977).

Qārī al-Baghdādī, Abū al-Ḥasan 'Alī, *Manāqib Ibn 'Arabī*, ed. Ṣālāḥ ad-Dīn al-Munajjid, Mu'assasat at-Turāth al-'Arabī, Beirut (1959).

Qiyarī, Ḥamūd, "Edition of Dīwān al-futūḥ," unpublished M.A. thesis, Cairo University (1988).

Rāzī, Aḥmad, b. 'Abd Allāh, *Tārīkh Madīnat Ṣan'ā'*, 3rd ed., ed. Ḥusayn 'Abd Allāh al-'Amrī, Dār al-Fikr, Damascus (1409/1989).

Sa'īd, 'Abd al-Karīm, *Qaḍāyā wa ishkāliyyāt at-taṣawwuf 'ind Ibn 'Alwān*, Maktabat Murād, Ṣan'ā' (1997).

Sakhāwī, Muḥammad b. 'Abd ar-Raḥmān, *aḍ-Ḍaw' al-lāmi' li-ahl al-qarn at-tāsi'*, 12 vols., Manshūrāt Dār Maktabat al-Ḥayāh, Beirut (n.d.).

Shahrastānī, Muḥammad, *al-Milal wa n-niḥal*, ed. William Cureton, Otto Horrassowitz, Leipzig (1923).

Shahrastānī, Muḥammad, *al-Milal wa n-niḥal*, ed. William Cureton, Gorgias Press (2002).

Shākir, Mustafā, *at-Tārīkh al-'arabī wa'l-mu'arrikhūn*, vol. 2, Dār al-'Ilm Li'l-Malāyyīn, Beirut (1979).

Shamāḥī, 'Abd Allāh, *al-Yaman: al-insān wa'l-ḥaḍāra*, Dār al-Kutub, Cairo (1972).

Shāmī, Aḥmad b. Muḥammad, *Ma'a ash-shi'r al-mu'āṣir fī'l-Yaman*, Dār an-Nafā'is, Beirut (1980).

Shāmī, Aḥmad b. Muḥammad, *al-Quṭūf ad-dawānī min shi'ir Ibrāīm al-Ḥaḍrānī*, Manshūrāt al-'Aṣr al-Ḥadīth, Dār al-Manāhil, Beirut (1991).

Shāmī, Aḥmad b. Muḥammad, *Riyāḥ at-taghyyīr fī'l-Yaman,* al-Maṭba'a al-'Arabiyah, Jiddah (1984).

Shāmī, Aḥmad b. Muḥammad, *Tārīkh al-Yaman al-fikrī fī'l-'aṣr al-'Abbāsī*, vol. 1, Manshūrāt al-'Aṣr al-Ḥadīth, Beirut (1987).

Sharaf, Muḥammad Jalāl, *Dirāsāt fī at-taṣawwuf al-Islāmī*, Dār al-Ma'rifah al-Jāmi'iyyah, Cairo (1999).

Sharaf, Muḥammad Jalāl, *at-Taṣawwuf al-islāmī: madārisuh wa naẓariyyātuh*, Dār al-'Ulūm al-'Arabiyyah, Beirut (1990).

Sharaf ad-Dīn, Aḥmad Ḥusayn, *Tārīkh al-fikr al-Islāmī fī'l-Yaman*, Maṭba'at al-Kīlānī, Cairo (1968).

Sha'rānī, 'Abd al-Wahhāb, *aṭ-Ṭabaqāt al-Kubrā*, vol. 1, ed. Ahmad Abd ar-Raḥīm al-Sā'iḥ and Tawfīq Ali Wahbah, Maktabat ath-Thaqāfa ad-Dīniyya, Cairo (2005).

Sharjī, Aḥmad b. Muḥammad, *Ṭabaqāt al-khawāṣṣ: ahl aṣ-ṣidq wa'l-ikhlāṣ*, ad-Dār al-Yamaniyyah li'n-Nashr wa't-Tawzī' (1986).

Shawkānī, Muḥammad b. 'Alī, *Adab aṭ-ṭalab wa muntahā al-arab*, ed. 'Abd Al-lāh Yaḥyā as-Surayḥī, Dār Ibn Ḥazm, Beirut (1998).

Shawkānī, Muḥammad b. 'Alī, *al-Badr aṭ-ṭāli' bi-maḥāsin man ba'd al-qarn as-sābi'*, 2 vols., Dār al-Ma'rifa, Beirut (n.d.).

Shawkānī, Muḥammad b. 'Alī, *Dīwān ash-Shawkānī aslāk al-jawāhir wa'l-ḥayāt al-fikriyya was-sīyāsiyya fī 'aṣrih*, 2nd ed., ed. Ḥusayn al-'Amrī, Dār al-fikr, Damascus (1986).

Shawkānī, Muḥammad b. 'Alī, *ad-Durr an-naḍīd fī ikhlāṣ kalimat at-tawḥīd*, ed. Abū 'Abd Allāh al-Ḥalabī, Dār Ibn Khuzayma (1414/1993).

Shawkānī, Muḥammad b. 'Alī, *Nayl al-awṭār min aḥādīth sayyid al-akhyār sharḥ muntqā al-akhbār*, ed. Muḥammad Sālim Hāshim, 8 vols., Dār al-Kutub al-'Ilmiyya, Beirut (1995).

Shawkānī, Muḥammad b. 'Alī, *Qaṭr al-walyy 'alā aḥādīth al-walī*, ed. Ibrāhim Hilāl, Dār al-Kutub al-Ḥadītha, Cairo (1969).

Shawkānī, Muḥammad b. 'Alī, *Sharḥ aṣ-ṣudūr fī taḥrīm raf' al-qubūr* in Majmū'at ar-rasā'il fī 'ilm at-tawḥīd, ed. al-Qāḍī 'Abd ar-Raḥmān b. Yaḥyā al-Iryānī, Dār al-Fikr, Damascus (1983).

Shillī, Muhammad b. Abū Bakr, *al-Mashra' al-rawī fī manāqib al-sāda al-kirām Āl Abī 'Alawī,* Cairo (1319/1901).

Ṣubḥī, Aḥmad Muḥammad, *az-Zaydiyya*, az-Zahrā' l'l-I'lām al-'Arabī, Cairo (1984).

Subkī, Tāj ad-Dīn 'Abd al-Wahhāb b. 'Alī, *Ṭabaqāt ash-shāfi'iyya al-kubrā*: 10 vols., ed. Maḥmūd Muḥammad at-Tanāhī and 'Abd al-Fattāḥ Muḥammad al-Ḥilw, 'Isā al-Bābī al-Ḥalabī, Cairo (1964–1976).

Sūdī, 'Abd al-Hādī, *Shi'ruh, rasā'iluh, manāqibuh*, ed. 'Abd al-'Azīz al-Manṣūb, Dār al-Fikr al-Mu'āṣir, Beirut (1995).

Sullamī, Abū 'Abd ar-Raḥmān Muḥammad, *Kitāb ṭabaqāt aṣ-ṣūfiyya al-kubrā*, ed. Johannes Pederson: E. J. Brill, Leiden (1960).

Ṭabarī, Ibn Jarīr, *Tārīkh al-umam war-rusul wal-mulūk*, vol. 2, Maṭba'at al-Istiqāmah, Cairo (1939).

Ṭabarī, Ibn Jarīr, *The History of al-Ṭabarī*, vol. 39, trans. Ella Landau-Tasseron, State University of New York Press (c. 1998).

Taftazānī, Abū l-Wafā, *Madkhal ilā at-tṣawwuf al-Islamī,* Dār ath-Thaqāfa, Cairo (1976).

Taminian, Lucine, ed., with the assistance of 'Abd al-Karīm al-'Aug, *al-Yaman kamā yarāhu al-ākhar*, vol. 2, American Institute for Yemeni Studies (1997).

'Umarī, Shihāb ad-Dīn Aḥmad b. Yaḥyā, *Masālik al-abṣār fī mamālik al-amṣār* ed. Ayman Fu'ad Sayyid, Institut Francais d'archéologie orientale, Cairo (1985).

'Uthmān, Gameel Muḥammad Sulṭān, "The Poetry of Mysticism of Aḥmad b. 'Alwān," M.A. thesis (no. 9920301006), University of Āl al-Bayt, Amman, Jordan (2002).

Wāsi'ī, Abd al-Wāsi' b. Yaḥyā, *Tārīkh al-Yaman*, 2nd ed., Maktabat al-Yaman al-Kubrā, Ṣan'ā' (1991).

Wazīr, 'Abd Allāh b. 'Alī, *Tārīkh al-Yaman khilāl al-qarn al-ḥādī 'ashar*, ed. Muḥammad 'Abd ar-Raḥmān Jāzim, Dār al-Masīrah, Beirut (1985).

Yāfi'ī, 'Abd Allāh b. As'ad, *Mir'āt al-janān wa 'ibrat al-yaqzān*, 4 vols., Dā'irat al-Ma'ārif an-Niẓāmiyyah, Hayderabad (1921).

Yāfi'ī, 'Abd Allāh b. As'ad, *Mir'at* al-*janān wa 'ibrat al-yaqḍān*, vol. 4, 2nd ed., Manshūrāt Mu'ssasat al-A'lamī lil-Maṭbū'āt, Beirut (1390/1970).

Yāfi'ī, 'Abd Allāh b. As'ad, *Nashr al-Maḥāsin al-ghāliya* in the margin of *Jāmi' karāmāt al-awliyā'* by an-Nabhānī, vol. 2, Dār Ṣādir, Beirut (n.d.).

Yāfi'ī, 'Abd Allāh b. As'ad, *Rawḍ ar-rayāḥīn fī ḥikāyāt aṣ-ṣālḥīn al-mulaqqab nuzhat al'uyūn an-nawāḍir*, 2 vols., Maktabat wa Maṭba'at Muṣṭafā al-Bābī al-Ḥalabī wa Awlādih, Egypt (1955).

Yaḥyā b. al-Ḥusayn, *Ghāyat al-amānī fī akhbār al-quṭr al-Yamānī*, ed. Sa'īd 'Abd al-Fattāḥ 'Āshūr, revised by Muṣṭafā Ziyādah, vol. 1., Dār al-Kātib al-'Arabī, Cairo (1388/1968).

Zabārah, Muḥammad b. Muḥammad Yaḥyā, *A'immat al-Yaman*, ad-Dār al-Yamaniyyah, Ṣan'ā' (1984).

Zabārah, Muḥammad b. Muḥammad Yaḥyā, *Nuzhat an-naẓar fī rijāl al-qarn ar-rābi' 'ashar*, Markaz ad-Dirāsāt wa'l-Buḥūth al-Yamaniyya, Ṣan'ā' (1979).

Zaydān, Yūsuf, *al-Fikr aṣ-ṣūfī 'ind 'Abd al-Karīm al-Jīlī*, Dār an-Nahḍa al-'Arabiyyah, Beirut (1988).

Ziriklī, Khayr ad-Dīn, *al-A'lām: qāmūs tarājim li-ashhar ar-rijāl wa'n-nisā' min al-'arab wa'l-musa'ribīn wa'l-mustashriqīn*. 4th ed., 8 vols., Dār al-'Ilm lil-Malāyīn, Beirut (1979).

References in European Languages

Abrahamov, Binyamin, *Islamic Theology: Traditionalism and Rationalism*, Edinburgh University Press (1998).

Aḥmad 'Alī, *Qur'ān*, trans., Princeton University Press (1994).

Ali, Abdullah Yusuf, *The Qur'ān Translation*, Tahrike Tarsile Qur'an, New York (2002).

'Amrī, Ḥusayn b. 'Abdallāh, *Al-Imām ash-Shawkānī: dirāsa fī fiqhih wa fikrih*, Dār al-Fikr al-Mu'āṣir, Beirut (1990).

'Amrī, Ḥusayn b. 'Abdullah, *The Yemen in 18th and 19th Centuries: A Political and Intellectual History*, Ithaca Press, London (1983).

Arberry, Arthur, *The Doctrines of the Sufis*, Ashraf Press, Lahore (1966).

Arbery, Arthur J., *The Mawāqif and Mukhāṭabāt of Muḥammad Ibn 'Abdi'l-Jabbār an Niffarī*, Luzac, London (1935).

Arberry, Arthur J., *The Qur'ān Interpreted*, trans., Touchstone (1955).

Arberry, Arthur J., *The Rubā'iyyāt of Jalāl ad-Dīn Rumī*, Emery Walker, London (1949).

Arberry, Arthur J., *Sufism*, Dover Publications, Mineola, N.Y. (2002).

Armstrong, Karen, *Isalm: A Short History*, Phoenix (2005).

Aẓamī, Muḥammad, *On Shacht's Origin of Muhammadan Jurisprudence*, King Saud University (1985).

Aziz, Muhammad Ali, "Abū l-Ghayth b. Jamīl," in *EI*[3] (2008).

Aziz, Muhammad Ali, "Aḥmad b. 'Alwān," in *EI*[3] (2008).

Aziz, Muhammad Ali, "A Short Survey of Sufism in Yemen from Its Inception to the Thirteenth Century," *American Journal of Islamic Social Sciences*, 26/1 (Winter 2009), pp. 1–19.

Aziz, Muhammad Ali, "al-Yāfi'ī," in *The I. B.Tauris Biographical Dictionary of Islamic Civilization*, ed. Mustafa Shah and Muhammad Abdel Haleem, London, forthcoming.

Ba'albaki, Munir, *Al-Mawrid: A Modern English-Arabic Dictionary*, Dar El-Ilm Lil-Malayen (1982).

Ba'albaki, Rohi, *Al-Mawrid: A Modern Arabi-English Dictionary*, Dar El-Ilm Lil-Malayen (2002).

Baldick, Julian, *Mystical Islam*, New York University Press (1992).

Brockelmann, Carl, *Geschichte der Arabischen Litteratur*, vol. 1, E. J. Brill, Leiden (1996).

Brown, Peter, *The Cult of the Saints: Its Rise and Function in Latin Christianity*, Oxford University Press, Oxford (1999).

Brown, Peter, "The Rise and Function of the Holy Man in Late Antiquity," *The Journal of Roman Studies* (*JRS*), 61, London (1971).

Browne, E. G., *A Literary History of Persia*, vol. 1, Iranbooks (1997).

Buchman, David, *The Pedagogy of Perfection: Levels of Complementarity within and between the Beliefs and Practices of the Shādhiliyyah/'Alawiyyah Sufi Order of San'ā' Yemen*, Ph.D. thesis in anthropology, State University of New York (1998).

Buchman, David, "Translator's Introduction," *al-Ghazālī's The Niche of Lights*, Brigham Young University Press, Provo, Utah (1998).

Cazelles, Brigitte, "Introduction," *Images of Sainthood in Medieval Europe*, ed. Renate Blumenfeld-Kosinski and Timea Szell, Cornell University Press, Ithaca, N.Y. (1991).

Chittick, William, *The Self-Disclosure of God*, State University of New York Press (1998).

Chittick, William C., *The Sufi Path of Knowledge*, State University of New York Press (1989).

Chittick, William C., "Waḥdat al-wujūd in Islamic Thought," *Bulletin of the Henry Martyn Institute of Islamic Studies* (Hyderabad), 10 (January–March 1991), pp. 7–27.

Cook, Michael, "On the Origions of Wahhābism," *Journal of the Royal Asiatic Society*, 2 (1992).

Cornell, Vincent J., *Realm of the Saint*, University of Texas Press, Austin (1998).

Cornell, Vincent J., *The Way of Abū Madyan: Doctrinal and Poetic Works of Abū Madyan Shu'ayb ibn al-Ḥusayn al-Anṣārī*, Cambridge (1996).
Daftary, Farhad, "Ismā'īlī-Sufi Relations in Early Post-Alamūt and Safavid Persia," in *The Heritage of Sufism*, ed. Leonard Lewisohn and David Morgan, vol. 3, Oneworld, Oxford (1999).
Daftary, Farhad, *The Ismā'īlīs,* Cambridge University Press (1990).
Delooz, Pierre, *Sociologie et Canonisations*, Liege (1969).
Delooz, Pierre, "Towards a Sociological Study of Canonized Sainthood," in *Saints and Their Cults: Studies in Religious Sociology, Folklore, and History,* ed. Stephen Wilson, Cambridge (1983).
De Jong, Frederik, "Les confreries mystiques musulmanes au Machreq arabe." In *Les orders mystiques dans l'Islam: Cheminements et situation actuelle*, ed. A. Popovic and G. Veinstein, Editions de l'Ecole des Hautes Etudes en Sciences Sociales, Paris (1985), pp. 205–243.
Eickelman, Dale, *Moroccan Islam,* University of Texas Press, Austin (1976).
Encyclopedia of Islam, 2nd ed. (*EI*²), E. J. Brill (1994).
Encyclopedia of Islam, 3rd ed. (*EI*³), E. J. Brill (2008).
Ernest, Carl W., "Traditionalism: The Perennial Philosophy, and Islamic Studies," *MESA Bulletin*, 28 (1994), pp. 176–180.
Ewing, Katherine, *Arguing Sainthood*, Duke University Press (1997).
Fakhrī, Majid, *A History of Islamic Philosophy*, 2nd ed., Columbia University Press, New York (1983).
Farid, Jabre, *La notion de certitude selon Ghazali*, Paris (1958).
Fayẓee, A. A. A., "Three Sulaymani Da'is: 1936–1939," *Journal of the Bombay Branch of the Royal Asiatic Society,* Bombay, 14 (1940).
Fierro, Maribel, "The Polemic about *Karāmāt Al-Awliyā'* and the Development of Sufism in Al-Andalus (Fourth/Tenth–Fifth/Eleventh Centuries)," *Bulletin of the School of Oriental and African Studies*, 55/2 (1992).
Fisher, Humphrey J., *Aḥmadiyyah: A Study in Contemporary Islam on the West African Coast,* Oxford University Press (1963).
Geddes, Charles L., "The Apostasy of 'Alī b. al-Faḍl," in *Arabian and Islamic Studies: Articles Presented to R. B. Serjeant*, ed. Robert L. Bidwell and G. Rex Smith, Longman, London (1983), pp. 80–85.
Gellner, Ernnest, *Saints of the Atlas,* Weidenfeld and Nicolson, London (1969).
Ghazālī, Abū Ḥāmid, *The Incoherence of the Philosophers*, translated, introduced, and annotated by Michael E. Marmura, Brigham Young University Press, Provo, Utah (2000).
Ghazālī, Abū Hāmid, *Mishkāt al-anwār*, trans. David Buchman, Brigham Young University Press, Provo, Utah (1998).
Ghazālī, Abū Ḥāmid, *Mishkāt al-anwār*, trans. W. H. T. Gairdner, Ashraf Press, Lahore (1952).
Gibb, H. A. R., and J. H. Kramers, eds., *Shorter Encyclopedia of Islam*, E. J. Brill, Leiden (1995).
Giffen, Lois, *Theory of Profane Love among the Arabs*, New York University Press, New York (1971).
Gochenour, David, "The Penetration of Zaydi Islam into Early Medieval Yemen," unpublished Ph.D. dissertation, Harvard University (1984).

Goldziher, Ignaz, *Introduction to Islamic Theology and Law*, trans. Andras and Ruth Hamori, Princeton University Press, Princeton, New Jersey (1979).

Goldziher, Ignaz, "The Veneration of Saints in Islam," in *Muslim Studies*, ed. Ignaz Goldziher, translated from German by C. R. Barber and S. M. Stern, vol. 2, Chicago (1971).

Graham, T., "Shāh Ni'matullāhī Walī: Founder of the Ni'matullāhī Sufi Order," in *The Legacy of Mediaeval Persian Sufism,* ed. Leonard Lewisohn, London (1992).

Gutas, Dimitri, *Greek Thought, Arabic Culture,* reprint ed., Routledge (1999).

Hallaq, Wael, *A History of Islamic Legal Theories*, Cambridge University Press (1997).

Halm, Heinz, *The Empire of the Mahdī: The Rise of the Fāṭimids*, trans. Michael Bonner, E. J. Brill (1996).

Hamdānī, Ḥusayṇ, Faiḍ Allāh, "Fāṭimid History and Historians," in *Religion, Learning and Science in the 'Abbāsid Period*, ed. M. J. L. Young, J. D. Latham, and R. B. Serjeant, Cambridge University Press, Cambridge (1990).

Hammoudi, Abdellah, *Master and Disciple*, University of Chicago Press, Chicago (1997).

Haykel, Bernard, "Ash-Shawkānī and the Jurisprudential Unity of Yemen," *La Revu du Musulman et de la Méditerranée,* 67/1 (1993).

Haykel, Bernard, *Revival and Reform in Islam: The Legacy of Muhammad al-Shawkānī*, Cambridge University Press (2003).

Hodgson, M. G. S. *The Venture of Islam*, 3 vols., University of Chicago Press (1977).

Homerin, Emil, *From Arab Poet to Muslim Saint*, American University in Cairo Press (2001).

Hujwīrī, 'Alī b. 'Uthmān, *The Kashf al-maḥjūb: The Oldest Persian Treatise on Sufism*, trans. Reynold A. Nicholson, with a foreword by Shahidullah Faridi, Islamic Book Foundation, Lahore (1976).

Ḥusaynī, as-Sayyid Aḥmad, *Mu'allafāt al-Zaydiyya*, 3 vols., Manshūrāt Maktabat Āyat Allāh al-'Uẓmā al-Mar'ashiyy an-Najafiyy, Qumm (1413/1993).

Jackson, Sherman, "Ibn Taymiyya on Trial in Damascus," *Journal of Semitic Studies* (Cambridge), 29/1 (1994).

Jackson, Sherman, *On the Boundaries of Theological Tolerance in Islam: Abū Ḥāmid al-Ghazālī's Fayṣal at-tafriqah*, Oxford University Press (2002).

Kamālī, Muḥammad Hāshim, *Principles of Islamic Jurisprudence*, reprint ed., Islamic Texts Society (1997).

Kennedy, H. N., "The 'Abbāsid Caliphate: A Historical Introduction," in *'Abbāsid Belles-Lettres*, Cambridge University Press (1990).

Knysh, Alexander, "The Cult of Saints in Hadramawt: An Overview," *New Arabian Studies*, 1 (1993), pp. 137–152.

Knysh, Alexander, *Ibn 'Arabī in the Later Islamic Tradition*, State University of New York Press (1999).

Knysh, Alexander, *Islamic Mysticism: A Short History*, Brill, Leiden (2000).

Knysh, Alexander, "The Sāda in History: A Critical Essay on Ḥaḍramī Historiography," in *Journal of the Royal Asiatic Society,* 9/2 (July 1999).

Lane-Poole, Stanley, *The Mohammedan Dynasties*, vol. 2, reprint ed., Routledge, London (2000).

Laoust, Henri, *Essai sur les doctrines sociales et politiques de Taki-D-Din Ahmad b. Taimiya,* Imprimerie de l'Institut Francais d'Archeologie Orientale, Cairo (1939).
Laoust, Henri, *La Profession de Foi D'Ibn Taymiyya: Texte, traduction et commentaire de la Wāsiṭiyya*, Librairie Orientaliste Pau Geuthner, Paris (1986).
Madelung, Wilferd, *Arabic Texts Concerning the History of the Zaydī Imams of Ṭabaristān, Daylamān and Gilān*, Beirut (1987).
Madelung, Wilferd, "Zaydī Attitudes to Sufism," in *Islamic Mysticism Contested: Thirteen Centuries of Controversies and Polemics*, ed. Frederick De Jong and Bernd Radtke, Brill, Leiden (1999).
Mad'aj, 'Abd al-Muḥsin, *The Yemen in Early Islam: A Political History*, Ithaca Press, London (1988).
Makdisi, George, "Ash'arī and the Ash'arites in Islamic Religious History," *Studia Islamica*, vol. 17 (1962).
Massignon, Louis, *The Passion of al-Hallāj: Mystic and Martyr of Islam*, trans. Herbert Madon, vol. 2, Princeton University Press (1982).
Meri, Josef W., "The Etiquette of Devotion in the Islamic Cult of Saints," in *The Cult of Saints in Late Antiquity and the Early Middle Ages: Essays on the Contribution of Peter Brown*, ed. James Howard-Johnston and Paul Antony Hayward, Oxford University Press (2002).
Messick, Brinkley, *The Calligraphic State*, University of California Press, Berkeley (1993).
Mitchell, Richard P., *The Society of the Muslim Brothers,* Oxford University Press (1993).
Momen, Moojan, *An Introduction to Shi'ī Islam*, Yale University Press, London (1985).
Morris, James Winston, "How to Study the 'Futūḥāt: Ibn 'Arabī's Own Advice," in *Muhyiddin Ibn 'Arabi. A Commemorative Volume*, ed. Stephen Hirtenstein and Michael Tiernan, Element. Brisbane, (1993), pp. 73–89.
Naṣr, Seyyed Ḥossein, *An Introduction to Islamic Cosmological Doctrine: Conceptions of Nature and Methods Used for Its Study by the Ikhwān aṣ-Ṣafā', al-Biruni and Ibn Sina,* Belknap Press of Harvard University Press, Cambridge, Mass. (1964).
Nicholson, Reynold Alleyne, *Studies in Islamic Mysticism*, reprint ed., Curzon Press, London (1994).
O'Fahey, R. S., *Enigmatic Saint: Ahmad Ibn Idris and the Idrisi Tradition*, Northwestern University Press, Evanston, Illinois (1990).
Ohlander, Erik, *Sufism in an Age of Transition: 'Umar al-Suhrawardī and the Rise of the Islamic Mystical Brotherhoods,* Brill, Leiden (2008).
Peskes, Esther, *Muḥammad b. 'Abdalwahhāb im Widerstreit*, Orient-Institut, Beirut (1993).
Qādirī, Muḥammad Riaz, *The Sultan of the Saints,* Abbasi Publications, Pakistan (2000).
Raḥmān, Faẓlur, *Islam*, 2nd ed., Chicago, University of Chicago Press (1979).
Rihani, Ameen, *Around the Coasts of Arabia*, Constable, London (1930).
Ruffing, Janet, "An Introduction," *Mysticism and Social Transformation*, ed. Janet Ruffing, Syracuse University Press (2001).

Sachedina, Abdulaziz Abdulhussein, *Islamic Messianism*, State University of New York Press (1981).
Schimmel, Annemarie, "Man and His Perfection in Islam," in *The World Treasury of Modern Religious Thought*, ed. Jaroslav Pelikan with a foreword by Clifton Fadiman, Little Brown, Boston (1990).
Schimmel, Annemarie, *Mystical Dimensions of Islam*, University of North Carolina Press (1975).
Sedgwick, Mark, *Saints and Sons: The Making and Remaking of the Rashīdī Aḥmadī Sufi Order, 1799–2000*, Brill, Leiden (2005).
Serjeant, Robert, "The Sayyids of Ḥaḍramawt," inaugural lecture delivered on June 5, 1956, School of Oriental and African Studies, University of London (1957).
Shami, A., and Serjeant, Robert, "Regional Literature: The Yemen," in *'Abbasid Belles-Lettres*, Cambridge University Press (1990).
Smith, G. Rex, "The Ayyubids and Rasulids: The Transfer of Power in 7th/13th Century Yemen," in *Islamic Culture* (Hyderabad), 43 (1969).
Smith, G. Rex, "The Ayyūbids and Rasūlids: The Transference of Power in 7th/13th Century Yemen," in *Studies in the Medieval History of the Yemen and South Arabia*, Variorum (1997).
Smith, G. Rex, "The Political History of the Islamic Yemen down to the First Turkish Invasion (1–945/622–1538)," in *Yemen: 3000 Years of Art and Civilization in Arabia Felix*, ed. Werner Daum, Pinguin, Innsbruck (1988), pp. 129–139.
Smith, G. Rex, ed. *The Ayyubids and Early Rasulids in the Yemen*, 2 vols., Luzac, London (1974–1978).
Smith, Margaret, *Early Mysticism in the Near and Middle East*, Oxford (1995).
Smith, Margaret, *An Early Mystic of Baghdad: A Study of the Life and Teaching of Harith b. Asad al-Muhasibi,* Sheldon Press, London (1935).
Stookey, Robert W., *Yemen: The Politics of the Yemen Arab Republic*, Westview Press, Boulder, Colo. (1978).
Trimingham, J. Spencer, *A History of Islam in West Africa,* reprint ed., Oxford University Press, Oxford (1982).
Triminghan, J. Spenser, *The Sufi Orders in Islam*, Oxford University Press (1998).
Tritton, Arthur, *The Rise of the Imams of Sanaa*, reprint ed., Hyperion Press, Westpoint, Conn. (1981).
Varisco, Daniel, "Texts and Pretexts: The Unity of the Rasūlid State under al-Malik al-Muẓaffar," *La Revu du Musulman et de la Méditerranée* (*REMMM*), vol. 67/1 (1993).
Vikor, Knut S., *Sufi and Scholar on the Desert Edge*, Hurst, London (1995).
Voll, John O., "Sufi Orders," in *The Oxford Encyclopedia of Modern Islamic World*, vol. 4, Oxford University Press (1995).
Watt, W. M., *The Formative Period of Islamic Thought*, Oneworld (1998).
Watt, W. M., *Islamic Philosophy and Theology*, reprint ed., Edinburgh University Press (1995).
Wehr, Hans, *Arabic English Dictionary*, ed. J. M. Cowan, 3rd ed., Spoken Language Services, New York (1976).
Woolf, Henry Bosley, ed., *Webster's New Collegiate Dictionary* (1977).

INDEX